core JSTL

Mastering the JSP™ Standard Tag Library

DAVID M. GEARY

PRENTICE
HALL
PTR

Prentice Hall PTR, Upper Saddle River, NJ 07458
www.phptr.com

Sun Microsystems Press
A Prentice Hall Title

The publisher offers discounts on this book when ordered in bulk quantities. For more information,
contact Corporate Sales Department, Prentice Hall PTR, One Lake Street, Upper Saddle River, NJ
07458. Phone: 800-382-3419; FAX: 201-236-7141. E-mail: corpsales@prenhall.com.

Editorial/production supervision: *Patti Guerrieri*
Cover design director: *Jerry Votta*
Art director: *Gail Cocker-Bogusz*
Series interior design: *Meg Van Arsdale*
Manufacturing manager: *Alexis R. Heydt-Long*
Marketing manager: *Debby vanDijk*
Executive editor: *Gregory G. Doench*
Associate editor: *Eileen Clark*
Editorial assistant: *Brandt Kenna*
Sun Microsystems Press publisher: *Michael Llwyd Alread*

10 9 8 7 6 5 4 3 2 1

ISBN 0-13-100153-1

Sun Microsystems Press
A Prentice Hall Title

About Prentice Hall Professional Technical Reference

With origins reaching back to the industry's first computer science publishing program in the 1960s, Prentice Hall Professional Technical Reference (PH PTR) has developed into the leading provider of technical books in the world today. Formally launched as its own imprint in 1986, our editors now publish over 200 books annually, authored by leaders in the fields of computing, engineering, and business.

Our roots are firmly planted in the soil that gave rise to the technological revolution. Our bookshelf contains many of the industry's computing and engineering classics: Kernighan and Ritchie's *C Programming Language,* Nemeth's *UNIX System Administration Handbook,* Horstmann's *Core Java,* and Johnson's *High-Speed Digital Design.*

PH PTR acknowledges its auspicious beginnings while it looks to the future for inspiration. We continue to evolve and break new ground in publishing by providing today's professionals with tomorrow's solutions.

PRENTICE
HALL
PTR

Contents

Preface

Until recently, JavaServer Pages (JSP) has, for the most part, been accessible only to Java developers. That's because JSP did not provide a standard set of tags for common functionality or a scripting language for page authors. The lack of those essential features meant that JSP developers had to embed Java code in JSP pages or implement custom tags that encapsulated that Java code. Either way, they had to be well versed in the Java programming language to effectively use JSP.

To implement maintainable and extensible Web applications, developers must decouple business and presentation logic. Without an expression language or standard tag library, JSP pages often contained a great deal of Java code, which allowed easy access to business logic. That Java code and the inevitable related business logic tightly coupled JSP pages with the underlying data model, which resulted in brittle systems that were difficult to modify or extend.

The JSP Standard Tag Library (JSTL) provides a scripting language and set of standard tags that make JSP accessible to page authors and make it much easier to separate business and presentation logic. Those benefits allow page authors to focus on a Web application's presentation, while Java developers implement business logic, which in turn makes those applications much easier to implement, maintain, and extend. Because JSTL has such a profound effect on the development of Java-based Web applications as a whole, it is one of the most important new developments for server-side Java.

1.1 What This Book Is About

This book discusses all aspects of JSTL, including a thorough examination of the expression language and JSTL's tags (which are commonly known as actions). I assume that readers are already familiar with the basics of servlets and JSP, so those topics are not discussed in this book. See "This Book's Audience" for more information about what level of experience is assumed for readers.

1.2 The Servlet and JSP APIs This Book Depends Upon

JSTL only works with servlet containers that support the Servlet 2.3 and JSP 1.2 APIs. To run this book's examples, you will need such a servlet container; for example, Resin 2.1.2 or Tomcat 4.1.3; see "Downloading and Installing a Servlet Container" on page 26 for more information about downloading and installing those servlet containers.

1.3 The Book's Web Site

This book has a companion Web site at `http://www.corejstl.com`. That Web site provides documented source code for all of this book's examples.

1.4 How This Book's Code Was Tested

All of the code examples in this book were tested with Resin 2.1.2 and Tomcat 4.1.3. See "The Book's Web Site" for more information about downloading that code.

1.5 This Book's Audience

This book was written for Java developers with a basic understanding of servlets and JSP. If you are new to servlets and JSP, I recommend the following books for your first book on those topics:

- *Core Servlets and JSP* by Marty Hall, Sun Microsystems Press
- *Advanced JavaServer Pages* by David Geary, Sun Microsystems Press
- *Java Servlet Programming* by Jason Hunter, O'Reilly
- *Web Development with JavaServer Pages* by Fields and Kolb, Manning

1.6 How To Use This Book

The majority of this book is written in a tutorial style that illustrates how to make the most of JSTL's expression language and actions. The last chapter in the book is a reference for the JSTL actions. That reference provides detailed syntax information for each JSTL action, in addition to a short description of the action and its constraints and error handling. Each action also is accompanied by an *In a Nutshell* section that provides enough information about the action to get you started.

You can use the reference chapter in one of two ways. First, it may be a good place to start when you are using a JSTL action for the first time. Once you understand the action's syntax and its intent, you will probably want to read more about the action in the applicable chapter where it's discussed in detail. Second, you should use the reference to help you use JSTL actions after you understand their purpose and intent; for example, the <fmt:formatNumber> action, which is discussed in detail in "Formatting and Parsing Numbers" on page 310 and summarized in "Formatting Actions" on page 509 provides 12 attributes. It can be difficult to remember all of those attributes and how they work together. Instead of trying to unearth that specific information from the "Formatting Actions" chapter beginning on page 308, you would be better off looking up those attributes in the "JSTL Reference" chapter beginning on page 464.

1.7 Conventions Used in This Book

Table P-1 shows the coding conventions used in this book.

Table P-1 Coding Conventions

Convention	Example
Class names have initial capital letters.	`public class ClassName`
Method names have initial lower case, and the rest of the words have an initial capital letter.	`getLength`
Variable names have initial lower case, and the rest of the words have an initial capital letter.	`private int length` `private int bufferLength`

Note that, for the most part, methods are referred to without their arguments; however, arguments are included when the discussion warrants them.

Table P-2 shows the typographic conventions used in this book.

Table P-2 Typographic Conventions

Typeface or Symbol	Description
`courier`	Indicates a command, file name, class name, method, argument, Java keyword, HTML tag, file content, code excerpt, or URL.
bold courier	Indicates a sample command-line entry.
italics	Indicates definitions, emphasis, a book title, or a variable that should be replaced with a valid value.

Acknowledgments

After writing six Java books over the past five years, I've learned that it's crucial to have a good set of reviewers. For this book, I was fortunate enough to have the best set of reviewers an author could possibly have.

First, I'd like to thank Marty Hall, the author of *Core Servlets and JSP* and *More Servlets and JSP* for his thorough and insightful review of this book. Marty's review comments added considerably to the quality of this book.

Second, I'd like to thank Jan Luehe for providing excellent review comments that went way above and beyond the call of duty. Jan was one of the handful of developers that implemented the JSTL Reference Implementation, and he pointed out many inconsistencies and misunderstandings that I originally had about JSTL, especially the internationalization and database actions, which can be rather complicated to initialize and use. Like Marty, Jan considerably increased the quality of this book by his sage observations.

Many other people also provided excellent review comments that I relentlessly incorporated into the book. I was fortunate to have Pierre Delisle, who is the lead engineer for JSTL, agree to review this book. Pierre provided many review comments that only someone in his position could make. Norbert Lindenberg, who is an internationalization specialist at Sun provided numerous comments on the internationalization and formatting chapters. Ryan Lubke, who implemented the test kit for the JSTL also provided numerous pithy comments, along with Lance Anderson and Carole Mah, whom I recruited from the Jakarta Taglibs mailing list to review the database chapter. Scott Ferguson, the developer of the excellent Resin app server,was also gracious enough to review another of my books. Lars Garshol, who has worked on the Goldfarb XML series from Prentice Hall helped me out considerably with the XML chapter. Finally, my good friend and resident Java expert, Rob Gordon, also provided me with excellent review comments.

core

JSTL
Mastering the JSP™
Standard Tag Library

INTRODUCTION

Topics in This Chapter

- JSTL Overview
- Getting Started
- A Simple JSTL Web Application
- JSTL Design Principles

Chapter 1

Since its introduction in 1995, Java has become the programming language of choice for developing e-business applications.[1] One of the main reasons for Java's success is its extensive class library, which lets developers implement complex applications with relative ease. Until now, server-side Java developers have had little in the way of a server-side class library beyond the servlet and JavaServer Pages (JSP) APIs. But as three major JSP specifications come to fruition in the latter part of 2002—JSP 2.0, JavaServer Faces, and the JSP Standard Tag Library (JSTL)—server-side Java developers will suddenly be standing on a very broad set of shoulders.

This book is an in-depth examination of JSTL, which offers two invaluable capabilities that substantially simplify the implementation of JSP-based Web applications: an expression language and a comprehensive set of fundamental JSP tags (hereafter known as actions).

Before JSTL, JSP's most glaring weakness was, ironically, it's *raison d'etre*: the use of JSP expressions and scriptlets to intersperse Java code with HTML. For example, if you have a color preference bean in session scope, you can access that bean's foreground color with this JSP expression:

```
<%= ((beans.ColorPreferences)pageContext.
    getAttribute("user", PageContext.SESSION_SCOPE)).
    getForeground() %>
```

---

1. According to a study by the Cutter Consortium in November, 1999: see
   http://www.cutter.com/press/991130.html

The preceding expression accesses a bean through the JSP `pageContext` object and invokes the bean's `getForeground` method. That Java code is contained in a JSP expression, so the output is sent to the current `JspWriter`.

JSP scriptlets and expressions, such as the expression in the preceding code, make JSP pages more difficult to understand and maintain. They also require knowledge of the Java programming language, which narrows the field of JSP programmers. As if that weren't enough, JSP scriptlets and expressions provide a direct conduit to business logic. As long as your business logic is implemented in the Java programming language, developers can access it with reckless abandon from JSP pages. Mixing presentation and business logic makes applications more difficult to maintain and extend.

With the JSTL expression language and the <c:out> action, the previous JSP expression can be written like this:

```
<c:out value='${user.foreground}'%>
```

To say that the preceding code fragment is more user friendly than the preceding JSP expression involves a good dose of understatement. The expression language does not allow direct invocation of an object's methods, but it does allow you to specify a property name, which the expression language converts to an appropriate JavaBeans-compliant getter method; for example, the preceding code fragment results in a call to `user.getForeground()`.

The expression language alone is a vast improvement for JSP; in fact, it's such a crucial capability that it will be incorporated into the JSP 2.0 specification, which will be finalized in the latter part of 2002. But JSTL offers more than just an expression language—its comprehensive suite of actions will make JSP development much easier and greatly reduce the reinvention of the wheel for everyday JSP tasks. For example, before JSTL, the common task of database access was not included in JSP's repertoire, so a developer could look for an existing database tag library or implement his own. That all changes with JSTL because it supports a set of database actions. The following JSP page shows how easy it is to make a database query and display the query results in an HTML table:

```
<!DOCTYPE HTML PUBLIC "-//W3C//DTD HTML 4.0 Transitional//EN">
<html>
   <head>
      <title>Accessing Database Queries</title>
   </head>

   <body>
      <%@ taglib uri='http://java.sun.com/jstl/core' prefix='c' %>
      <%@ taglib uri='http://java.sun.com/jstl/sql'  prefix='sql'%>
```

```
<%-- Execute a database query --%>
<sql:query var='customers'>
    SELECT * FROM CUSTOMERS
</sql:query>

<%-- Access the rowCount property of the query --%>
<p>There are <c:out value='${customers.rowCount}'/> rows
 in the customer query. Here they are:</p>

<%-- Create a table with column names and row data --%>
<p><table border='1'>
    <tr>
        <%-- Create table headers --%>
        <c:forEach var='columnName'
                items='${customers.columnNames}'>
            <th><c:out value='${columnName}'/></th>
        </c:forEach>
    </tr>

    <%-- Create table rows and data --%>
    <c:forEach var='row' items='${customers.rowsByIndex}'>
        <tr>
            <c:forEach var='rowData' items='${row}'>
                <td><c:out value='${rowData}'/></td>
            </c:forEach>
        </tr>
    </c:forEach>
</table>
 </body>
</html>
```

The preceding JSP page executes an SQL query that selects all customers in a database. Subsequently, the JSP page uses the <c:forEach> action to iterate over column names and row data to create an HTML table that displays the query result. If you want to read more about the preceding JSP page and see the output that it produces, see "Querying a Database" on page 378.

Now that we have a basic understanding of JSTL and how we can use it, let's take a closer look at what JSTL is and what it can do for you.

1.1 JSTL Overview

In late 1997, Sun Microsystems introduced the Servlet API. Servlets were a godsend to CGI developers because servlets are much more elegant, efficient, powerful, and portable than CGI.[2] But it soon became apparent that the Servlet API had a serious shortcoming: *developers created user interfaces by emitting HTML with servlet print statements, which is a terrible way to implement maintainable and extensible code.* That servlet shortcoming was addressed with the introduction of JavaServer Pages (JSP), which lets you embed Java code in HTML.

But, as is often the case, the solution to the problem turned out to have a serious shortcoming of its own: *embedding Java code in HTML can quickly lead to complicated JSP pages that mix presentation and business logic and are, therefore, difficult to understand and maintain.* Also, with only a limited set of standard tags, such as <jsp:useBean> and <jsp:include>, JSP was great for Java developers who could write scriptlets, but difficult for page authors with no Java experience. In reaction to that shortcoming, Java developers quickly took advantage of JSP's mechanism for implementing custom tags, and a profusion of JSP custom tags soon arose, including the Jakarta Taglibs hosted by the Apache Software Foundation.[3]

From the crucible of Jakarta Taglibs and developer discontent with the JSP status quo, the JavaServer Pages Standard Tag Library (JSTL) was born. With an expression language and a comprehensive standard tag library, JSTL nearly eradicates the need for JSP scriptlets and expressions.

In late 2000, the Java Community Process (JCP) selected an expert group for JSTL. Since that time, the expert group has defined the JSTL specification and produced a reference implementation. JSTL is designed to work with servlet containers that support Servlet 2.3 and JSP 1.2 or higher. See "Getting Started" on page 23 for more information about JSTL prerequisites.

Core Warning

JSTL works only with servlet containers that support the Servlet 2.3 and JSP 1.2 APIs.

What Is JSTL?

JSTL is composed of:

- An expression language
- Standard Action Libraries (42 actions in four libraries)
- Tag Library Validators (2 validators)

---

2. CGI stands for Common Gateway Interface.
3. See http://jakarta.apache.org/taglibs/index.html for more information about Jakarta Taglibs.

The expression language is arguably JSTL's single most important feature. The expression language makes it easy to access implicit objects such as the servlet request and response and *scoped variables*, meaning objects stored in a JSP scope (page, request, session, or application). The expression language drastically reduces the need for JSP expressions and scriptlets, which in turn increases maintainability and extensibility of JSP-based Web applications. Starting with JSP 2.0, the expression language will be defined in the JSP specification. See Chapter 2, "The JSTL Expression Language," for more details.

The standard action libraries provide a solid base of functionality for building Web applications, from general actions that iterate over collections or import URLs to more specialized actions that you can use to internationalize your website, access databases and manipulate XML.

JSTL also provides two tag library validators that let you restrict the use of scriptlets and tag libraries used in JSP pages. Those validators are provided as a proof of concept and are not part of JSTL's core functionality.

Core Definition

Scoped variable: An object stored in one of the four JSP scopes.

The JSTL Expression Language

The JSTL expression language is a simple language based on ECMAScript and XPath. It provides expressions and identifiers; arithmetic, logical, and relational operators; and automatic type conversion.

One of the most significant features of the expression language is the implicit objects it defines. Those implicit objects let you access request parameters and headers, context initialization parameters, scoped variables, and cookies. The `pageContext` implicit object lets you access the page context, which has references to the request, response, session, servlet context, servlet config, etc. For example, the following code fragment displays the value of a request parameter named `name`:

```
<c:out value='${param.name}'/>
```

In the preceding code fragment, the `param` identifier is an implicit object that's a map of request parameters. You can also use the expression language to access context initialization parameters; for example, the following code fragment iterates over the application's context initialization parameters and displays their values:

```
<%-- Loop over the JSTL initParam implicit object,
     which is a map --%>
<c:forEach items='${initParam}' var='parameter'>
   <ul>
      <%-- Display the key of the current item, which
           corresponds to the name of the init param --%>
      <li>Name: <c:out value='${parameter.key}'/></li>

      <%-- Display the value of the current item, which
           corresponds to the value of the init param --%>
      <li>Value: <c:out value='${parameter.value}'/></li>
   </ul>
</c:forEach>
```

The preceding code fragment uses the <c:forEach> action to iterate over context initialization parameters. The initParam identifier is an implicit object that's a map of context initialization parameters. Each item in that map is a map entry, so the body of the <c:forEach> action accesses the keys and values of each map entry.

The JSTL expression language is discussed in detail in Chapter 2, "The JSTL Expression Language," and JSTL implicit objects are discussed in "Implicit Objects" on page 64.

The JSTL Tag Libraries

Although its name suggests that JSTL is a single tag library, it's actually composed of four libraries that contain a total of 42 actions. Those libraries are listed in Table 1.1.

Table 1.1   JSTL Libraries

Library	Actions	Description
Core	14	**Fundamentals**: if/then statements and switch constructs; creating output; creating and destroying scoped variables; manipulating properties of JavaBeans components; handling exceptions; iterating over collections; constructing URLs and importing their content.
Formatting	12	**Internationalization and Formatting**: Setting locales and resource bundles; localizing text and compound messages; formatting and parsing numbers, percents, currencies, and dates.
SQL	6	**Database Access**: Specifying a data source; executing queries, updates, and transactions; iterating over query results.
XML	10	**XML Parsing and Transforming**: Parsing XML; accessing and transforming XML with XPath and XSLT, respectively.

As you can see from Table 1.1, JSTL actions are pretty well distributed among the four libraries listed above. Each of those libraries is discussed, in the order listed in Table 1.1, starting at "Core Actions" on page 11.

Twin Libraries

Most JSTL actions have *dynamic attributes*—attributes that can have runtime values; for example, you can specify a runtime expression for the <c:out> action, which evaluates an expression and sends the result to the current JspWriter, like this:

```
<%@ taglib uri='http://java.sun.com/jstl/core' prefix='c' %>

<c:out value='${user.preferences.backgroundColor}'/>
```

The preceding code fragment uses the <c:out> action and the JSTL expression language to display the background color stored in a user's preferences.

The JSTL expression language is not nearly as powerful as the Java programming language, so sometimes you might need to specify a JSTL action attribute with a Java expression. Because of that need, JSTL provides *two versions* of each of its libraries, one that supports the JSTL expression language—known as the EL library—and another that supports JSP expressions—known as the RT library. The RT library knows nothing about the JSTL expression language; instead, you specify dynamic attributes for the actions in that library with JSP expressions; for example, the following code fragment uses the <c_rt:forEach> action to iterate over the locales available for formatting dates:[4]

```
<%@ taglib uri='http://java.sun.com/jstl/core_rt' prefix='c_rt' %>
<%@ taglib uri='http://java.sun.com/jstl/core' prefix='c' %>
...
<form>
   <table>
      ...
      <%-- Create an HTML select element whose name is locale --%>
      <select name='locale'>
         <%-- For each of the available locales for date
              formatting, create an HTML option element --%>
         <c_rt:forEach var='thisLocale'
                   items='<%= java.text.DateFormat.
                                        getAvailableLocales()%>'>
            <%-- Begin the <option> start tag --%>
            <option

            <%-- See if the locale request parameter is the same
```

---

4. The following code fragment is discussed in "Formatting and Parsing Dates and Times" on page 333.

```
                     as the locale that we're creating an option for
              --%>
              <c:if test='${param.locale == thisLocale}'>
                 <%-- Now we've generated: <option selected --%>
                 selected
              </c:if>

              <%-- Generate the ending bracket for the <option> start
                     tag and specify the value of the current locale
                     as the value for the option element --%>
              ><c:out value='${thisLocale}'/>

              <%-- Generate the <option> end tag --%>
              </option>
          </c_rt:forEach>
       </select>
    </table>
</form>
```

The preceding code fragment creates an HTML select element whose option elements represent the locales available for formatting dates. For access to those locales, it's necessary to write a scriptlet or use the <c_rt:forEach> action, which accepts a JSP expression for its items attribute.

Notice the taglib declarations in the preceding code fragments. The RT version of the Core library is specified with a URI of http://java.sun.com/jstl/core_rt and a prefix of c_rt, whereas the EL library is specified with a URI of http://java.sun.com/jstl/core and a prefix of c. Those URIs are the standard URIs that you use to access the core actions for JSP expressions and EL expressions, respectively.

The prefixes used in the preceding code fragment are recommended by the JSTL specification. Table 1.2 and Table 1.3 list the URIs and prefixes for all of the JSTL libraries.

Table 1.2   JSTL Taglib URIs for the EL Libraries

Library	URI	Prefix[a]
Core	http://java.sun.com/jstl/core	c
Formatting	http://java.sun.com/jstl/fmt	fmt
SQL	http://java.sun.com/jstl/sql	sql
XML	http://java.sun.com/jstl/xml	x

a. The prefix is merely a recommendation; you can use any prefix you choose.

Table 1.3   JSTL Taglib URIs for the RT Libraries

Library	URI	Prefix[a]
Core	http://java.sun.com/jstl/core_rt	c_rt
Formatting	http://java.sun.com/jstl/fmt_rt	fmt_rt
SQL	http://java.sun.com/jstl/sql_rt	sql_rt
XML	http://java.sun.com/jstl/xml_rt	x_rt

a.   The prefix is merely a recommendation; you can use any prefix you choose.

Although it's not strictly necessary, adhering to the prefixes listed in the two preceding tables is a good idea, if for no other reason than doing so will make your code easier for other JSP developers to understand.

The _rt suffixes added to the URIs and prefixes stand for *runtime expression values*, which is the name for values assigned to dynamic action attributes.[5]

The rest of this section briefly introduces each of the libraries listed in Table 1.2, in the order in which they are listed. "Getting Started" on page 23 shows you how to download and install the software that you need to get started with JSTL and "A Simple JSTL Web Application" on page 30 shows you how to implement a simple JSTL-based application. Finally, this chapter concludes with "JSTL Design Principles" on page 34, which discusses some of the JSTL design principles that affect your everyday use of JSTL actions.

Core Approach

The JSTL expression language is rich enough that you will rarely need to use the RT (runtime) libraries. Because the RT and EL (expression language) libraries are identical except for the language used to specify dynamic attributes, this book covers the EL libraries almost exclusively.

Core Actions

The JSTL core actions embody fundamental functionality that is implemented by many JSP pages. That functionality includes:

- Send output to the current JspWriter
- Create and destroy scoped variables

---

5.   That's what <rtexprvalue>—used to specify that an attribute can be set to a runtime expression value in a tag library descriptor—stands for (*runtime expression value*).

- Manipulate JavaBeans component (bean) properties and collections
- Manipulate entries in a map
- Implement if/then constructs and switch statements
- Handle exceptions
- Iterate over data structures, integer values, or strings
- Create URLs and import resources
- Redirect servlet responses

The core JSTL actions are listed in Table 1.4.

Table 1.4   Core Actions

Action	Description
<c:catch>	Catches exceptions thrown in the action's body
<c:choose>	Chooses one of potentially many code fragments
<c:forEach>	Iterates over a collection of objects, or iterates a fixed number of times
<c:forTokens>	Iterates over tokens in a string
<c:if>	Conditionally performs some functionality
<c:import>	Imports a URL
<c:otherwise>	Specifies default functionality in a <c:choose> action
<c:out>	Sends output to the current JspWriter
<c:param>	Specifies a URL parameter for <c:import> or <c:url>
<c:redirect>	Redirects a response to a specified URL
<c:remove>	Removes a scoped variable
<c:set>	Creates a scoped variable
<c:url>	Creates a URL, with URL rewriting as appropriate
<c:when>	Specifies one of several conditions in a <c:choose> action

Until JSP 2.0 is finalized, the <c:out> action will probably be the most heavily used JSTL action. The <c:out> action evaluates an EL expression and sends the result to the current JspWriter; for example, the following code fragment uses the <c:out> action to display the value of a request parameter named amount.

```
<c:if test='${not empty param.amount}'>
   <c:out value='${param.amount}'/>
</c:if>
```

In the preceding example, the <c:if> action evaluates an EL expression that tests to see whether a request parameter named amount exists and has a non-null value;[6] if it does, the <c:if> action evaluates its body content.

The JSP 2.0 specification incorporates the JSTL expression language, which means that JSP template text will accommodate EL expressions; so, for example, with JSP 2.0, you could rewrite the preceding code fragment like this:

```
<%-- This code fragment will only work with JSP 2.0 --%>
<c:if test='${not empty param.amount}'>
   ${param.amount}
</c:if>
```

In the preceding example, the <c:out> action is not needed because JSP 2.0 template text is JSTL-expression-aware.

There's a lot more to the Core library than evaluating expressions and displaying the result; for example, you can implement if/then statements and switch constructs. The following code fragment implements the former: if a request parameter named name exists and has a non-null value, the code prints a greeting; otherwise, it asks users to enter their name and includes a JSP page that contains a registration form.

```
<html>
   ...
   <body>
      <%@ taglib uri='http://java.sun.com/jstl/core' prefix='c' %>

      <c:choose>
         <c:when test='${not empty param.name}'>
            Hello <c:out value='${param.name}'/>.
         </c:when>

         <c:otherwise>
            <font color='red'>
               Please enter your name:<p>
            </font>

            <jsp:include page='index.jsp'/>
         </c:otherwise>
      </c:choose>
   </body>
</html>
```

---

6. See "The empty Operator" on page 60 for more information about the empty operator.

Besides handling exceptions with JSP's error page mechanism, you can use the <c:catch> action to catch an exception and deal with it in the same JSP page; for example, the following code fragment uses <c:catch> to catch an exception:

```
<c:catch var='exception'>
   <%-- Actions that could possibly throw exceptions... --%>
</c:catch>

<%-- If the exception scoped variable is not
     empty, handle the exception here --%>
<c:if test='${not empty exception}'>
   <%-- Display an error message --%>
</c:if>
```

If an exception is thrown within the <c:catch> body, the <c:catch> action stores that exception in a scoped variable. In the preceding code fragment, that exception, named `exception`, is accessed in the body of the <c:if> action.

JSTL also provides URL actions that simplify importing resources and creating URLs. For example, the <jsp:include> action can import resources, but only from the same Web application. The <c:import> action can do that too, but it can also import resources from absolute URLs and foreign contexts.[7] For example, the following code fragment imports content from an absolute URL:

```
<c:import url='http://www.mysite.com/mydoc.txt'/>
```

The following code fragment imports content from a resource in a foreign context (another Web application) on the same server.

```
<c:import url='/jsp/test_2.jsp' context='/core-jstl'/>
```

The preceding examples are just some of the things that the Core library actions can do. Chapters 3–5 in this book discuss all of the Core library actions in detail.

Formatting Actions

The JSTL formatting actions let you internationalize your Web applications so you can easily localize them for different locales. You can:

- Specify a resource bundle used to localize messages
- Specify a locale used for formatting and parsing
- Localize messages
- Format and parse numbers, currencies, and percents

---

7. A foreign context is another Web application in a website.

- Format and parse dates
- Set a request encoding

The formatting JSTL actions are listed in Table 1.5.

Table 1.5 Formatting Actions

Action	Description
<fmt:bundle>	Sets a localization context for enclosed <fmt:message> and formatting actions
<fmt:setBundle>	Sets a localization context for <fmt:message> and formatting actions
<fmt:setLocale>	Sets the locale used by <fmt:message> and formatting actions
<fmt:formatDate>	Formats a date in a locale-sensitive manner
<fmt:formatNumber>	Formats a number, currency, or percent in a locale-sensitive manner
<fmt:message>	Retrieves a message from a resource bundle
<fmt:param>	Supplies a parameter for an enclosing <fmt:message> action
<fmt:parseDate>	Parses a date in a locale-sensitive manner
<fmt:parseNumber>	Parses a number, currency, or percent in a locale-sensitive manner
<fmt:requestEncoding>	Sets the request encoding for a JSP page
<fmt:setTimeZone>	Sets the time zone used by date and time formatting actions
<fmt:timeZone>	Sets the time zone used by enclosed date and time formatting actions

The most heavily used action listed in Table 1.5 is undoubtedly <fmt:message>, which retrieves localized messages from a resource bundle; for example, the following code fragment uses <fmt:message> to display a company name and slogan:

```
<html>
...
  <body>
    <%-- Use <fmt:message> to display localized messages
         from a resource bundle --%>
    <font size='5'>
      <fmt:message key='company.name'/>
    </font>

    <p><fmt:message key='company.slogan'/>
    <hr>
  </body>
</html>
```

The <fmt:message> action's mandatory key attribute specifies a key in a resource bundle; the <fmt:message> action retrieves the corresponding object—typically a string—associated with that key, coerces that object to a string, and sends it to the current JspWriter.

Besides localizing messages, the formatting actions also let you format and parse numbers, currencies, percents, dates, and times; for example, the following code fragment formats the current date and time for the U.S. English locale:

```
<fmt:setLocale value='en-US'/>
<jsp:useBean id='today' class='java.util.Date'/>
<fmt:formatDate value='${today}' type='both'/>
```

The preceding code fragment sets the locale for formatting actions with <fmt:setLocale> and creates an instance of java.util.Date with <jsp:useBean>. That date is subsequently passed to <fmt:formatDate>, which formats both the date and time according to the locale set by <fmt:setLocale>.

SQL Actions

The JSTL SQL actions let you:

- Specify a data source
- Execute database queries and access the query result
- Execute database updates and transactions
- Execute prepared statements

The SQL JSTL actions are listed in Table 1.6.

Table 1.6   SQL Actions

Action	Description
<sql:dateParam>	Specifies a date parameter for <sql:query> or <sql:update>
<sql:param>	Specifies a parameter for <sql:query> or <sql:update>
<sql:query>	Executes a database query
<sql:setDataSource>	Sets a data source for <sql:query>, <sql:update>, and <sql:transaction> actions
<sql:transaction>	Wraps a transaction around enclosed <sql:query> and <sql:update> actions
<sql:update>	Executes a database update

On page 4, we saw how to execute database queries and iterate over the result. You can also use the SQL actions to perform database updates and execute transactions; for example:[8]

```
<sql:transaction>
    <%-- Withdraw money from the "from" customer's account --%>
    <sql:update>
        UPDATE ACCOUNTS SET BALANCE = BALANCE - ?  WHERE CUST_ID = ?

        <sql:param value='${param.amount}'/>
        <sql:param value='${param.fromCustomer}'/>
    </sql:update>

    <%-- Deposit the money withdrawn from the "from"
        customer's account in the "to" customer's account --%>
    <sql:update>
        UPDATE ACCOUNTS SET BALANCE = BALANCE + ?  WHERE CUST_ID = ?

        <sql:param value='${param.amount}'/>
        <sql:param value='${param.toCustomer}'/>
    </sql:update>
</sql:transaction>
```

The preceding JSP page uses the <sql:transaction> action to perform a database transaction that consists of two database updates that transfer funds from one account to another.

XML Actions

The JSTL XML actions let you manipulate XML documents. Those actions offer the following functionality:

- Parse an XML document
- Transform an XML document with XSLT
- Set a system ID for resolving external entities
- Apply a SAX filter to an XML document

---

8. See "Executing Database Transactions" on page 411 for a discussion of that code.

The XML actions are listed in Table 1.7.

Table 1.7   XML Actions

Action	Description
<x:choose>	XML version of <c:choose>
<x:forEach>	XML version of <c:forEach>
<x:if>	XML version of <c:if>
<x:otherwise>	XML version of <c:otherwise>
<x:out>	XML version of <c:out>
<x:param>	XML version of <c:param>; specifies a transformation parameter for an <x:transform> action
<x:parse>	Parses an XML document
<x:set>	XML version of <c:set>
<x:transform>	Transforms an XML document
<x:when>	XML version of <c:when>

Although there are many XML actions, all but two of those actions are XML versions of JSTL core actions. The core actions, such as <c:out>, <c:set> and <c:if>, accept EL expressions, whereas the corresponding XML actions, such as <x:out>, <x:set>, and <x:if>, accept XPath expressions.[9] The only two XML actions that are not XML versions of core actions—<x:parse> and <x:transform>—let you parse and transform XML documents.

To get an idea of how to use the XML actions, let's parse a simple XML document and display the result. A partial listing of that XML document is listed below.

```
<rolodex>
   <contact>
      <firstName>Anna</firstName>
      <lastName>Keeney</lastName>
      <email>anna.keeney@worldlink.net</email>
      <phone type="work">716-873-9644</phone>
      <phone type="home">716-834-8772</phone>
   </contact>
   ...
</rolodex>
```

---

9. You can also use JSP expressions with the RT libraries; see "Twin Libraries" on page 9 for more information.

The preceding XML document is a Rolodex that keeps track of a collection of contacts. For brevity, only the first entry in the Rolodex is listed above. The code fragment listed below parses that document and creates an HTML table that shows the data associated with each entry in the address book:[10]

```
<c:import var='rolodex_xml' url='rolodex.xml'/>
<x:parse var='document' xml='${rolodex_xml}'/>

<table>
    <x:forEach select='$document//contact'>
        <table>
            <tr><td>First Name:</td>
                <td><x:out select='firstName'/></td></tr>
            <tr><td>Last Name:</td>
                <td><x:out select='lastName'/></td></tr>
            <tr><td>Email:</td>
                <td><x:out select='email'/></td></tr>
            <tr><td>Work Phone:</td>
                <td><x:out select='phone[@type="work"]'/></td></tr>

            <x:if select='phone[@type="home"]'>
                <tr><td>Home Phone:</td>
                    <td><x:out select='phone[@type="home"]'/></td>
            </x:if>
        </table><br>
    </x:forEach>
</table>
```

The preceding code fragment uses the <x:parse> action to parse the Rolodex XML document. Subsequently, it uses the <x:forEach>, <x:out>, and <x:if> actions to show the contacts in an HTML table; that output looks like this:

```
First Name:     Anna

Last Name:      Keeney

Email:          anna.keeney@worldlink.net

Work Phone:     716-873-9644

Home Phone:     716-834-8772

...
```

---

10. See "Parsing XML" on page 432 for more information about that code.

The JSTL Tag Library Validators

JSTL lets you eliminate almost all JSP scriptlets and expressions from your JSP code, which makes your code more maintainable and extensible. It will take some discipline on your part, however, to keep scriptlets and expressions out of your code; occasionally, you might have to implement a servlet or custom action to assist you in that endeavor.

Instead of relying on discipline to keep JSP scriptlets and expressions out of your code, you can use one of the JSTL tag library validators to enforce that restriction. That validator lets you allow or disallow the following:

- JSP declarations
- JSP expressions
- JSP scriptlets
- Runtime expression values

You don't have to write any code to use the JSTL validators, but you must create a tag library descriptor (TLD) because tag library validators are associated with a tag library;[11] for example, the following TLD specifies a `validator` element that disallows scriptlets:

```
<?xml version="1.0" encoding="ISO-8859-1"?>
<!DOCTYPE taglib PUBLIC
  "-//Sun Microsystems, Inc.//DTD JSP Tag Library 1.2//EN"
  "http://java.sun.com/j2ee/dtds/web-jsptaglibrary_1_2.dtd">

<taglib>
   <tlib-version>1.0</tlib-version>
   <jsp-version>1.2</jsp-version>
   <short-name>Core JSTL Validation Example Tag</short-name>
   <description>
      This library has a validator that allows
      JSP declarations, expressions, and
      runtime expression values but disallows scriplets
   </description>

   <validator>
      <validator-class>
         javax.servlet.jsp.jstl.tlv.ScriptFreeTLV
      </validator-class>

      <init-param>
         <param-name>allowDeclarations</param-name>
```

---

11. But validators have access to the entire JSP page, so they can perform general validation.

```
         <param-value>true</param-value>
      </init-param>

      <init-param>
         <param-name>allowScriptlets</param-name>
         <param-value>false</param-value>
      </init-param>

      <init-param>
         <param-name>allowExpressions</param-name>
         <param-value>true</param-value>
      </init-param>

      <init-param>
         <param-name>allowRTExpressions</param-name>
         <param-value>true</param-value>
      </init-param>
   </validator>

   <tag>
      <name>DoNothingTag</name>
      <tag-class>tags.DoNothingAction</tag-class>
   </tag>
</taglib>
```

The other JSTL validator restricts the tag libraries that can be used in a JSP page; the following TLD lets you use only the JSTL core and formatting libraries:

```
<?xml version="1.0" encoding="ISO-8859-1" ?>
<!DOCTYPE taglib PUBLIC
   "-//Sun Microsystems, Inc.//DTD JSP Tag Library 1.2//EN"
   "http://java.sun.com/j2ee/dtds/web-jsptaglibrary_1_2.dtd">

<taglib>
   <tlib-version>1.0</tlib-version>
   <jsp-version>1.2</jsp-version>
   <short-name>Core JSTL Validation Example Tag</short-name>
   <description>
      This library has a validator that restricts the tag libraries
      that a JSP developer can use
   </description>

   <validator>
      <validator-class>
         javax.servlet.jsp.jstl.tlv.PermittedTaglibsTLV
      </validator-class>

      <init-param>
         <param-name>permittedTaglibs</param-name>
```

```
      <param-value>
          http://java.sun.com/jstl/core
          http://java.sun.com/jstl/fmt
      </param-value>
    </init-param>
  </validator>

  <tag>
     <name>DoNothingTag</name>
     <tag-class>tags.DoNothingAction</tag-class>
  </tag>
</taglib>
```

Notice that both of the preceding TLDs include a `tag` element because at least one `tag` element is required for each TLD. The `name` and `tag-class` elements are required for the `tag` element, so the preceding listing specifies those values. The tag class is a tag handler that, as its name suggests, does nothing; it looks like this:

```
package tags;

import javax.servlet.jsp.JspException;
import javax.servlet.jsp.tagext.TagSupport;

public class DoNothingAction extends TagSupport {
   public int doStartTag() throws JspException {
      return SKIP_BODY;
   }
}
```

To use the validators, you simply add a `taglib` declaration at the top of your JSP pages, like this:

```
<!DOCTYPE HTML PUBLIC "-//W3C//DTD HTML 4.0 Transitional//EN">
<html>
   <head>
      <%@ taglib uri='WEB-INF/restrictJavaCode.tld' prefix='rjc' %>
      <%@ taglib uri='WEB-INF/restrictTaglibs.tld'  prefix='rtl' %>
      <%@ taglib uri='http://java.sun.com/jstl/fmt' prefix='fmt' %>

      <title><fmt:message key='index.window-title'/></title>
   </head>

   <body>
      <% new java.util.Date(); %>
      <h2><fmt:message key='index.greeting'/></h2>
   </body>
</html>
```

At translation time, the preceding JSP page will throw an exception because it has a scriptlet, which violates the first TLD declared in the page.

Now that you know what JSTL is and what it offers, let's get started by downloading and installing the necessary software and implementing a simple Web application that uses JSTL.

1.2 Getting Started

Getting started with JSTL is easy; you need:

- The Java 2 Platform, either J2SE (Standard Edition) or J2EE (Enterprise Edition)
- A servlet container that supports the Servlet 2.3 and JSP 1.2 APIs
- JSTL

If you don't plan to use J2EE features such as Java Naming and Directory Interface (JNDI) or Enterprise JavaBeans (EJB), you're probably better off with J2SE, which is a subset of J2EE.

You can download the J2SE, which is available for Linux, Solaris, and Windows, at `http://java.sun.com/j2se/1.4/download.html`; you can download J2EE at `http://java.sun.com/j2ee/sdk_1.3`. For other platforms, such as Mac OSX, check to see if a Java 2 implementation is preinstalled.

JSTL requires a servlet container that supports the Servlet 2.3 and JSP 1.2 APIs. For running the Web applications discussed in this book, I recommend either Tomcat 4.1.3 (or later) or Resin 2.1.2 (or later). See "Tomcat" on page 26 and "Resin" on page 28, for more information about those servlet containers.

Finally, of course, you need a JSTL implementation. Some servlet containers, such as Resin, already offer their own JSTL implementations, but as this book went to press, those implementations were immature. To test this book's examples, I recommend you use the JSTL Reference Implementation, which is discussed in "The JSTL Reference Implementation" on page 24.

This section shows you how to download the JSTL specification and download and install Tomcat, Resin, and the JSTL Reference Implementation. "A Simple JSTL Web Application" on page 30 discusses a simple JSTL example to get you started.

The JSTL Specification

You may find it useful to have the JSTL specification on hand while you use JSTL, so before we discuss downloading servlet containers and JSTL, let's take a look at how to download the specification. If you're not interested in the specification, you may prefer to skip ahead to one of the following destinations:

- "The JSTL Reference Implementation" on page 24
- "Downloading and Installing a Servlet Container" on page 26
- "A Simple JSTL Web Application" on page 30

You can download the JSTL specification at this URL: `http://jcp.org/aboutJava/communityprocess/final/jsr052/`. The specification is a PDF file, so you will probably use Acrobat to view it, as shown in Figure 1–1.

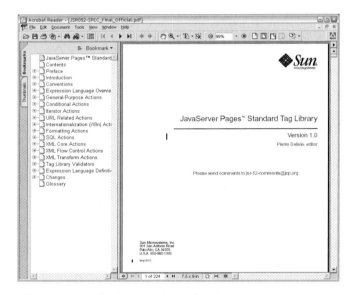

Figure 1–1   The JSTL 1.0 Specification

It's not necessary to download the JSTL specification, but you might find it useful anyhow, especially for legalistic issues. From here on out, our discussion will revolve around the software required for JSTL: a JSTL implementation (which may be bundled with your servlet container) and a servlet container.

The JSTL Reference Implementation

The JSTL Reference Implementation is a mature JSTL implementation that's the last word on any ambiguities in the specification. But it's not fast. For a speedy implementation, you should look to your servlet container; for example, Resin's JSTL is called *Fast JSTL*. If your servlet container does not provide a JSTL implementation, then you must come up with one of your own. Fortunately, the JSTL Reference Implementation is freely available; you can download it from this URL: `http://jakarta.apache.org/builds/jakarta-taglibs/releases/standard`. That webpage is shown in Figure 1–2.

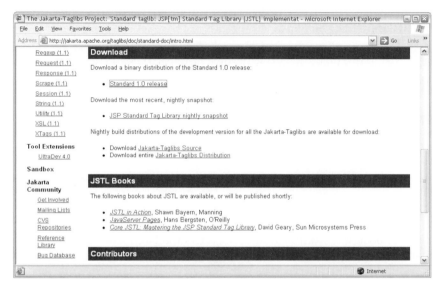

Figure 1–2   Downloading the JSTL Binary Distribution

As you can see from Figure 1–2, you have two choices: you can download either the 1.0 release or a nightly build. I recommend that you download the former for the sake of reliability. If you download the 1.0 release, you can choose between ZIP and TAR files.

Once you've downloaded the Reference Implementation, you can unzip or untar the file that you downloaded in a directory of your choice. Decompressing that file will produce a top-level directory, so you don't have to worry about scattering files about in the directory of your choice.

Now you know how to download and install the reference implementation. In "A Simple JSTL Web Application" on page 30, we discuss how to use it.

The following two sections discuss how to download and install Tomcat and Resin. If you already have a servlet container installed that supports the Servlet 2.3 and JSP 1.2 APIs, you can skip those sections and start reading at "A Simple JSTL Web Application" on page 30.

Downloading and Installing a Servlet Container

You can use the JSTL Reference Implementation with any servlet container that supports Servlet 2.3 and JSP 1.2. I recommend that, if possible, you use two servlet containers installed on your desktop to test your Web applications. Using servlet containers that are stored on your machine will give you more control over how those containers are configured and used. Using more than one servlet container to test your code will ensure that you don't inadvertently use nonportable constructs.

This section discusses downloading two servlet containers: Tomcat 4.1.3 and Resin 2.1.2. All of the code in this book was tested with both of those servlet containers.

Core Approach

Use two servlet containers to test your code to ensure quality and portability.

Tomcat

At the time this book was written, Tomcat 4.1.3 was the latest version of the reference implementation for the Servlet and JSP APIs. You can download Tomcat at this URL: `http://jakarta.apache.org/builds/jakarta-tomcat-4.0/`. That webpage is shown in Figure 1–3.

Figure 1–3   Downloading Tomcat

As you can see from Figure 1–3, you can download the latest Tomcat 4 *milestone* or *nightly* releases. I suggest that, for stability, you download the latest milestone release. Like the JSTL Reference Implementation, you can download Tomcat in a ZIP or TAR file. Once you have downloaded that file, decompress it and a top-level directory will be created.

By default, Tomcat will run on port 8080 instead of the standard port—80—to avoid conflicts with other Web services that may be using the standard port. If you're not using the standard port, you might want to reconfigure Tomcat to run on that port so you don't have to include the port number in your URLs. To change that port, just edit the file $TOMCAT/conf/server.xml, where $TOMCAT represents the top-level directory that was created when you decompressed the ZIP or TAR file that you downloaded.

Once you open that file, search for the string port=8080 and change 8080 to 80, like this:

```
<!-- Define a non-SSL Coyote HTTP/1.1 Connector on port 8080 -->

<Connector className="org.apache.coyote.tomcat4.CoyoteConnector"
             port="80" minProcessors="5" maxProcessors="75"
        enableLookups="true" redirectPort="8443"
          acceptCount="10" debug="0" connectionTimeout="20000"
useURIValidationHack="false" />
```

Now you're ready to run Tomcat. In the $TOMCAT/bin directory, you will find the files startup.sh and startup.bat that you use to start Tomcat for UNIX and Windows, respectively. The files shutdown.sh and shutdown.bat in the same directory shut down Tomcat on UNIX and Windows, respectively. For convenience, I recommend that you create desktop icons for starting up and shutting down.

After you start Tomcat, access this URL to make sure Tomcat is working: http://localhost.[12] You should see a webpage similar to the one shown in Figure 1–4.

---

12. If you're not using port 80, use this URL: http://localhost:*XXXX*, where *XXXX* represents the port number.

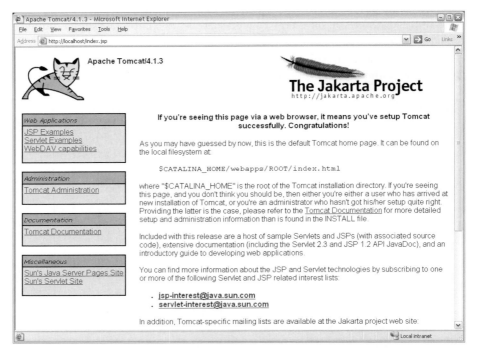

Figure 1–4   Running Tomcat

Once you have Tomcat installed and running, you're ready to start using JSTL. See "A Simple JSTL Web Application" on page 30 for details on how to do that.

Resin

Resin is one of the most popular servlet containers because it's stable and fast, with numerous unique features that support XML. The process for downloading and installing Resin is similar to the same process for Tomcat: Download Resin, decompress the file that you downloaded, thereby creating a top-level directory, and modify the port number, if desired. You can download Resin at this URL: `http://www.caucho.com/download`. That webpage is shown in Figure 1–5.

As you can see from Figure 1–5, you can download a ZIP file or a TAR file. Once you've downloaded the file, decompress it and a top-level directory will be created.

As with Tomcat, you may want to change the port that Resin runs on to the standard 80 port so that you don't have to include the port number in your URLs. To

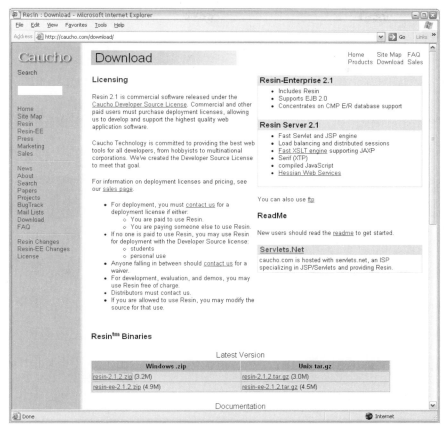

Figure 1–5   Downloading Resin

do that, edit the file `$RESIN/conf/resin.conf` and change the port number like this:[13]

```
<http port='80'/>
```

In the `$RESIN/bin` directory you will find an executable for Resin named `httpd.exe` for Windows and `httpd.sh` for Unix. Unlike Tomcat, Resin has no application for shutting itself down, because Resin creates a small window that lets you restart Resin or shut it down.

---

13. `$RESIN` represents the top-level directory created when you decompressed the downloaded file.

Once you've started Resin, you can verify that it's working by accessing the `http://localhost` URL, as shown in Figure 1–6.

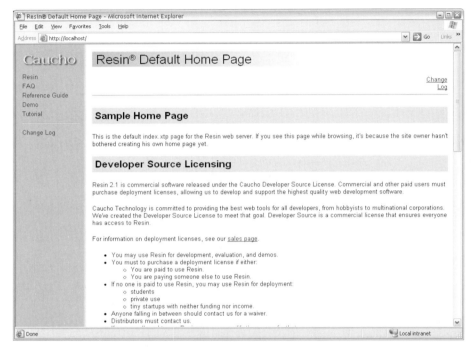

Figure 1–6   Running Resin

1.3 A Simple JSTL Web Application

Now that you have the necessary software installed, let's implement a simple JSTL Web application, shown in Figure 1–7.

Figure 1–7   A Simple JSTL Web Application

The preceding JSP page uses the JSTL <fmt:message> action to set the window's title and display a greeting. Before we discuss the code, let's take a look at the Web application's files, which are shown in Figure 1–8.

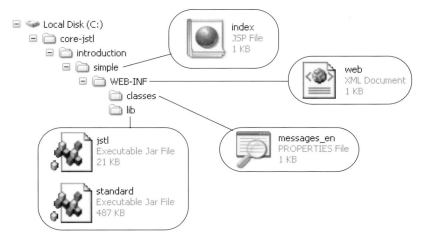

Figure 1–8   The Web Application's Files

The Web application has a deployment descriptor, one JSP page, two JAR files, and a properties file. The JAR files are from the JSTL Reference Implementation distribution. Although the Reference Implementation comes with other JAR files, such as `xalan.jar` for the XML actions, most applications will only use `jstl.jar` and `standard.jar`. The former contains the classes and interfaces defined under the `javax.servlet.jsp.jstl` package, and the latter contains classes and interfaces specific to the JSTL reference implementation.

The properties file defines an English resource bundle that the <fmt:message> action uses to localize text. The deployment descriptor defines two JSTL configuration settings—one that sets the locale and another that sets the base name of the resource bundle used by the application.[14]

---

14. See "Configuration Settings" on page 230 for more information about JSTL configuration settings.

The JSP page is listed in Listing 1.1.

Listing 1.1   *index.jsp*

```
<!DOCTYPE HTML PUBLIC "-//W3C//DTD HTML 4.0 Transitional//EN">
<html>
   <head>
     <%@ taglib uri='http://java.sun.com/jstl/fmt' prefix='fmt' %>
     <title><fmt:message key='index.window-title'/></title>
   </head>

   <body>
      <h2><fmt:message key='index.greeting'/></h2>
   </body>
</html>
```

The preceding JSP page uses only the JSTL formatting library, which is accessible through the `taglib` declaration. That declaration must come before the first use of any formatting action, so in this case, the `taglib` directive is in the HTML `head` section. Typically, `taglib` directives are placed at the top of the `body` section.

The JSP page uses the <fmt:message> action to localize text. That action retrieves from a resource bundle the values that correspond to the action's `key` attribute; for example, `index.greeting` corresponds to `Welcome to JSTL`. But how does the <fmt:message> action know which resource bundle to use? That can be specified in a number of ways;[15] this application specifies the resource bundle in the deployment descriptor, which is listed in Listing 1.2.

The preceding deployment descriptor specifies two JSTL configuration settings that define a locale and resource bundle base name, `en-US` and `messages`, respectively.

Because of those settings, the <fmt:message> action will retrieve localized messages from the `messages_en.properties` file located in `WEB-INF/classes`. That properties file is listed in Listing 1.3.

The preceding properties file defines two key/value pairs for the window title and greeting.

If you want to localize this application for another language, you can simply specify a different locale in the deployment descriptor and provide a properties file that defines a resource bundle for that locale. Even if you don't plan to support multiple locales, you should still use <fmt:message> to localize all the text that your application displays to users, for two reasons. First, placing all of the text in one location—a properties file—makes it easier to find and change that text. Second, if

---

15. See "Localization Context Lookup" on page 268 for more information about specifying resource bundles.

| Listing 1.2 | *WEB-INF/web.xml* |

```
<?xml version="1.0" encoding="ISO-8859-1"?>

<!DOCTYPE web-app
    PUBLIC "-//Sun Microsystems, Inc.//DTD Web Application 2.2//EN"
    "http://java.sun.com/j2ee/dtds/web-app_2.2.dtd">

<web-app>
    <context-param>
        <param-name>
            javax.servlet.jsp.jstl.fmt.locale
        </param-name>
        <param-value>
            en-US
        </param-value>
    </context-param>

    <context-param>
        <param-name>
            javax.servlet.jsp.jstl.fmt.localizationContext
        </param-name>
        <param-value>
            messages
        </param-value>
    </context-param>

    <welcome-file-list>
        <welcome-file>
            index.jsp
        </welcome-file>
    </welcome-file-list>
</web-app>
```

| Listing 1.3 | *WEB-INF/classes/messages_en.properties* |

```
index.window-title=A JSTL Application
index.greeting=Welcome to the JSTL
```

you later decide to support more locales, supporting multiple locales is a simple matter of creating new resource bundles and modifying the locale configuration setting. See "I18N Actions" on page 248 for more information about internationalization, and see "Formatting Actions" on page 308 for information about formatting and parsing numbers, currencies, percents, and dates.

When you deploy your application, you have two choices: Create a Web archive (WAR) file and place it in your servlet container's webapps directory, or modify your servlet container's configuration file. To create a WAR file, you can use the JAR command; for example, `jar cvf $TOMCAT/webapps/simpleJSTL.war *` executed in a Web application's top-level directory will create a WAR file in Tomcat's webapps directory.[16] The next time you start Tomcat, it will load your application.

For Tomcat, you can add a Web application in the configuration file—`$TOMCAT/conf/server.xml`—like this:

```
...
<!-- Tomcat 4.1.3 context -->

<Context path="/core-jstl/introduction"
        docBase="C:/core-jstl/introduction/simple"/>
...
```

Tomcat refers to Web applications as contexts, so you specify a URL path for the context and its corresponding directory, known as a document base. Resin, on the other hand, refers to Web applications as Web apps and refers to document bases as application directories; here's how you specify your Web application in the Resin configuration file:

```
...
<!-- Resin 2.1.2 web app -->

<web-app id="/core-jstl/introduction"
        app-dir="C:/core-jstl/introduction/simple"/>
...
```

Regardless of whether you are using Tomcat or Resin, the URL for the preceding application is `http://localhost/core-jstl/introduction`, assuming your servlet container is running on your desktop on port 80.

1.4 JSTL Design Principles

This chapter concludes with a discussion of some fundamental JSTL design principles. To make the best use of JSTL, you should understand those design principles; they apply to many, if not all, of the JSTL actions. The design principles discussed in this section are:

- Naming conventions
- Scoped variables
- Dynamic attributes

---

16. `$TOMCAT` represents the Tomcat top-level directory.

- Error handling
- Configuration settings

Naming Conventions for JSTL Actions

JSTL actions and their attributes use the Java naming convention—they start with lower case, and subsequent words begin with upper case; for example:

```
<c:out value='${param.amount}'/>
<c:forEach var='item' items='${names}' varStatus='status'>
```

Some attribute names, such as `var` and `scope`, are used by many JSTL actions and always have the same semantic value. The next section discusses those attributes.

Scoped Variables vs. Scripting Variables

Actions are a conduit between JSP pages and Java code. Through that conduit flows information from JSP page to Java code, and vice versa. For example, consider this code:

```
<c:forEach var='item' begin='1' end='10'>
   value = <c:out value='${item}'/><br>
</c:forEach>
```

In the preceding code fragment, the JSP page uses the <c:forEach> action to send information—such as the value of the `var` attribute, which represents the current item in the iteration—to the tag's handler, which is written in the Java programming language. The tag handler exports an object named `item` and makes it available, as a scoped variable, to the body of the <c:forEach> action.

Many JSTL actions export scoped variables that you can easily access through the expression language, as is the case for the preceding code fragment. Realize that this is in contrast to most JSP custom actions, which typically make objects available to JSP pages with scripting variables, which are accessed with JSP expressions and scriptlets.

The `var` and `scope` Attributes

If a JSTL action makes a scoped variable available to one or more JSP pages, it will have an attribute named `var` that lets you specify the name of that scoped variable. Actions that make that scoped variable available outside their body also have a `scope` attribute that lets you specify the scoped variable's scope. For example, the following code fragment uses <fmt:message> to store a localized message in a scoped variable:

```
<fmt:message key='index.greeting' var='msg' scope='request'/>
```

If you don't specify the `var` and `scope` attributes, the <fmt:message> action will send the localized message corresponding to the specified key to the current

JspWriter. If you specify the var attribute, <fmt:message> stores the localized message in a scoped variable whose name corresponds to the var attribute's value; for example, in the preceding code fragment the <fmt:message> action stores the value corresponding to the index.greeting key in a scoped variable named msg that resides in request scope.

If a JSTL action has var and scope attributes, you can leave the scope unspecified, and it will default to page scope; for example, the preceding code fragment could be modified like this:

```
<fmt:message key='index.greeting' var='msg'/>
```

The <fmt:message> action listed above also stores a localized message in a scoped variable named msg, but because the scope attribute was not specified, that variable resides in page scope.

Some JSTL actions can export more than one scoped variable; in those cases, the primary scoped variable is named with the var attribute and its scope is specified with the scope attribute, whereas the names of other scoped variables are specified with an attribute named varXXX and their corresponding scope attribute, if available, is named scopeXXX, where XXX represents the semantics of the scoped variable. For example, the <x:parse> action has var and scope attributes for the parsed XML document, but you can specify the varDOM and scopeDOM attributes instead if you want to force <x:parse> to use the Document Object Model (DOM).

Scoped Variable Visibility

Scoped variables created by JSTL actions are visible either within the body of the action or after the action's end tag. The scope of the former is referred to as *nested*, and the scope of the latter is referred to as *at-end*. The life cycle of an at-end scoped variable depends on its scope.

Static vs. Dynamic Action Attributes

Values specified for JSTL action attributes can be static or dynamic. Dynamic attributes can be specified with EL expressions for actions in the EL library or with JSP expressions for actions in the RT library. Static attributes are specified with strings.

Nearly all JSTL action attributes are dynamic, except for the var and scope attributes (and varXXX and scopeXXX attributes) discussed in "The var and scope Attributes" on page 35 and the select attribute for the JSTL XML actions. Requiring static values for those attributes is beneficial to tools, with few drawbacks for JSP developers.

Error Handling

JSTL does all it can to avoid throwing exceptions, so in many cases if you specify an action's value as `null` or an empty string, that value will be coerced—see "Type Coercion" on page 62—to a harmless constant; for example, if you look at "JSTL Type Coercion" on page 62, you can see that `null` values are coerced to 0 when an attribute expects a number.

Besides the expression language's built-in type coercion, the library actions themselves do their best to interpret nonsensical values as harmless constants; for example, the <c:forEach> action will do nothing if you specify a `null` value for its `items` attribute. That default behavior, for example, makes it practical to iterate over form data that contains unchecked checkboxes.

Table 1.8 shows how JSTL handles errors for certain types of attributes.

Table 1.8 JSTL Attribute Error Handling

Attribute	If value is invalid:
`var`	Translation-time validation error
`scope`	Translation-time validation error
Dynamic, *with* a fixed-set of possible values	If the value is `null`, it's coerced to a default value; otherwise, other invalid values will cause an exception to be thrown.
Dynamic, *without* a fixed-set of possible values	If the value is `null`, the result is action dependent; other invalid values will cause an exception to be thrown.

Exceptions caused by an action's body content, the action itself, the expression language, or XPath are always propagated. You can use the <c:catch> action to catch those exceptions; see "The <c:catch> Action" on page 126 for more information about the <c:catch> action.

Configuration Settings

Some of the more specialized JSTL actions, such as the SQL and formatting actions, use JSTL configuration settings to specify a value that's shared among a set of JSTL actions. A configuration setting is a combination of a context initialization parameter and a configuration variable that can be used to override that initialization parameter for a particular JSP scope. See Chapter 6, "Configuration Settings," for more information about configuration settings.

THE JSTL EXPRESSION LANGUAGE

Topics in This Chapter

- Expression Language Overview
- Expressions
- Identifiers
- Operators
- Type Coercion
- Literal Values
- Implicit Objects
- Method Invocation
- EL Expressions in Custom Actions
- Common Mistakes

Chapter 2

Although JSTL, as its name implies, provides a set of standard tags, its single most important feature may well be the expression language it defines. That expression language greatly reduces the need for specifying tag attribute values with Java code and significantly simplifies accessing all sorts of application data, including beans, arrays, lists, maps, cookies, request parameters and headers, context initialization parameters, and so on. In fact, the JSTL expression language adds so much value to JSP that it will be incorporated into JSP 2.0.[1]

This chapter examines the JSTL expression language in detail, starting with expressions and identifiers and ending with sections on using the expression language for custom action attributes and common mistakes that developers make when using the expression language.

Note: To illustrate the JSTL expression language, this chapter uses a number of JSTL actions, such as <c:out>, <c:if>, and <c:forEach>, that have not yet been formally discussed in this book. However, the use of those actions is intuitive and this chapter does not use any of those action's advanced features. See Chapter 3, "General-Purpose and Conditional Actions," and "Iteration Actions" on page 150 for formal discussions of the actions used throughout this chapter.

---

1. The JSP expert group will do everything possible to ensure that the JSP 2.0 expression language is backward-compatible with the JSTL 1.0 expression language.

2.1 Expression Language Overview

The JSTL expression language is a simple language inspired by ECMAScript (also known as JavaScript) and XPath. The expression language provides:

- Expressions and identifiers
- Arithmetic, logical, and relational operators
- Automatic type coercion
- Access to beans, arrays, lists, and maps
- Access to a set of implicit objects and servlet properties

All of the features listed above are described in this chapter.

Throughout this book, for convenience the expression language is referred to with the acronym EL and JSTL expressions are referred to as EL expressions.

How the Expression Language Works

Nearly all of the JSTL actions have one or more dynamic attributes that you can specify with an EL expression;[2] for example, you can specify a request parameter with the <c:out> action's `value` attribute like this:

```
<c:out value='${param.emailAddress}'/>
```

The preceding expression displays the value of a request parameter named `emailAddress`. You can also use EL expressions to perform conditional tests, for example:

```
<c:if test='${not empty param.emailAddress}'>...</c:if>
```

The body of the preceding <c:if> action is evaluated if the `emailAddress` request parameter is not empty, meaning neither `null` nor an empty string.

If you're using JSTL with JSP 1.2, you can only use JSTL expressions to specify values for JSTL action attributes, as illustrated above.[3] All JSTL actions that have dynamic attributes interpret EL expressions before they are passed to the action's tag handler, so the expression language is applied—and values are typically coerced—before the tag handler gets them.

---

2. Dynamic values for JSTL actions from the runtime (RT) library can be specified as JSP expressions.
3. Starting with JSP 2.0, you will be able to use EL expressions in JSP template text. See "Expressions" on page 41 for more information.

How to Use the Expression Language

Attributes of JSTL actions can be specified with EL expressions in one of three ways. First, an attribute can be specified with a single expression like this:[4]

```
<jstl:action value='${expr}'/>
```

In the preceding code fragment, the expression `${expr}` is evaluated and its value is coerced to the type expected by the `value` attribute.

Attribute values can also be specified as strings, like this:

```
<jstl:action value='text'/>
```

The string specified for the `value` attribute in the preceding code fragment is coerced to the type expected by that attribute.

Finally, attribute values can consist of one or more expressions intermixed with strings, like this:

```
<jstl:action value='${expr}text${expr}${expr}more text${expr}'/>
```

In the previous code fragment, each of the four expressions is evaluated in order from left to right, coerced to a string, and concatenated with the intermixed text. The resulting string is subsequently coerced to the value expected by the `value` attribute.

2.2 Expressions

EL expressions are invoked with this syntax: `${expr}`, where `expr` represents an expression. Expressions can consist of:

- Identifiers—see "Identifiers" on page 43

- Binary and unary operators—see "Operators" on page 44

- String, boolean, integer, and floating-point literals and `null`—see "Literal Values" on page 63

- Implicit objects, such as `param`, `cookie`, or `header`—see "Implicit Objects" on page 64

---

4. The action <jstl:action> represents any JSTL action.

Until JSP 2.0, when the JSTL expression language is scheduled to be incorporated into the JSP specification, you can only use EL expressions to specify attributes of JSTL actions; for example, the following code fragment from the Database Actions chapter specifies an SQL data source as a comma-separated string constructed with four EL expressions and three commas:[5]

```
<sql:setDataSource dataSource='${url},${driver},${user},${pwd}'
                   scope='session'/>
```

If you upgrade to JSP 2.0, you can have EL expressions in template text; for example, you will be able to execute an SQL query like this:[6]

```
<%-- This only works with containers that support JSP 2.0 --%>

<sql:query>
   ${customerQuery}
</sql:query>
```

The customerQuery scoped variable referenced by the EL expression in the preceding code fragment is a string that specifies a particular query.

Until JSP 2.0, you are restricted to using EL expressions to specify attributes for JSTL actions; for example, you can still execute the query listed in the preceding code fragment like this:

```
<%-- This works with containers that support JSP 1.2 --%>

<sql:query sql='${customerQuery}'/>
```

Alternatively, you could use the <c:out> action if you had to specify the query in the body of the action like this:

```
<%-- This also works with containers that support JSP 1.2 --%>

<sql:query>
   <c:out value='${customerQuery}'/>
</sql:query>
```

The <c:out> action in the preceding code fragment sends the string stored in the customerQuery scoped variable to the current JspWriter, which points to the <sql:query> action's body, so the preceding code fragment is functionally equivalent to the two preceding code fragments.

---

5. See "Specify Your Data Source with <sql:setDataSource>" on page 369.
6. The JSP 2.0 specification is scheduled to be completed in late 2002.

2.3 Identifiers

Identifiers in the expression language represent the names of objects stored in one of the JSP scopes: page, request, session, or application. Those types of objects are referred to throughout this book as *scoped variables*.

When the expression language encounters an identifier, it searches for a scoped variable with that name in the page, request, session, and application scopes, in that order; for example, the following code fragment stores a string in page scope and accesses that string with an EL expression:

```
<% // Create a string
   String s = "Richard Wilson";

   // Store the string in page scope
   pageContext.setAttribute("name", s); %>

<%-- Access the string with an EL expression --%>
<c:out value='${name}'/>
```

In the preceding code fragment, the expression $\${name}$ resolves to a reference to the string named name that was placed in page scope by the scriptlet. That reference is specified for the <c:out> action's value attribute. When the <c:out> action is confronted with an object reference for its value attribute, it coerces that object to a string by invoking its toString method, which in this case produces the value of the string, so the output of the preceding code fragment is Richard Wilson. If the name string had been placed in a different scope, the expression $\${name}$ would still resolve to that string, as long as there was not another object with the same name in another scope that was searched first. For example, if two objects named name are stored in request and application scopes, the expression $\${name}$ would resolve to the object stored in request scope.[7]

Identifiers must adhere to the syntax for Java programming language identifiers; for example, you cannot use characters such as - or / in an identifier.

The two sections that follow—"Accessing JavaBeans Components" and "Accessing Objects Stored in Arrays, Lists, and Maps" on page 52—illustrate how to use identifiers to access beans and collections, respectively, that are stored in JSP scopes.

---

7. Storing beans that have the same name in different scopes is not recommended because the JSP specification allows one of those beans to override the other.

2.4 Operators

JSTL offers a small set of operators, listed in Table 2.1.

Table 2.1   Expression Language Operators

Type	Operators
Arithmetic	`+ - * / (div) % (mod)`
Grouping	`( )`
Identifier Access	`. []`
Logical	`&& (and) || (or) ! (not) empty`
Relational	`== (eq) != (ne) < (lt) > (gt) <= (le) >= (ge)`
Unary	`-`

You need to know three things about the operators in Table 2.1. First, you need to know the operators' syntax; for example, the + operator is used like this: A + B. That material is not covered here because you use EL expressions just like you use their Java equivalents. The second thing you need to know is operator precedence, so you can deduce that 1 + 3 * 5 is 16 but (1 + 3) * 5 is 20. Operator precedence is discussed in "Operator Precedence" on page 45. The third thing you need to know about the operators listed in Table 2.1 is what data types they prefer and how the EL performs type coercion. The former is briefly discussed here and the latter is discussed in "Type Coercion" on page 62.

All of the binary arithmetic operations prefer Double values and all of them will resolve to 0 if either of their operands is null. The operators + - * % will try to coerce their operands to Long values if they cannot be coerced to Double.

The grouping operators, which are parentheses, can be used to force operator precedence, as discussed above. The identifier access operators are discussed in "The . and [] Operators" on page 45, so that discussion is not repeated here.

The relational operators all have textual equivalents; for example, either == or eq will suffice for the equality operator. Those equivalents are provided for XML generation. Like binary arithmetic operations, all of the relational operators prefer Double values but will make do with Long values if the operands cannot be converted to Double.

The logical operators prefer to work with `Boolean` operands. You can use the `empty` operator to see if a value is either `null` or an empty string (`""`). That operator comes in handy when you are interpreting request parameters.

Operator Precedence

The precedence for EL operators is listed below:

- `[] .`
- `()`
- `- (unary) not ! empty`
- `* / div % mod`
- `+ - (binary)`
- `< > <= >= lt gt le ge`
- `== != eq ne`
- `&& and`
- `|| or =`

The operators are listed above from left to right and top to bottom according to precedence; for example, the `[]` operator has precedence over the `.` operator, and the modulus (`%` or `mod`) operator, which represents a division remainder, has precedence over the logical operators.

The `.` and `[]` Operators

The JSTL expression language provides two operators—`.` and `[]`—that let you access scoped variables and their properties. The `.` operator is similar to the Java `.` operator, but instead of invoking methods, you access bean properties; for example, if you have a `Name` bean stored in a scoped variable named `name` and that bean contains `firstName` and `lastName` properties, you can access those properties like this:

```
First Name: <c:out value='${name.firstName}'/>
Last Name: <c:out value='${name.lastName}'/>
```

Assuming that there is a bean named `name` that has readable properties `firstName` and `lastName` in one of the four JSP scopes—meaning methods named `getFirstName` and `getLastName`—the preceding code fragment will display those properties.

You can also use the `[]` operator to access bean properties; for example, the preceding code fragment could be rewritten like this:

```
First Name: <c:out value='${name["firstName"]}'/>
Last Name: <c:out value='${name["lastName"]}'/>
```

The `[]` operator is a generalization of the `.` operator, which is why the two previous code fragments are equivalent, but the `[]` operator lets you specify a *computed value*. "A Closer Look at the [] Operator" on page 56 takes a closer look at how the `[]` operator works.

You can also use the `[]` operator to access objects stored in maps, lists, and arrays; for example, the following code fragment accesses the first object in an array:

```
<% String[] array = { "1", "2", "3" };
   pageContext.setAttribute("array", array); %>


<c:out value='${array[0]}'/>
```

The preceding code fragment creates an array of strings and stores it in page scope with a scriptlet. Subsequently, the <c:out> action accesses the first item in the array with `${array[0]}`.

The following sections—"Accessing JavaBeans Components" and "Accessing Objects Stored in Arrays, Lists, and Maps" on page 52—explore in greater detail the use of the `.` and `[]` operators to access bean properties and objects stored in collections.

Accessing JavaBeans Components

This section shows you how to use the `.` and `[]` operators to access bean properties, including nested beans. Listing 2.1, Listing 2.2, and Listing 2.3 list the implementation of three beans: Name, Address, and UserProfile.

The preceding beans are simple JavaBean components. The Name bean has two properties: firstName and lastName. The Address bean has four properties: streetAddress, city, state, and zip. The UserProfile bean has two properties: name and address. UserProfile beans contain references to Name and Address beans.

Figure 2–1 shows a JSP page that creates a user profile and accesses its properties with EL expressions.

Listing 2.1   *WEB-INF/classes/beans/Name.java*

```java
package beans;

public class Name {
   private String firstName, lastName;

   // JavaBean accessors for first name
   public void setFirstName(String firstName) {
      this.firstName = firstName;
   }
   public String getFirstName() {
      return firstName;
   }

   // JavaBean accessors for last name
   public void setLastName(String lastName) {
      this.lastName = lastName;
   }
   public String getLastName() {
      return lastName;
   }
}
```

Listing 2.2   *WEB-INF/classes/beans/Address.java*

```java
package beans;

public class Address {
   private String streetAddress, city, state;
   private int zip;

   // JavaBean accessors for street address
   public void setStreetAddress(String streetAddress) {
      this.streetAddress = streetAddress;
   }
   public String getStreetAddress() {
      return streetAddress;
   }

   // JavaBean accessors for city
   public void setCity(String city) {
      this.city = city;
   }
```

| Listing 2.2 | *WEB-INF/classes/beans/Address.java (cont.)* |

```java
 public String getCity() {
     return city;
 }
// JavaBean accessors for state
   public void setState(String state) {
       this.state = state;
   }
   public String getState() {
       return state;
   }

   // JavaBean accessors for zip
   public void setZip(int zip) {
       this.zip = zip;
   }
   public int getZip() {
       return zip;
   }
}
```

| Listing 2.3 | *WEB-INF/classes/beans/UserProfile.java* |

```java
package beans;

public class UserProfile {
   private Name name;
   private Address address;

   // JavaBean accessors for name
   public void setName(Name name) {
       this.name = name;
   }
   public Name getName() {
       return name;
   }

   // JavaBean accessors for address
   public void setAddress(Address address) {
       this.address = address;
   }
   public Address getAddress() {
       return address;
   }
}
```

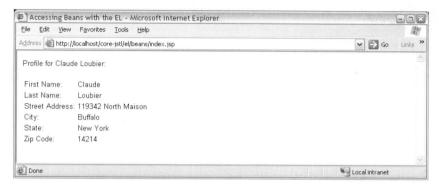

Figure 2–1 Accessing Beans with the Expression Language

The JSP page shown in Figure 2–1 is listed in Listing 2.4.

Listing 2.4 *Accessing JavaBean Properties*

```
<!DOCTYPE HTML PUBLIC "-//W3C//DTD HTML 4.0 Transitional//EN">
<html>
   <head>
      <title>Accessing Beans with the EL</title>
   </head>
   <body>
      <%@ taglib uri='http://java.sun.com/jstl/core' prefix='c' %>

      <%-- Create a Name bean and store it in page scope --%>
      <jsp:useBean id='name' class='beans.Name'>
         <%-- Set properties with strings --%>
         <jsp:setProperty name='name'
                     property='firstName' value='Claude'/>
         <jsp:setProperty name='name'
                     property='lastName'  value='Loubier'/>
      </jsp:useBean>

<%-- Create an Address bean and store it in page scope --%>
      <jsp:useBean id='address' class='beans.Address'>
         <%-- Set properties with strings --%>
         <jsp:setProperty name='address'
                     property='streetAddress'
                        value='119342 North Maison'/>
         <jsp:setProperty name='address'
                     property='city'  value='Buffalo'/>
<jsp:setProperty name='address'
                     property='state' value='New York'/>
```

Listing 2.4   *Accessing JavaBean Properties (cont.)*

```
<jsp:setProperty name='address'
                     property='zip'    value='14214'/>
    </jsp:useBean>

    <%-- Create a UserProfile bean and store it in
        page scope --%>
    <jsp:useBean id='profile'
            class='beans.UserProfile'>
      <%-- Set properties with the name bean and address
          bean stored in page scope --%>
      <jsp:setProperty name='profile'
          property='name'
            value='<%= (beans.Name)
                      pageContext.getAttribute("name") %>'/>

      <jsp:setProperty name='profile'
          property='address'
            value='<%= (beans.Address)
                      pageContext.getAttribute("address") %>'/>
    </jsp:useBean>

    <%-- Show profile information --%>

    Profile for
    <%-- Access the name bean's firstName property directly,
        without specifying scope --%>
    <c:out value='${name["firstName"]}'/>

    <%-- Access the name bean's lastName property through the
        profile bean by explicitly specifying scope --%>
    <c:out value='${pageScope.profile.name.lastName}'/>:
    <p>
    <table>
      <tr>
        <%-- Access the UserProfile bean's properties without
            explicitly specifying scope --%>
        <td>First Name:</td>
        <td><c:out value='${profile["name"].firstName}'/></td>
      </tr><tr>
        <td>Last Name:
        <td><c:out value='${profile.name["lastName"]}'/></td>
      </tr><tr>
        <td>Street Address:
        <td><c:out value='${profile.address.streetAddress}'/>
        </td>
```

Listing 2.4	*Accessing JavaBean Properties (cont.)*

```
    </tr><tr>
            <td>City:
            <td><c:out value='${profile.address.city}'/></td>
        </tr><tr>
            <td>State:
            <td><c:out value='${profile.address.state}'/></td>
        </tr><tr>
            <td>Zip Code:
            <td><c:out value='${profile.address.zip}'/></td>
        </tr>
    </table>
  </body>
</html>
```

The preceding JSP page creates three beans: a name bean, an address bean, and a user profile bean; the name and address beans are used to create the user profile. All three beans are stored in page scope.

The JSP page listed in Listing 2.4 uses EL expressions to access properties of the user profile. First, the JSP page accesses the name bean's firstName property with the expression ${name["firstName"]}, which is equivalent to this expression: ${name.firstName}.

Next, the JSP page accesses the name bean's lastName property with this expression: ${pageScope.profile.name.lastName}. The expression starts with the pageScope identifier, which is an implicit object that provides access to all page-scoped attributes.[8] The user profile bean—named profile—that exists in page scope is accessed by name with an identifier, and its enclosed name bean is also accessed with an identifier. Finally, the lastName property of that name bean is accessed with another identifier.

The rest of the JSP page accesses the profile bean's properties by using the . and [] operators. Remember that the . and [] operators are interchangeable when accessing bean properties, so the expression ${profile["name"].firstName} is equivalent to ${profile.name.firstName} and ${profile.name["lastName"]} is equivalent to ${profile.name.lastName}.

Now that we've seen how to access bean properties, let's see how to access objects stored in arrays, lists, and maps.

---

8. See "Implicit Objects" on page 64 for more information about the JSTL implicit objects.

Accessing Objects Stored in Arrays, Lists, and Maps

In "Accessing JavaBeans Components" on page 46 we discussed a Web application that created user profiles and accessed their properties, all in a single JSP page. For a change of pace, this section discusses a Web application that creates user profiles in a servlet and accesses their properties in a JSP page.[9] Figure 2–2 shows the Web application's JSP page.

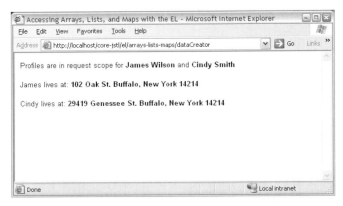

Figure 2–2   Accessing Arrays, Lists, and Maps with the JSTL Expression Language

The JSP page shown in Figure 2–2 is accessed indirectly with the URL /dataCreator. That URL invokes a servlet that creates user profiles and forwards to the JSP page. Listing 2.5 lists the application's deployment descriptor, which maps the /dataCreator URL to the dataCreator servlet.

The dataCreator servlet is listed in Listing 2.6.

The preceding servlet creates two user profiles and stores those profiles in an array, a map, and a list. Subsequently, the servlet stores the array, map, and list in request scope and forwards to a JSP page named showData.jsp. That JSP page is shown in Figure 2–2 and listed in Listing 2.7.

As the preceding JSP page illustrates, you access objects in an array with the [] operator, just as you would in Java by specifying a 0-based index into the array; for example, the expression ${profileArray[0].name.firstName} accesses the first name of the first profile stored in the profileArray.

---

9. Creating application data in a servlet separates the model from its presentation, which results in more flexible and extensible software.

Listing 2.5   *WEB-INF/web.xml*

```xml
<?xml version="1.0" encoding="ISO-8859-1"?>

<!DOCTYPE web-app
  PUBLIC "-//Sun Microsystems, Inc.//DTD Web Application 2.3//EN"
  "http://java.sun.com/j2ee/dtds/web-app_2.3.dtd">

<web-app>
   <servlet>
      <servlet-name>dataCreator</servlet-name>
      <servlet-class>DataCreatorServlet</servlet-class>
   </servlet>

   <servlet-mapping>
      <servlet-name>dataCreator</servlet-name>
      <url-pattern>/dataCreator</url-pattern>
   </servlet-mapping>
</web-app>
```

Listing 2.6   *WEB-INF/classes/DataCreatorServlet.java*

```java
import java.io.IOException;
import java.util.*;
import javax.servlet.*;
import javax.servlet.http.*;
import beans.*;

public class DataCreatorServlet extends HttpServlet {
   public void doGet(HttpServletRequest request,
                     HttpServletResponse response)
                     throws IOException, ServletException {
      // Create an array, map, and list
      UserProfile[] profileArray = createProfiles();
      HashMap        profileMap = new HashMap();
      LinkedList     profileList = new LinkedList();

      // Populate the list and map
      for(int i=0; i < profileArray.length; ++i) {
         UserProfile profile = profileArray[i];

profileList.add(profile);

         String firstName = profile.getName().getFirstName(),
                lastName = profile.getName().getLastName(),
                key = firstName + " " + lastName;
```

Listing 2.6	*WEB-INF/classes/DataCreatorServlet.java (cont.)*

```
profileMap.put(key, profile);
    }

    // Store the array, map, and list in request scope
    request.setAttribute("profileArray", profileArray);
    request.setAttribute("profileMap",   profileMap);
    request.setAttribute("profileList",  profileList);

    // Forward the request and response to /showData.jsp
    RequestDispatcher rd =
      getServletContext().getRequestDispatcher("/showData.jsp");

    rd.forward(request, response);
  }
  private UserProfile[] createProfiles() {
    // Create an array of user profiles
    UserProfile[] userProfiles = {
      new UserProfile(new Name("James", "Wilson"),
                  new Address("102 Oak St.", "Buffalo",
                          "New York", 14214)),
      new UserProfile(new Name("Cindy", "Smith"),
                  new Address("29419 Genessee St.",
                          "Buffalo", "New York", 14214))
    };
    return userProfiles;
  }
}
```

You access objects stored in a list with the same syntax used for accessing objects in arrays; for example, in the preceding JSP page, the expression `${profileList[1].name.firstName}` accesses the first name of the second profile stored in the `profileList`.

The Java class libraries offer quite a few different types of maps, including hash tables, hash maps, attributes, and tree maps. All of those data structures store *key/value* pairs of objects. To access those objects using the EL, you specify a key, enclosed in double quotes, with the `[]` operator; for example, the JSP page listed in Listing 2.7 accesses Cindy Smith's last name with this expression: `${profileMap["Cindy Smith"].name.lastName}`.

As you can tell from the JSP pages listed in Listing 2.4 on page 49 and Listing 2.7, accessing nested bean properties can be rather verbose, although it's much more succinct than accessing properties with a JSP expression. You can reduce that verbosity by creating page-scoped variables that directly reference beans stored in

Listing 2.7 *showData.jsp*

```
<!DOCTYPE HTML PUBLIC "-//W3C//DTD HTML 4.0 Transitional//EN">
<html>
    <head>
        <title>Accessing Arrays, Lists, and Maps with the EL</title>
    </head>
    <body>
        <%@ taglib uri='http://java.sun.com/jstl/core' prefix='c' %>

        <%-- Access the first and last names stored in the two
             user profiles through the array, list, and map --%>
        Profiles are in request scope for <b>
         <c:out value='${profileArray[0].name.firstName}'/>
         <c:out value='${profileArray[0].name.lastName}'/></b>
        and <b>
         <c:out value='${profileList[1].name.firstName}'/>
         <c:out value='${profileMap["Cindy Smith"].name.lastName}'/>
         </b><p>

        <%-- Store the two profiles in page-scoped variables --%>
        <c:set var='jamesProfile'
               value='${profileMap["James Wilson"]}'/>

        <c:set var='cindyProfile'
               value='${profileList[1]}'/>

        <%-- Show address information, through the page-scoped
             variables --%>
        <c:out value='${jamesProfile.name.firstName}'/> lives at:<b>
        <c:out value='${jamesProfile.address.streetAddress}'/>
        <c:out value='${jamesProfile.address.city}'/>,
        <c:out value='${jamesProfile.address.state}'/>
        <c:out value='${jamesProfile.address.zip}'/></b>

        <p>

        <c:out value='${cindyProfile.name.firstName}'/> lives at:<b>
        <c:out value='${cindyProfile.address.streetAddress}'/>
        <c:out value='${cindyProfile.address.city}'/>,
        <c:out value='${cindyProfile.address.state}'/>
        <c:out value='${cindyProfile.address.zip}'/>

    </body>
</html>
```

data structures. For example, the JSP page listed in Listing 2.7 stores James Wilson's user profile in a page-scoped variable named `jamesProfile`. That JSP page also creates a page-scoped variable named `cindyProfile` that directly references the user profile for Cindy Smith. Those page-scoped variables make it easier to access the user profiles; for example, instead of accessing Cindy's first name through the profile map like this: `${profileMap["Cindy Smith"].name.firstName}`, you can access it like this: `${cindyProfile.name.firstName}`.

In this and the preceding section, we discussed how to use the `[]` operator to access bean properties and beans stored in arrays, lists, and maps. In the next section, we take a closer look at how the `[]` operator works and why you might prefer that operator to the `.` operator when accessing beans.

A Closer Look at the `[]` Operator

As discussed in "Accessing JavaBeans Components" on page 46 and "Accessing Objects Stored in Arrays, Lists, and Maps" on page 52, you use the `[]` operator with this syntax: `${identifier[subexpression]}`. Here's how expressions with that syntax are evaluated:

1. Evaluate the `identifier` and the `subexpression`; if either resolves to `null`, the expression is `null`.

2. If the identifier is *a bean*: The `subexpression` is coerced to a `String` value and that string is regarded as a name of one of the bean's properties. The expression resolves to the value of that property; for example, the expression **${name.["lastName"]}** translates into the value returned by **name.getLastName()**.

3. If the identifier is *an array*: The `subexpression` is coerced to an `int` value—which we'll call `subexpression-int`—and the expression resolves to `identifier[subexpression-int]`. For example, for an array named `colors`, **colors[3]** represents the fourth object in the array. Because the subexpression is coerced to an `int`, you can also access that color like this: **colors["3"]**; in that case, JSTL coerces "3" into 3. *That feature may seem like a very small contribution to JSTL, but because request parameters are passed as strings, it can be quite handy.*

4. If the identifier is *a list*: The `subexpression` is also coerced to an `int`—which we will also call `subexpression-int`—and the expression resolves to the value returned from `identifier.get(subexpression-int)`, for example: **colorList[3]** and **colorList["3"]** both resolve to the fourth element in the list.

5. If the identifier is *a map*: The `subexpression` is regarded as one of the map's keys. That expression is not coerced to a value because map keys can be any type of object. The expression evaluates to `identifier.get(subexpression)`, for example, **`colorMap[Red]`** and **`colorMap["Red"]`**. The former expression is valid only if a scoped variable named `Red` exists in one of the four JSP scopes and was specified as a key for the map named `colorMap`.

Table 2.2 lists the methods that the EL invokes on your behalf.

Table 2.2   Methods That the EL Invokes for You

Identifier Type	Example Use	Method Invoked
JavaBean component	`${colorBean.red}` `${colorBean["red"]}`	`colorBean.getRed()`
Array	`${colorArray[2]}` `${colorArray["2"]}`	`Array.get(colorArray, 2)`
List	`colorList[2]` `colorList["2"]`	`colorList.get(2)`
Map	`colorMap[red]`	`colorMap.get(pageContext.findAttribute("red"))`
	`colorMap["red"]`	`colorMap.get("red")`

JSTL developers rely heavily on maps because the EL provides 11 indispensable implicit objects, of which 10 are maps. Everything, from request parameters to cookies, is accessed through a map. Because of this reliance on maps, you need to understand the meaning of the last row in Table 2.2. You access a map's values through its keys, which you can specify with the `[]` operator, for example, in Table 2.2, `${colorMap[red]}` and `${colorMap["red"]}`. The former specifies an *identifier* for the key, whereas the latter specifies a *string*. For the identifier, the `PageContext.findAttribute` method searches all four JSP scopes for a scoped variable with the name that you specify, in this case, `red`. On the other hand, if you specify a string, it's passed directly to the map's `get` method.

The [] Operator's Special Ability

Although it may not be obvious from our discussion so far, the `[]` operator has a special ability that its counterpart, the `.` operator, does not have—it can operate on an *expression*, whereas the `.` operator can only operate on an *identifier*. For example, you can do this: `${colorMap[param.selectedColor]}`, which uses the string value of the selectedColor request parameter as a key for a map named colorMap.[10] That's something that you can't do with the . operator.

Figure 2–3 shows a Web application that uses the [] operator's special ability to show request header values.

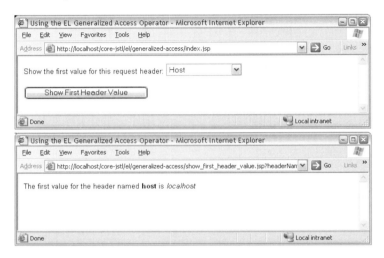

Figure 2–3   Illustrating an Advantage of the [] Operator

The top picture in Figure 2–3 shows a JSP page that lets you select a request header. After you activate the Show First Header Value button, the JSP page shown in the bottom picture shows the first value for the request header that was selected.

The JSP page shown in the top picture in Figure 2–3 is listed in Listing 2.8.

The preceding JSP page uses the header JSTL implicit object to iterate over request headers. The names of those request headers are used to create an HTML select element named headerName. The select element resides in a form whose action is show_first_header_value.jsp, so that the JSP page is loaded when you activate the Show First Header Value button. That JSP page is listed in Listing 2.9.

The preceding JSP page uses two JSTL implicit objects: param, which is a map of request parameters, and header, which is a map of request headers. The subexpression param.headerName accesses the headerName request parameter's value, and the expression ${header[param.headerName]} resolves to the first value for that request header.

---

10. The param implicit object lets you access request parameters; see "Implicit Objects" on page 64 for more information.

Listing 2.8 *Selecting a Request Header*

```
<!DOCTYPE HTML PUBLIC "-//W3C//DTD HTML 4.0 Transitional//EN">
<html>
    <head>
        <title>Using the EL Generalized Access Operator</title>
    </head>
    <body>
        <%@ taglib uri='http://java.sun.com/jstl/core' prefix='c' %>

        <form action='show_first_header_value.jsp'>
            Show the first value for this request header:

            <select name='headerName'>
                <c:forEach var='hdr' items='${header}'>
                    <option value='<c:out value="${hdr.key}"/>'>
                        <c:out value='${hdr.key}'/>
                    </option>
                </c:forEach>
            </select>

            <p><input type='submit' value='Show First Header Value'/>
        </form>
    </body>
</html>
```

Listing 2.9 *Using the [ ] Operator with a Request Parameter*

```
<!DOCTYPE HTML PUBLIC "-//W3C//DTD HTML 4.0 Transitional//EN">
<html>
    <head>
        <title>Using the EL Generalized Access Operator</title>
    </head>
    <body>
        <%@ taglib uri='http://java.sun.com/jstl/core' prefix='c' %>

        The first value for the header named <b>
        <c:out value='${param.headerName}'/></b> is <i>
        <c:out value='${header[param.headerName]}'/></i>
    </body>
</html>
```

The `empty` Operator

Testing for the existence of request parameters can be tricky because they evaluate to `null` if they don't exist but they evaluate to an empty string (`" "`) if their value was not specified. Most of the time, when you check for the existence of request parameters, you don't have to distinguish the former from the latter; you just want to know whether a value was specified. For that special task, you can use the `empty` operator, which tests whether an identifier is `null` or doesn't exist, as illustrated by the Web application shown in Figure 2–4.

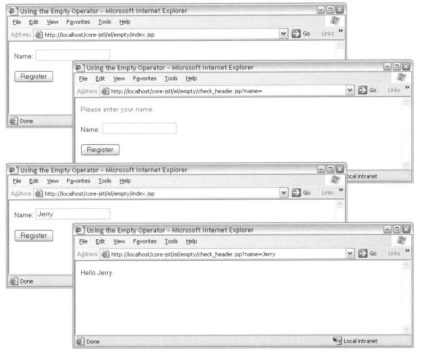

Figure 2–4   Using the `empty` Operator to Test for the Existence of Request Parameters

The Web application shown in Figure 2–4 consists of two JSP pages, one that lets you enter a name and another that checks for a corresponding request parameter. As illustrated by the top two pictures in Figure 2–4, if you don't enter anything in the name field, the latter JSP page prints an error message and includes the referring JSP page. The bottom two pictures illustrate successful access to the `name` request parameter. The JSP page with the `name` input field is listed in Listing 2.10.

The preceding JSP page includes form.jsp, which is listed in Listing 2.11.

The action for the form in the preceding JSP page is `check_header.jsp`, which is listed in Listing 2.12.

Listing 2.10   *index.jsp*

```
<!DOCTYPE HTML PUBLIC "-//W3C//DTD HTML 4.0 Transitional//EN">
<html>
   <head>
      <title>Using the Empty Operator</title>
   </head>
   <body>
      <jsp:include page='form.jsp'/>
   </body>
</html>
```

Listing 2.11   *form.jsp*

```
<form action='check_header.jsp'>
   Name: <input type='text' name='name'/>
   <p><input type='submit' value='Register'/>
</form>
```

Listing 2.12   *check_header.jsp*

```
<!DOCTYPE HTML PUBLIC "-//W3C//DTD HTML 4.0 Transitional//EN">
<html>
   <head>
      <title>Using the Empty Operator</title>
   </head>
   <body>
      <%@ taglib uri='http://java.sun.com/jstl/core' prefix='c' %>

      <c:choose>
         <c:when test='${not empty param.name}'>
            Hello <c:out value='${param.name}'/>.
         </c:when>

         <c:otherwise>
            <font color='red'>
               Please enter your name:<p>
            </font>

            <jsp:include page='form.jsp'/>
         </c:otherwise>
      </c:choose>
   </body>
</html>
```

The preceding JSP page combines the not and empty operators to see whether the name request parameter was specified; if so it displays a personalized greeting; otherwise, it prints an error message and includes the referring JSP page.

2.5 Type Coercion

The EL defines a comprehensive set of coercion rules for various data types. Those rules are summarized in Table 2.3.

Table 2.3   JSTL Type Coercion[a]

convert to —>	Boolean	Character	Number	String
Boolean	——	ERROR	ERROR	x.toString()
Character	ERROR	——	(short)x	x.toString()
Number	ERROR	(char)x	——	x.toString()
String (not empty)	Boolean. valueOf(x)	x.charAt(0)	N.valueOf(x)	——
Other	ERROR	ERROR	ERROR	x.toString()
null	Boolean.false	(char)0	0	" "
" "	Boolean.false	(char)0	0	" "

a. *x* represents the object being converted, *N* represents a Number subclass, and " " represents an empty string

In the preceding table, types in the left column are converted into the types specified in the table's header. For example, if you specify an action attribute's value as a string and that attribute's type is Character, the EL will convert that string to the first character in the string by invoking the method x.charAt(0), where x represents the string. Likewise, strings are coerced to Boolean values with the static Boolean.valueOf(x), where x represents the string.

Table 2.3 also shows how null values and empty strings are converted into booleans, characters, numbers, and strings. JSTL actions typically avoid throwing exceptions because the coercions shown in Table 2.3 are applied to their attribute values before they receive them.

If you specify a `null` value or an empty string in an expression, the EL's coercion rules ensure that sensible default values are used instead; for example:

```
<c:out value='${count + param.increment}'/>
```

In the preceding code fragment, the expression specified for the `value` attribute coerces a *string* (a request parameter value named `increment`) to an *integer* which is added to the `count` scoped variable and sent to the current `JspWriter` by the `<c:out>` action.

If the `increment` request parameter does not exist, `param.increment` resolves to `null`. If it exists, but no value was specified for it—perhaps it represents an HTML `input` element in a form that was left blank—it resolves to an empty string. Either way, as you can see from Table 2.3, the EL coerces the string value of `param.increment` to 0, and the expression `${count + param.increment}` evaluates to the value of the `count` scoped variable.

In general, JSTL actions avoid throwing exceptions, instead favoring sensible default values like 0 for `null` and empty strings.

Another thing you don't have to worry about is throwing a `null` pointer exception if you try to access an identifier that is `null`; for example, the expression `${userProfile.address.city}` resolves to `null` if `userProfile`, `address` or `city` is `null` because the EL coerces that value into one of the appropriate values in Table 2.3.

2.6 Literal Values

The JSTL expression language defines boolean, integer, floating-point, string, and `null` literals, as shown in Table 2.4.

Table 2.4   JSTL Literal Values

Type	Examples
Boolean	`Boolean.true Boolean.false`
Integer	`143 +3 -4 2435`
Double	`1.43 -2.35 2.34E9`
String	`"string in double quotes"` `'a string in single quotes'`
Null	`null`

2.7 Implicit Objects

Arguably, the most useful feature of the JSTL expression language is the implicit objects it defines for accessing all kinds of application data. Those implicit objects are listed in Table 2.5.

Table 2.5   JSTL Implicit Objects

Implicit Object	Type	Key[a]	Value
cookie	Map	Cookie name	Cookie
header	Map	Request header name	Request header value
headerValues	Map	Request header name	String[] of request header values
initParam	Map	Initialization parameter name	Initialization parameter value
param	Map	Request parameter name	Request parameter value
paramValues	Map	Request parameter name	String[] of request parameter values
pageContext	PageContext	N/A	N/A
pageScope	Map	Page-scoped attribute name	Page-scoped attribute value
requestScope	Map	Request-scoped attribute name	Request-scoped attribute value
sessionScope	Map	Session-scoped attribute name	Session-scoped attribute value
applicationScope	Map	Application-scoped attribute name	Application-scoped attribute value

a. All keys are strings.

There are three types of JSTL implicit objects:

- Maps for a single set of values, such as request headers and cookies:

  `param, paramValues, header, headerValues, initParam, cookie`

- Maps for scoped variables in a particular scope:

  `pageScope, requestScope, sessionScope, applicationScope`

- The page context: `pageContext`

The rest of this section examines each of the JSTL implicit objects in the order listed above; the first category begins at "Accessing Request Parameters" below, the second category begins at "Accessing Scoped Attributes" on page 78, and use of the `pageContext` implicit object begins at "Accessing JSP Page and Servlet Properties" on page 80.

Accessing Request Parameters

Request parameters are the lifeblood of most Web applications, passing information from one Web component to another. That crucial role makes the `param` and `paramValues` implicit objects, both of which access request parameters, the most heavily used JSTL implicit objects.

The `param` and `paramValues` implicit objects are both maps of request parameters. For both the `param` and `paramValues` maps, keys are request parameter names, but the values corresponding to those keys are different for `param` and `paramValues`; `param` stores the *first value* specified for a request parameter, whereas `paramValues` stores a `String` array that contains *all the values* specified for a request parameter.[11]

Most often, the overriding factor that determines whether you use `param` or `paramValue` is the type of HTML element a request parameter represents; for example, Figure 2–5 shows a Web application that uses both `param` and `paramValues` to display request parameters defined by a form.

---

11. Two of the implicit objects listed in Table 2.5 have plural names: `paramValues` and `headerValues`; both are maps that associate keys with `String` arrays. The other implicit objects associate keys with scalar values.

Figure 2–5   Accessing Request Parameters with the `param` and `paramValues` Implicit Objects

The Web application shown in Figure 2–5 consists of two JSP pages, one that contains a form (top picture) and another that interprets the form's data (bottom picture). Listing 2.13 lists the JSP page that contains the form.

Listing 2.13   *index.jsp*

```
<!DOCTYPE HTML PUBLIC "-//W3C//DTD HTML 4.0 Transitional//EN">
<html>
   <head>
      <title>EL Implicit Objects: Request Parameters</title>
   </head>

   <body>
      <form action='param.jsp'>
```

Listing 2.13	*index.jsp (cont.)*

```
<table>
        <tr>
          <td>First Name:</td>
          <td><input type='text' name='firstName'/></td>
        </tr>
        <tr>
          <td>Last Name:</td>
          <td><input type='text' name='lastName'/></td>
        </tr>
        <tr>
          <td>
              Select languages that you have worked with:
          </td>
          <td>
              <select name='languages' size='7'
                  multiple='true'>
              <option value='Ada'>Ada</option>
              <option value='C'>C</option>
              <option value='C++'>C++</option>
              <option value='Cobol'>Cobol</option>
              <option value='Eiffel'>Eiffel</option>
              <option value='Objective-C'>
                  Objective-C
              </option>
              <option value='Java'>Java</option>
              </select>
          </td>
        </tr>
      </table>
      <p><input type='submit' value='Finish Survey'/>
    </form>
  </body>
</html>
```

The preceding JSP page is unremarkable; it creates an HTML form with two textfields and a `select` element that allows multiple selection. That form's action, `param.jsp`, is the focus of our discussion. It is listed in Listing 2.14.

Listing 2.14	*param.jsp*

```
<!DOCTYPE HTML PUBLIC "-//W3C//DTD HTML 4.0 Transitional//EN">
<html>
    <head>
        <title>Accessing Request Parameters</title>
```

Listing 2.14   *param.jsp (cont.)*

```
    </head>
<body>
      <%@ taglib uri='http://java.sun.com/jstl/core' prefix='c' %>

      <font size='5'>
         Skillset for:
      </font>

      <%-- Access the lastName and firstName request parameters
           parameters by name --%>
      <c:out value='${param.lastName}'/>,
      <c:out value='${param.firstName}'/>

      <%-- Show all request parameters and their values --%>
      <p><font size='5'>
         All Request Parameters:
      </font><p>

      <%-- For every String[] item of paramValues... --%>
      <c:forEach var='parameter' items='${paramValues}'>
         <ul>
            <%-- Show the key, which is the request parameter
                 name --%>
            <li><b><c:out value='${parameter.key}'/></b>:</li>

            <%-- Iterate over the values -- a String[] --
                 associated with this request parameter --%>
            <c:forEach var='value' items='${parameter.value}'>
               <%-- Show the String value --%>
               <c:out value='${value}'/>
            </c:forEach>
         </ul>
      </c:forEach>

      <%-- Show values for the languages request parameter --%>
      <font size='5'>
         Languages:
      </font><p>

      <%-- paramValues.languages is a String [] of values for the
           languages request parameter --%>
      <c:forEach var='language' items='${paramValues.languages}'>
         <c:out value='${language}'/>
      </c:forEach>

      <p>
```

Listing 2.14   *param.jsp (cont.)*

```
<%-- Show the value of the param.languages map entry,
         which is the first value for the languages
         request parameter --%>
    <c:out value="${'${'}param.languages} = ${param.languages}"/>
   </body>
</html>
```

The preceding JSP page does four things of interest. First, it displays the
lastName and firstName request parameters, using the param implicit object.
Since we know that those request parameters represent textfields, we know that they
are a single value, so the param implicit object fits the bill.

Second, the JSP page displays all of the request parameters and their values, using
the paramValues implicit object and the <c:forEach> action.[12] We use the
paramValues implicit object for this task since we know that the HTML select
element supports multiple selection and so can produce multiple request parameter
values of the same name.

Because the paramValues implicit object is a map, you can access its values
directly if you know the keys, meaning the request parameter names. For example,
the third point of interest in the preceding JSP page iterates over the array of strings
representing selected languages—paramValues.languages. The selected
languages are accessed through the paramValues map by use of the key
languages.

To emphasize the difference between param and paramValues, the fourth
point of interest is the value of the param.languages request parameter, which
contains only the first language selected in the HTML select element. A <c:out>
action uses the EL expression ${'${'} to display the characters ${ and another
EL expression—${param.languages}—to display the first value for the
languages request parameter.

Accessing Request Headers

You can access request headers just as you can access request parameters, except that
you use the header and headerValues implicit objects instead of param and
paramValues.

Like the param and paramValues implicit objects, the header and
headerValues implicit objects are maps, but their keys are request header names.

---

12. See "The <c:forEach> Action" on page 154 for more information about <c:forEach>.

The header map's values are the first value specified for a particular request header, whereas the headerValues map contains arrays of all the values specified for that request header.

Figure 2–6 shows a JSP page that uses the header implicit object to display all of the request headers and the first value defined for each of them.

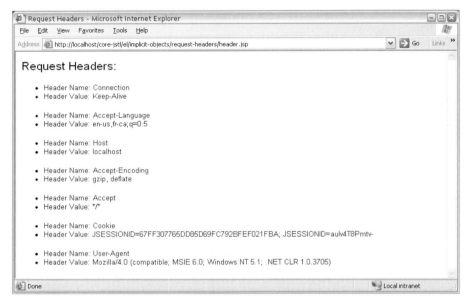

Figure 2–6   Accessing Request Headers with the header Implicit Object

The JSP page shown in Figure 2–6 is listed in Listing 2.15.

The keys stored in the header map are request header names and the corresponding values are strings representing request header values. You can also use the headerValues implicit object to iterate over request headers, like this:

```
<%-- Loop over the JSTL headerValues implicit object,
     which is a map --%>
<c:forEach items='${headerValues}' var='hv'>
   <ul>
      <%-- Display the key of the current item; that item
           is a Map.Entry --%>
      <li>Header name: <c:out value='${hv.key}'/></li>

      <%-- The value of the current item, which is
           accessed with the value method from
           Map.Entry, is an array of strings
```

Listing 2.15	*Accessing Requests Headers with the* `header` *Implicit Object*

```
<!DOCTYPE HTML PUBLIC "-//W3C//DTD HTML 4.0 Transitional//EN">
<html>
    <head>
        <title>Request Headers</title>
    </head>

    <body>
        <%@ taglib uri='http://java.sun.com/jstl/core' prefix='c' %>

        <font size='5'>
            Request Headers:
        </font><p>

        <%-- Loop over the JSTL header implicit object, which is a
             map --%>
        <c:forEach items='${header}' var='h'>
            <ul>
                <%-- Display the key of the current item, which
                     represents the request header name and the
                     current item's value, which represents the
                     header value --%>
                <li>Header Name: <c:out value='${h.key}'/></li>
                <li>Header Value: <c:out value='${h.value}'/></li>
            </ul>
        </c:forEach>
    </body>
</html>
```

```
                representing request header values, so
                we iterate over that array of strings --%>
        <c:forEach items='${hv.value}' var='value'>
            <li>Header Value: <c:out value='${value}'/></li>
        </c:forEach>
    </ul>
</c:forEach>
```

Unlike request parameters, request headers are rarely duplicated; instead, if multiple strings are specified for a single request header, browsers typically concatenate those strings separated by semicolons. Because of the sparsity of duplicated request headers, the `header` implicit object is usually preferred over `headerValues`.

Accessing Context Initialization Parameters

You can have only one value per context initialization parameter, so there's only one JSTL implicit object for accessing initialization parameters: `initParam`. Like the implicit objects for request parameters and headers, the `initParam` implicit object is a map. The map keys are context initialization parameter names and the corresponding values are the context initialization parameter values.

Figure 2–7 shows a JSP page that iterates over all the context initialization parameters and prints their values. That JSP page also accesses the parameters directly.

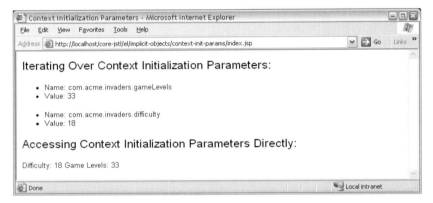

Figure 2–7   Accessing Initialization Parameters with the `initParam` Implicit Object

Before we discuss the listing for the JSP page shown in Figure 2–7, let's look at the deployment descriptor, listed in Listing 2.16, which defines two context initialization parameters: `com.acme.invaders.difficulty` and `com.acme.invaders.gameLevels`.

The context initialization parameters defined above are accessed by the JSP page shown in Figure 2–7 and listed in Listing 2.17.

The preceding JSP page uses the <c:forEach> action to iterate over the key/value pairs stored in the `initParam` map. The body of that action displays each key/value pair.

In the example discussed in "Accessing Request Parameters" on page 65, we accessed a request parameter by name like this: `${paramValues.languages}`. In the preceding JSP page, can we access an initialization parameter in a similar fashion with the `initParam` implicit object? The answer is yes, but in this case we have a problem because the initialization parameter name has `.` characters, which have special meaning to the expression language. If we try to access the `com.acme.invaders.difficulty` parameter like this: `${initParam.com.acme.invaders.difficulty}`,   the   expression

Listing 2.16 *WEB-INF/web.xml*

```
<?xml version="1.0" encoding="ISO-8859-1"?>

<!DOCTYPE web-app
  PUBLIC "-//Sun Microsystems, Inc.//DTD Web Application 2.3//EN"
  "http://java.sun.com/j2ee/dtds/web-app_2.3.dtd">

<web-app>
  <!-- Application-wide default values for the Acme Invaders
       online game -->
  <context-param>
    <param-name>com.acme.invaders.difficulty</param-name>
    <param-value>18</param-value>
  </context-param>

  <context-param>
    <param-name>com.acme.invaders.gameLevels</param-name>
    <param-value>33</param-value>
  </context-param>

  <welcome-file-list>
    <welcome-file>
       index.jsp
    </welcome-file>
  </welcome-file-list>
</web-app>
```

Listing 2.17 *Accessing Context Initialization Parameters*

```
<!DOCTYPE HTML PUBLIC "-//W3C//DTD HTML 4.0 Transitional//EN">
<html>
   <head>
      <title>Context Initialization Parameters</title>
   </head>

   <body>
      <%@ taglib uri='http://java.sun.com/jstl/core' prefix='c' %>

      <font size='5'>
         Iterating Over Context Initialization Parameters:
      </font><p>

<%-- Loop over the JSTL initParam implicit object,
         which is a map --%>
<c:forEach items='${initParam}' var='parameter'>
```

Listing 2.17   *Accessing Context Initialization Parameters (cont.)*

```
   <ul>
            <%-- Display the key of the current item, which
                 corresponds to the name of the init param --%>
            <li>Name: <c:out value='${parameter.key}'/></li>

            <%-- Display the value of the current item, which
                 corresponds to the value of the init param --%>
            <li>Value: <c:out value='${parameter.value}'/></li>
         </ul>
      </c:forEach>

      <font size='5'>
         Accessing Context Initialization Parameters Directly:
      </font><p>

      Difficulty:
      <c:out value='${initParam["com.acme.invaders.difficulty"]}'/>

      Game Levels:
      <c:out value='${initParam["com.acme.invaders.gameLevels"]}'/>

   </body>
</html>
```

language will interpret that expression as an object's property named `difficulty`, which is not the interpretation we want.

The solution to this difficulty is to use the `[]` operator, which evaluates an expression and turns it into an identifier; for example, you can access the `com.acme.invaders.difficulty` initialization parameter like this: `${initParam["com.acme.invaders.difficulty"]}`. See "A Closer Look at the [] Operator" on page 56 for more information about the `[]` operator.

Accessing Cookies

It's not uncommon to read cookies in JSP pages, especially cookies that store user-interface-related preferences. The JSTL expression language lets you access cookies with the `cookie` implicit object. Like all JSTL implicit objects, the `cookie` implicit object is a map.[13] That map's keys represent cookie names, and the values are the cookies themselves.

Figure 2–8 shows a JSP page that reads cookie values, using the `cookie` implicit object.

---

13. The sole exception is the `pageContext` implicit object, which is not a map.

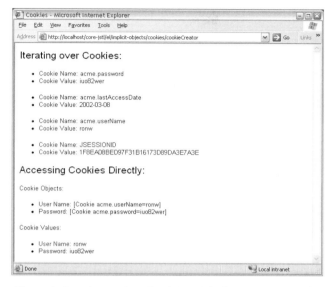

Figure 2–8 Accessing Cookies with the `cookie` Implicit Object

The JSP page shown in Figure 2–8 uses the `cookie` implicit object to iterate over all cookies and also accesses `Cookie` objects and their values directly. That JSP page is invoked with the URL `/cookieCreator`, which is mapped to a servlet that creates cookies. That servlet, after creating cookies, forwards to the JSP page shown in Figure 2–8. Listing 2.18 lists the Web application's deployment descriptor, which maps the URL `/cookieCreator` to the `CookieCreatorServlet` class.

Listing 2.18 *WEB-INF/web.xml*

```
<?xml version="1.0" encoding="ISO-8859-1"?>

<!DOCTYPE web-app
  PUBLIC "-//Sun Microsystems, Inc.//DTD Web Application 2.3//EN"
  "http://java.sun.com/j2ee/dtds/web-app_2.3.dtd">

<web-app>
   <servlet>
      <servlet-name>cookieCreator</servlet-name>
      <servlet-class>CookieCreatorServlet</servlet-class>
   </servlet>

   <servlet-mapping>
      <servlet-name>cookieCreator</servlet-name>
      <url-pattern>/cookieCreator</url-pattern>
   </servlet-mapping>
</web-app>
```

The `CookieCreatorServlet` class is listed in Listing 2.19.

Listing 2.19 *WEB-INF/classes/CookieCreatorServlet.java*

```java
import java.io.IOException;
import javax.servlet.*;
import javax.servlet.http.*;

public class CookieCreatorServlet extends HttpServlet {
   public void doGet(HttpServletRequest request,
                     HttpServletResponse response)
                     throws IOException, ServletException {
      String[] cookieNames = {"acme.userName", "acme.password",
                              "acme.lastAccessDate"};
      String[] cookieValues = {"ronw", "iuo82wer", "2002-03-08"};

      // Create cookies and add them to the HTTP response
      for(int i=0; i < cookieNames.length; ++i) {
         Cookie cookie = new Cookie(cookieNames[i],
                                    cookieValues[i]);
         response.addCookie(cookie);
      }

      // Forward the request and response to cookies.jsp
      RequestDispatcher rd =
         request.getRequestDispatcher("cookies.jsp");
         rd.forward(request, response);
   }
}
```

The cookie creator servlet creates three cookies and adds them to the response before forwarding to `cookies.jsp`. That JSP page is listed in Listing 2.20.

Listing 2.20 *cookies.jsp*

```html
<!DOCTYPE HTML PUBLIC "-//W3C//DTD HTML 4.0 Transitional//EN">
<html>
   <head>
      <title>Cookies</title>
   </head>

   <body>
      <%@ taglib uri='http://java.sun.com/jstl/core' prefix='c' %>

      <p><font size='5'>
         Iterating over Cookies:
      </font><p>
```

Listing 2.20   *cookies.jsp (cont.)*

```
<%-- Loop over the JSTL cookie implicit object, which is a
        map. If there are no cookies, the <c:forEach> action
        does nothing. --%>
    <c:forEach items='${cookie}' var='mapEntry'>
        <ul>
            <%-- The mapEntry's key references the cookie name --%>
            <li>Cookie Name: <c:out value='${mapEntry.key}'/></li>

            <%-- The mapEntry's value references the Cookie
                object, so we show the cookie's value --%>
            <li>Cookie Value:
                <c:out value='${mapEntry.value.value}'/></li>
        </ul>
    </c:forEach>

    <p><font size='5'>
        Accessing Cookies Directly:
    </font><p>

    Cookie Objects:
    <ul>
        <li>
            User Name: <c:out value='${cookie["acme.userName"]}'/>
        </li>
        <li>
            Password:   <c:out value='${cookie["acme.password"]}'/>
        </li>
    </ul>

    Cookie Values:
    <ul>
        <li>
            User Name:
            <c:out value='${cookie["acme.userName"].value}'/>
        </li>
        <li>
            Password:
            <c:out value='${cookie["acme.password"].value}'/>
        </li>
    </ul>
    </body>
</html>
```

The preceding JSP page uses the <c:forEach> action to iterate over the entries contained in the cookie map. For each entry, the body of the <c:forEach> action displays the cookie's name and value. Notice that cookie values are accessed with the expression `${mapEntry.value.value}`. The map entry's value is a cookie, which also has a `value` property.

The rest of the JSP page accesses cookie objects and their values directly. Because the cookie names contain `.` characters, they cannot be used as identifiers, so the preceding JSP page uses the `[]` operator to directly access cookies and their values.

Accessing Scoped Attributes

Since we started discussing JSTL implicit objects at "Implicit Objects" on page 64, we've seen how to access four types of objects:

- Request parameters
- Request headers
- Context initialization parameters
- Cookies

In addition to the specific types listed above, you can access any type of object that's stored in one of the four JSP scopes: page, request, session, or application. The expression language provides one implicit object for each scope:

- `pageScope`
- `requestScope`
- `sessionScope`
- `applicationScope`

Remember from our discussion in "Identifiers" on page 43 that identifiers refer to scoped variables; for example, the expression `${name}` refers to a scoped variable named name. That scoped variable can reside in page, request, session, or application scope. The expression language searches those scopes, in that order, for scoped variables.

The implicit objects listed above let you explicitly access variables stored in a specific scope; for example, if you know that the name scoped variable resides in session scope, the expression `${sessionScope.name}` is equivalent to `${name}`, but the latter unnecessarily searches the page and request scopes before finding the name scoped variable in session scope. Because of that unnecessary searching, `${sessionScope.name}` should be faster than `${name}`.

The scope implicit objects listed above—`pageScope`, `requestScope`, `sessionScope`, and `applicationScope`—are also handy if you need to iterate over attributes stored in a particular scope; for example, you might look for a timestamp attribute in session scope. The scope implicit objects give you access to a map of attributes for a particular scope.

Figure 2–9 shows a Web application that displays all of the attributes from the scope of your choosing. The top picture in Figure 2–9 shows a JSP page that lets you select a scope, and the bottom picture shows a JSP page that lists the attributes for the selected scope.

Figure 2–9   Accessing Scoped Variables for a Specific Scope with the `pageScope` Implicit Object

The JSP page shown in the top picture in Figure 2–9 is listed in Listing 2.21.

Listing 2.21   *Choosing a Scope*

```
<!DOCTYPE HTML PUBLIC "-//W3C//DTD HTML 4.0 Transitional//EN">
<html>
   <head>
      <title>Select a Scope</title>
   </head>

   <body>
      <form action='show_scope_attributes.jsp'>
         Select a scope:
         <select name='scope'>
            <option value='page'>page</option>
            <option value='request'>request</option>
            <option value='session'>session</option>
            <option value='application'>application</option>
         </select>

         <p><input type='submit' value='Show Scope Attributes'/>
      </form>
   </body>
</html>
```

The preceding JSP page creates an HTML form that lets you select a scope. That form's action is `show_scope_attributes.jsp`, which is listed in Listing 2.22.

The preceding JSP page is passed a request parameter named `scope` whose value is `"page"`, `"request"`, `"session"`, or `"application"`. The JSP page creates a page-scoped variable, also named `scope`, and sets it to the appropriate JSTL implicit object—`pageScope`, `requestScope`, `sessionScope`, or `applicationScope`—based on the `scope` request parameter. Then the JSP page loops over that implicit object and displays each scoped variable's name and value.

Accessing JSP Page and Servlet Properties

Now that we've seen how to access request parameters and headers, initialization parameters, cookies, and scoped variables, the JSTL implicit objects have one more feature to explore: accessing servlet and JSP properties, such as a request's protocol or server port, or the major and minor versions of the servlet API your container supports. You can find out that information and much more with the `pageContext` implicit object, which gives you access to the request, response, session, and application (also known as the servlet context). Useful properties for the `pageContext` implicit object are listed in Table 2.6.

Listing 2.22 *Showing Scoped Variables for a Specific Scope*

```
<!DOCTYPE HTML PUBLIC "-//W3C//DTD HTML 4.0 Transitional//EN">
<html>
    <head>
        <title>Scoped Variables</title>
    </head>

    <body>
        <%@ taglib uri='http://java.sun.com/jstl/core' prefix='c' %>

        <%-- Set a page-scoped attribute named scope to
             pageScope, requestScope, sessionScope, or
             applicationScope, depending on the value of a
             request parameter named scope --%>
        <c:choose>
          <c:when test='${param.scope == "page"}'>
            <c:set var='scope' value='${pageScope}'/>
          </c:when>
          <c:when test='${param.scope == "request"}'>
            <c:set var='scope' value='${requestScope}'/>
          </c:when>
          <c:when test='${param.scope == "session"}'>
            <c:set var='scope' value='${sessionScope}'/>
          </c:when>
          <c:when test='${param.scope == "application"}'>
            <c:set var='scope' value='${applicationScope}'/>
          </c:when>
        </c:choose>

        <font size='5'>
          <c:out value='${param.scope}'/>-scope attributes:
        </font><p>

        <%-- Loop over the JSTL implicit object, stored in the
             page-scoped attribute named scope that was set above.
             That implicit object is a map --%>
        <c:forEach items='${scope}' var='p'>
          <ul>
            <%-- Display the key of the current item, which
                 represents the parameter name --%>
            <li>Parameter Name: <c:out value='${p.key}'/></li>

            <%-- Display the value of the current item, which
                 represents the parameter value --%>
            <li>Parameter Value: <c:out value='${p.value}'/></li>
          </ul>
        </c:forEach>
    </body>
</html>
```

Table 2.6 `pageContext` Properties

Property	Type	Description
request	ServletRequest	The current request
response	ServletResponse	The current response
servletConfig	ServletConfig	The servlet configuration
servletContext	ServletContext	The servlet context (the application)
session	HttpSession	The current session

The `pageContext` properties listed in Table 2.6 give you access to a lot of information; for example, you can access a client's host name like this: `${pageContext.request.remoteHost}`, or you can access the session ID like this: `${pageContext.session.id}`.

The following four tables list useful request, response, session, and application properties, all of which are available through the `pageContext` implicit object.

Table 2.7 `pageContext.request` Properties

Property	Type	Description
characterEncoding	String	The character encoding for the request body
contentType	String	The MIME type of the request body
locale	Locale	The user's preferred locale
locales	Enumeration	The user's preferred locales
new	boolean	Evaluates to `true` if the server has created a session, but the client has not yet joined
protocol	String	The name and version of the protocol for the request; for example: `HTTP/1.1`
remoteAddr	String	The IP address of the client
remoteHost	String	The fully qualified host name of the client, or the IP address if the host name is undefined
scheme	String	The name of the scheme used for the current request; i.e.: HTTP, HTTPS, etc.
serverName	String	The host name of the server that received the request

Table 2.7   `pageContext.request` Properties *(cont.)*

Property	Type	Description
serverPort	int	The port number that the request was received on
secure	boolean	Indicates whether this was made on a secure channel such as HTTPS

Table 2.8   `pageContext.response` Properties

Property	Type	Description
bufferSize	int	The buffer size used for the response
characterEncoding	String	The character encoding used for the response body
locale	Locale	The locale assigned to the response
committed	boolean	Indicates whether the response has been committed

Table 2.9   `pageContext.session` Properties

Property	Type	Description
creationTime	long	The time the session was created (in milliseconds since January 1, 1970, GMT)
id	String	A unique session identifier
lastAccessedTime	long	The last time the session was accessed (in milliseconds since January 1, 1970, GMT)
maxInactiveInterval	int	The time duration for no activities, after which the session times out

Table 2.10   `pageContext.servletContext` Properties

Property	Type	Description
majorVersion	int	The major version of the Servlet API that the container supports
minorVersion	int	The minor version of the Servlet API that the container supports
serverInfo	Set	The name and version of the servlet container
servletContextName	String	The name of the Web application specified by the display-name attribute in the deployment descriptor

The JSP page shown in Figure 2–10 accesses some of the information available in the preceding tables: the request port, protocol, and locale; the response locale; the session ID and maximum inactive interval; and the servlet API version supported by the JSP container.

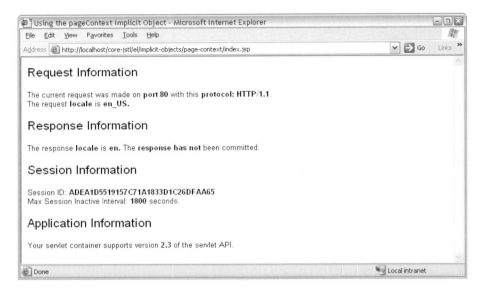

Figure 2–10   Using the `pageContext` Implicit Object

The JSP page shown in Figure 2–10 is listed in Listing 2.23.

Listing 2.23   *Accessing Servlet and JSP Properties*

```
<!DOCTYPE HTML PUBLIC "-//W3C//DTD HTML 4.0 Transitional//EN">
<html>
   <head>
      <title>Using the pageContext Implicit Object</title>
   </head>

   <body>
      <%@ taglib uri='http://java.sun.com/jstl/core' prefix='c' %>

      <%-- Show Request Information --%>
      <font size='5'>Request Information</font><p>

         <%-- Use the request object to show the server port and
               protocol --%>
The current request was made on <b>port
         <c:out value='${pageContext.request.serverPort}'/></b>
```

Listing 2.23   *Accessing Servlet and JSP Properties (cont.)*

```
with this <b>protocol:
      <c:out value='${pageContext.request.protocol}'/></b>.<br>

      <%-- Use the request object to show the user's preferred
           locale --%>
      The request <b>locale</b> is
      <b><c:out value='${pageContext.request.locale}'/>.</b>

      <p>

   <%-- Show Response Information --%>
   <font size='5'>Response Information</font><p>

      The response <b>locale</b> is
      <b><c:out value='${pageContext.response.locale}'/>.</b>

      <%-- Use the response object to show whether the response
           has been committed --%>
      The <b>response
      <c:choose>
         <c:when test='${pageContext.response.committed}'>
            has
         </c:when>

         <c:otherwise>
            has not
         </c:otherwise>
      </c:choose>
      </b> been committed.

      <p>

   <%-- Show Session Information --%>
   <font size='5'>Session Information</font><p>

      Session ID:
      <b><c:out value='${pageContext.session.id}'/></b><br>
      Max Session Inactive Interval:<b>
      <c:out
         value='${pageContext.session.maxInactiveInterval}'/>
      </b>seconds.

      <p>

   <%-- Show Application Information --%>
   <font size='5'>Application Information</font><p>
```

```
<%-- Store the servlet context in a page-scoped variable
        named app for better readability --%>
    <c:set var='app' value='${pageContext.servletContext}'/>

    <%-- Use the application object to show the major and
         minor versions of the servlet API that the container
         supports --%>
    Your servlet container supports version<b>
    <c:out
       value='${app.majorVersion}.${app.minorVersion}'/></b>
    of the servlet API.
  </body>
</html>
```

The preceding JSP page accesses request, response, session, and application properties, using the `pageContext` implicit object. The end of that JSP page creates a page-scoped variable named `app` that references the servlet context (meaning the application). That page-scoped variable is subsequently used to access the Servlet API version supported by the JSP container. Sometimes it's convenient, for the sake of readability, to store a reference to one of the objects listed in Table 2.6 on page 82 in a page-scoped variable, as does the preceding JSP page.

2.8 Method Invocation

One of the most hotly debated topics within the JSTL expert group was whether the expression language should let you invoke arbitrary methods.

The major point of contention was whether that ability fit the philosophy of the expression language and whether it would encourage Java code in JSP pages. As you may have discerned so far and as you will learn more about as you explore JSTL actions throughout the rest of this book, the expression language and JSTL actions are implemented so that developers don't need to be concerned with types; for example, you iterate over a list, array, or comma-separated string in exactly the same fashion, without regard to their types, with the <c:forEach> action and EL expressions. If you could also invoke arbitrary methods on objects, that capability could compromise that intent and would open the door to another kind of expression language that contains EL expressions and Java statements.

The final decision for JSTL 1.0 was to *disallow direct method invocation* in the expression language.[14] You can only *indirectly* invoke a strict subset of methods for certain kinds of objects by specifying JavaBeans property names or array, list, or map indexes; see "A Closer Look at the [] Operator" on page 56 for more information.

Although that decision was probably for the best, you can still run into the need for method invocation pretty quickly; for example, consider the JSP page shown in Figure 2–11, which accesses the first item in a list.

Figure 2–11 Accessing the First Item in a List

The JSP page shown in Figure 2–11 is listed in Listing 2.24.

Listing 2.24 *Accessing the First Item in a List*

```
<!DOCTYPE HTML PUBLIC "-//W3C//DTD HTML 4.0 Transitional//EN">
<html>
   <head>
      <title>Invoking Methods</title>
   </head>

   <body>
      <%@ taglib uri='http://java.sun.com/jstl/core' prefix='c' %>
      <%@ page import='java.util.LinkedList' %>

      <%
         LinkedList list = new LinkedList();
         list.add("item one");
         list.add("item two");
         list.add("item three");
         list.add("item four");
         list.add("item five");

         pageContext.setAttribute("list", list);
      %>

      The list starts with <b><c:out value='${list[0]}'/></b>
   </body>
</html>
```

14. An early draft of the JSP 2.0 specification includes direct method invocation for the expression language, but that feature may not make it into the final JSP 2.0 specification.

The preceding JSP page is simple: In a scriptlet, it creates a linked list and stores that list in page scope under the name `list`. Subsequently, the expression `${list[0]}` is used to access the first item in the list, and the output is `item one`.

So far, so good. But what if you want to access the last item in the list? To do that, you need to know how many items are in the list so that you can specify the proper position in the list. If you look at the Java documentation for the `LinkedList` class, you'll see that it has a `size` method that returns the number of items in the list. You might try to access the last item in the list like this:

```
<%-- Beware! this code will throw an exception --%>

The list starts with <b><c:out value='${list[0]}'/></b>
and ends with <b><c:out value='${list[list.size-1]}'/></b>
```

As you might guess, the preceding code fragment will throw an exception like the one shown in Figure 2–12.

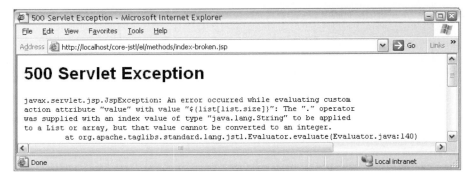

Figure 2–12   Trying to Access the Last Item in a List

The problem is that we are trying to invoke the list's `size` method (which is a valid `LinkedList` method), but it's *not a JavaBeans-compliant getter method*, so the expression `list.size-1` *cannot be evaluated*.

There are two ways to address this dilemma. First, you can use the RT Core library, like this:

```
<c_rt:out value='<%= list[list.size()-1] %>'/>
```

Second, if you want to avoid Java code in your JSP pages, you can implement a simple wrapper class that contains a list and provides access to the list's `size` property with a JavaBeans-compliant getter method. That bean is listed in Listing 2.25.

The preceding wrapper class has two JavaBeans properties: `list` and `size`; the former provides access to the list, and the latter provides access to the list's size. Listing 2.26 lists a JSP page that uses one of those wrappers.

Listing 2.25   *WEB-INF/classes/beans/ListWrapper.java*

```java
package beans;

import java.util.List;

public class ListWrapper {
   private List list;

   // JavaBean accessors for first name
   public ListWrapper(List list) {
      this.list = list;
   }
   public List getList() {
      return list;
   }
   public int getSize() {
      return list.size();
   }
}
```

Listing 2.26   *Using a Wrapper to Access an Object's Properties*

```html
<!DOCTYPE HTML PUBLIC "-//W3C//DTD HTML 4.0 Transitional//EN">
<html>
   <head>
      <title>Invoking Methods</title>
   </head>

   <body>
      <%@ taglib uri='http://java.sun.com/jstl/core' prefix='c' %>
      <%@ page import='java.util.LinkedList' %>
      <%@ page import='beans.ListWrapper' %>

      <%
         LinkedList list = new LinkedList();
         list.add("item one");
         list.add("item two");
         list.add("item three");
         list.add("item four");
         list.add("item five");

         ListWrapper listWrapper = new ListWrapper(list);
         pageContext.setAttribute("listWrapper", listWrapper);
      %>

      The first item is
      <b><c:out value='${listWrapper.list[0]}'/></b>
```

Listing 2.26   *Using a Wrapper to Access an Object's Properties (cont.)*

```
        and the last item is
        <b>
            <c:out value='${listWrapper.list[listWrapper.size-1]}'/>
        </b>

        <p>

        Here are all the items in the list:

        <p>

        <ul>
            <c:forEach var='item' items='${listWrapper.list}'>
                <li><c:out value='${item}'/></li>
            </c:forEach>
        </ul>
    </body>
</html>
```

Like the JSP page listed in Listing 2.24 on page 87, the preceding JSP page
creates a list and populates it. But this time, the list is stored in a wrapper and the
wrapper is stored in page scope. The JSP page accesses the list with the expression
`listWrapper.list` and accesses the list's size with the expression
`listWrapper.size`.

The JSP page listed in Listing 2.26 is shown in Figure 2–13.

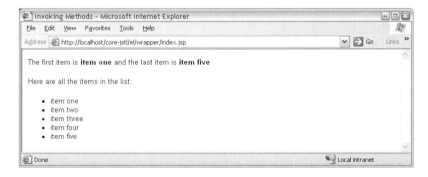

Figure 2–13   Using a JavaBeans Wrapper to Access a List's Size

The JSP page shown in Figure 2–13 and listed in Listing 2.26 displays the first and last items in the list and iterates over all of the items in the list. See "Iteration Actions" on page 150 for more information about iterating over collections.

2.9 EL Expressions in Custom Actions

The JSTL expression language is one of JSTL's most exciting features. If you implement JSP custom actions, you may be wondering how you can use the expression language for your own action attributes.

You can incorporate the expression language into your custom actions, but for JSTL 1.0, you cannot do it portably. Here's why: The JSP expert group is ultimately responsible for the expression language, which will be incorporated into JSP 2.0. When JSTL 1.0 was finalized—well before JSP 2.0—the JSP expert group had not yet defined a portable API for accessing the expression language. Because of that scheduling mismatch, until JSP 2.0 you will have to make do with writing code specific to the JSTL Reference Implementation.[15] JSP 2.0 will define a portable mechanism for accessing the expression language.[16]

This section shows you how to implement a custom action that permits EL expressions for an attribute using the JSTL 1.0 Reference Implementation.

Core Warning

For JSTL 1.0, it's not possible to use the EL for custom action attributes in a portable fashion.

Figure 2–14 shows a JSP page that uses a custom action to display values contained in a map. The maps shown in Figure 2–14 are accessed through some of the JSTL implicit objects discussed in "Implicit Objects" on page 64.

---

15. As this book went to press, negotiations were underway to put the expression language implementation of the JSTL Reference Implementation in Jakarta Commons.
16. See http://java.sun.com/products/jsp/ to download the JSP 2.0 specification.

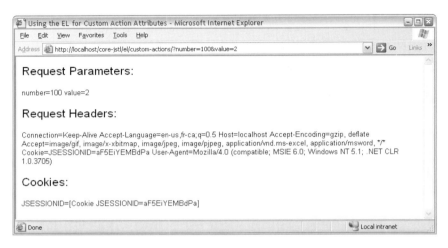

Figure 2–14   A Custom Action That Processes EL Expressions for Its Attribute

The JSP page shown in Figure 2–14 is listed in Listing 2.27.

Listing 2.27   *index.jsp*

```
<!DOCTYPE HTML PUBLIC "-//W3C//DTD HTML 4.0 Transitional//EN">
<html>
   <head>
      <title>Using the EL for Custom Action Attributes</title>
   </head>
   <body>
      <%@ taglib uri='WEB-INF/core-jstl.tld' prefix='core-jstl' %>

      <font size='5'>Request Parameters:</font>
      <p><core-jstl:showMap map='${param}'/>

      <p><font size='5'>Request Headers:</font>
      <p><core-jstl:showMap map='${header}'/>

      <p><font size='5'>Cookies:</font>
      <p><core-jstl:showMap map='${cookie}'/>
   </body>
</html>
```

The preceding JSP page uses a custom action—<core-jstl:showMap>—that displays values stored in a map. That custom action is unspectacular except for one feature: you can use the expression language to specify the action's map attribute.

Let's see how that custom action is implemented. First, we must specify a tag library descriptor (TLD) that defines the library and its lone action. That TLD, specified in `WEB-INF/core-jstl.tld`, is listed in Listing 2.28.

Listing 2.28 *WEB-INF/core-jstl.tld*

```
<?xml version="1.0" encoding="ISO-8859-1" ?>
<!DOCTYPE taglib
   PUBLIC "-//Sun Microsystems, Inc.//DTD JSP Tag Library 1.2//EN"
   "http://java.sun.com/dtds/web-jsptaglibrary_1_2.dtd">

<taglib>
   <tlib-version>1.0</tlib-version>
   <jsp-version>1.2</jsp-version>
   <short-name>JSTL Examples</short-name>
   <description>
      A custom action that shows how to incorporate the JSTL
      expression language for custom action attributes
   </description>

   <tag>
      <name>showMap</name>
      <tag-class>tags.ShowMapAction</tag-class>
      <body-content>JSP</body-content>
      <description>
         This action shows the values stored in a map
      </description>

      <attribute>
        <name>map</name>
        <required>true</required>
        <rtexprvalue>true</rtexprvalue>
        </attribute>
   </tag>
</taglib>
```

The preceding TLD specifies the name of the action—showMap—and the action's one required attribute, named `map`. The TLD also specifies the action's tag handler: `tags.ShowMapAction`, which is listed in Listing 2.29.

The preceding tag handler for the <core-jstl:showMap> action uses the Apache expression evaluator manager to evaluate the value specified for the `map` attribute with the `setMap` method. You pass the `ExpressionEvaluatorManager.evaluate` method the attribute's name, the expression specified for that attribute, the type that you expect the attribute to be, a reference to the tag handler and its page context. That method evaluates the expression and returns the appropriate object.

Listing 2.29 *WEB-INF/classes/tags/ShowMapAction.java*

```
package tags;

import java.util.*;
import javax.servlet.jsp.*;
import javax.servlet.jsp.tagext.*;

// WARNING: non-standard class
import org.apache.taglibs.standard.lang.support.Expression
EvaluatorManager;

public class ShowMapAction extends TagSupport {
   private String mapName;
   private Map map;

   public void setMap(String mapName) {
      this.mapName = mapName;
   }
   public int doStartTag() throws JspException {
      // EL expressions must be evaluated in doStartTag()
      // and not in attribute setter methods, because servlet
      // containers can reuse tags, and if an attribute takes a
      // string literal, the setter method might not be called
      // every time the tag is encountered.
      map = (Map)ExpressionEvaluatorManager.evaluate(
            "map",                   // attribute name
            mapName,                 // expression
            java.util.Map.class,     // expected type
            this,                    // this tag handler
            pageContext);            // the page context

      if(map == null)
         return SKIP_BODY;

      Iterator it = map.keySet().iterator();
      JspWriter out = pageContext.getOut();

      while(it.hasNext()) {
         Object key = it.next(), value = map.get(key);

         try {
            if(value instanceof String[]) {
               String[] strings = (String[])value;

               for(int i=0; i < strings.length; ++i) {
                  out.println(strings[i]);
```

| Listing 2.29 | *WEB-INF/classes/tags/ShowMapAction.java (cont.)* |

```
}
            }
            else {
               out.println(key + "=" + value);
            }
         }
         catch(java.io.IOException ex) {
            throw new JspException(ex);
         }
      }
      return SKIP_BODY;
   }
}
```

2.10 Common Mistakes

All languages have their idiosyncrasies and pitfalls to avoid, and the JSTL expression language is no different. This section discusses some common mistakes that you are apt to make repeatedly. Once you are aware of them, it's easier to avoid them. Here are five of the most common JSTL expression language mistakes:

1. Forgetting curly braces
2. Forgetting `taglib` declarations
3. Neglecting to store variables in a scope
4. Using illegal characters for attribute names
5. Inadvertently using implicit objects

Forgetting Curly Braces

When you first start using the expression language, it can take awhile to remember to use the dollar sign and the *curly braces* for your expressions. Just as important, it can take awhile for expressions to look odd when the curly braces have been omitted. Here's a classic example:

```
<c:if test='counter.count == 1'>
   <%-- Do something the first time... --%>
</c:if>
```

The expression specified for the <c:if> test attribute will always evaluate to
`false` because the value is a string that does not equal `"true"`.[17] Instead, you
need to do this for the comparison to work:

```
<c:if test='${counter.count == 1}'>
   <%-- Do something the first time... --%>
</c:if>
```

Forgetting `taglib` Declarations

Even if you haven't yet read the Iteration Actions chapter in this book, you probably
have a good idea what the following code fragment does:

```
<c:forEach var='item' begin='1' end='10'>
   <c:out value='${item}'/>
</c:forEach>
```

At first glance, it looks as though the preceding code fragment will print values
from 1 to 10, inclusive; however, that's not necessarily the case. If you *forget the
`taglib` directive* for the JSTL core actions, the preceding code fragment will do
nothing.

To make sure that the preceding code works as you expect, you need to remember
the `taglib` directive, like this:

```
<%@ taglib uri='http://java.sun.com/jstl/core' prefix='c' %>

<c:forEach var='item' begin='1' end='10'>
   <c:out value='${item}'/>
</c:forEach>
```

Neglecting to Store Variables in a Scope

Although it's not recommended for production code, it is not uncommon for developers to create some temporary objects in a scriptlet that act as placeholders for data
that will eventually come from another source; for example, you can create a hash
map in a scriptlet that you can subsequently access with an EL expression, like this:

```
<%
   java.util.HashMap map = new java.util.HashMap();
   map.put("key One", "value One");
```

---

17. That criterion is from the Java documentation for `Boolean.valueOf(String)`. See
    Table 2.3 on page 62 for more information about expression language type coercions.

```
    map.put("key Two", "value Two");
    map.put("key Three", "value Three");
    map.put("key Four", "value Four");
    map.put("key Five", "value Five");
%>

<c:out value='${map["key One"]}'/>
```

You may think that the preceding code fragment will display the value of the first entry added to the map, but in actuality, it will display nothing at all because *the map created in the scriptlet was never stored in one of the JSP scopes.*

Once the map is placed in one of the JSP scopes, it can be accessed with an EL expression. Here is the corrected code fragment:

```
<%
    java.util.HashMap map = new java.util.HashMap();
    map.put("key One", "value One");
    map.put("key Two", "value Two");
    map.put("key Three", "value Three");
    map.put("key Four", "value Four");
    map.put("key Five", "value Five");

    pageContext.setAttribute("map", map);
%>

<c:out value='${map["key One"]}'/>
```

You can iterate over the items stored in the map created above like this:

```
<c:forEach var='item' items='${map}'>
   <c:out value='Key=${item.key}, Value=${item.value}'/>
</c:forEach>
```

Using Illegal Characters for Attribute Values

The preceding code fragment will print the key and value for each entry in a map. The following code, however, will not do the same:

```
<%-- The name an-item is not legal, so this produces no output --%>
<c:forEach var='an-item' items='${map}'>
   <c:out value='Key=${an-item.key}, Value=${an-item.value}'/>
</c:forEach>
```

The preceding code fragment will not produce any output because the name chosen for the scoped variable created by <c:forEach> is not a valid Java identifier—because it contains a dash—and therefore the preceding code will fail silently.

Inadvertently Using Implicit Objects

One final word of caution. Be careful that you don't inadvertently use the names of the JSTL implicit objects; for example, the following code fragment displays all of the request parameters, similar to the example discussed in "Accessing Request Parameters" on page 65:

```
<html>
   <head>
      ...
   </head>

   <body>
      <%@ taglib uri='http://java.sun.com/jstl/core' prefix='c' %>
      ...
      <%-- For every String[] item of paramValues... --%>
      <c:forEach var='parameter' items='${paramValues}'>
         <ul>
            <%-- Show the key, which is the request parameter
                 name --%>
            <li><b><c:out value='${parameter.key}'/></b>:</li>
            <%-- Iterate over the values -- a String[] --
                 associated with this request parameter --%>
            <c:forEach var='value' items='${parameter.value}'>
               <%-- Show the String value --%>
               <c:out value='${value}'/>
            </c:forEach>
         </ul>
      </c:forEach>
      ...
   </body>
</html>
```

The preceding code fragment works as advertised, but if you make this seemingly innocuous change—

```
...
<c:forEach var='param' items='${paramValues}'>
   <ul>
      ...
      <li><b><c:out value='${param.key}'/></b>:</li>
      ...
```

```
    <c:forEach var='value' items='${param.value}'>
      ...
    </c:forEach>
  </ul>
</c:forEach>
...
```

—the preceding code fragment will not work like the previous code fragment because `param` is an implicit object, not the current object of the iteration.

GENERAL-PURPOSE AND CONDITIONAL ACTIONS

Topics in This Chapter

- General-Purpose Actions
- Conditional Actions
- Using Conditional and General-Purpose Actions Together
- Conditional Custom Actions

Chapter 3

Some of the most basic tasks that JSP developers perform involve producing output, setting and accessing scoped variables and JavaBean properties, implementing conditional code, and handling exceptions. All of those tasks are discussed in this chapter, which explores the JSTL general-purpose and conditional actions. The general-purpose actions are discussed in "General-Purpose Actions" on page 102, and the conditional actions are discussed in "Conditional Actions" on page 127.

Besides showing you how to use the JSTL general-purpose and conditional actions, this chapter also illustrates how to perform a number of common tasks for JSP-based applications, including:

- "Setting Attributes for HTML Elements" on page 104
- "Retaining Values for HTML Text Elements" on page 106
- "Accessing Bean Properties" on page 108
- "Setting Bean Properties and Map Entries" on page 112
- "Retaining Values for HTML Option Elements" on page 129
- "Implementing If/Else Constructs" on page 133
- "Implementing Switch Statement Constructs" on page 136

This chapter concludes with a section on implementing conditional custom actions and a section that shows you how to use the general-purpose and conditional actions together in a simple case study.

3.1 General-Purpose Actions

JSTL provides four general-purpose actions:

- <c:out>
- <c:set>
- <c:remove>
- <c:catch>

The actions listed above represent the most fundamental JSTL actions. Each of those actions is discussed in the following sections.

The <c:out> Action

The JSTL expression language (EL), which is discussed in "The JSTL Expression Language" on page 38, is not incorporated into JSP 1.2 or earlier versions.[1] Currently, you can only use Java code in JSP expressions, scriptlets, and declarations; for example, you can access the Host request header with a JSP expression like this:

```
<%= request.getHeader("host") %>
```

Because JSP does not currently provide support for the EL, JSTL includes a <c:out> action, which evaluates an EL expression, coerces the resulting value to a string, and forwards that string to the current JspWriter. The <c:out> action is the EL equivalent of a JSP expression; for example, you can use <c:out> to access the Host request header like this:

```
<c:out value='${header.host}'/>
```

The preceding code fragment uses the JSTL header implicit object to access the Host request header.[2] The two preceding code fragments produce identical results.

The <c:out> action is easy to use, as the preceding code fragment illustrates. There are two ways that you can use <c:out>; here is one syntax:[3]

<c:out value [default] [escapeXml]/>

---

1. EL support is planned for JSP 2.0.
2. See "The JSTL Expression Language" on page 38 for more information about JSTL implicit objects.
3. Items in brackets are optional. See "<c:out>" on page 469 for a more complete description of <c:out> syntax.

The `value` attribute, which is required, can be an EL expression or a string. The `default` attribute—which replaces the `value` attribute if the value evaluates to `null`—is handy when you try to access a value that might not exist, for example:

```
Name: <c:out value='${param.name}' default='Not Specified'/>
```

The preceding code fragment tries to access a request parameter named `name`; if that request parameter does not exist, the `<c:out>` action will send the string `Not Specified` to the current `JspWriter`.

You can also specify the default value in the body of the `<c:out>` action with this syntax:

> *<c:out value [escapeXml]>*
> *   default*
> *</c:out>*

If you don't specify a default value, the default value itself defaults to an empty string; for example:

```
Name: <c:out value='${param.name}'/>
```

The `<c:out>` action in the preceding code fragment will not produce any output if the `name` request parameter does not exist or evaluates to `null`.

By default, `<c:out>` converts certain characters to XML escape sequences, as shown in Table 3.1.

Table 3.1   `<c:out>` Default Character Conversions

Character	Character Entity Code
<	<
>	>
&	&
'	&#039
"	&#034

Sometimes, however, you don't want those characters to be converted, for example:

```
<c:set var='opt1' value='Red'/>
<c:set var='opt2' value='Blue'/>
<c:set var='opt3' value='Green'/>
```

```
<form>
  <select>
    <c:out value='<option value=${opt1}>${opt1}</option>'
      escapeXml='false'/>
    <c:out value='<option value=${opt2}>${opt2}</option>'
      escapeXml='false'/>
    <c:out value='<option value=${opt3}>${opt3}</option>'
      escapeXml='false'/>
  </select>
</form>
```

The preceding code fragment generates an HTML select element with scoped variables created by the <c:set> action.[4] In that case, you don't want to escape the < and > characters because the select elements will not be properly generated. Because the <c:out> actions in the preceding code fragment set the escapeXml attribute to false, those characters will not be converted to their corresponding XML escape sequences.

The JSTL runtime library has a <c_rt:out> action that corresponds to the <c:out> action from the expression language library. Instead of specifying an EL expression for the value attribute, as is the case for <c:out>, a Java expression is specified for the <c_rt:out> action's value attribute, like this:

```
<c_rt:out value='<%= new Integer(5) %>'/>
```

The <c_rt:out> action is provided only for symmetry between the JSTL RT and EL libraries.[5] In practice, that action is rarely—if ever—used because it's simpler to just specify a JSP expression; for example:

```
<%= new Integer(5) %>
```

The preceding JSP expression is equivalent to the previous code fragment that uses the <c_rt:out> action.

Now that we have a basic understanding of the <c:out> action, let's take a look at three situations in which that action is especially useful: setting attributes for HTML elements, retaining values for HTML text elements, and accessing properties of beans and maps.

Setting Attributes for HTML Elements

You can use <c:out> to specify attributes for HTML elements; for example, the JSP page shown in Figure 3–1 uses <c:out> to set the value of the submit button to whatever value you specify in the textfield.

---

4. See "The <c:set> Action" on page 111 for more information about the <c:set> action.
5. See "Twin Libraries" on page 9 for more information about the RT and EL libraries.

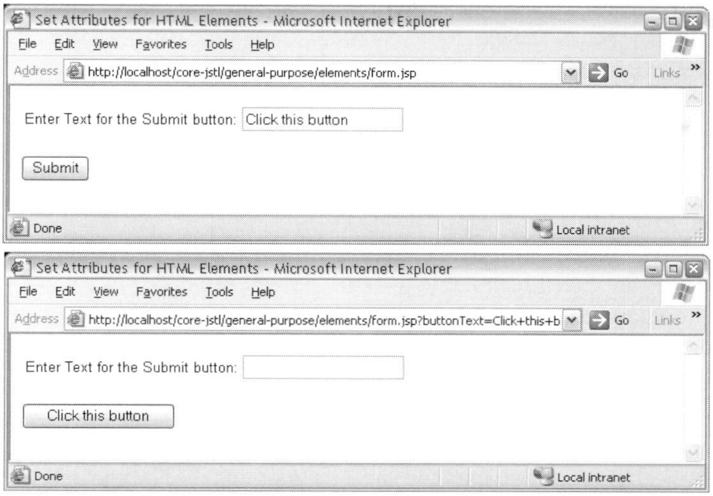

Figure 3–1 Setting HTML Element Attributes with <c:out>

The top picture in Figure 3–1 shows the JSP page after it's first loaded and a user has entered a string in the textfield. The bottom picture shows the JSP page after the user has subsequently activated the submit button.

The JSP page shown in Figure 3–1 is listed in Listing 3.1.

In the preceding JSP page, the value for the submit button is specified with a <c:out> action. The value specified for that action is the value of the `buttonText` request parameter. Notice that the <c:out> action also specifies a default value, which is used when the `buttonText` request parameter does not exist, as illustrated by the top picture in Figure 3–1.

When you use <c:out> to specify a value for a tag (HTML or otherwise) attribute, you must quote the <c:out> action and its attribute values. You can use single quotes to quote the <c:out> action and double quotes to quote that action's attribute value as is the case for the preceding JSP page, or vice versa; for example:

```
<input type='submit'
     value="<c:out value='${param.buttonText}'
                default='Submit'/>"/>
```

As you can see from Figure 3–1, the textfield in the preceding JSP page does not retain its value when the page is reloaded. It's often desirable for HTML elements to retain their values; for example, when a form that's not properly filled out is redisplayed. You can use the <c:out> action to retain HTML `text` element values, as discussed in the next section.

| Listing 3.1 | *Set HTML Element Attributes* |

```
<!DOCTYPE HTML PUBLIC "-//W3C//DTD HTML 4.0 Transitional//EN">
<html>
   <head>
      <title>Set Attributes for HTML Elements</title>
   </head>

   <body>
      <%@ taglib uri='http://java.sun.com/jstl/core' prefix='c' %>

      <%-- Because the following form has no action, this JSP
           page will be reloaded when the form is submitted --%>
      <form>
         <table>
           <tr>
              <td>Enter Text for the Submit button:</td>
              <td><input name='buttonText' type='text'></td>
           </tr>
         </table>

         <p><input type='submit'
                  value='<c:out value="${param.buttonText}"
                              default="Submit"/>'/>
      </form>
   </body>
</html>
```

Retaining Values for HTML Text Elements

Figure 3–2 shows a JSP page that retains its textfield's values when the page is reloaded. The top picture in Figure 3–2 shows the JSP page when it's first loaded and the user has entered values for the First Name and Last Name textfields. The bottom picture shows the same JSP page after the user has activated the submit button and the page has been reloaded.

The JSP page shown in Figure 3–2 is listed in Listing 3.2.

The preceding JSP page uses <c:out> actions to access the values previously specified for the textfields. Those values are used to set the textfield's value attributes so that the textfields retain their values when the page is reloaded.

The JSP pages discussed in the two previous sections use <c:out> actions to access request parameters. Another popular use for <c:out> is accessing bean properties, which is discussed in the next section.

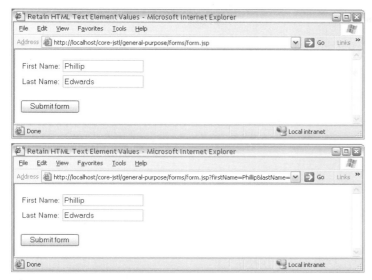

Figure 3–2 Retaining Values for HTML Text Elements with <c:out>

Listing 3.2 *Retaining HTML Text Element Values*

```
<!DOCTYPE HTML PUBLIC "-//W3C//DTD HTML 4.0 Transitional//EN">
<html>
   <head>
      <title>Retain HTML Text Element Values</title>
   </head>

   <body>
      <%@ taglib uri='http://java.sun.com/jstl/core' prefix='c' %>

      <%-- Because the following form has no action, this JSP
      page will be reloaded when the form is submitted --%>
      <p><form>
         <table>
            <tr>
               <td>First Name:</td>
               <td><input type='text'
                     name='firstName'
                  value='<c:out value="${param.firstName}"/>'/>
               </td>
            </tr>

            <tr>
```

Listing 3.2 *Retaining HTML Text Element Values (cont.)*

```
            <td>Last Name:</td>
            <td>
               <input type='text'
                      name='lastName'
                      value='<c:out value="${param.lastName}"/>'/>
            </td>
         </tr>
      </table>

      <p><input type='submit' value='Submit form'/>
   </form>
 </body>
</html>
```

Accessing Bean Properties

It's easy to access bean properties with <c:out>, but to illustrate that feature, we need to have a bean that we can access. Listing 3.3 lists a simple color preference bean that stores background and foreground colors. Instances of that bean are used throughout this chapter.

Listing 3.3 *WEB-INF/classes/beans/ColorPreferences.java*

```java
package beans;

public class ColorPreferences {
   private String background = "white",
                  foreground = "black";

   public void setForeground(String foreground) {
      this.foreground = foreground;
   }
   public String getForeground() {
      return foreground;
   }
   public void setBackground(String background) {
      this.background = background;
   }
   public String getBackground() {
      return background;
   }
}
```

The color preference bean listed above provides JavaBeans-compliant setter and getter methods for its background and foreground colors. The JSTL expression language lets you access bean properties through accessor methods that conform to the JavaBeans specification, but it does not provide support for invoking random methods on an object.[6]

The color preference bean listed above is used in the JSP page shown in Figure 3–3 to set foreground and background colors for an HTML table.

Figure 3–3   Accessing Bean Properties with <c:out>

The JSP page shown in Figure 3–3 is listed in Listing 3.4.

The preceding JSP page uses <jsp:useBean> to create a color preference bean and store that bean in page scope. The body of the <jsp:useBean> action contains <jsp:setProperty> actions that set the bean's background and foreground colors. Subsequently, the JSP page creates an HTML table and specifies the background color for that table with the <c:out> action, which accesses the bean's background color. The color of the text displayed in the table is also set with a <c:out> action that accesses the bean's foreground color.

Notice that the first <c:out> action in the preceding JSP page accesses the bean without specifying its scope, whereas the second <c:out> action explicitly specifies the bean's scope by accessing the bean with the `pageScope` JSTL implicit object. When you access a bean with an EL expression, you don't have to specify that bean's scope, so the second <c:out> action in the preceding JSP page could have accessed the bean's foreground color with `${bean.foreground}`. The only reason the second <c:out> action explicitly specified that bean's scope was to show you that it can be done. Sometimes, if you have beans that have the same name and reside in different scopes, you may have to explicitly specify a bean's scope.[7]

The preceding JSP page uses <jsp:setProperty> in conjunction with <jsp:useBean>. Instead of using <jsp:setProperty>, you can use the <c:set> action,

---

6. See "Method Invocation" on page 86 for more information about invoking methods with the JSTL expression language.

7. Storing beans that have the same name in different scopes is not recommended because the JSP specification allows one of those beans to override the other.

Listing 3.4 *Access Bean Properties*

```
<!DOCTYPE HTML PUBLIC "-//W3C//DTD HTML 4.0 Transitional//EN">
<html>
    <head>
        <title>Access Bean Properties</title>
    </head>

    <body>
        <%@ taglib uri='http://java.sun.com/jstl/core' prefix='c'%>

        <%-- Create a color preferences bean and store it in
             page scope --%>
        <jsp:useBean id='bean' class='beans.ColorPreferences'>
            <%-- The following <jsp:setProperty> actions are
                 invoked when the bean is created, which happens
                 every time this page is accessed because the bean
                 resides in page scope --%>

            <%-- Set the bean's background color --%>
            <jsp:setProperty name='bean' property='background'
                        value='black'/>

            <%-- Set the bean's foreground color --%>
            <jsp:setProperty name='bean' property='foreground'
                        value='white'/>
        </jsp:useBean>

        <%-- Create a table with the background color stored
             in the bean's background property --%>
        <table align='center' border='3'
             bgcolor='<c:out value="${bean.background}"/>'>
            <tr>
                <td>
                    <%-- Create table data with the font color stored
                         in the bean's foreground property --%>
                    <font size='7'
                        color='<c:out
                            value="${pageScope.bean.foreground}"/>'>
                        JSTL
                    </font>
                </td>
            </tr>
        </table>
    </body>
</html>
```

which allows you to use the expression language—that's something that you currently cannot do with <jsp:setProperty>. The <c:set> action is discussed in the next section.

The <c:set> Action

The <c:set> action is quite versatile; it lets you do the following:

- Store a value in a scoped variable
- Delete a scoped variable
- Set a bean's property to a specified value
- Set a bean's property to `null`
- Store an entry (a key/value pair) in a Java map
- Modify an entry in a Java map
- Remove an entry from a Java map

The <c:set> action supports four syntaxes; two of those syntaxes let you manipulate scoped variables and the other two let you manipulate beans or maps. You can set or remove a scoped variable with the following syntax:[8]

<c:set value var [scope]/>

The mandatory `var` and `value` attributes specify the name of the scoped variable and its value, respectively. Optionally, you can specify the variable's scope with the `scope` attribute. By default, <c:set> stores scoped variables in page scope. The following code fragment stores the HTTP request method—either `GET`, `POST`, `PUT`, `HEAD`, `DELETE`, `OPTIONS`, or `TRACE`—in a scoped variable stored in request scope:

```
<c:set var='aScopedVariable' scope='request'
    value='${pageContext.request.method}'/>
```

You can access the scoped variable referenced in the preceding code fragment with <c:out>, like this:

```
<c:out value='${aScopedVariable}'/>
```

If you specify the `var` attribute and a `null` value for the `value` attribute, <c:set> will delete the specified scoped variable, for example:

---

8. Items in brackets are optional. See "<c:set>" on page 471 for a more complete description of <c:set> syntax.

```
<c:set var='aScopedVariable' value='${null}'/>
```

The preceding code fragment removes the scoped variable named `aScopedVariable` from page scope. You can also specify the value for <c:set> in the action's body with this syntax:

> *<c:set var [scope]>*
>   *value*
> *</c:out>*

The syntax listed above is most useful when you want to store output from another action, for example:

```
<c:set var='substring'>
   <str:substring start='3' end='7'>
      0123456789
   </str:substring>
</c:set>

<c:out value='${substring}'/>
```

The preceding code fragment uses Apache's Jakarta String Tag Library to extract a substring from the string `0123456789`.[9] The <c:set> action stores the output from the <str:substring> action in a page-scoped variable named `substring`. Subsequently, <c:out> displays the value of the `substring` scoped variable. The output from the preceding code fragment is `3456`.

Setting Bean Properties and Map Entries

You can set a bean's property with this <c:set> syntax:

> *<c:set target property value/>*

In the preceding syntax, the `target` attribute is a reference to a bean, the `property` attribute is the name of the bean's property, and the `value` attribute represents the property's value. You can also specify the property value in the body of the <c:set> action with this syntax:

> *<c:set target property>*
>   *value*
> *</c:set>*

---

9. You can download any of the Jakarta tag libraries from
   `http://jakarta.apache.org/taglibs/index.html`.

Besides setting bean properties, you can also use the two preceding <c:set> syntaxes to set, remove, and modify entries in a map. In that case, the `target` attribute is a reference to a map, the `property` attribute represents the *key* for the map entry, and the `value` attribute represents the map entry's *value*.

The following sections—"Setting Bean Properties" and "Setting Compound Bean Properties"—show you how to use <c:set> to set bean properties, and "Adding, Removing, and Modifying Map Entries" on page 119 shows you how to add, remove, and modify map entries.

Setting Bean Properties

Figure 3–4 shows a JSP page that lets you specify a color preference bean's foreground and background colors. That bean's colors are used to set the foreground and background colors for the table shown in Figure 3–4. The top picture in Figure 3–4 shows the JSP page when it's first loaded and a user has selected background and foreground colors, and the bottom picture shows the JSP page after the user has activated the submit button.

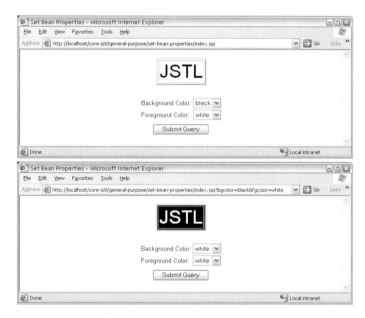

Figure 3–4   Setting Bean Properties with <c:set>. Because the textfields do not retain their values, the values specified in the textfields in the bottom picture are out of sync with the table displayed above them.

The JSP page shown in Figure 3–4 is listed in Listing 3.5.

Listing 3.5   *Setting Bean Properties*

```
<!DOCTYPE HTML PUBLIC "-//W3C//DTD HTML 4.0 Transitional//EN">
<html>
   <head>
      <title>Set Bean Properties</title>
   </head>

   <body>
      <%@ taglib uri='http://java.sun.com/jstl/core' prefix='c' %>

      <%-- Create a color preferences bean and store it in
           page scope --%>
      <jsp:useBean id='bean' class='beans.ColorPreferences'/>

      <%-- If there are no bgcolor or fgcolor request parameters
           (as is the case when this page is first loaded),
           the following <c:set> actions set the bean's
           properties to null --%>

      <%-- Set the bean's background property to the value of the
           bgcolor request parameter --%>
      <c:set target='${bean}' property='background'
           value='${param.bgcolor}'/>

      <%-- Set the bean's foreground property to the value of the
           fgcolor request parameter. Notice that the action's
           value is specified in the body of the action, for no
           other reason than to show it can be done. --%>
      <c:set target='${bean}' property='foreground'>
         <c:out value='${param.fgcolor}'/>
      </c:set>

      <table align='center'>
         <tr>
            <td colspan='2' align='center'></td>
               <%-- Create a table with the background color
                    stored in the bean's background property --%>
               <table border='3' align='center'
                    bgcolor='<c:out value="${bean.background}"/>'>
                  <tr>
                    <td>
                    <%-- Create table data with the font color
                         stored in the bean's foreground
                         property --%>
                    <font size='7'
                     color='<c:out value="${bean.foreground}"/>'>
                       JSTL
                    </font>
                    </td>
```

Listing 3.5 *Setting Bean Properties (cont.)*

```
                    </tr>
                </table><p>
            </td>
        </tr>

        <tr>
            <%-- Because the following form has no action, this JSP
                 page will be reloaded when the form
                 is submitted --%>
            <form>
                <table align='center'>
                    <tr>
                        <td>Background Color:</td>
                        <td>
                            <%-- Create the HTML select element for
                                 background color --%>
                            <select name='bgcolor'>
                                <option value='white'>white</option>
                                <option value='black'>black</option>
                            </select>
                        </td>
                    </tr>

                    <tr>
                        <td>Foreground Color:</td>
                        <td>
                            <%-- Create the HTML select element for
                                 foreground color --%>
                            <select name='fgcolor'>
                                <option value='white'>white</option>
                                <option value='black'>black</option>
                            </select>
                        </td>
                    </tr>

                    <tr>
                        <table align='center'>
                            <tr>
                                <td><input type='submit'></td>
                            </tr>
                        </table>
                    </tr>
                </table>
            </form>
        </tr>
    </table>
  </body>
</html>
```

The preceding JSP page uses <jsp:useBean> to create a color preference bean. Subsequently, two <c:set> actions are used to set the bean's background and foreground colors with the values specified in the page's form. The JSP page then uses that bean to set the background color for its table and the font color for the table's text. Finally, the JSP page creates the form that lets you select foreground and background colors.

Two things are noteworthy about the preceding JSP page. First, the JSP page could dispense entirely with the color preference bean by using the bgcolor and fgcolor request parameters to set the table's background color and the font foreground color, respectively; instead, the JSP page stores the request parameters in a bean and uses that bean to set the table's background color and the font color. The only reason for using the bean is to illustrate how you can use <c:set> to set a bean's properties.

Second, solely for the sake of illustration, the <c:set> actions that set the bean's background and foreground colors use both syntaxes discussed in "Setting Bean Properties and Map Entries" on page 112, even though it was not necessary to do so—both actions could use the same syntax. The first <c:set> action uses the value attribute like this:

```
<c:set target='${bean}' property='background'
       value='${param.bgcolor}'/>
```

The second <c:set> action specifies its value in its body like this:

```
<c:set target='${bean}' property='foreground'>
  <c:out value='${param.fgcolor}'/>
</c:set>
```

You should note that you cannot use <c:out> for a JSTL action's attribute; for example, the following code fragment will not produce the same result as the previous two code fragments:

```
<%-- This code fragment won't produce desirable results --%>

<c:set target='${bean}' property='foreground'
       value='<c:out value="${param.fgcolor}"/>'/>
```

If you set the foreground color to black, the preceding code fragment will set the bean's foreground property to the string <c:out value="black"/>, which will not be interpreted by the table as the color black. You might think that this behavior is a bug, but it's valid because the value attribute is interpreted as an EL expression, so the expression ${param.fgcolor} is interpreted as black and embedded into the rest of the string specified for the value attribute. Note that this behavior is in contrast to using <c:out> to specify an attribute of an HTML tag, which works as expected and is discussed in "Setting Attributes for HTML Elements" on page 104.

Finally, Figure 3–4 on page 113 might be rather puzzling at first glance because the textfields do not retain their values, so the bottom picture in Figure 3–4 displays white in the Background Color select element, even though the background color for the table is black in that picture. As "Retaining Values for HTML Text Elements" on page 106 illustrated, it's a simple matter to retain values in textfields; however, retaining values for HTML select elements is more of a challenge. See "Retaining Values for HTML Option Elements" on page 129 for more information about how you can retain values for HTML option elements.

Most of the time the beans that you use in Web applications are compound, meaning one bean contains a reference to another. As is the case for simple beans, it's easy to access properties for compound beans, as the next section illustrates.

Setting Compound Bean Properties

This section shows you how to use <c:set> to set properties for compound beans, which are beans that contain references to other beans, but before we can illustrate that approach, we need a compound bean. Listing 3.6 lists a simple Name bean that stores first and last names.

| Listing 3.6 | *WEB-INF/classes/beans/Name.java* |

```java
package beans;

public class Name {
   private String first, last;

   public void   setFirst(String first) { this.first = first; }
   public String getFirst()              { return first; }

   public void   setLast(String last)    { this.last = last; }
   public String getLast()               { return last; }
}
```

The name bean listed above is a compound bean because it contains references to strings. Name beans are referenced by another compound bean—Subscriber— listed in Listing 3.7.

Listing 3.7	*WEB-INF/classes/beans/Subscriber.java*

```
package beans;

public class Subscriber {
   private Name name;
   private String email;

   public void setName(Name name) { this.name = name; }
   public Name getName()          { return name; }

   public void  setEmail(String email) { this.email = email; }
   public String getEmail()             { return email; }
}
```

Listing 3.8 illustrates how you can access the first and last names of a subscriber.

Listing 3.8	*Setting Nested Bean Properties*

```
<!DOCTYPE HTML PUBLIC "-//W3C//DTD HTML 4.0 Transitional//EN">
<html>
   <head>
      <title>Setting Nested Bean Properties</title>
   </head>

   <body>
      <%@ taglib uri='http://java.sun.com/jstl/core' prefix='c' %>

      <jsp:useBean id='name' class='beans.Name'>
         <c:set target='${name}' property='first' value='John'/>
         <c:set target='${name}' property='last'  value='Tate'/>
      </jsp:useBean>

      <jsp:useBean id='subscriber' class='beans.Subscriber'>
         <c:set target='${subscriber}'
               property='name' value='${name}'/>
      </jsp:useBean>

      <c:out value='${subscriber.name.first}'/>
      <c:out value='${subscriber.name.last}'/>
   </body>
</html>
```

The preceding JSP page uses <jsp:useBean> to create a name bean and sets the `first` and `last` name properties for that bean with the <c:set> action. Subsequently, the JSP page creates a subscriber bean and uses <c:set> to specify the subscriber's name. Finally, two <c:out> actions display the subscriber's first and last names with the EL expressions `${subscriber.name.first}` and `${subscriber.name.last}`. The output of the JSP page is `John Tate`.

Adding, Removing, and Modifying Map Entries

In addition to using <c:set> to set bean properties, you can also use it to add, remove, and modify entries in a map.[10] Figure 3–5 shows a simple Web application that lets you do just that.

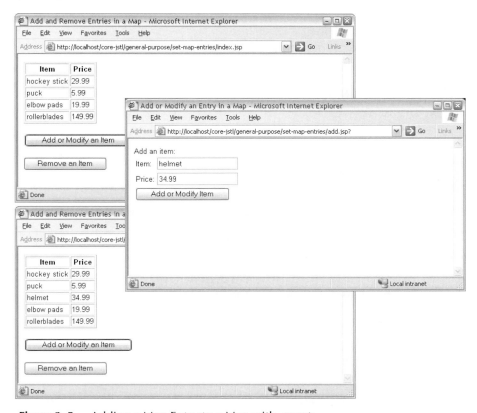

Figure 3–5   Adding a Map Entry to a Map with <c:set>

---

10. A map is an object that implements the `java.util.Map` interface, which maintains a collection of key/value pairs.

The top picture in Figure 3–5 shows a JSP page that displays key/value pairs stored in a hashtable, which is just one of many kinds of Java maps.[11] The JSP page has two buttons corresponding to JSP pages that allow you to add, modify, or remove entries from the map. The middle picture shows the JSP page that's loaded if you activate the Add or Modify an Item button in the JSP page shown in the top picture. The bottom picture shows the result of activating the Add or Modify Item button in the JSP page shown in the middle picture. As you can see, the item and price—in this case a helmet that costs $34.99—is added to the hashtable.

The JSP page shown in the top picture in Figure 3–5 is listed in Listing 3.9.

Listing 3.9	*index.jsp*

```
<!DOCTYPE HTML PUBLIC "-//W3C//DTD HTML 4.0 Transitional//EN">
<html>
   <head>
      <title>Add and Remove Entries in a Map</title>
   </head>

   <body>
      <%@ taglib uri='http://java.sun.com/jstl/core' prefix='c' %>

      <%-- Create a hash map and store it in session scope --%>
      <jsp:useBean id='map' class='java.util.HashMap'
                        scope='session'>
         <%-- Add initial key/value pairs stored in the hash
               map. The following <c:set> actions are only invoked
               when the hash map is created. --%>
         <c:set target='${map}' property='inline skates'
                           value='149.99'/>
         <c:set target='${map}' property='hockey stick'
                           value='29.99'/>
         <c:set target='${map}' property='elbow pads'
                           value='19.99'/>
         <c:set target='${map}' property='puck'
                           value='5.99'/>
      </jsp:useBean>

      <%-- Add an entry to the map, modify an existing entry,
            or remove an entry, all with the following <c:set>
            action, depending on the values of the key and
            value request parameters. Those request parameters
            are set by add.jsp and remove.jsp, which are invoked
```

---

11. Other types of Java maps include Attributes, HashMap, and TreeMap.

Listing 3.9   *index.jsp (cont.)*

```
            depending on which button is selected from this
            page. --%>
<c:set target='${map}'
       property='${param.key}' value='${param.value}'/>

    <table border='1'>
       <tr>
          <th>Item</th>
          <th>Price</th>
       </tr>

       <%-- Use <c:forEach> to create an HTML table that shows
            the map entries --%>
       <c:forEach var='entry' items='${map}'>
          <tr>
             <td><c:out value='${entry.key}'/></td>
             <td><c:out value='${entry.value}'/></td>
          </tr>
       </c:forEach>
    </table>

    <form action='add.jsp'>
       <input type='submit' value='Add or Modify an Item'/>
    </form>

    <form action='remove.jsp'>
       <input type='submit' value='Remove an Item'/>
    </form>
   </body>
</html>
```

The preceding JSP page uses <jsp:useBean> to create a hashtable and store it in session scope. The body of the <jsp:useBean> action contains <c:set> actions that add the initial key/value pairs to the hash map. Two things are noteworthy about those <c:set> actions. First, those actions are executed only when the hash map is created by <jsp:useBean> because they reside in the body of that <jsp:useBean> action. Second, you cannot replace those <c:set> actions with <jsp:setProperty> actions because <jsp:setProperty> can set existing properties only in a bean; <jsp:setProperty> cannot add key/value pairs to a hash map.

After the hash map has been created and the initial key/value pairs have been added, a <c:set> action accesses request parameters that it uses to add, modify, or remove an entry in the hashtable. Those request parameters are set by the JSP pages (add.jsp and remove.jsp) that are loaded when one of the submit buttons in the preceding JSP page is activated. The first time that JSP page is loaded, the key and value request parameters are not specified, so the <c:set> action does nothing.

Although the <c:forEach> action has not yet been discussed in this book, it is used in the preceding JSP page—in the interest of simplicity—to create the HTML table. You can read more about the <c:forEach> action in "The <c:forEach> Action" on page 154.

If you activate the Add or Modify an Item button in the preceding JSP page, add.jsp will be loaded in the browser. That JSP page is listed in Listing 3.10.

Listing 3.10 *add.jsp*

```
<!DOCTYPE HTML PUBLIC "-//W3C//DTD HTML 4.0 Transitional//EN">
<html>
    <head>
        <title>Add or Modify an Entry in a Map</title>
    </head>

    <body>
        <form action='index.jsp'>
            Add an item:<br>
            <table>
                <tr>
                    <td>Item:</td>
                    <td><input type='text' name='key'/></td>
                </tr><tr>
                    <td>Price:</td>
                    <td><input type='text' name='value'></td>
                </tr><tr>
                    <td colspan='2'>
                        <input type='submit' value='Add or Modify Item'/>
                    </td>
                </tr>
            </table>
        </form>
    </body>
</html>
```

The preceding JSP page contains a form whose action is the JSP page listed in Listing 3.9. The preceding JSP page contains textfields that set the key and value request parameters used by the <c:set> action in Listing 3.9 to modify the hashtable.

In addition to creating a new entry in the hashtable created by the JSP page listed in Listing 3.9, you can also use the Web application shown in Figure 3–5 to modify an existing entry in the hashtable, as illustrated in Figure 3–6.

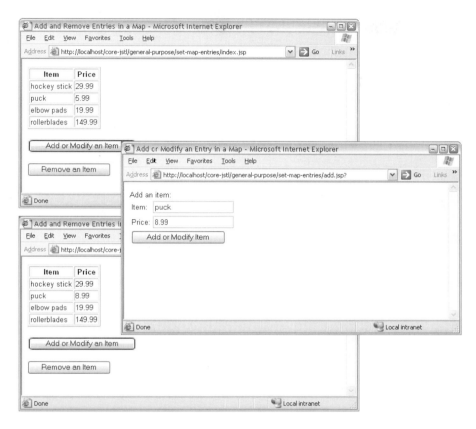

Figure 3–6   Modifying a Map Entry's Value with <c:set>

Figure 3–6 is nearly identical to Figure 3–5 on page 119, except Figure 3–6 shows how you can modify an existing entry in the hashtable by specifying an item name that already exists. In Figure 3–6, that item is puck, and its value is changed from 5.99 to 8.99.

Figure 3–7 shows how you can use <c:set> to remove an entry from a map. The top picture in Figure 3–7 shows the JSP page listed in Listing 3.9 on page 120 and the middle picture shows the JSP page—remove.jsp—that's loaded when you activate the Remove an Item button in the JSP page shown in the top picture. If you activate the Remove Item button in the JSP page shown in the middle picture, the JSP page shown in the top picture is reloaded and is passed the name of the selected item as the key request parameter and null for the value request parameter. As you can see from the bottom picture in Figure 3–7, the item selected in the JSP page shown in the middle picture is removed from the hashtable.

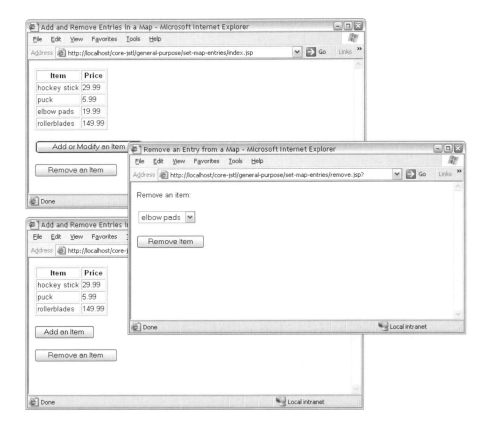

Figure 3–7   Removing a Map Entry from a Map with <c:set>

The JSP page shown in the middle picture in Figure 3–7 is listed in Listing 3.11.

The preceding JSP page, like the JSP page listed in Listing 3.9 on page 120, uses the <c:forEach> action in the interest of simplicity to create the HTML option elements for the select element. See "The <c:forEach> Action" on page 154 for more information about the <c:forEach> action.

The preceding JSP page stores the select element's name in the key request parameter and creates a hidden field whose name is value and whose value is null. When the Remove Item button is activated in the JSP page, the JSP page listed in Listing 3.9 on page 120 is loaded and passed the key and value request

---

Listing 3.11 *remove.jsp*

```
<!DOCTYPE HTML PUBLIC "-//W3C//DTD HTML 4.0 Transitional//EN">
<html>
    <head>
        <title>Remove an Entry from a Map</title>
    </head>

    <body>
        <%@ taglib uri='http://java.sun.com/jstl/core' prefix='c' %>

        <form action='index.jsp'>
            Remove an item:<p>
            <table>
                <tr>
                    <td>
                        <select name='key'>
                            <c:forEach var='entry' items='${map}'>
                                <option
                                    value='<c:out value="${entry.key}"/>'>
                                    <c:out value='${entry.key}'/>
                                </option>
                            </c:forEach>
                        <select>
                    </td>
                </tr>
            </table>

            <p><input type='submit' value='Remove Item'/>

            <text type='hidden' name='value'
                value='<c:out value="${null}"/>'/>
        </form>
    </body>
</html>
```

---

parameters. Those parameters are used by <c:set> to remove the selected item from the hashtable.

The <c:remove> Action

As we saw in "The <c:set> Action" on page 111, you can use <c:set> to create scoped variables. Sometimes it's necessary to remove those variables, as evidenced by the example discussed in "Using Conditional and General-Purpose Actions Together" on page 137. JSTL provides a <c:remove> action that removes a scoped variable. You use that action with this syntax:[12]

<c:remove var [scope]/>

You must specify the name of the scoped variable that you want to remove with the var attribute. Optionally, you can specify that variable's scope with the scope attribute. If you don't specify the scope attribute, <c:remove> will search the page, request, session, and application scopes—in that order—for a scoped variable with the name that you specified with the var attribute; <c:remove> removes the first variable that it finds with that name.

The <c:catch> Action

JSP pages usually handle page-specific exceptions with the JSP page directive by specifying the errorPage attribute like this:

```
<%@ page errorPage='relative URL' %>
```

If an exception is thrown in a JSP page that has a page directive like the one listed above, the JSP container forwards control to the error page specified by the relative URL. Error pages specify a JSP page directive of their own, like this:

```
<%@ page isErrorPage='true' %>
```

JSP error pages have access to an exception variable that references the exception thrown by the original JSP page.

The exception handling mechanism described above is sufficient for handling exceptions in many situations, but sometimes it's convenient to handle exceptions in the page where those exceptions are thrown. The <c:catch> action lets you do just that. Here's the syntax for the <c:catch> action:[13]

<c:catch [var]>
   body content, presumably with nested actions that can throw exceptions
</c:catch>

---

12. Items in brackets are optional. See "<c:remove>" on page 473 for a more complete description of <c:remove> syntax.
13. Items in brackets are optional. See "<c:catch>" on page 474 for a more complete description of <c:catch> syntax.

The <c:catch> action has one optional attribute—var—that specifies the name of a page-scoped variable. If an exception is thrown in the body of a <c:catch> action, <c:catch> stores the exception in that scoped variable. You can subsequently access that scoped variable only in the page on which the corresponding <c:catch> action resides. If you don't specify the var attribute, exceptions are caught but not saved.

JSTL goes to great lengths to avoid exceptions; for example, if you specify null for the <c:out> action's value, that action will not throw an exception; instead, it will not produce any output. In fact, none of the actions that we have discussed so far in this book throw an exception, so we must introduce an action that we have not yet discussed—<c:import>—that throws an exception to illustrate the <c:catch> action.

The <c:import> action, which is discussed in "The <c:import> Action" on page 201, lets you import a resource from your Web application, a foreign context, or an external URL, but if you specify a URL that does not exist, <c:import> will throw an exception. The following code fragment, which attempts to import a nonexistent resource with <c:import>, throws an exception.

```
<c:catch var='urlException'>
   <c:import url='http://aNonexistentURL.com'/>
</c:catch>

<c:if test='${not empty urlException}'>
   Sorry, couldn't find:
   <c:out value='${urlException.message}'/>
</c:if>
```

In the preceding code fragment, the <c:catch> action catches the exception thrown by <c:import> and stores it in a page-scoped variable named urlException. Subsequently, the code fragment uses that variable to print an error message.

Besides <c:import>, the preceding code fragment uses another action—<c:if>— that we have not yet formally discussed. That action, along with JSTL's other conditional actions, is discussed in the next section.

3.2 Conditional Actions

Conditional statements are essential for any programming language, but before JSTL, JSP did not provide an explicit means to express conditional statements. JSTL offers the following conditional actions:

- <c:if>
- <c:choose>

- <c:when>
- <c:otherwise>

JSTL supports two types of conditions: *simple* and *mutually exclusive*. Simple conditions perform an action if a test condition is true, whereas mutually exclusive conditions perform one of several actions depending upon the value of a test condition. Simple conditions are supported by the <c:if> action, and mutually exclusive conditions are supported by the <c:choose>, <c:when>, and <c:otherwise> actions; the <c:if> action is discussed below and the <c:choose>, <c:when>, and <c:otherwise> actions are discussed in "Mutually Exclusive Conditions" on page 132.

Simple Conditions

You can use the <c:if> action with the following syntax:[14]

```
<c:if test [var] [scope]>
    body content that's processed if the value of the test attribute is true
</c:out>
```

The test attribute, which is required, is a boolean expression that determines whether the body of the <c:if> action is evaluated. That attribute is an EL expression for the <c:if> action and a Java expression for the <c_rt:if> action. The optional var and scope attributes specify a scoped variable that stores the boolean result of the expression specified with the test attribute. The following code fragment uses <c:if> to test the existence of a non-null request parameter named name:

```
<c:if test='${not empty param.name}'>
   <c:out value='${param.name}'/>
</c:if>
```

If the name request parameter exists and is not null, the preceding code fragment displays its value. You can also use the var and scope attributes like this:

```
<c_rt:if var='zipTest' scope='request'
      test='<%= request.getHeader("accept-encoding").
                indexOf("gzip") != -1%>'>
   GZIP is supported
</c_rt:if>
```

The preceding code fragment uses the <c_rt:if> action to see if the current HTTP requests supports GZIP encoding; if so, the message GZIP is supported is

---

14. Items in brackets are optional. See "<c:if>" on page 475 for a more complete description of <c:if> syntax.

displayed. The <c_rt:if> action in the preceding code fragment also stores the result of the test condition in a request-scoped variable named zipTest. Later on, for the same request and presumably in a different JSP page, you can test to see whether the current request supports the GZIP encoding, like this:

```
<c:if test='${zipTest}'>
    GZIP is supported
</c:if>
```

The preceding code fragment uses <c:if> to test the value of the zipTest scoped variable; if that variable is true, the body of the <c:if> action is evaluated.

Most of the time, if you store the result of a test condition in a scoped variable, as is the case for the preceding code fragment, you don't need a body for the <c:if> or <c_rt:if> action that creates the scoped variable. JSTL supports that use case with the following syntax:

<c:if test var [scope]/>

In the preceding code fragment, if you don't need to display a message if the GZIP encoding is supported for a particular request but you want to store a boolean variable that you can test against later, you can do this:

```
<c_rt:if var='zipTest' scope='request'
        test='<%= request.getHeader("accept-encoding").
                 indexOf("gzip") != -1%>'/>
```

The <c:if> action and its corresponding <c_rt:if> action are easy to understand and use, as the preceding code fragments illustrate. One popular use for the <c:if> action is to retain values for HTML option elements, which is discussed in the next section.

Retaining Values for HTML Option Elements

In "Retaining Values for HTML Text Elements" on page 106, we saw how to retain values for HTML text elements with the <c:out> action. In this section we explore how to retain values for HTML option elements with the <c:if> action.

The JSP page shown in Figure 3–8 contains a form with two textfields and an HTML select element, which is populated with HTML option elements. The action for that form is unspecified, so when you activate the submit button, the JSP page is reloaded. As you can see from Figure 3–8, the textfields and the select element all retain their values when the JSP page is reloaded. The top picture in Figure 3–8 shows the JSP page when it's first loaded and a user has filled out the form, and the bottom picture shows the JSP page after the user has activated the submit button and the page has been reloaded.

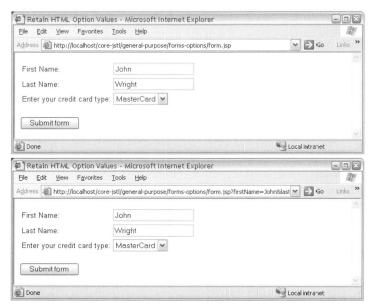

Figure 3–8   Retaining Values for HTML Option Elements with <c:if>

The JSP page shown in Figure 3–8 is listed in Listing 3.12.

Listing 3.12   *Retaining HTML Option Values*

```
<!DOCTYPE HTML PUBLIC "-//W3C//DTD HTML 4.0 Transitional//EN">
<html>
   <head>
      <title>Retain HTML Option Values</title>
   </head>

   <body>
      <%@ taglib uri='http://java.sun.com/jstl/core' prefix='c' %>

      <%-- Because the following form has no action, this JSP
           page will be reloaded when the form is submitted --%>
      <form>
         <table>
            <tr>
               <td>First Name:</td>
               <td><input type='text'
                     name='firstName'
                     value='<c:out value="${param.firstName}"/>'/>
```

Listing 3.12 *Retaining HTML Option Values (cont.)*

```
            </td>
        </tr>

        <tr>
            <td>Last Name:</td>
            <td><input type='text'
                    name='lastName'
                 value='<c:out value="${param.lastName}"/>'/>
            </td>
        </tr>

        <tr>
            <td>Enter your credit card type:</td>
            <td>
                <%-- Create the HTML select element for
                    credit card type --%>
                <select name='cardType'>
                    <%-- Create option elements and select the
                         previously selected credit card type --%>
                    <option value='Visa'
                        <c:if test='${param.cardType == "Visa"}'>
                            selected
                        </c:if>
                        >Visa</option>
                    <option value='MasterCard'
                  <c:if test='${param.cardType == "MasterCard"}'>
                            selected
                        </c:if>
                        >MasterCard</option>
                    <option value='Discover'
                    <c:if test='${param.cardType == "Discover"}'>
                            selected
                        </c:if>
                        >Discover</option>
                </select>
            </td>
        </tr>
    </table>
    <p><input type='submit' value='Submit form'/>
    </form>
</body>
</html>
```

The preceding JSP page retains values for its textfields with the <c:out> action and retains values for its option elements with the <c:if> action. Each option element is declared in three stages, like this:

```
<select name='cardType'>
...
   <option value='Visa'
     <c:if test='${param.cardType == "Visa"}'>
        selected
     </c:if>
   >Visa</option>
...
</select>
```

First, the start tag for the option element is specified without the closing angle bracket. Second, if the cardType request parameter is the same as the name of the current option, the string selected is added to the option start tag. Third, the start tag is completed with the closing angle bracket, the display value is specified, and the option end tag is added. For the preceding code fragment, if Visa was the last card type selected, the following will be generated:

```
<option value='Visa' selected>Visa</option>
```

If the last card type selected was not Visa, the following will be generated:

```
<option value='Visa'>Visa</option>
```

The <c:if> action is handy for simple conditions, but it will not suffice for mutually exclusive actions, such as if/else or switch constructs. The following section shows you how to specify those constructs.

Mutually Exclusive Conditions

Sometimes you need to execute code if one of several conditions is true. This section shows you how to do that with the <c:choose>, <c:when>, and <c:otherwise> actions.

When you specify a mutually exclusive condition with JSTL, the <c:choose> action is always the outermost action; the syntax for that action looks like this:[15]

```
<c:choose>
    body content that can only consist of one or more <c:when> actions followed
    by an optional <c:otherwise> action
</c:choose>
```

---

15. See "<c:choose>" on page 476 for a more complete description of <c:choose> syntax.

The body content of <c:choose> actions can only contain one or more <c:when> actions and, optionally, one <c:otherwise> action. The <c:otherwise> action, if specified, must be the last action in the body of the <c:choose> action. The <c:when> action has the following syntax:[16]

<c:when test>
   body content that's evaluated if this is the first <c:when> contained in a <c:choose> whose test evaluates to true
</c:choose>

The <c:when> action is similar to the <c:if> action—both actions have a `test` attribute that determines whether the action's body content is evaluated. Unlike the <c:if> action, <c:when> actions do not have `var` and `scope` attributes, so you cannot store the result of a <c:when> action's boolean test in a scoped variable.

The <c:otherwise> action's body content is evaluated only if none of the preceding <c:when> actions nested in the same <c:choose> action evaluated to true. Here is the syntax for the <c:otherwise> action:[17]

<c:otherwise>
   body content that's evaluated if none of the preceding <c:when> actions evaluated to true
</c:otherwise>

You can use the <c:choose>, <c:when>, and <c:otherwise> actions together to emulate if/else constructs or switch statements. The former is discussed in the next section and the latter is discussed in "Implementing Switch Statement Constructs" on page 136.

Implementing If/Else Constructs

An if/else statement is implemented with <c:choose>, <c:when>, and <c:otherwise> actions like this:

```
<c:choose>
   <%-- The <c:when> action represents the if clause --%>
   <c:when test='boolean expression'>
      <%-- Do something if the preceding test condition is true --%>
   </c:when>

   <%-- The <c:otherwise> action represents the else clause --%>
   <c:otherwise>
```

---

16. See "<c:when>" on page 477 for a more complete description of <c:when> syntax.
17. See "<c:otherwise>" on page 478 for a more complete description of <c:otherwise> syntax.

```
      <%-- Do something if the <c:when> condition is false --%>
   </c:otherwise>
</c:choose>
```

In the preceding code fragment, the <c:when> action represents the if clause and the <c:otherwise> action represents the else clause.

Let's see how to put that construct to use with a JSP page—shown in Figure 3–9—that simulates rolling dice.

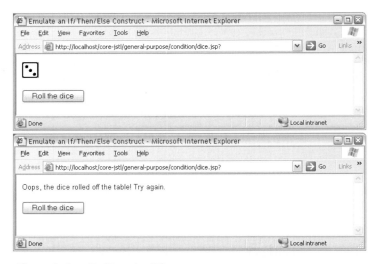

Figure 3–9   Rolling the Dice

When you activate the Roll the dice button in the JSP page shown in Figure 3–9, a random number is generated from 0 to 6, inclusive. If that number is greater than 0, the JSP page displays a die with the corresponding number. If that number is 0, the JSP page displays a message indicating that the roll was invalid. The top picture shown in Figure 3–9 shows a valid roll and the bottom picture depicts an invalid roll.

The JSP page shown in Figure 3–9 is listed in Listing 3.13.

The preceding JSP page uses the <c_rt:set> action to store a random number between 0 and 6 inclusive in a page-scoped variable named roll. Subsequently, an if/else construct is implemented with a single <c:when> action and a single <c:otherwise> action nested in a <c:choose> action. The <c:when> action tests the value stored in the roll scoped variable. If that variable contains a valid number for a dice roll, the body of the <c:when> action displays an image. The name of that image is constructed with the roll scoped variable with this EL expression: dice-${roll}.jpg. If the value stored in the roll scoped variable is 1, the image

Listing 3.13 *Emulating the If/Else Construct*

```
<!DOCTYPE HTML PUBLIC "-//W3C//DTD HTML 4.0 Transitional//EN">
<html>
    <head>
        <title>Emulate an If/Then/Else Construct</title>
    </head>

    <body>
        <%@ taglib uri='http://java.sun.com/jstl/core' prefix='c' %>
        <%@ taglib uri='http://java.sun.com/jstl/core_rt'
                prefix='c_rt' %>

        <%-- Roll the dice --%>
        <c_rt:set var='roll'>
            <%= (int)(Math.random() * 7) %>
        </c_rt:set>

        <%-- Emulate an if/then construct --%>
        <c:choose>
            <%-- If it was a good roll --%>
            <c:when test='${roll >= 1 && roll <= 6}'>
                <img src='<c:out value="dice-${roll}.jpg"/>'>
            </c:when>

            <%-- If it was a bad roll --%>
            <c:otherwise>
                Oops, the dice rolled off the table! Try again.
            </c:otherwise>
        </c:choose>

        <%-- Because the following form has no action, this JSP
                page will be reloaded when the form is submitted --%>
        <form>
            <input type='submit' value='Roll the dice'/>
        </form>

    </body>
</html>
```

dice-1.jpg will be displayed; if the value is 2, the image dice-2.jpg will be displayed, and so on. If the roll scoped variable does not contain a valid number for a dice roll, the <c:otherwise> action displays a message that indicates an invalid roll.

If you need to choose between more than two conditions, you can emulate a switch statement simply by adding more <c:when> actions in the body of a <c:choose> action, as illustrated in the next section.

Implementing Switch Statement Constructs

Listing 3.14 lists a variation of the JSP page shown in Figure 3–9 on page 134 that illustrates how you can emulate a switch statement with the <c:choose>, <c:when>, and <c:otherwise> actions.

Listing 3.14   *Implementing Switch Statement Constructs*

```
<!DOCTYPE HTML PUBLIC "-//W3C//DTD HTML 4.0 Transitional//EN">
<html>
   <head>
     <title>Emulate a Switch Statement</title>
   </head>

   <body>
     <%@ taglib uri='http://java.sun.com/jstl/core' prefix='c' %>
     <%@ taglib uri='http://java.sun.com/jstl/core_rt'
            prefix='c_rt' %>

     <%-- Roll the dice --%>
     <c_rt:set var='roll'>
        <%= (int)(Math.random() * 7) %>
     </c_rt:set>

     <%-- Emulate a switch statement --%>
     <c:choose>
        <%-- If the roll was equal to 1 --%>
        <c:when test='${roll == 1}'>
           <img src='<c:out value="dice-${roll}.jpg"/>'>
        </c:when>

        <%-- If the roll was equal to 2 --%>
        <c:when test='${roll == 2}'>
           <img src='<c:out value="dice-${roll}.jpg"/>'>
        </c:when>

        <%-- If the roll was equal to 3 --%>
        <c:when test='${roll == 3}'>
           <img src='<c:out value="dice-${roll}.jpg"/>'>
        </c:when>

        <%-- If the roll was equal to 4 --%>
        <c:when test='${roll == 4}'>
           <img src='<c:out value="dice-${roll}.jpg"/>'>
        </c:when>

        <%-- If the roll was equal to 5 --%>
```

Listing 3.14 *Implementing Switch Statement Constructs (cont.)*

```
            <c:when test='${roll == 5}'>
                <img src='<c:out value="dice-${roll}.jpg"/>'>
            </c:when>

            <%-- If the roll was equal to 6 --%>
            <c:when test='${roll == 6}'>
                <img src='<c:out value="dice-${roll}.jpg"/>'>
            </c:when>

            <%-- Here, <c:otherwise> is the equivalent of a default
                 in a switch statement --%>
            <c:otherwise>
                Oops, the dice rolled off the table! Try again.
            </c:otherwise>
        </c:choose>

        <%-- Because the following form has no action, this JSP
             page will be reloaded when the form is submitted --%>
        <form>
            <input type='submit' value='Roll the dice'/>
        </form>

    </body>
</html>
```

The preceding JSP page is functionally equivalent to the JSP page listed in Listing 3.13. The preceding JSP page tests each value that constitutes a valid dice role with individual <c:when> actions. In this case, we are testing for one condition out of seven, but you can easily generalize the JSP page to select one condition out of any number of conditions that you desire.

3.3 Using Conditional and General-Purpose Actions Together

This chapter has covered a lot of ground. We've discussed the JSTL general-purpose and conditional actions and shown how those actions can be useful for specific purposes such as retaining HTML element values and emulating if/else constructs and switch statements. Now let's see how to use those actions together to implement a simple Web application, shown in Figure 3–10, that lets you change background and foreground colors for all pages in the application.

Figure 3–10   Setting Color Preferences

The top picture in Figure 3–10 shows the Web application's welcome page, which provides a link to a color preferences JSP page that lets you modify your color preferences. The middle page in Figure 3–10 shows the color preferences page, which contains a simple form with two HTML `select` elements that let you select background and foreground colors. When you click the submit button in the color preferences page, you return to the previous page, which adjusts its colors to the background and foreground colors that you specified, as shown in the bottom picture in Figure 3–10.

The application shown in Figure 3–10 has a few special features. First, the button in the color preferences page displays the name of the previously displayed page, as you can see from the middle picture in Figure 3–10. Second, the application will not let you specify the same colors for the foreground and background because you won't be able to see anything if you do. If the same colors are specified for the foreground and background, the color preferences page is redisplayed with an error message, as shown in Figure 3–11. Third, the error message displayed in the color preferences page displays the name of the JSP page that was last displayed.

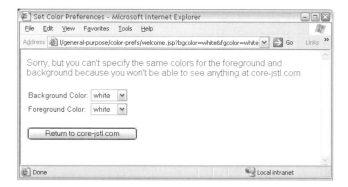

Figure 3–11   Handling a Bad Color Combination

The application shown in Figure 3–10 consists of two JSP pages: welcome.jsp and set-colors.jsp. The former is listed in Listing 3.15.

Listing 3.15   *welcome.jsp*

```
<!DOCTYPE HTML PUBLIC "-//W3C//DTD HTML 4.0 Transitional//EN">
<html>
   <head>
      <%-- The taglib declaration is in the <head> section because
           <c:out> is used by the <body> element below --%>
      <%@ taglib uri='http://java.sun.com/jstl/core' prefix='c'%>

      <title>Welcome to core-jstl.com</title>
   </head>

   <%-- Specify a background color for the body that matches the
        bgcolor request parameter --%>
   <body bgcolor='<c:out value="${param.bgcolor}"/>'>

      <%-- Store the name of this page in a session-scoped
           variable. That variable is used below to generate an
           error message and in set_colors.jsp to set the
           submit button's text --%>
      <c:set var='lastPage' scope='session'
value='core-jstl.com'/>
```

Listing 3.15   *welcome.jsp (cont.)*

```
<%-- If request parameters for foreground and background
       colors exist... --%>
<c:if test='${! empty param.fgcolor && ! empty
param.bgcolor}'>
       <%-- ...create a color preferences bean and store it in
              session scope so that those color preferences can
              be used by other JSP pages in the application --%>
       <jsp:useBean id='bean' scope='session'
              class='beans.ColorPreferences'/>

       <%-- Set the bean's background property to the
            background color specified with the bgcolor
            request parameter and... --%>
       <c:set target='${bean}' property='background'
              value='${param.bgcolor}'/>

       <%-- ...set the bean's foreground property to the
              foreground color specified with the fgcolor --%>
       <c:set target='${bean}' property='foreground'
              value='${param.fgcolor}'/>

       <%-- If the bean's foreground and background colors
            are the same... --%>
       <c:if test='${bean.background == bean.foreground}'>
          <%-- ...store an error message in session scope
               and...--%>
          <c:set var='colorErrorMessage' scope='session'>
             Sorry, but you can't specify the same colors for the
             foreground and background because you won't
             be able to see anything at
             <c:out value='${sessionScope.lastPage}'/>
          </c:set>

          <%-- ...go back to set_colors.jsp --%>
          <jsp:forward page='set_colors.jsp'/>
       </c:if>
</c:if>

<%-- Set font characteristics --%>
<font size='6' face='Arial,Helvetica'
    color='<c:out value="${bean.foreground}"/>'/>
   Welcome to core-jstl.com
</font>

<hr><p>
```

Listing 3.15	*welcome.jsp (cont.)*

```
    <%-- Reset font size --%>
    <font color='<c:out value="${bean.foreground}"/>'/>
        <i>Core JSTL</i> is an in-depth examination of the
        JavaServer Pages Standard Tag Library (JSTL), which
        provides a standard set of custom tags including:
        <ul>
            <li>General Purpose Actions
            <li>Conditional and Iteration Actions
            <li>URL Actions
            <li>Database Actions
            <li>Internationalization Actions
            <li>XML Actions
        </ul>

        <hr>
        Click <a href='set_colors.jsp'>here</a> to change your
        color preferences.
    </font>
  </body>
</html>
```

The first thing you should notice about the preceding JSP page (known hereafter as the welcome page) is that the `taglib` declaration for the JSTL core actions resides in the HTML `head` section, instead of the `body` section, as is the case for the other JSP pages discussed in this chapter. That's because the HTML <body> tag uses the <c:out> action to set the background color to the color specified with the `bgcolor` request parameter, so the `taglib` declaration must come before the <body> tag. The `bgcolor` parameter is set in the color preferences page, so if you access the welcome page directly, that request parameter will not exist and the <c:out> action will not produce any output. So the first time the welcome page is accessed, the background color will be the default color, as you can see from the top picture in Figure 3–10 on page 138.

After the welcome page sets its background color, it uses <c:set> to store the name of the welcome page in a session-scoped variable named `lastPage`. That scoped variable is used to set the text of the submit button in the color preferences page and is also used later on in the welcome page to generate an error message if the foreground and background colors are the same.

After setting the background color and storing the name of the welcome page in a scoped variable, the welcome page tests to see if the `fgcolor` and `bgcolor` request parameters exist; if so, the welcome page is being accessed from the color preferences page, so the welcome page creates a color preference bean and stores it in session scope.[18] Consequently, the welcome page stores the colors specified with the `fgcolor` and `bgcolor` request parameters in the bean's `foreground` and `background` properties, respectively, with the <c:set> action.

Subsequently, the welcome page checks to see if the bean's `foreground` and `background` properties are the same; if so, the welcome page creates a session-scoped variable that references an error message. Notice that the error message contains the name of the welcome page, which was previously stored in the `lastPage` scoped variable. Finally, if the foreground and background colors are the same, the welcome page forwards to the color preferences page; otherwise, the welcome page displays its content, which includes a link to the color preferences page.

The color preferences page—set_colors.jsp—is listed in Listing 3.16.

Listing 3.16   *set_colors.jsp*

```
<!DOCTYPE HTML PUBLIC "-//W3C//DTD HTML 4.0 Transitional//EN">
<html>
   <head>
      <title>Set Color Preferences</title>
   </head>

   <body>
      <%@ taglib uri='http://java.sun.com/jstl/core' prefix='c' %>

      <c:choose>
         <%-- If there's an error message about a bad color
               combination... --%>
        <c:when test='${not empty sessionScope.colorErrorMessage}'>
            <%-- ...set the font size and color,... --%>
            <font size='4' color='red'>
              <%-- ...display the error message and... --%>
             <c:out value='${sessionScope.colorErrorMessage}'/><p>
            </font>

            <%-- ...remove the error message from session scope.
                  Note: it's not necessary to specify the scope
                  attribute for <c:remove>, but it's good
                  practice. --%>
            <c:remove var='colorErrorMessage' scope='session'/>
        </c:when>
         <%-- If there's not an error message about a bad color
               combination, ask the user to set colors --%>
```

---

18. That bean is created only once per user (or per session) by the <jsp:useBean> action. That bean is an instance of `ColorPreferences`, which is listed in Listing 3.3 on page 108.

Listing 3.16   *set_colors.jsp (cont.)*

```
    <c:otherwise>
       Please set your background and foreground colors:
    </c:otherwise>
</c:choose>

<%-- Store the preferred colors stored in the color
     preferences bean in page-scoped variables, for better
     readability in the <c:if> actions used for the HTML
     options below --%>
<c:set var='prefBgColor'
     value='${sessionScope.bean.background}'/>

<c:set var='prefFgColor'
     value='${sessionScope.bean.foreground}'/>

<%-- The form --%>
<p><form action='welcome.jsp'>
    <table>
       <tr>
          <td>Background Color:</td>
          <td>
             <%-- Create the HTML select element for
                  background color --%>
             <select name='bgcolor'>
                <%-- Create option elements and select the
                     previously selected background color --%>
                <option value='white'
                   <c:if test='${prefBgColor == "white"}'>
                      selected
                   </c:if>
                   >white</option>
                <option value='yellow'
                   <c:if test='${prefBgColor == "yellow"}'>
                      selected
                   </c:if>
                   >yellow</option>
                <option value='black'
                   <c:if test='${prefBgColor == "black"}'>
                      selected
                   </c:if>
                   >black</option>
                <option value='blue'
                   <c:if test='${prefBgColor == "blue"}'>
                      selected
```

Listing 3.16 *set_colors.jsp (cont.)*

```
                    </c:if>
                    >blue</option>
                </select>
            </td>
        </tr>

        <tr>
            <td>Foreground Color:</td>
            <td>
                <%-- Create the HTML select element for
                     foreground color --%>
                <select name='fgcolor'>
                    <%-- Create option elements and select the
                         previously selected foreground color --%>
                    <option value='white'
                        <c:if test='${prefFgColor == "white"}'>
                            selected
                        </c:if>
                        >white</option>
                    <option value='yellow'
                        <c:if test='${prefFgColor == "yellow"}'>
                            selected
                        </c:if>
                        >yellow</option>
                    <option value='black'
                        <c:if test='${prefFgColor == "black"}'>
                            selected
                        </c:if>
                        >black</option>
                    <option value='blue'
                        <c:if test='${prefFgColor == "blue"}'>
                            selected
                        </c:if>
                        >blue</option>
                </select>
            </td>
        </tr>
    </table>

    <%-- Create the submit button text, using the name of the
         last page stored in session scope --%>
    <c:set var='submitButtonText'>
        Return to <c:out value='${sessionScope.lastPage}'/>
    </c:set>
```

Listing 3.16 *set_colors.jsp (cont.)*

```
          <%-- Create the submit button, using the value of the
               page-scoped variable created above as the
               button's text --%>
          <p><input type='submit'
                 value='<c:out value="${submitButtonText}"/>'/>
     </form>
   </body>
</html>
```

The color preferences page firsts checks to see if there's an error message in session scope named `colorErrorMessage`; if so, the color preferences page changes the font color to red and displays the message. After the message is displayed, the color preferences page removes it from session scope with the `<c:remove>` action.

After it deals with the error message, the color preferences page stores the color preference bean's background and foreground colors in page-scoped variables solely for better readability when those colors are accessed further down the page. Then the color preferences page creates its form, using the `<c:if>` action to retain the values displayed by its HTML `select` elements, as discussed in "Retaining Values for HTML Option Elements" on page 129. Finally, the color preferences page creates the submit button, which includes the name of the last page accessed, which is stored in the session-scoped variable named `lastPage`.

3.4 Conditional Custom Actions

The JSTL conditional actions should be sufficient for nearly all your conditional code needs, but just in case they're not, JSTL provides the infrastructure that you need to implement your own conditional actions. That infrastructure consists of one class—`ConditionalTagSupport`—that resides in the `javax.servlet.jsp.jstl.core` package. This section shows you how to use that class to implement conditional custom actions.

The JSP page listed in Listing 3.15 on page 139 used the `<c:if>` action to test whether a color preference bean's background and foreground colors were the same, like this:

```
<html>
   ...
   <body bgcolor='<c:out value="${param.bgcolor}"/>'>
```

```
   ...
      <%-- If the bean's foreground and background colors
         are the same... --%>
      <c:if test='${bean.background == bean.foreground}'>
         <%-- ...store an error message in
               session scope and...--%>
         <c:set var='colorErrorMessage' scope='session'>
            Sorry, but you can't specify the same colors for the
            foreground and background because you won't
            be able to see anything at
            <c:out value='${sessionScope.lastPage}'/>
         </c:set>

         <%-- ...go back to set_colors.jsp --%>
         <jsp:forward page='set_colors.jsp'/>
      </c:if>
   ...
   </body>
</html>
```

The preceding code fragment tests to see if the bean's background and foreground colors are the same, but what it's really testing for is an inadequate combination of background and foreground colors. It would be better to encapsulate that test in a custom action so that the definition of *inadequate combination of background and foreground colors* can change over time; for example, we might want to extend that definition to include background and foreground color combinations that are difficult to read, such as black on blue or yellow on orange.

The following code fragment shows a custom action that replaces the <c:if> action in the preceding code fragment.

```
<html>
   ...
   <body bgcolor='<c:out value="${param.bgcolor}"/>'>
      <%@ taglib uri='WEB-INF/core-jstl.tld' prefix='core-jstl'%>
      ...
      <%-- If the bean's foreground and background colors
         are the same... --%>
      <core-jstl:ifBadColorCombination target='bean'>
         <%-- ...store an error message in
               session scope and...--%>
         <c:set var='colorErrorMessage' scope='session'>
            Sorry, but you can't specify the same colors for the
            foreground and background because you won't
            be able to see anything at
            <c:out value='${sessionScope.lastPage}'/>
         </c:set>
```

```
        <%-- ...go back to set_colors.jsp --%>
        <jsp:forward page='set_colors.jsp'/>
    </core-jstl:ifBadColorCombination>
    ...
  </body>
</html>
```

The <core-jstl:ifBadColorCombination> action has one attribute, named
target, which specifies a color preference bean. The action compares the
background and foreground colors of the specified bean.

Implementing the <core-jstl:ifBadColorCombination> custom action used in the
preceding code fragment is a simple two-step procedure. First, we implement the
action's tag handler, which is listed in Listing 3.17.

Listing 3.17 *WEB-INF/classes/tags/IfBadColorCombinationAction.java*

```java
package tags;

import javax.servlet.jsp.JspTagException;
import javax.servlet.jsp.jstl.core.ConditionalTagSupport;
import beans.ColorPreferences;

public class IfBadColorCombinationAction
            extends ConditionalTagSupport {
   private String targetName;

   // Setter method for the target attribute, which is a string
   public void setTarget(String targetName) {
      this.targetName = targetName;
   }

   // Compare bean colors and return true if it's a bad
   // combination; otherwise, return false
   protected boolean condition() throws JspTagException {
      ColorPreferences bean = (ColorPreferences)
                         pageContext.findAttribute(targetName);

      return bean.getBackground().equals(bean.getForeground());
   }
}
```

Implementing the tag handler could not be much simpler. We simply extend
ConditionalTagSupport and implement the abstract condition
method. That method returns true if the condition—in this case, whether the
background and foreground colors are equal—is true and returns false otherwise.

The second step in implementing the custom action is creating a tag library descriptor, which describes the tag library and its lone action.

The preceding tag library descriptor declares the <core-jstl:ifBadColorCombination> action and its attributes. Notice that, in addition to the `target` attribute, the preceding tag library descriptor also declares `var` and `scope` attributes. Those attributes are declared because they are supported by the `ConditionalTagSupport` class, which means that the <core-jstl:ifBadColorCombination> action can also be used like this:

```
<html>
   ...
   <body bgcolor='<c:out value="${param.bgcolor}"/>'>
      <%@ taglib uri='WEB-INF/app-tlds/app.tld'
                 prefix='core-jstl'%>
      ...
         <core-jstl:ifBadColorCombination target='bean'
                                          var='badColorCombo'
                                          scope='page'/>
         <c:if test='${badColorCombo}'>
            <%-- ...store an error message in
                    session scope and...--%>
            <c:set var='colorErrorMessage' scope='session'>
               Sorry, but you can't specify the same colors for
               the foreground and background because you wont
               be able to see anything at
               <c:out value='${sessionScope.lastPage}'/>
            </c:set>

            <%-- ...go back to set_colors.jsp --%>
            <jsp:forward page='set_colors.jsp'/>
         </c:if>
      ...
   </body>
</html>
```

In the preceding code fragment, the <core-jstl:ifBadColorCombination> action stores the boolean value returned from the tag handler's `condition` method in a page-scoped variable specified with the `var` and `scope` attributes. That scoped variable is subsequently used with a <c:if> action. The preceding code fragment is functionally equivalent to the code fragment that precedes it.

You should realize that in order for your custom action to use the infrastructure provided by the `ConditionalTagSupport` class for the `var` and `scope` attributes, *you must declare those attributes in your tag library descriptor*. Because of that requirement, it's always a good idea to declare the `var` and `scope` attributes in your tag library descriptor unless you want to explicitly prevent their use, as shown in Listing 3.18.

Listing 3.18 *WEB-INF/core-jstl.tld*

```
<?xml version="1.0" encoding="ISO-8859-1"?>
<!DOCTYPE taglib
  PUBLIC "-//Sun Microsystems, Inc.//DTD JSP Tag Library 1.2//EN"
  "http://java.sun.com/dtd/web-jsptaglibrary_1_2.dtd">
<taglib>
  <tlib-version>1.0</tlib-version>
  <jsp-version>1.2</jsp-version>
  <short-name>Core JSTL Custom Actions</short-name>
  <display-name>
     Core JSTL Custom Actions for the Conditional Actions chapter
  </display-name>
  <description>
     A library containing a custom action that determines whether
     colors stored in a bean are incompatible
  </description>

  <tag>
    <name>ifBadColorCombination</name>
    <tag-class>tags.IfBadColorCombinationAction</tag-class>
    <body-content>JSP</body-content>
    <description>
      This action decides whether colors stored in a bean are
      incompatible. This action leverages JSTL functionality by
      extending the
      javax.servlet.jsp.jstl.core.ConditionalTagSupport class.
    </description>
    <attribute>
       <name>target</name>
       <required>true</required>
       <rtexprvalue>false</rtexprvalue>
    </attribute>
    <attribute>
       <name>var</name>
       <required>false</required>
       <rtexprvalue>false</rtexprvalue>
    </attribute>
    <attribute>
       <name>scope</name>
       <required>false</required>
       <rtexprvalue>false</rtexprvalue>
    </attribute>
  </tag>
</taglib>
```

ITERATION ACTIONS

Topics in This Chapter

- The <c:forEach> Action
- The <c:forTokens> Action
- Iteration Status
- Custom Iteration Actions

Chapter 4

In any programming language, the ability to iterate over a set of values is essential. Before JSTL, JSP did not provide an explicit means to accomplish that fundamental task, so developers had two choices: use a scriptlet or implement a custom action, neither of which is very attractive.

JSTL provides two actions that iterate over a set of values: <c:forEach> and <c:forTokens>. JSTL also exposes an interface and two classes that you can use to implement custom iteration actions: LoopTag, LoopTagSupport, and LoopTagStatus, respectively.[1] This chapter describes the <c:forEach> and <c:forTokens> actions and shows you how to implement custom actions using the LoopTag interface and the LoopTagSupport and LoopStatus classes.

To iterate over a set of values with a scriptlet, you must be proficient in the Java programming language and you must also understand how Java and HTML interact within JSP pages. For example, consider the following code fragment:

```
<% int[] values = (int[])request.getAttribute("primitiveValues");

   for(int i=0; i < values.length; ++i) { %>
      value = <%= values[i] %><br>
<% } %>
```

---

1. LoopTag, LoopTagSupport, and LoopTagStatus all reside in the javax.servlet.jsp.jstl.core directory.

The preceding scriptlet iterates over an array of `ints` stored in request scope. That scriptlet is short, but it requires you to be familiar with the following constructs:

- Casting: `(int[])request.getAttribute(...)`
- `for` loop syntax: `for(;;)`
- Array `length` property: `values.length`
- Accessing array values: `values[i]`
- JSP Expression Syntax: `<%= ... %>`
- Mixing Java and HTML: `<% int[]... { %> ... <% } %>`

Even for seasoned Java developers, it's not uncommon to forget the required cast in the preceding code fragment. If you are a page author and you're not familiar with the constructs listed above, or if you're a veteran Java developer and you want to avoid scriptlets, the JSTL iteration actions are for you. Consider the simplicity of the following code fragment, which is functionally identical to the preceding scriptlet:

```
<c:forEach items='${primitiveValues}' var='item'>
  value = <c:out value='${item}'/><br>
</c:forEach>
```

The preceding code fragment uses the <c:forEach> action to iterate over the same array that the scriptlet accesses. Although that code is not much shorter than its scriptlet counterpart, it's much simpler because none of the constructs listed above are required. In the preceding code fragment, two of the <c:forEach> action's attributes are specified: `items` and `var`; the former specifies the set of values that <c:forEach> iterates over, and the latter specifies the name of a scoped variable that references the current item of the iteration. The `var` scoped variable is only available within the body of the <c:forEach> action.

Not only does <c:forEach> simplify iteration, it also lets you iterate over many different types of data structures. Also, no matter what type of data you iterate over, the code that you write will be nearly identical to the preceding code fragment. The only difference is the value of the <c:forEach> `items` attribute.[2]

Figure 4–1 shows a JSP page that contains both of the preceding code fragments.

The JSP page shown in Figure 4–1 is listed in Listing 4.1.

Perhaps the most difficult aspect of iterating with JSTL actions is that you must remember to specify the `taglib` directive for the JSTL core actions. If you forget that declaration, the <c:forEach> and <c:forTokens> actions will do nothing.[3]

---

2. The exception is maps, which require you to access a map entry's key and value; see "Iterating Over Data Structures" on page 158 for more information about iterating over maps with <c:forEach>.

3. See "Common Mistakes" on page 95 for more information about missing `taglib` declarations.

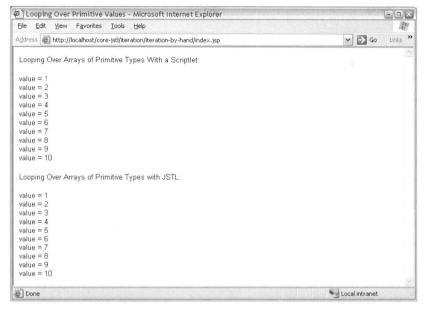

Figure 4–1   Looping Over Primitive Types with a Scriptlet vs. Looping with JSTL

Listing 4.1   *Looping with a Scriptlet vs. Using JSTL*

```
<!DOCTYPE HTML PUBLIC "-//W3C//DTD HTML 4.0 Transitional//EN">
<html>
   <head>
      <title>Looping Over Primitive Values</title>
   </head>

   <body>
      <%-- The taglib directive for the JSTL core actions --%>
      <%@ taglib uri='http://java.sun.com/jstl/core' prefix='c' %>

      <%-- Create an array of ints and store them in request
           scope --%>
      <% int[] primitiveValues = {1,2,3,4,5,6,7,8,9,10};
         pageContext.setAttribute("primitiveValues",
                                  primitiveValues,
                                  PageContext.REQUEST_SCOPE);
      %>
```

Listing 4.1	*Looping with a Scriptlet vs. Using JSTL (cont.)*

```
<%-- Loop over the array and print its values using
       a scriptlet --%>
Looping Over Arrays of Primitive Types With a Scriptlet:<p>

<%
   int[] values = (int[])request.getAttribute(
                             "primitiveValues");

   for(int i=0; i < values.length; ++i) { %>
      value = <%= values[i] %><br>
<%    }
%>

<p>

<%-- Loop over the array and print its values using
       JSTL's <c:forEach> action --%>
Looping Over Arrays of Primitive Types with JSTL:<p>

<c:forEach items='${primitiveValues}' var='item'>
   value = <c:out value='${item}'/><br>
</c:forEach>
</body>
</html>
```

4.1 The <c:forEach> Action

You can use the <c:forEach> action in two ways: to iterate over a range of integer values or to iterate over the items contained in a data structure. To accomplish those tasks, the <c:forEach> action offers the following attributes:

- `items`: The items that <c:forEach> iterates over; valid data structures for this attribute are listed in Table 4.1 on page 159. This attribute is not specified when you iterate over explicit integer values.

- `var`: The name of a scoped variable that references the iteration's current item. If you iterate over explicit integer values, that scoped variable contains the current integer value; if you iterate over a data structure, it contains the current object from that data structure.

- `varStatus`: The name of a scoped variable that references an object that has properties corresponding to the status of the iteration. That object's type is `LoopTagStatus`.

- `begin`: If you iterate over explicit integer values, this attribute specifies the starting value. If you iterate over a data structure, this attribute specifies the index of the first item that's accessed in that data structure. If you specify this attribute, its value must be greater than or equal to 0.

- `end`: If you iterate over explicit integer values, this attribute specifies the ending value. If you iterate over a data structure, this attribute specifies the index of the last item that's potentially accessed in that data structure. If you specify this attribute, its value must be greater than or equal to the value specified for the `begin` attribute.

- `step`: The amount that the loop index is incremented for every round of an iteration. If you specify this attribute, its value must be greater than or equal to 1.

All of the attributes listed above, with the exception of `var` and `varStatus`, can be specified with dynamic values, either runtime expressions for the RT library or EL expressions for the EL library.

The only attributes that you use within the body of <c:forEach> are `var` and `varStatus`, which define the names of scoped variables representing the current item in the iteration and a status object, respectively. That status object is discussed in "Iteration Status" on page 171.

Now that we have a basic understanding of the <c:forEach> action, let's take a look at how you use it to iterate over integer values.

Iterating Over Integer Values

If you don't specify the <c:forEach> action's `items` attribute, you can specify integer values for the `begin` and `end` attributes; for example, the following code fragment iterates over the values between 5 and 10, inclusive:

```
<c:forEach var='item' begin='5' end='10'>
   value = <c:out value='${item}'/><br>
</c:forEach>
```

The preceding code fragment produces the following output: 5 6 7 8 9 10. You can also specify the `step` attribute, which represents the increment for each round of the iteration; for example:

```
<c:forEach var='item' begin='5' end='10' step='2'>
   <c:out value='${item}'/>
</c:forEach>
```

The output of the preceding code fragment is: 5 7 9.

There are some restrictions on the begin, end, and step attributes:

• The begin, end, and step attributes must all be integer values.

• The value of the begin attribute must be greater than or equal to 0.

• The value of the end attribute must be greater than the value of the begin attribute. (Backward iteration is not allowed.)

• The value of the step attribute must be greater than 0.

Figure 4–2 shows a JSP page that lets you iterate over integer values by specifying the begin, end, and step attributes for the <c:forEach> action.

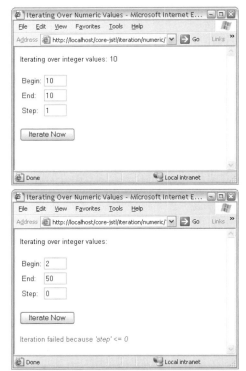

Figure 4–2   Iterating Over Integer Values with begin, end, and step Attributes

The top-left picture in Figure 4–2 iterates over the numbers 2 through 50, inclusive, with a step of 3. The top-right picture shows what happens if you specify the same value for the begin and end attributes—<c:forEach> will iterate exactly once in that case. The bottom pictures in Figure 4–2 illustrate illegal combinations of values for the begin, end, and step attributes. The bottom-left picture shows a `step` attribute value of 0, which is illegal because the iteration would never advance. The bottom-right picture shows a `begin` value that's greater than the `end` value, which is illegal because backward iterations are not allowed.

The JSP page shown in Figure 4–2 is listed in Listing 4.2.

Listing 4.2   *Iterating Over Explicit Integer Values*

```
<!DOCTYPE HTML PUBLIC "-//W3C//DTD HTML 4.0 Transitional//EN">
<html>
   <head>
      <title>Iterating Over Numeric Values</title>
   </head>

   <body>
      <%@ taglib uri='http://java.sun.com/jstl/core' prefix='c' %>

      <%-- Loop over numeric values with looping attributes
           specified with request parameters --%>
      <c:catch var='exception'>
         Iterating over integer values:
         <c:forEach var='item' begin='${param.begin}'
                               end='${param.end}'
                               step='${param.step}'>
             <c:out value='${item}'/>
         </c:forEach>
      </c:catch>

      <%-- Because this form does not have an action, this
           JSP page will be reloaded when the submit button
           is activated --%>
      <form>
         <table>
           <tr>
              <td>Begin:</td>
              <td><input type='text' size='3'
                     value='<c:out value="${param.begin}"/>'
                      name='begin'/>
              </td>
           </tr>

           <tr>
              <td>End:
              <td><input type='text' size='3'
                     value='<c:out value="${param.end}"/>'
                      name='end'/>
              </td>
           </tr>
```

Listing 4.2   *Iterating Over Explicit Integer Values (cont.)*

```
        <tr>
           <td>Step:
           <td><input type='text' size='3'
                     value='<c:out value="${param.step}"/>'
                     name='step'/>
           </td>
        </tr>
     </table>

     <p><input type='submit' value='Iterate Now'/>
  </form>

  <%-- Handle exceptions thrown by <c:forEach> --%>
  <c:if test='${not empty exception}'>
     <font color='red'>
        Iteration failed because<i>
        <c:out value='${exception.message}'/></i>
     </font>
  </c:if>
 </body>
</html>
```

If you specify an illegal combination of begin, end, and step attributes, the <c:forEach> action will throw an exception. In the preceding JSP page, those exceptions are caught by the <c:catch> action, which stores the exception in a scoped variable. At the end of the JSP page, the code handles those exceptions by displaying an error message.

One more thing: you can only specify integer values for the begin, end, and step attributes. If you specify a floating-point value for any of those attributes, the <c:forEach> action will throw an exception, as illustrated in Figure 4–3.

Iterating over integer values is the easiest way to use the <c:forEach> action. You can also iterate over data structures, which is not much more difficult, but requires you to know which data structures <c:forEach> will accept. Iterating over data structures with <c:forEach> is the topic of the next section.

Iterating Over Data Structures

The <c:forEach> action can iterate over a wide range of data structures, which are listed in Table 4.1.

As you can see from Table 4.1, <c:forEach> can iterate over collections, maps, comma-separated strings, and arrays of primitive types. All of those data structures are specified with the items attribute.

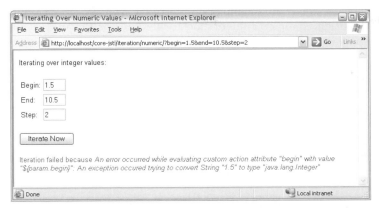

Figure 4–3   The <c:forEach> Action Iterates Over Integer Values

Table 4.1   Data Structures That <c:forEach> Can Iterate Over

Data Type	Description
java.util.Collection	Any type of collection, including List, LinkedList, Vector, ArrayList, Stack, and Set. The current item of the iteration is the object stored in the collection; that item can be any Java type.
java.util.Map	Any type of map, including Hashtable, HashMap, TreeMap, and WeakHashMap. The current item of the iteration is an instance of Map.Entry, which has key and value properties.
java.lang.Object[]	An array of Java objects. The current item of the iteration is an object in the array; that item can be any Java type.
java.lang.String	A comma-separated string; (i.e., "one,two,three"). You can iterate over strings that have delimiters other than commas with the <c:forTokens> action, which is discussed in "The <c:forTokens> Action" on page 166.
Arrays of primitive types	Arrays that contain primitive types: boolean, byte, char, short, int, long, float, and double. The current item in the iteration is a Java object that wraps the primitive type; for example, for an array of ints, the current item in the iteration will be an instance of java.lang.Integer.
java.util.Iterator, java.util.Enumeration	Any iterator or enumeration. The current item of the iteration can be any Java object. **Warning:** *iterators and enumerations cannot be reset, so you can only iterate over them once.*

You can also specify an iterator or an enumeration with the items attribute, and <c:forEach> will use that iterator or enumeration to iterate over the underlying collection. If you use an iterator or an enumeration, you should be aware that they *can only be used once because iterators and enumerations are not resettable.*

The beauty of the <c:forEach> action is that it doesn't matter what kind of data structure it iterates over—you always use <c:forEach> in the same manner. For example, consider the following code fragment, which iterates over an array of primitive types (ints) and an array of Java objects:

```
Iterating Over Arrays of Primitive Types:
<% int[] primitiveValues = {1,2,3,4,5,6,7,8,9,10};

    pageContext.setAttribute("primitiveValues",
                             primitiveValues);
%>

<c:forEach items='${primitiveValues}' var='item'>
    <c:out value='${item}'/>
</c:forEach>

Iterating Over Arrays of Objects:
<% Object[] objectValues = {
            new Integer(1), new Integer(2), new Integer(3),
            new Integer(4), new Integer(5), new Integer(6),
            new Integer(7), new Integer(8), new Integer(9),
            new Integer(10) };

    pageContext.setAttribute("objectValues",
                             objectValues ,
                             PageContext.REQUEST_SCOPE);
%>

<c:forEach items='${objectValues}' var='item'>
    <c:out value='${item}'/>
</c:forEach>
```

In the preceding code fragment, notice that it doesn't matter whether you iterate over primitive types or Java objects; in both cases, you just specify the items and var attributes and you access the current item in the iteration in the same manner. For both uses of <c:forEach> in the code fragment, the output will be 1 2 3 4 5 6 7 8 9 10. Also, notice that the array of ints is stored in page scope, but the array of Java objects is stored in request scope; that fact, however, is of no consequence to <c:forEach> because <c:forEach> only needs to know the name of the scoped variable and not its scope.

There is one exception to the uniform manner in which you access items in data structures with <c:forEach>—maps are handled a little differently, for example:

```
Iterating Over A Map:
<% java.util.Hashtable h = new java.util.Hashtable();
                       h.put("key1", "value1");
                       h.put("key2", "value2");
                       h.put("key3", "value3");
                       h.put("key4", "value4");

   pageContext.setAttribute("map", h);
%>

<c:forEach items='${map}' var='mapItem'>
   <%-- Remember that items in a Hashtable don't necessarily
        come out in the same order they went in. --%>
        (<c:out value='${mapItem.key}'/>
         <c:out value='${mapItem.value}'/>)
</c:forEach>
```

Maps get their name by virtue of the fact that they store keys that are *mapped* to values. One example of a map is a hashtable, like the one in the preceding code fragment. When you use <c:forEach> to iterate over a map, the current value of the iteration is an instance of Map.Entry, which has key and value properties. In the preceding code fragment those properties are used to access the keys and values stored in the hashtable. The output of the code fragment is this: Iterating Over A Map: (key4 value4) (key3 value3) (key2 value2) (key1 value1).

The JSP page shown in Figure 4–4 uses <c:forEach> to access request headers and their values.

Figure 4–4   Iterating Over Request Headers: A Map That Contains Arrays

The JSP page shown in Figure 4–4 is listed in Listing 4.3.

Listing 4.3 | *Iterating Over Data Structures*

```
<!DOCTYPE HTML PUBLIC "-//W3C//DTD HTML 4.0 Transitional//EN">
<html>
   <head>
      <title>Iterating Over Data Structures</title>
   </head>

   <body>
      <%@ taglib uri='http://java.sun.com/jstl/core' prefix='c' %>

      Looping Over Request Headers:<p>

      <%-- Loop over the JSTL headerValues implicit object,
           which is a map --%>
      <c:forEach items='${headerValues}' var='hv'>
         <ul>
            <%-- Display the key of the current item; that item
                 is a Map.Entry --%>
            <li><b><c:out value='${hv.key}'/></b><br>
            <ul>
               <%-- The value of the current item, which is
                    accessed with the value method from
                    Map.Entry, is an array of strings
                    representing request header values, so
                    we iterate over that array of strings --%>
               <c:forEach items='${hv.value}' var='value'>
                  <li><c:out value='${value}'/>
               </c:forEach>
            </ul>
         </ul>
      </c:forEach>
   </body>
</html>
```

The preceding JSP page uses the <c:forEach> action twice, with one action nested inside the other. The outer <c:forEach> action iterates over the JSTL headerValues implicit object, which is a map of request headers. Each item in that map is an instance of Map.Entry, which is the case for all maps. The key property of that entry references the request header name, and the value property references an array of strings representing the request header's values. The inner <c:forEach> action iterates over that array of strings.

Using the `begin`, `end`, and `step` Attributes for Data Structures

If you specify the `items` attribute for the <c:forEach> action—meaning you are iterating over a data structure—the `begin` and `end` attributes have different meanings than when you iterate over integer values. When you iterate over a data structure, the `begin` attribute specifies the starting index in the data structure and the `end` attribute specifies the ending index. The `step` attribute specifies the amount that the index is incremented for each round of the iteration.

The JSP page shown in Figure 4–5 iterates over a vector of strings and lets you specify the `begin`, `end`, and `step` attributes for the iteration. The strings in the vector represent numbers from 1 to 10.

The top picture in Figure 4–5 shows the JSP page when it iterates over all of the strings contained in the vector. The `begin` attribute is set to 0, which means that the first item in the iteration will be the first item in the data structure; in this case, that's the first string—`"ONE"`—in the vector. The `end` attribute is set to 1000, which is well beyond the last index in the vector. If you specify an `end` attribute greater than the last index in a data structure, <c:forEach> will stop iterating after the last item in that data structure.

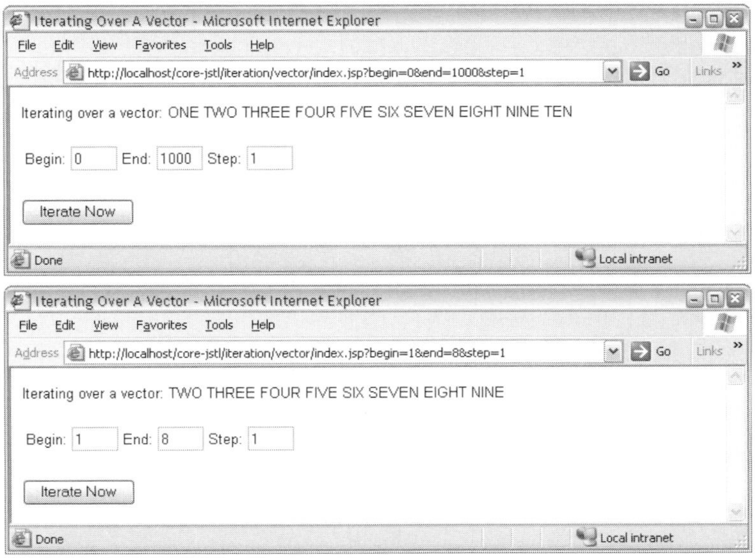

Figure 4–5   Iterating Over a Vector with `begin`, `end`, and `step` Attributes

The bottom picture in Figure 4–5 shows the JSP page when it iterates over a subset of the strings contained in the vector; the begin attribute is set to 1 and the end attribute is set to 8. Data structure indexes are zero-based, so in this case, the begin attribute specifies the second string in the vector, and the end attribute specifies the second-last string.

The JSP page shown in Figure 4–5 is listed in Listing 4.4.

Listing 4.4 *Iterating Over a Vector with begin, end, and step Attributes*

```
<!DOCTYPE HTML PUBLIC "-//W3C//DTD HTML 4.0 Transitional//EN">
<html>
   <head>
      <title>Iterating Over A Vector</title>
   </head>

   <body>
      <%@ taglib uri='http://java.sun.com/jstl/core' prefix='c' %>
      <%@ page import='java.util.Vector' %>

      <% // Create a vector of strings
         Vector v= new Vector();
         v.add("ONE");   v.add("TWO");   v.add("THREE");
         v.add("FOUR");  v.add("FIVE");  v.add("SIX");
         v.add("SEVEN"); v.add("EIGHT"); v.add("NINE");
         v.add("TEN");

         // Store the vector in page scope
         pageContext.setAttribute("vector", v);
      %>
      <%-- Loop over a vector with looping attributes specified
           with request parameters --%>
      <c:catch var='exception'>
         Iterating over a vector:
         <c:forEach items='${vector}'
                        var='item' begin='${param.begin}'
                                    end='${param.end}'
                                   step='${param.step}'>
            <c:out value='${item}'/>
         </c:forEach>
      </c:catch>
```

Listing 4.4	*Iterating Over a Vector with* begin, end, *and* step *Attributes (cont.)*

```
<%-- Because this form does not specify an action, this
     JSP page will be reloaded when the submit button
     is activated --%>
<form>
   <table>
      <tr>
         <td>Begin:</td>
         <td><input type='text' size='3'
                  value='<c:out value="${param.begin}"/>'
                  name='begin'/>
         </td>

         <td>End:</td>
         <td><input type='text' size='3'
                  value='<c:out value="${param.end}"/>'
                  name='end'/>
         </td>

         <td>Step:</td>
         <td><input type='text' size='3'
                  value='<c:out value="${param.step}"/>'
                  name='step'/>
         </td>
      </tr>
   </table>
   <p><input type='submit' value='Iterate Now'/>
</form>
<%-- Handle exceptions thrown by <c:forEach> --%>
<c:if test='${not empty exception}'>
   <font color='red'>
      Iteration failed because<i>
      <c:out value='${exception.message}'/></i>
   </font>
</c:if>
   </body>
</html>
```

Like the JSP page listed in Figure 4–2, the preceding JSP page contains a form that lets you specify the begin, end, and step attributes. Also, the preceding JSP page uses <c:forEach> to iterate over a vector of strings stored in page scope with the begin, end, and step attributes specified in the form.

4.2 The <c:forTokens> Action

You can use <c:forEach> to iterate over a comma-separated string, like this:

```
<c:forEach items='ONE, TWO, THREE, FOUR' var='item'>
   <c:out value='${item}'/>
</c:forEach>
```

The output of the preceding code fragment is ONE TWO THREE FOUR. But the <c:forEach> action can only iterate over strings delimited with commas. If you want to iterate over a string with delimiters other than commas, you can use the <c:forTokens> action, like this:

```
<c:forTokens items='ONE | TWO | THREE | FOUR'
            delims='|' var='item'>
   <c:out value='${item}'/>
</c:forTokens>
```

The preceding code fragment, which produces the same output as the previous code fragment, uses <c:forTokens> with a | character as a delimiter. There is no default delimiter for <c:forTokens>, so the delims attribute is mandatory. You can also specify more than one delimiter for <c:forTokens>, like this:

```
<c:forTokens items='(A B C)-(D E F)'
            delims='()' var='item'>
   <c:out value='${item}'/><br>
</c:forTokens>
```

How many times does the <c:forTokens> action in the preceding code fragment iterate? The answer is 3 because there are three tokens between the specified delimiters.[4] The output of the preceding code fragment is:

```
A B C
-
D E F
```

The first token consists of the characters A B C, which reside between the first pair of (and) delimiters. The second token is the – character, which resides between the) and (delimiters, and the third token is the string D E F, which resides between the second pair of (and) delimiters.

Like <c:forEach>, <c:forTokens> has var, varStatus, begin, end, and step attributes. Unlike <c:forEach> whose begin and end attributes have different

---

4. Tokens are strings between delimiters.

meanings depending on whether <c:forEach> iterates over integer values or a data structure, <c:forTokens> has `begin` and `end` attributes that always represent indexes into the tokens that it iterates over. For example, the following code fragment uses the <c:forTokens> `begin`, `end`, and `step` attributes:

```
<c:forTokens items='(A B C)-(D E F)-(G H I)-(J K L)-(M N O)-(P Q R)'
          delims='()' var='item'
            begin='2' end='8' step='2'>
  <c:out value='${item}'/><br>
</c:forTokens>
```

The string that <c:forTokens> iterates over in the preceding code fragment contains 11 tokens, but that action only executes four rounds of iterations which begin with the third token and end with the ninth token because the `begin` and `end` attributes are specified as 2 and 8, respectively. The output of the code fragment is:

```
D E F
G H I
J K L
M N O
```

Using <c:forTokens> with multiple delimiters is most useful when you have nested data. For example, consider the JSP page shown in Figure 4–6, which creates an HTML table from a single string in which table headings and table data are delimited with brackets and data for each column is delimited with commas.

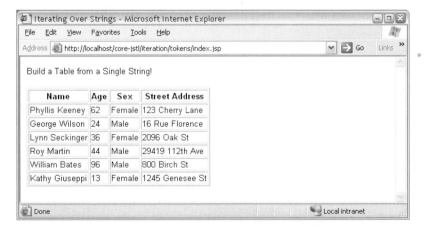

Figure 4–6   Using <c:forTokens> to Create an HTML Table from a Single String

The JSP page shown in Figure 4–6 is listed in Listing 4.5.

Listing 4.5 *Iterating Over Strings with <c:forEach> and <c:forTokens>*

```
<!DOCTYPE HTML PUBLIC "-//W3C//DTD HTML 4.0 Transitional//EN">
<html>
   <head>
      <title>Iterating Over Strings</title>
   </head>

   <body>
      <%@ taglib uri='http://java.sun.com/jstl/core' prefix='c' %>

      Build a Table from a Single String!
      <%
         // This string, which could ultimately come from a data
         // source such as a flat file, could be stored in
         // request scope (or any other scope) by a business
         // component. The page author just needs to know the
         // name of the corresponding scoped variable and
         // the delimiters.

         // The first token delimited with the characters []
         // represents table column names. The rest of the tokens
         // represent table data.

         String s = "[Name, Age, Sex, Street Address]" +
             "[Phyllis Keeney, 62, Female,123 Cherry Lane]" +
             "[George Wilson, 24, Male, 16 Rue Florence]" +
             "[Lynn Seckinger, 36, Female, 2096 Oak St]" +
             "[Roy Martin, 44, Male, 29419 112th Ave]" +
             "[William Bates, 96, Male, 800 Birch St]" +
             "[Kathy Giuseppi, 13, Female, 1245 Genesee St]";

         // Store the string in request scope
         pageContext.setAttribute("dataForSimpleTable", s,
                            PageContext.REQUEST_SCOPE);
      %>

      <%-- Create the HTML table with <c:forTokens> and
           <c:forEach> --%>

      <p><table border='1'>
         <c:forTokens var='tableData' varStatus='status'
                 items='${dataForSimpleTable}'
                 delims='[]'>
```

Listing 4.5	*Iterating Over Strings with <c:forEach> and <c:forTokens> (cont.)*

```
<c:choose>
    <%-- If it's the first token, create the
        table headers --%>
    <c:when test='${status.first}'>
        <tr>
            <%-- Instead of <c:forEach> we could've used
                <c:forTokens> with commas for delimiters,
                as we do below --%>
            <c:forEach var='tableHeader'
                    items='${tableData}'>
                <th><c:out value='${tableHeader}'/></th>
            </c:forEach>
        </tr>
    </c:when>

    <%-- If it's not the first token, create the
        table rows --%>
    <c:otherwise>
        <tr>
            <%-- Instead of <c:forTokens> with commas for
                delimiters, we could've used
                <c:forEach>, as we did above --%>
            <c:forTokens var='rowData'
                    items='${tableData}'
                    delims=','>
                <td><c:out value='${rowData}'/>
            </c:forTokens>
        </tr>
    </c:otherwise>
</c:choose>
        </c:forTokens>
    </table>
</body>
</html>
```

The preceding JSP page creates one long string in a scriptlet and stores that string in request scope. Subsequently, the JSP page iterates over that string with three iterations, like this:

```
<p><table border='1'>
    <c:forTokens var='tableData' varStatus='status'
            items='${dataForSimpleTable}'
```

```
                    delims='[]'>

        <c:choose>
            <%-- If it's the first token, create the
                table headers --%>
            <c:when test='${status.first}'>
                <tr>
                    <%-- Instead of <c:forEach> we could've used
                        <c:forTokens> with commas for delimiters,
                        as we do below --%>
                    <c:forEach var='tableHeader'
                            items='${tableData}'>
                        <th><c:out value='${tableHeader}'/></th>
                    </c:forEach>
                </tr>
            </c:when>

            <%-- If it's not the first token, create the
                table rows --%>
            <c:otherwise>
                <tr>
                    <%-- Instead of <c:forTokens> with commas for
                        delimiters, we could've used
                        <c:forEach>, as we did above --%>
                    <c:forTokens var='rowData'
                            items='${tableData}'
                            delims=','>
                        <td><c:out value='${rowData}'/>
                    </c:forTokens>
                </tr>
            </c:otherwise>
        </c:choose>
    </c:forTokens>
  </table>
 </body>
</html>
```

In the preceding JSP page, the outermost <c:forTokens> action iterates over tokens between brackets; since there are seven sets of brackets, that action will iterate seven times. Also, notice that the outermost <c:forTokens> action specifies the string status for the varStatus attribute, so a scoped variable named status—accessible in the body of the <c:forTokens> action—provides access to the status of the iteration. If it's the first iteration, a nested <c:forEach> action iterates over the comma-separated string that represents table headers. If it's not the first iteration, a nested <c:forTokens> action iterates over the comma-separated strings that represent the table's data. The JSP page uses both a <c:forEach> action and a <c:forTokens> action to reiterate that both of those actions can iterate over comma-separated strings.

The preceding JSP page specifies the varStatus attribute of the <c:forTokens> action and uses the resulting scoped variable to detect the first iteration. That scoped variable is an object whose type is LoopTagStatus, which is discussed in the next section.

4.3 Iteration Status

You can specify a varStatus attribute for both the <c:forEach> and <c:forTokens> actions. The value of that attribute represents the name of a scoped variable that you can use to obtain information about the status of the iteration performed by those two actions; Table 4.2 lists the properties that you can access with that status object.

Table 4.2 LoopTagStatus Properties

Property	Type	Description
current	Object	The current item in the iteration.
index	int	If you are iterating over integer values, this property has the same value as the current item. If you are iterating over a data structure, this property represents the 0-based index of the current item; it tells you the index of the current item with respect to the underlying collection.
count	int	A 1-based count of the current round of the iteration.
first[a]	boolean	This property tells whether the current round of the iteration is the first round—it's only true when count is equal to 1.
last[b]	boolean	This property tells whether the current round of the iteration is the last round—it's only true when count is equal to n, where n represents the total number of iteration rounds.
begin	Integer	The value specified for the begin attribute.
end	Integer	The value specified for the end attribute.
step	Integer	The value specified for the step attribute.

a. The corresponding accessor method for the first property is isFirst, not get-First.
b. The corresponding accessor method for the last property is isLast, not getLast.

The next two sections describe how to use status objects when you iterate over integer values with <c:forEach> and when you iterate over data structures with <c:forEach> or strings with <c:forTokens>.

Iteration Status for Integer Iterations

Figure 4–7 shows a JSP page that uses <c:forEach> to iterate over integer values. That JSP page lets you specify the begin, end, and step attributes for the <c:forEach> action and also displays information about the status of each round of the iteration.

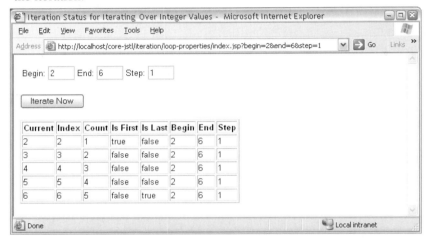

Figure 4–7   Iteration Status for Iterating Over Integer Values

The JSP page shown in Figure 4–7 is listed in Listing 4.6.

The preceding JSP page uses the <c:forEach> varStatus attribute to specify a scoped variable that is available only within the body of that action. That scoped variable is a status object that has the properties listed in Table 4.2 on page 171. The JSP page uses that scoped variable to print all of the status properties for each round of the iteration that <c:forEach> performs.

The picture shown in Figure 4–7 shows the result of specifying a begin attribute of 2, an end attribute of 6, and a step attribute of 1. Notice that the index of the iteration is equal to the value of the current item, which is always the case when you iterate over integer values. The count property specifies the current round of the iteration and always starts with a value of 1 and increments by 1 for each round of the iteration. The isFirst property is true for the first round of the iteration, which coincides with a value of 1 for the count property. The isLast property is only true for the last round of the iteration, and the begin, end, and step properties

---

| **Listing 4.6** | *Iteration Status for Iterating Over Integer Values* |

```
<!DOCTYPE HTML PUBLIC "-//W3C//DTD HTML 4.0 Transitional//EN">
<html>
    <head>
        <title>
            Iteration Status for Iterating Over Integer Values
        </title>
    </head>

    <body>
        <%@ taglib uri='http://java.sun.com/jstl/core' prefix='c' %>

        <%-- Because this form does not specify an action, this
             JSP page will be reloaded when the submit button
             is activated --%>
        <form>
            <table>
                <tr>
                    <td>Begin:</td>
                    <td><input type='text' size='3'
                                value='<c:out value="${param.begin}"/>'
                                name='begin'/></td>
                    <td>End:</td>
                    <td><input type='text' size='3'
                                value='<c:out value="${param.end}"/>'
                                name='end'/></td>
                    <td>Step:</td>
                    <td><input type='text' size='3'
                                value='<c:out value="${param.step}"/>'
                                name='step'/></td>
                </tr>
            </table>

            <p><input type='submit' value='Iterate Now'/>
        </form>

        <c:if test='${not empty param.begin and
                      not empty param.end and
                      not empty param.step}'>
            <table border='1'>
                <tr>
                    <%-- Create table headers --%>
                    <c:forEach var='item' items='Current,Index,Count,
                                                  Is First,Is Last,
                                                  Begin,End,Step'>
                        <th><c:out value='${item}'/></th>
```

| Listing 4.6 | *Iteration Status for Iterating Over Integer Values (cont.)* |

```
            </c:forEach>
        </tr>

        <%-- Loop over numeric values specified with
             request parameters --%>
        <c:catch var='exception'>
            <c:forEach varStatus='status'
                            begin='${param.begin}'
                              end='${param.end}'
                             step='${param.step}'>
                <tr>
                    <%-- Create table data --%>
                    <td><c:out value='${status.current}'/></td>
                    <td><c:out value='${status.index}'/></td>
                    <td><c:out value='${status.count}'/></td>
                    <td><c:out value='${status.first}'/></td>
                    <td><c:out value='${status.last}'/></td>
                    <td><c:out value='${status.begin}'/></td>
                    <td><c:out value='${status.end}'/></td>
                    <td><c:out value='${status.step}'/></td>
                </tr>
            </c:forEach>
        </c:catch>
    </table>
</c:if>
<%-- Handle exceptions thrown by <c:forEach> --%>
<c:if test='${not empty exception}'>
    <font color='red'>
        Iteration failed because<i>
        <c:out value='${exception.message}'/></i>
    </font>
</c:if>
    </body>
</html>
```

coincide with the values specified for the begin, end, and step attributes of the <c:forEach> (or <c:forTokens>) action, respectively.

Besides using status objects for integer iterations, you can also use them when you iterate over data structures, as illustrated in the next section.

Iteration Status for Data Structure Iterations

Using status objects for data structure iterations is the same as using them for integer iterations, but the index property or data structure iterations are different from the index property for integer iterations.

Figure 4–8 shows a JSP page that iterates over an array of strings representing numbers from 1 to 10. That JSP page lets you specify the begin, end, and step attributes for the iteration.

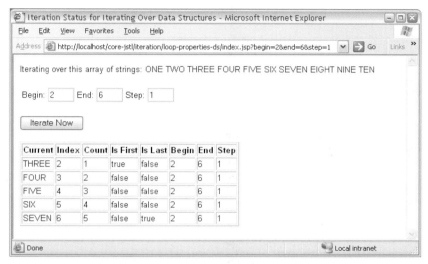

Figure 4–8   Iteration Status for Iterating Over Data Structures

The JSP page shown in Figure 4–8 is listed in Listing 4.7.

The preceding JSP page is similar to the JSP page shown in Figure 4–7 on page 172 and listed in Listing 4.6 on page 173. Both of those JSP pages use <c:forEach> to perform an iteration, and they both let you specify values for the <c:forEach> begin, end, and step attributes. Finally, both JSP pages use a status object, whose name is specified with the <c:forEach> varStatus attribute, to print all of the status properties.

In both cases, the results are similar: the count property represents the current round of the iteration and starts with 1. The isFirst and isLast properties are boolean properties that reveal whether the current round of the iteration is the first or last, respectively. Finally, the begin, end, and step properties are fixed values that coincide with the begin, end, and step attributes specified for the <c:forEach> action.

The index status property is the only property that differs depending on whether you iterate over integer values or a data structure. As Figure 4–7 on page 172 illustrates, when you iterate over integer values, the index property coincides with the current property, but when you iterate over a data structure, the index property represents the index of the current item with respect to the underlying data structure. In the preceding JSP page, the starting index is specified with the <c:forEach> begin attribute as 2, and therefore the first item in the iteration is the

| Listing 4.7 | *Iterating Over an Array* |

```
<!DOCTYPE HTML PUBLIC "-//W3C//DTD HTML 4.0 Transitional//EN">
<html>
   <head>
      <title>
         Iteration Status for Iterating Over Numeric Values
      </title>
   </head>

   <body>
      <%@ taglib uri='http://java.sun.com/jstl/core' prefix='c' %>

      <% // Create an array of strings
         String[] values = { "ONE", "TWO", "THREE", "FOUR",
                             "FIVE","SIX", "SEVEN", "EIGHT",
                             "NINE","TEN" };

         // Store the array in page scope
         pageContext.setAttribute("values", values);
      %>
      <%-- Show the array of strings --%>
      Iterating over this array of strings:
      <c:forEach var='item' items='${values}'>
         <c:out value='${item}'/>
      </c:forEach>

      <%-- Because this form does not specify an action, this
           JSP page will be reloaded when the submit button
           is activated --%>
      <form>
         <table>
            <tr>
               <td>Begin:</td>
               <td><input type='text' size='3'
                       value='<c:out value="${param.begin}"/>'
                       name='begin'/></td>
               <td>End:</td>
               <td><input type='text' size='3'
                       value='<c:out value="${param.end}"/>'
                       name='end'/></td>
               <td>Step:</td>
               <td><input type='text' size='3'
                       value='<c:out value="${param.step}"/>'
                       name='step'/></td>
            </tr>
         </table>

         <p><input type='submit' value='Iterate Now'/>
```

Listing 4.7   *Iterating Over an Array (cont.)*

```
    </form>

    <c:if test='${not empty param.begin and
                not empty param.end and
                not empty param.step}'>
        <table border='1'>
            <tr>
                <%-- Create table headers --%>
                <c:forEach var='item' items='Current,Index,Count,
                                    Is First,Is Last,Begin,
                                        End,Step'>
                    <th><c:out value='${item}'/></th>
                </c:forEach>
            </tr>

            <%-- Loop over an array of strings with looping
                attributes specified with request parameters --%>
            <c:catch var='exception'>
                <c:forEach items='${values}'
                        varStatus='status'
                            begin='${param.begin}'
                              end='${param.end}'
                             step='${param.step}'>
                    <tr>
                        <%-- Create table data --%>
                        <td><c:out value='${status.current}'/></td>
                        <td><c:out value='${status.index}'/></td>
                        <td><c:out value='${status.count}'/></td>
                        <td><c:out value='${status.first}'/></td>
                        <td><c:out value='${status.last}'/></td>
                        <td><c:out value='${status.begin}'/></td>
                        <td><c:out value='${status.end}'/></td>
                        <td><c:out value='${status.step}'/></td>
                    </tr>
                </c:forEach>
            </c:catch>
        </table>
    </c:if>
    <%-- Handle exceptions thrown by <c:forEach> --%>
    <c:if test='${not empty exception}'>
        <font color='red'>
            Iteration failed because<i>
            <c:out value='${exception.message}'/></i>
        </font>
    </c:if>
  </body>
</html>
```

third string in the array—remember that indexes for a collection are 0-based, so the first item in a collection has the index 0, the second item has the index 1, the third item has the index 2, and so on. Like the `index` status property for integer iterations, the `index` property for data structure iterations increases by the value that you specify for the <c:forEach> `step` attribute (which defaults to 1), as you can see from both Figure 4–8 on page 175 and Figure 4–7 on page 172.

4.4 Custom Iteration Actions

The <c:forEach> and <c:forTokens> actions should be sufficient for most of your iteration needs, but you may find that you need a custom action that provides more functionality than those actions or a custom action that simplifies their use. JSTL provides support for two types of custom iteration actions:

- Collaboration custom actions
- Iteration custom actions

Each of those types of custom actions is discussed in the following sections.

Collaboration Custom Actions

Collaboration custom actions work in concert with existing iteration actions. Typically, collaboration custom actions provide functionality related to the status of an iteration; for example, a custom action that implements some functionality for the first round of an iteration.

The <c:forEach> and <c:forTokens> actions are implemented with tag handlers that implement the `LoopTag` interface; the methods defined by that interface are listed in Table 4.3.

Table 4.3   `LoopTag` Methods

Method	Description
`Object getCurrent()`	Returns the current item in the iteration. If you call this method, the iteration will not advance (unlike, for example, Java iterators, whose `next` method returns the current item and advances the iteration).
`LoopTagStatus getLoopStatus()`	Returns an instance of `LoopTagStatus`, which has the properties defined in Table 4.2 on page 171.

Collaboration custom actions obtain a reference to the tag handler for their enclosing <c:forEach> or <c:forTokens> action and access the current object in the iteration or the iteration's status by invoking that tag handler's `LoopTag` methods listed in Table 4.3.

In "The <c:forTokens> Action" on page 166 we discussed how you can use <c:forTokens> to create an HTML table from a single string delimited with brackets and commas. That example, which is listed in its entirety in Listing 4.5 on page 168, looked something like this:

```
<table border='1'>
   <c:forTokens var='tableData' varStatus='status'
              items='${dataForSimpleTable}'
              delims='[]'>
      <c:choose>
         <c:when test='${status.first}'>
            . . .
         </c:when>

         <c:otherwise>
            . . .
         </c:otherwise>
      </c:choose>
   </c:forTokens>
</table>
```

In Listing 4.5, represented by the preceding code fragment, we created the table headers during the first round of the iteration and created the rest of the table's data during the subsequent rounds of the iteration. That required us to differentiate between the first round of the iteration and the subsequent rounds, as illustrated by the preceding code fragment. That differentiation required us to use the <c:forTokens> `varStatus` attribute to access a status object and to use that status object with the <c:choose>, <c:when>, and <c:otherwise> actions. If we implement two custom actions, one that detects the first round of an iteration and another that detects all other rounds, we can significantly reduce that complexity, like this:

```
<table border='1'>
   <c:forTokens var='tableData'
              items='${dataForSimpleTable}'
              delims='[]'>

      <core-jstl:firstRound>
         . . .
      </core-jstl:firstRound>

      <core-jstl:notFirstRound>
         . . .
      </core-jstl:notFirstRound>
```

```
     </c:forTokens>
</table>
```

Listing 4.8 lists a revision of Listing 4.5 on page 168 that uses the custom actions described above.

Listing 4.8	*Using a Collaborative Custom Action*

```
<!DOCTYPE HTML PUBLIC "-//W3C//DTD HTML 4.0 Transitional//EN">
<html>
   <head>
      <title>Testing Iteration Custom Actions</title>
   </head>

   <body>
      <%@ taglib uri='http://java.sun.com/jstl/core' prefix='c'  %>
      <%@ taglib uri='WEB-INF/core-jstl.tld' prefix='core-jstl'%>

      <% // This string, which could ultimately come from a data
         // source such as a flat file, could be stored in
         // request scope (or any other scope) by a business
         // component. The page author just needs to know the
         // name of the corresponding scoped variable and
         // the delimiters.

         // The first token delimited with the characters []
         // represents table column names. The rest of the tokens
         // represent table data.

         String s = "[Name, Age, Sex, Street Address]"          +
                    "[Phyllis Keeney, 62, Female,123 Cherry Lane]" +
                    "[George Wilson, 24, Male, 16 Rue Florence]"   +
                    "[Lynn Seckinger, 36, Female, 2096 Oak St]"    +
                    "[Roy Martin, 44, Male, 29419 112th Ave]"      +
                    "[William Bates, 96, Male, 800 Birch St]"      +
                    "[Kathy Giuseppi, 13, Female, 1245 Genesee St]";

         // Store the string in page scope
         pageContext.setAttribute("dataForSimpleTable", s);
      %>

      <p><table border='1'>
         <%-- For each token in the string delimited with [] --%>
         <c:forTokens var='tableData' delims='[]'
                  items='${dataForSimpleTable}'>

            <%-- This custom action includes its body content if
                 it's the first round of the iteration --%>
```

| Listing 4.8 | *Using a Collaborative Custom Action (cont.)* |

```
      <core-jstl:firstRound>
         <tr>
            <c:forEach var='tableHeader'
                     items='${tableData}'>
               <th><c:out value='${tableHeader}'/></th>
            </c:forEach>
         </tr>
      </core-jstl:firstRound>

      <%-- This custom action includes its body content if
           it's NOT the first round of the iteration --%>
      <core-jstl:notFirstRound>
         <tr>
            <c:forEach var='rowData' items='${tableData}'>
               <td><c:out value='${rowData}'/></td>
            </c:forEach>
         </tr>
      </core-jstl:notFirstRound>
      </c:forTokens>
    </table>
  </body>
</html>
```

The tag handler for the <core-jstl:firstRound> custom action is listed in Listing 4.9.

The tag handler shown in Listing 4.9 uses the `findAncestorWithClass` method from `javax.servlet.jsp.tagext.TagSupport` to obtain a reference to an enclosing action, such as <c:forEach> or <c:forTokens>, that implements the `LoopTag` interface. If no ancestor action fits that requirement, the preceding tag handler throws an exception. If the ancestor action is found, the tag handler accesses the iteration status by invoking that ancestor's `getLoopStatus` method, which returns an object whose type is `LoopTagStatus`. That status object is subsequently used to determine whether the current round of iteration is the first; if so, the body of the action is evaluated; if not, the action's body is skipped.

The tag handler for the <core-jstl:notFirstRound> action is listed in Listing 4.10.

The preceding tag handler is almost identical to the tag handler listed in Listing 4.9 except the preceding tag handler evaluates its body content if the current round of iteration is *not* the first round.

Note: The common functionality implemented by the two preceding tag handlers could be encapsulated in a base class, thereby reducing the amount of code that needs to be written and making maintenance of those tag handlers easier. In the interest of simplicity, the two preceding tag handlers do not share that common base class.

Listing 4.9   *WEB-INF/classes/tags/FirstRoundAction.java*

```
package tags;

import javax.servlet.jsp.JspException;
import javax.servlet.jsp.tagext.TagSupport;

import javax.servlet.jsp.jstl.core.LoopTag;
import javax.servlet.jsp.jstl.core.LoopTagStatus;

public class FirstRoundAction extends TagSupport {
   public int doStartTag() throws JspException {
      Class klass = javax.servlet.jsp.jstl.core.LoopTag.class;

      LoopTag ancestor = (LoopTag)findAncestorWithClass(
                              this, klass);
      if(ancestor != null) {
         LoopTagStatus status = ancestor.getLoopStatus();
         if(status.isFirst())
            return EVAL_BODY_INCLUDE;
      }
      else {
         throw new JspException("This tag can only be nested " +
            "in the body of a tag that implements " +
            "javax.servlet.jsp.jstl.core.LoopTag");
      }
      return SKIP_BODY;
   }
}
```

The tag library containing the two custom actions used in Listing 4.8 on page 180 are declared in the tag library descriptor (TLD) listed in Listing 4.11.

The preceding TLD declares the <core-jstl:firstRound> and <core-jstl:notFirstRound> actions and their associated tag handlers. That TLD is referenced with a taglib directive in Listing 4.8 on page 180.

Iteration Custom Actions

In addition to implementing collaboration custom actions as described in "Collaboration Custom Actions" on page 178, you can also implement custom actions that iterate by implementing the LoopTag interface. The easiest way to do that is to extend the LoopTagSupport class which implements the LoopTag interface and provides a number of protected variables and methods that greatly simplify

Listing 4.10 | *WEB-INF/classes/tags/NotFirstRoundAction.java*

```
package tags;

import javax.servlet.jsp.JspException;
import javax.servlet.jsp.tagext.TagSupport;

import javax.servlet.jsp.jstl.core.LoopTag;
import javax.servlet.jsp.jstl.core.LoopTagStatus;

public class NotFirstRoundAction extends TagSupport {
    public int doStartTag() throws JspException {
        Class klass = javax.servlet.jsp.jstl.core.LoopTag.class;

        LoopTag ancestor = (LoopTag)findAncestorWithClass(
                                    this, klass);
        if(ancestor != null) {
            LoopTagStatus status = ancestor.getLoopStatus();
            if(!status.isFirst())
                return EVAL_BODY_INCLUDE;
        }
        else {
            throw new JspException("This tag can only be nested " +
                "in the body of a tag that implements " +
                "javax.servlet.jsp.jstl.core.LoopTag");
        }
        return SKIP_BODY;
    }
}
```

implementing custom iteration actions. Table 4.4 lists the `LoopTagSupport` `protected` variables.

The `protected` variables listed above give you direct access to the `begin`, `end`, `step`, `var` (`itemId`), and `varStatus` (`statusID`) attributes. You can also find out whether the `begin`, `end`, and `step` attributes were specified with the `beginSpecified`, `endSpecified`, and `stepSpecified` variables.

The `LoopTagSupport` class defines three `abstract` methods that subclasses must implement; those methods are listed in Table 4.5.[5]

The methods listed in Table 4.5 are always called in the order they are listed in Table 4.5. The `prepare` method is called by the `LoopTagSupport.doStartTag` method before an iteration starts. Subsequently, the `LoopTagSupport` superclass

---

5. `LoopTagSupport` subclasses must implement those `abstract` methods if they are to be considered concrete classes.

Listing 4.11 *WEB-INF/core-jstl.tld*

```xml
<?xml version="1.0" encoding="ISO-8859-1"?>
<!DOCTYPE taglib
  PUBLIC "-//Sun Microsystems, Inc.//DTD JSP Tag Library 1.2//EN"
  "http://java.sun.com/dtd/web-jsptaglibrary_1_2.dtd">
<taglib>
  <tlib-version>1.0</tlib-version>
  <jsp-version>1.2</jsp-version>
  <short-name>Core JSTL Custom Actions</short-name>
  <display-name>
      Core JSTL Custom Actions for the Iteration Actions chapter
  </display-name>
  <description>
    A library containing two custom actions that determine
    whether a round is or is not the first round in an
    iteration.
  </description>

  <tag>
    <name>firstRound</name>
    <tag-class>tags.FirstRoundAction</tag-class>
    <body-content>JSP</body-content>
    <description>
      This action determines whether the current round in an
      iteration is the first. This action must be nested
      in an action that implements the
      javax.servlet.jsp.jstl.core.LoopTag interface.
    </description>
  </tag>

  <tag>
    <name>notFirstRound</name>
    <tag-class>tags.NotFirstRoundAction</tag-class>
    <body-content>JSP</body-content>
    <description>
      This action determines whether the current round in an
      iteration is NOT the first. This action must be nested
      in an action that implements the
      javax.servlet.jsp.jstl.core.LoopTag interface.
    </description>
  </tag>
</taglib>
```

Table 4.4   `LoopTagSupport` protected Variables

Variable	Description
`int begin`	The starting index in the collection that `LoopTagSupport` iterates over.
`int end`	The ending index in the collection that `LoopTagSupport` iterates over.
`int step`	The step for the iteration.
`java.lang.String itemId`	The name specified for the `var` attribute.
`java.lang.String statusId`	The name specified for the `varStatus` attribute.
`boolean beginSpecified`	Indicates whether the `begin` attribute was specified.
`boolean endSpecified`	Indicates whether the `end` attribute was specified.
`boolean stepSpecified`	Indicates whether the `step` attribute was specified.

Table 4.5   `LoopTagSupport` abstract Methods[a]

Method	Description
`boolean prepare()`	This method lets you prepare for an iteration. The `prepare` method is called once by the `LoopTagSupport.doStartTag` method.
`boolean hasNext()`	This method indicates whether the underlying collection has more elements. The `hasNext` method may be called more than once by `LoopTagSupport` for each round of an iteration.
`Object next()`	This method returns the next object in the iteration. It is called by `LoopTagSupport` once for each round of an iteration.

 a. All of the methods in this table are `protected` and can throw instances of `JspTagException`.

calls the `hasNext` method (possibly more than once) for each round of the iteration. Finally, the `next` method, which returns the next object in the iteration, is invoked by the `LoopTagSupport` superclass.

Typically, the three methods listed in Table 4.5 are the only methods you will need to implement for your iteration custom actions. The `LoopTagSupport` class also provides a number of convenience methods, which are listed in Table 4.6.

Table 4.6   `LoopTagSupport` Convenience Methods[a]

Method	Description
`Object getCurrent()`	Returns the current item in the iteration. If you call this method, the iteration will not advance (unlike, for example, Java iterators, whose `next` method returns the current item and advances the iteration).
`LoopTagStatus getLoopStatus()`	Returns an instance of `LoopTagStatus`, which has the properties defined in Table 4.2 on page 171.
`void setVar(String)`	Setter method for the `var` attribute.
`void setVarStatus(String)`	Setter method for the `varStatus` attribute.
`void validateBegin()`	Validates the value specified for the `begin` attribute. If that value is invalid—meaning the `begin` attribute is < 0—this method throws an exception.
`void validateEnd()`	Validates the value specified for the `end` attribute. If that value is invalid—meaning the `end` attribute is < 0—this method throws an exception.
`void validateStep()`	Validates the value specified for the `step` attribute. If that value is invalid—meaning the `step` attribute is <= 0—this method throws an exception.

a. The last three methods in this table are `protected` and can throw instances of `JspTagException`. All the rest are `public` and do not throw exceptions.

If you write enough iteration custom actions, you will probably find a use for all of the methods listed in Table 4.6 at one time or another, except for the `setVar` and `setVarStatus` methods, which are setter methods for the `var` and `varStatus` attributes, respectively.

The following two sections show you how to implement to custom actions: one that iterates over integer values, and another that iterates over a data structure.

Custom Actions That Iterate Over Integer Values

Remember from our discussion in "The <c:forEach> Action" on page 154 that the <c:forEach> action can be used in two ways: to iterate over integer values or a data structure. The differentiator that determines how <c:forEach> is used is whether you specify a data structure with the `items` attribute; if you specify that attribute, <c:forEach> iterates over the data structure. If you don't specify the `items`

attribute, <c:forEach> iterates over the integer values that you specify with the
begin and end attributes.

If you look at Table 4.5 and Table 4.6, which collectively list all of the
LoopTagSupport methods, you will see that the LoopTagSupport class does
not implement a setter method for the items attribute. That omission may lead you
to believe that custom actions whose tag handlers extend LoopTagSupport are
meant to iterate over integer values, but that assumption can get you into trouble.
Let's see how.

Listing 4.12 lists a simple tag handler, designed to iterate over integer values, that
extends LoopTagSupport.

Listing 4.12 *WEB-INF/classes/tags/SimpleIterationAction.java*

```
package tags;

import javax.servlet.jsp.JspTagException;
import javax.servlet.jsp.jstl.core.LoopTagSupport;

public class SimpleIterationAction extends LoopTagSupport {
   private int count;

   public void setBegin(int begin) throws JspTagException {
      this.begin = begin;
   }
   public void setEnd(int end) throws JspTagException {
      this.end = end;
   }
   protected void prepare() throws JspTagException {
      count = begin;
   }
   protected boolean hasNext() throws JspTagException {
      return count <= end;
   }
   protected Object next() throws JspTagException {
      return new Integer(count++);
   }
}
```

Because LoopTagSupport does not provide setter methods for the begin and
end properties, the preceding tag handler implements those methods. That tag
handler also implements the abstract methods defined by LoopTagSupport
listed in Table 4.5 on page 185. The prepare method sets a private count
variable to the value specified for the begin attribute, the hasNext method
returns true if the count variable is less than or equal to the value specified for the

end attribute, and the next method returns an integer value representing the current count and increments that count. Now that our tag handler is implemented, let's see how you can use that tag handler's associated custom action named <core-jstl:simpleIteration>.

Listing 4.13 lists a JSP page that iterates with <c:forEach> and <core-jstl:simpleIteration>. Identical attributes are specified for both actions: the begin attribute's value is set to 5 and the end attribute's value is set to 10.

Listing 4.13   *Using an Iteration Custom Action*

```
<!DOCTYPE HTML PUBLIC "-//W3C//DTD HTML 4.0 Transitional//EN">
<html>
    <head>
        <title>A Broken Custom Iteration Action</title>
    </head>

    <body>
        <%@ taglib uri='http://java.sun.com/jstl/core' prefix='c' %>
        <%@ taglib uri='WEB-INF/core-jstl.tld' prefix='core-jstl' %>

        <font size='4'>With &lt;c:forEach&gt;</font><p>
        <c:forEach var='item' begin='5' end='10'>
           Item:  <c:out value='${item}'/><br>
        </c:forEach>
        <p>
        <font size='4'>With the Custom Action</font><p>
        <core-jstl:simpleIteration var='item' begin='5' end='10'>
           Item:  <c:out value='${item}'/><br>
        </core-jstl:simpleIteration>
    </body>
</html>
```

The output of the preceding JSP page is shown in Figure 4–9.

As you can see from Figure 4–9, the <c:forEach> action properly iterates over the integer values 5 through 10 inclusive; however, the <core-jstl:simpleIteration> action only iterates once. The tag handler for the <core-jstl:simpleIteration> action couldn't be much simpler, but somewhere along the line, something went wrong.

The problem with the tag handler listed in Listing 4.12 is that it set the begin and end attributes stored in its superclass (LoopTagSupport). When you set those attributes, LoopTagSupport *interprets those values as indexes into an underlying collection*. But if you don't explicitly specify a collection, where does the

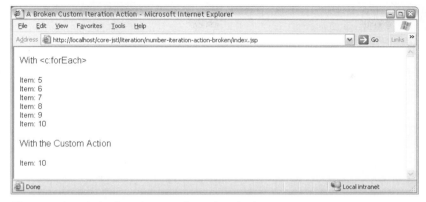

Figure 4–9 A Broken Custom Iteration Action

collection come from? The answer is that the values returned from the next method are interpreted by LoopTagSupport as a collection.

So then, why did the <core-jstl:simpleIteration> action only iterate once? Here is the answer—the values returned by the next method of the action's tag handler are 5 6 7 8 9 10. As mentioned above, those values are interpreted by LoopTagSupport as a collection, and therefore the begin and end attributes— in this case, 5 and 10—are interpreted as indexes into that collection. So LoopTagSupport starts iterating over the sixth item (remember that collection indexes are 0-based), which is the value 10. Because that value is the last item in the "collection," the iteration stops after that value.

So, how can we fix the tag handler for the <core-jstl:simpleIteration> action so that it properly iterates over integer values? The answer is simple: we implement that tag handler so that it does not set the begin and end attributes stored in its superclass (LoopTagSupport), and therefore LoopTagSupport will not interpret those values—because it won't know about them—as indexes into the values returned by the tag handler's next method. The easiest way to do that is to declare begin and end variables in the tag handler—that declaration hides the variables of the same name in the LoopTagSupport superclass. Listing 4.14 lists the revised tag handler.

With the revised tag handler listed above, the <core-jstl:simpleIteration> action will properly iterate over integer values, as you can see from Figure 4–10, which shows the output from the JSP page listed in Listing 4.13 on page 188.

Listing 4.14   *WEB-INF/classes/tags/SimpleIterationAction.java (revised)*

```java
package tags;

import javax.servlet.jsp.JspTagException;
import javax.servlet.jsp.jstl.core.LoopTagSupport;

public class SimpleIterationAction extends LoopTagSupport {
   private int count, begin, end;

   public void setBegin(int begin) throws JspTagException {
      this.begin = begin;
   }
   public void setEnd(int end) throws JspTagException {
      this.end = end;
   }
   protected void prepare() throws JspTagException {
      count = begin;
   }
   protected Object next() throws JspTagException {
      return new Integer(count++);
   }
   protected boolean hasNext() throws JspTagException {
      return count <= end;
   }
}
```

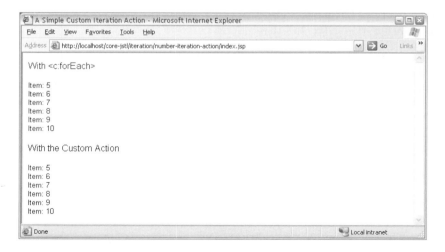

Figure 4–10   A Custom Iteration Action That Iterates Over Integer Values Properly

One note of caution before we move on. The preceding discussion is based on the
JSTL Reference Implementation. The JSTL specification is rather vague about how
the `LoopTagSupport` class should behave when used as a superclass, as in the
preceding example. Because of that vagueness, you may experience different results
if you try the preceding example with a JSTL implementation other than the JSTL
Reference Implementation.[6]

Finally, the tag library descriptor (TLD) for the tag library containing the
<core-jstl:simpleIteration> action is listed in Listing 4.15.

Listing 4.15   *WEB-INF/core-jstl.tld*

```
<?xml version="1.0" encoding="ISO-8859-1"?>
<!DOCTYPE taglib
    PUBLIC "-//Sun Microsystems, Inc.//DTD JSP Tag Library 1.2//EN"
    "http://java.sun.com/dtd/web-jsptaglibrary_1_2.dtd">

<taglib>
    <tlib-version>1.0</tlib-version>
    <jsp-version>1.2</jsp-version>
    <short-name>Core JSTL Custom Actions</short-name>
    <display-name>
        Core JSTL Custom Actions for the Iteration Action chapter
    </display-name>
    <description>
        A library containing a custom action that iterates over
        numeric values.
    </description>

  <tag>
    <name>simpleIteration</name>
    <tag-class>tags.SimpleIterationAction</tag-class>
    <body-content>JSP</body-content>
    <description>
      This action iterates over numeric values.
      This action leverages JSTL functionality by extending
      the javax.servlet.jsp.jstl.core.LoopTagSupport class.
    </description>
    <attribute>
       <name>var</name>
       <required>false</required>
       <rtexprvalue>false</rtexprvalue>
    </attribute>
    <attribute>
```

---

6.   Overall, JSTL is very well designed, but the JSTL Reference Implementation's
     implementation of the `LoopTagSupport` class is undoubtedly questionable.

Listing 4.15   *WEB-INF/core-jstl.tld (cont.)*

```
          <name>varStatus</name>
          <required>false</required>
          <rtexprvalue>false</rtexprvalue>
      </attribute>
      <attribute>
          <name>begin</name>
          <required>false</required>
          <rtexprvalue>true</rtexprvalue>
      </attribute>
      <attribute>
          <name>end</name>
          <required>false</required>
          <rtexprvalue>true</rtexprvalue>
      </attribute>
      <attribute>
          <name>step</name>
          <required>false</required>
          <rtexprvalue>true</rtexprvalue>
      </attribute>
    </tag>
</taglib>
```

Notice that the preceding TLD must list all of the attributes supported by the <core-jstl:simpleIteration> action, even though setter methods for some of those attributes, namely, the `var` and `varStatus` attributes, are implemented by the `LoopTagSupport` class.

Now that we've seen how to properly implement custom actions that iterate over integer values, let's see how to implement a custom action that iterates over a data structure.

Custom Actions That Iterate Over Data Structures

The JSP page shown in Figure 4–11 contains a login form that does not specify an action, so when you activate the `Log In` button, the JSP page is reloaded. The top picture in Figure 4–11 shows the JSP page just after the form has been filled out, and the bottom picture shows the JSP page after the `Log In` button has been activated and the page has been reloaded.

The JSP page shown in Figure 4–11 uses a custom action that iterates over request parameters and displays their values. That custom action comes in handy for debugging, especially for forms that post their data, such as the form contained in the JSP page shown in Figure 4–11.

The JSP page shown in Figure 4–11 is listed in Listing 4.16.

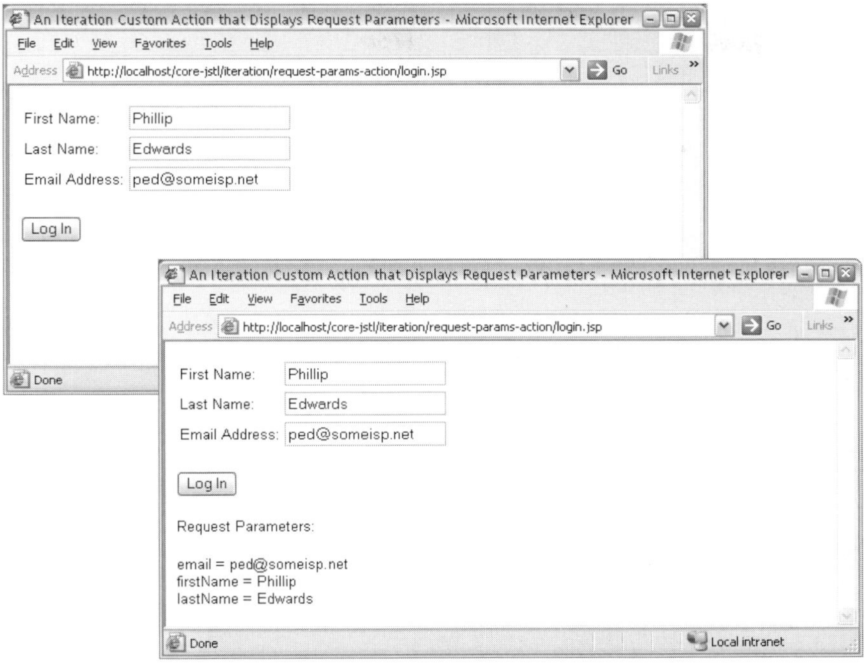

Figure 4–11 An Iteration Custom Action That Displays Request Parameters

---

Listing 4.16 *Displaying Request Parameters with a Custom Action*

```
<!DOCTYPE HTML PUBLIC "-//W3C//DTD HTML 4.0 Transitional//EN">

<html>
   <head>
      <title>
       An Iteration Custom Action that Displays Request Parameters
      </title>
   </head>

   <body>
      <%@ taglib uri='http://java.sun.com/jstl/core' prefix='c' %>
      <%@ taglib uri='WEB-INF/app-tlds/app.tld'
             prefix='core-jstl'%>

      <%-- This form does not specify an action, so this JSP
           page will be reloaded when the submit button
           is activated --%>
```

Listing 4.16 *Displaying Request Parameters with a Custom Action (cont.)*

```
<form method='post'>
    <table>
        <tr>
            <td>First Name:</td>
            <td><input type='text' name='firstName'
                    value='<c:out value="${param.firstName}"/>'/>
            </td>
        </tr>

        <tr>
            <td>Last Name:</td>
            <td><input type='text' name='lastName'
                    value='<c:out value="${param.lastName}"/>'/>
            </td>
        </tr>

        <tr>
            <td>Email Address:</td>
            <td><input type='text' name='email'
                    value='<c:out value="${param.email}"/>'/>
            </td>
        </tr>
    </table>

    <p><input type='submit' value='Log In'/>
</form>

<%-- If any of the fields in the form were filled in... --%>
<c:if test='${not empty param.firstName or
            not empty param.lastName or
            not empty param.email}'>
    Request Parameters:<p>

    <%-- Show all request parameters with the
        custom action --%>
    <core-jstl:requestParams var='item'>
        <c:out value='${item}'/><br>
    </core-jstl:requestParams>
</c:if>
    </body>
</html>
```

The preceding JSP page tests to see whether any of the form's fields have been filled in; if so, the <core-jstl:requestParams> action iterates over the request parameters, which are displayed by the <c:out> action in the body of the <core-jstl:requestParams> action.

The tag handler for the <core-jstl:requestParams> action is listed in Listing 4.17.

Listing 4.17	*WEB-INF/classes/tags/ShowRequest ParametersAction.java*

```java
package tags;

import java.util.*;
import javax.servlet.jsp.JspException;
import javax.servlet.jsp.JspTagException;
import javax.servlet.jsp.jstl.core.LoopTagSupport;

public class ShowRequestParametersAction extends LoopTagSupport {
    private Iterator entriesIterator;
    private StringBuffer nextItem = new StringBuffer();

    // Prepare for the next round of the iteration. The prepare
    // method is invoked once by LoopTagSupport.doStartTag()
    protected void prepare() throws JspTagException {
        // Get a reference to the map of request parameters
        Map parameterMap=pageContext.getRequest().getParameterMap();

        // Store the iterator from the request parameters map
        entriesIterator = parameterMap.entrySet().iterator();
    }

    // Determine whether there are any items left to iterate over
    protected boolean hasNext() throws JspTagException {
        return entriesIterator.hasNext();
    }

    // Return the next item in the collection
    protected Object next() throws JspTagException {
        // Get a reference to the next Map.Entry from the iterator
        // and get that entry's key and value.
        Map.Entry entry = (Map.Entry)entriesIterator.next();
        String     key = (String)entry.getKey();
        String[] values = (String[])entry.getValue();

        // Clear the nextItem string buffer
        nextItem.delete(0, nextItem.length());
```

Listing 4.17	WEB-INF/classes/tags/ShowRequest ParametersAction.java (cont.)

```
        // Add the map entry's key (which is the name of the request
        // parameter) to the nextItem string buffer
        nextItem.append(key + " = ");

        // Iterate over the map entry's value, which is an array of
        // strings representing the current request parameter's
        // values
        for(int i=0; i < values.length; ++i) {
            // Append the current value to the nextItem string buffer
            nextItem.append(values[i]);

            // If it's not the last value, append a comma to the
            // nextItem string buffer
            if(i != values.length-1)
                nextItem.append(",");
        }

        // Create a string from the nextItem string buffer and
        // return that string
        return nextItem.toString();
    }
}
```

The preceding tag handler implements the three `abstract` methods defined by the `LoopTagSupport` class: `prepare`, `hasNext`, and `next`.

The `prepare` method obtains a reference to a map of request parameters and their values, accesses an iterator for that map, and stores it in a `private` variable. The `hasNext` method uses the `Iterator.hasNext` method to determine whether any items are left to iterate over. The `next` method obtains a reference to the next item in the collection with the `Iterator.next` method and stores a string with the format *key=values* in a string buffer, where *key* is the name of the request parameter and *values* is a comma-separated string representing that parameter's values. Finally, the `next` method creates a string from that string buffer and returns it.

Listing 4.18 lists the tag library descriptor for the tag library that contains the <core-jstl:requestParams> action.

The preceding tag library descriptor declares the <core-jstl:requestParams> action and all of its attributes.

Listing 4.18   *WEB-INF/core-jstl.tld*

```xml
<?xml version="1.0" encoding="ISO-8859-1"?>
<!DOCTYPE taglib
  PUBLIC "-//Sun Microsystems, Inc.//DTD JSP Tag Library 1.2//EN"
  "http://java.sun.com/dtd/web-jsptaglibrary_1_2.dtd">
<taglib>
  <tlib-version>1.0</tlib-version>
  <jsp-version>1.2</jsp-version>
  <short-name>Core JSTL Custom Actions</short-name>
  <display-name>
      Core JSTL Custom Actions for the Iteration Action chapter
  </display-name>
  <description>
     A library containing a custom action that shows request
     parameters
  </description>

  <tag>
    <name>requestParams</name>
    <tag-class>tags.ShowRequestParametersAction</tag-class>
    <body-content>JSP</body-content>
    <description>
      This action prints all request parameters and their values.
      This action leverages JSTL functionality by extending
      the javax.servlet.jsp.jstl.core.LoopTagSupport class.
    </description>
    <attribute>
       <name>var</name>
       <required>false</required>
       <rtexprvalue>false</rtexprvalue>
    </attribute>
  </tag>
</taglib>
```

URL ACTIONS

Topics in This Chapter

Chapter 5

If you've developed Web applications with JavaServer Pages (JSP), you have probably found many uses for <jsp:include> and <jsp:forward>. The former includes the contents of a resource and the latter forwards control to a Web component, such as a servlet or another JSP page. On the other hand, you may have found that those actions have limited capabilities; for example, the URLs that you specify for those actions must be relative URLs, so you cannot use them to access URLs outside your Web application. JSTL provides a set of URL actions that augment the capabilities provided by <jsp:include> and <jsp:forward>; those actions are the subject of this chapter.

Before we discuss the JSTL URL actions, let's review some Web application basics and define a few terms used throughout this chapter. Java-based Web applications are stored in a directory on your filesystem; for example, Figure 5–1 illustrates a Web application that resides under the C:\core-jstl\webapp directory.

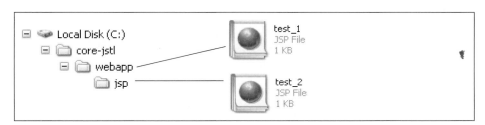

Figure 5–1   A Simple Java-Based Web Application

Java-based Web applications *reside* in a *directory*, but they are *defined* by a *context*; for example, the Web application depicted in Figure 5–1 could be defined in Tomcat's configuration file with a `Context` element, like this:[1]

```
<Context path="/core-jstl"
     docBase="C:/core-jstl/webapp"/>
```

The `path` attribute of the `Context` element defines a URL that you use to access a Web application that resides in a directory specified by the `docBase` attribute; for example, to access the Web application shown in Figure 5–1 you would use the URL `$SCHEME$HOSTNAME/core-jstl`, where `$SCHEME$HOSTNAME` represents a scheme and a host name. For example, if the scheme is `http://` and the host name is `localhost`, the URL for the Web application defined above would be `http://localhost/core-jstl`.

As websites grow, it is not uncommon for them to contain more than one Web application. From the perspective of a single Web application, the other Web applications in the same website are referred to as *foreign contexts*. For example, if your website has a registration Web application and a shopping application, the registration application is a foreign context relative to the shopping application, and vice versa.

When you access resources with <jsp:include>, you can specify either a *context-relative path* or a *page-relative path*; the former is relative to the top-level directory in a context (a Web application), and the latter is relative to the JSP page in which the <jsp:include> action resides.

Context-relative paths always start with a forward slash, whereas page-relative paths do not. For example, for the application shown in Figure 5–1, you can:

- Access `test_2.jsp` from `test_1.jsp`
  - with a context-relative path, like this:
    `<jsp:include page='/jsp/test_2.jsp'/>`
  - or with a page-relative path, like this:
    `<jsp:include page='jsp/test_2.jsp'/>`.

- Access `test_1.jsp` from `test_2.jsp`
  - with a context-relative path, like this:
    `<jsp:include page='/test_1.jsp'/>`
  - or with a page-relative path, like this:
    `<jsp:include page='../test_1.jsp'/>`.

---

1. Different JSP containers use different terms for context paths; for example, Resin calls them web-app ids.

Now that we have established some common vocabulary, let's take a look at the JSTL URL actions.

5.1 Overview

JSTL provides four URL actions that let you do the following:

- Import page-relative resources, context-relative resources, resources that reside in a foreign context, and external resources
- Redirect HTTP responses
- Create URLs with automatic URL rewriting and encoded request parameters

The JSTL URL actions are listed in Table 5.1.

Table 5.1   JSTL URL Actions

Action	Description
<c:import>	Imports the content of a URL-based resource
<c:redirect>	Redirects an HTTP response
<c:url>	Creates a URL, applying URL rewriting as necessary
<c:param>	Encodes a request parameter for <c:import>, <c:redirect>, or <c:url>

The actions listed in Table 5.1 are discussed—in the order in which they are listed—in the following sections. After we discuss those actions, we examine how they can be used in several real-world scenarios, such as scraping book information from Amazon.com, importing JSP pages from foreign contexts, and redirecting HTTP responses for logging access to external resources.

5.2 The <c:import> Action

The <jsp:include> action lets you encapsulate functionality in one JSP page and include it in another; for example, you could include company headers and footers, like this:

```
<!DOCTYPE HTML PUBLIC "-//W3C//DTD HTML 4.0 Transitional//EN">
<html>
   ...
   <body>
      <jsp:include page='/WEB-INF/jsp/company/companyHeader.jsp'/>

      <%-- Page content goes here--%>

      <jsp:include page='/WEB-INF/jsp/company/companyFooter.jsp'/>
   </body>
</html>
```

The preceding JSP page includes JSP files specified with context-relative URLs that reside in a /WEB-INF/jsp/company directory.[2] You can also specify request parameters for included files with the <jsp:param> action, like this:

```
<!DOCTYPE HTML PUBLIC "-//W3C//DTD HTML 4.0 Transitional//EN">
<html>
   ...
   <body>
      <jsp:include page='/WEB-INF/jsp/company/companyHeader.jsp'>
         <jsp:param name='user'
                   value='<%=session.getAttribute("userName")%>'/>
      </jsp:include>

      <%-- Page content goes here--%>

      <jsp:include page='/WEB-INF/jsp/company/companyFooter.jsp'/>
   </body>
</html>
```

In the preceding code fragment, companyHeader.jsp is passed a request parameter named user that references a user name stored in session scope.

As handy as the <jsp:include> action is, its capabilities are limited; for example, it cannot import external resources or resources stored in foreign contexts. The JSTL

---

2. Files stored under WEB-INF cannot be directly accessed by users.

<c:import> action can do all those things and more. Table 5.2 lists the features
supported by <jsp:include> and <c:import>.

Table 5.2   <jsp:include> vs. <c:import>

Feature	<jsp:include>	<c:import>
Access resources in the same Web application	Yes	Yes
Access resources in a foreign context[a]	No	Yes
Access external resources	No	Yes
Provide a performance boost option	No	Yes
Store imported content in a scoped variable	No	Yes
Specify a character encoding for the imported resource	No	Yes
Support the JSTL Expression Language	No	Yes

   a. This feature is not supported by all JSP containers.

You can use <c:import> instead of <jsp:include> to import resources in the same
Web application; for example, you could import company headers and footers like
this:

```
<!DOCTYPE HTML PUBLIC "-//W3C//DTD HTML 4.0 Transitional//EN">
<html>
   ...
   <body>
      <c:import url='/WEB-INF/jsp/company/companyHeader.jsp'/>

      <%-- Page content goes here--%>

      <c:import url='/WEB-INF/jsp/company/companyFooter.jsp'/>
   </body>
</html>
```

JSTL also provides a <c:param> action that you can use just like <jsp:param>; for
example, the code fragment listed on page 202 could be rewritten like this:

```
<!DOCTYPE HTML PUBLIC "-//W3C//DTD HTML 4.0 Transitional//EN">
<html>
   ...
   <body>
      <c:import url='/WEB-INF/jsp/company/companyHeader.jsp'>
         <c:param name='user'
```

```
                        value='${sessionScope.userName}'/>
        </c:import>

        <%-- Page content goes here--%>

        <c:import url='/WEB-INF/jsp/company/companyFooter.jsp'/>
    </body>
</html>
```

The <c:import> action applies URL rewriting as necessary to maintain sessions if cookies are disabled on the client. The <c:import> action has two syntaxes; here's one of them:[3]

<c:import url [context] [charEncoding] [var] [scope]>
   <c:param> actions
</c:import>

The `url` attribute is similar to the <jsp:include> action's `page` attribute—both attributes specify a URL, either context-relative or page-relative—whose content is included in the JSP page in which the respective actions reside. But the URL specified with the <c:import> `url` attribute can also represent an external resource or a resource that resides in a foreign context.

To access an external resource, you simply specify an absolute URL for the `url` attribute. To access a resource in a foreign context, you must specify a value for the `context` attribute that represents a context path for the foreign context in conjunction with the `url` attribute, which represents a context-relative path to the resource. For example, from another Web application in the same website, you could import `test_2.jsp` shown in Figure 5–1 on page 199 like this:

```
<c:import url='/jsp/test_2.jsp' context='/core-jstl'/>
```

See "Accessing External Resources" on page 210 for an example of importing external resources and "Accessing Resources in Foreign Contexts" on page 215 for an example of importing resources from a foreign context.

The `charEncoding` attribute specifies a character encoding, such as `UTF-8`, that <c:import> uses to decode characters that it imports;[4] for example, you could specify a character encoding of `Shift_JIS` to import a URL whose content is in Japanese like this:

---

3. Items in brackets are optional. See "<c:import>" on page 486 for a more complete description of <c:import> syntax.
4. See "Unicode and Charsets" on page 260 for more information about character encodings.

```
<c:import url='http://www.tcvb.or.jp/jp/index-j.htm'
 charEncoding='Shift_JIS'/>
```

By default, the <c:import> action writes the content of the URL that it imports to the current JspWriter; however, if you specify the var attribute, <c:import> will create a scoped variable whose name is specified with that attribute. That scoped variable references a string that contains the content that <c:import> imports. By default, <c:import> stores that scoped variable in page scope, but you can specify the scope attribute to store it in page, request, session, or application scope.

You can also use <c:import> with this syntax:

> *<c:import url [context] [charEncoding] varReader>*
>   *body content that uses the varReader scoped variable:*
>   ***<c:param> actions not allowed***
> *</c:import>*

The preceding syntax is the same as the first syntax, except that the var and scope attributes are replaced by a varReader attribute and <c:param> actions are disallowed in the body of the <c:import> action. The varReader attribute specifies the name of a reader that references the imported content. That reader is only accessible in the body of the <c:import> action, and because it must be available immediately after the <c:import> start tag, <c:param> actions are not allowed in the body of the <c:import> action. This syntax is provided for efficiency because the imported content is not stored in a string but instead is accessed directly with a reader. Figure 5–2 shows a JSP page that uses <c:import> with the preceding syntax to display the content of a URL.

Figure 5–2   Using <c:import> with a Reader

The JSP page shown in Figure 5–2 uses a custom action nested in the body of a <c:import> action. That custom action uses a reader created by <c:import> to directly access the content of a URL. That JSP page is listed in Listing 5.1.

The preceding JSP page uses <c:import> to read the content of another JSP page named someContent.jsp, which resides in the same directory as the preceding

Listing 5.1	*Using a Custom Action That Uses the Optional Reader Created by <c:import>*

```
<!DOCTYPE HTML PUBLIC "-//W3C//DTD HTML 4.0 Transitional//EN">
<html>
   <head>
      <title>
         Using the Reader Created by &lt;c:import&gt;
      </title>
   </head>

   <body>
      <%@ taglib uri='http://java.sun.com/jstl/core' prefix='c' %>
      <%@ taglib uri='WEB-INF/core-jstl.tld' prefix='core-jstl' %>

      <c:import url='someContent.jsp' varReader='reader'>
         <core-jstl:displayUrlContent reader='reader'/>
      </c:import>
   </body>
</html>
```

JSP page. The `varReader` attribute is specified so that <c:import> will create a reader and store it in page scope. The custom action—<core-jstl:displayUrlContent>—uses the reader to display the imported content. Notice that the custom action has a `reader` attribute that specifies the name of the reader. That attribute's value must be the same as the value specified for the enclosing <c:import> action's `varReader` attribute.

The JSP page imported by the preceding JSP page is listed in Listing 5.2.

Listing 5.2	*someContent.jsp*

CONTENT

The tag handler for the <core-jstl:displayUrlContent> custom action is listed in Listing 5.3.

The preceding tag handler's `doStartTag` method invokes the `PageContext.findAttribute` method to locate the reader created by an enclosing <c:import> action to read each character and write it to the current `JspWriter`.

Note: Unlike other JSTL actions, such as the iteration, SQL, and internationalization actions, the URL actions do not expose any classes or interfaces.

Listing 5.3   *WEB-INF/classes/tags/DisplayUrlAction.java*

```java
package tags;

import java.io.Reader;
import javax.servlet.jsp.JspException;
import javax.servlet.jsp.tagext.*;

public class DisplayUrlAction extends TagSupport {
   private String readerName;

   public void setReader(String readerName) {
      this.readerName = readerName;
   }
   public int doStartTag() throws JspException {
      int character;

      Reader reader = (Reader)
                     pageContext.findAttribute(readerName);

      if(reader == null) {
         throw new JspException("You can only use this action " +
                                "in the body of a "  +
                                "&lt;c:import&gt; "  +
                                "action that exposes a reader ");
      }
      try {
         while((character = reader.read()) != -1)
            pageContext.getOut().print((char)character);
      }
      catch(java.io.IOException ex) {
         throw new JspException(ex.getMessage());
      }
      return SKIP_BODY;
   }
}
```

If the <c:import> tag handler's class had been exposed, the preceding tag handler could check to make sure that it had an <c:import> ancestor action and could also obtain a reference to the reader that the enclosing <c:import> action created. However, because the URL actions do not expose any classes or interfaces, you must explicitly pass the tag handler the name of the reader created by its enclosing <c:import> action and the tag handler must also check to make sure that the reader is not null.

5.3 The <c:redirect> Action

The <c:redirect> action sends an HTTP redirect response to the client and aborts the processing of the JSP page in which the action resides. You can use <c:redirect> to redirect to an external resource or a resource in a foreign context with the following syntax:[5]

<c:redirect url [context]/>

As is the case for <c:import>, if you specify the context attribute for <c:redirect>, you must also specify a context-relative URL with the url attribute that points to a resource contained in that foreign context. You can also use <c:redirect> with <c:param> actions with this syntax:

<c:redirect url [context]>
  <c:param> actions
</c:redirect>

Like <c:import>, the <c:redirect> action applies URL rewriting as necessary. See "Redirecting a Response" on page 225 for an example of how you can use <c:redirect>.

5.4 The <c:url> Action

The <c:url> action processes a URL, applying URL rewriting—for relative URLs only—as necessary. The <c:url> action has two syntaxes; here's one of them:[6]

<c:url value [context] [var] [scope]/>

The mandatory value attribute specifies the URL that's processed by the <c:url> action. The context attribute lets you specify a foreign context. Like <c:import> and <c:redirect>, if you specify the context attribute for <c:url>, you must also specify a context-relative URL, with the value attribute, that points to a resource in that foreign context. By default, <c:url> sends the processed URL to the current

---

5. Items in brackets are optional. See "<c:redirect>" on page 489 for a more complete description of <c:redirect> syntax.
6. Items in brackets are optional. See "<c:url>" on page 490 for a more complete description of <c:url> syntax.

`JspWriter`, but you can store that URL in a scoped variable instead if you specify the `var` attribute and, optionally, the `scope` attribute.

Like <c:import> and <c:redirect>, you can specify request parameters that are encoded in the URL that <c:url> processes with nested <c:param> actions. You can do that with the following syntax:

> *<c:url value [context] [var] [scope]>*
>   *<c:param> actions*
> *</c:url>*

If you specify a context-relative or page-relative URL for the `value` attribute, <c:url> will prepend the context path of the Web application to the URL; for example, consider the following use of <c:url>:

```
<c:url value='/test_1.jsp'/>
```

If the context path of the Web application is `/core-jstl/webapp`, <c:url> will produce the following URL: `/core-jstl/webapp/test_1.jsp`, not taking into account possible URL rewriting. Because of this feature, you must not use <c:url> in conjunction with <c:import> or <c:redirect> for relative URLs because those actions also prepend the context path to relative URLs before passing the URL to the request dispatcher. For example, consider the following code:

```
<c:import url='/test_1.jsp'/>
```

The preceding code fragment is *not equivalent* to the following code fragment:

```
<%-- WARNING: this code fragment will throw an exception --%>

<c:url value='/test_1.jsp' var='processedURL'/>
<c:import url='${processedURL}'/>
```

The preceding code fragment will throw an exception because both <c:url> and <c:import> will try to prepend the context path to the relative URL. URLs processed by <c:url> actions are meant to be *sent directly to the browser*; for example:

```
<c:url value='/test_1.jsp' var='processedURL'/>
<a href='<c:out value="${processedURL}"/>'>Click Here</a>
```

The preceding code fragment creates a URL with <c:url> and uses the resulting URL with the HTML anchor element, which is how <c:url> is meant to be used.

The examples discussed in "Accessing External Resources" on page 210 and "Accessing Resources in Foreign Contexts" on page 215 both use <c:url> to process URLs that are sent directly to the browser.

Core Warning

*Don't use <c:url> to encode relative URLs used by <c:import> or
<c:redirect>.*

5.5 The <c:param> Action

The <c:param> action specifies a request parameter that is used by enclosing
<c:import>, <c:redirect>, or <c:url> actions. The <c:param> action can be used with
the following syntax:[7]

> *<c:param name value/>*

The <c:param> action encodes the values specified for its `name` and `value`
attributes. Instead of specifying the value for a request parameter with the `value`
attribute, you can also specify that value in the body of a <c:param> action with this
syntax:

> *<c:param name>*
> *value*
> *</c:param>*

Now that we have a basic understanding of the JSTL URL actions, let's see how to
put them to use with three real-world examples, as discussed in the following sections.

5.6 Accessing External Resources

This section discusses a Web application, shown in Figure 5–3, that illustrates how
you can use JSTL URL actions to access external resources by scraping book information from Amazon.com. The application consists of two JSP pages that use the
<c:import>, <c:url>, and <c:param> actions.

The top picture in Figure 5–3 shows the JSP page that serves as the application's
welcome page. That page creates four links that are created by HTML anchor
elements. The corresponding URLs for those links are created by <c:url> actions

---

7. See "<c:param>" on page 491 for a more complete description of <c:param> syntax.

with nested <c:param> actions. The rest of the pictures in Figure 5–3 show information for each of the books listed in the welcome page. That information is scraped from Amazon.com with a combination of <c:import> actions and the <str:nestedString> action from the Jakarta String Tag Library.[8]

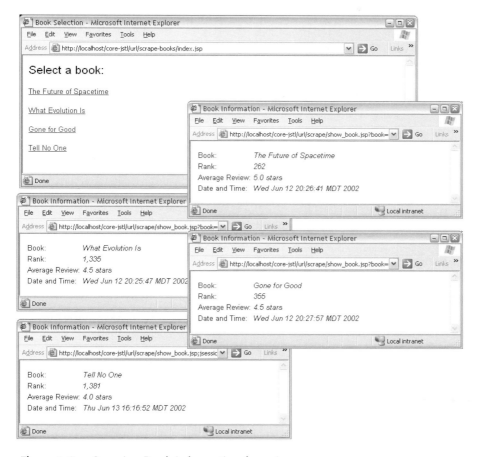

Figure 5–3   Scraping Book Information from Amazon.com

The JSP page shown in the top picture in Figure 5–3 is listed in Listing 5.4.

The preceding JSP page uses four <c:url> actions with nested <c:param> actions to create four URLs that all point to show_book.jsp. That JSP page is specified

8. You can download the Jakarta String Tag Library from
    http://jakarta.apache.org/builds/jakarta-taglibs/nightly/
    projects/string.

Listing 5.4   *Creating the Book URLs*

```
<!DOCTYPE HTML PUBLIC "-//W3C//DTD HTML 4.0 Transitional//EN">
<html>
   <head>
      <title>Book Selection</title>
   </head>

   <body>
      <%@ taglib uri='http://java.sun.com/jstl/core' prefix='c' %>

      <font size='5'>
         Select a book:
      </font><p>

      <%-- Create URLs for each book with a page-relative path
           to show_book.jsp and a request parameter named bookUrl
           whose value represents the book's URL on Amazon.com.
           Those URLs are stored in page-scoped variables that
           are used to create HTML links below --%>

      <c:url var='theFutureOfSpacetime' value='show_book.jsp'>
         <c:param name='bookUrl' value='http://www.amazon.com/exec/
obidos/ASIN/0393020223/ref=pd_sim_books_1/102-5303437-2118551'/>
      </c:url>

      <c:url var='whatEvolutionIs' value='show_book.jsp'>
         <c:param name='bookUrl' value='http://www.amazon.com/exec/
obidos/ASIN/0465044255/ref=pd_sim_books_4/102-5303437-2118551'/>
      </c:url>

      <c:url var='goneForGood' value='show_book.jsp'>
         <c:param name='bookUrl' value='http://www.amazon.com/exec/
obidos/ASIN/038533558X/ref=pd_sim_books_3/102-5303437-2118551'/>
      </c:url>

      <c:url var='tellNoOne' value='show_book.jsp'>
         <c:param name='bookUrl' value='http://www.amazon.com/exec/
obidos/ASIN/0440236703/qid=1023935482/sr=8-1/ref=sr_8_1/
104-6556245-7867920'/>
      </c:url>

      <%-- Create HTML links for each book using the URLs stored
           in page-scoped variables that were created above by
           <c:url> --%>
```

| Listing 5.4 | *Creating the Book URLs (cont.)* |

```
    <a href='<c:out value="${theFutureOfSpacetime}"/>'>
        The Future of Spacetime
    </a><p>

    <a href='<c:out value="${whatEvolutionIs}"/>'>
        What Evolution Is
    </a><p>

    <a href='<c:out value="${goneForGood}"/>'>
        Gone for Good
    </a><p>

    <a href='<c:out value="${tellNoOne}"/>'>
        Tell No One
    </a><p>

    </body>
</html>
```

with the <c:url> action's value attribute as a page-relative URL. Each of the four URLs created by the <c:url> actions also has a request parameter named bookUrl whose value represents an external URL that points to the respective book's page on Amazon.com. Each of the four <c:url> actions stores its processed URLs in page-scoped variables whose names correspond to the books that they represent. Subsequently, four HTML anchor elements are created to reference the values stored in those scoped variables. When a user clicks on one of those anchors, control is transferred to show_book.jsp, which is listed in Listing 5.5.

| Listing 5.5 | *show_book.jsp* |

```
<!DOCTYPE HTML PUBLIC "-//W3C//DTD HTML 4.0 Transitional//EN">
<html>
    <head>
        <title>Book Information</title>
    </head>

    <body>
        <%@ taglib uri='http://java.sun.com/jstl/core' prefix='c' %>

        <%-- Declare the Jakarta Strings tag library --%>
        <%@ taglib uri='WEB-INF/string.tld' prefix='str'%>
        <%-- Import the page from Amazon.com using the bookUrl
             request parameter --%>
```

Listing 5.5   *show_book.jsp (cont.)*

```
<c:import var='book' url='${param.bookUrl}'/>

<%-- Store today's date and time in page scope --%>
<jsp:useBean id='now' class='java.util.Date'/>

<table>
    <tr>
        <td>Book:</td>
        <td><i>
            <%-- Show the book title --%>
            <str:nestedString open='buying info: '
                              close='&lt;/title&gt;'>
                <c:out value='${book}'/>
            </str:nestedString>
        </td></i>
    </tr>
    <tr>
        <td>Rank:</td>
        <td><i>
            <%-- Show the book rank --%>
            <str:nestedString open='Sales Rank: &lt;/b&gt; '
                              close='&lt;/span&gt;'>
                <c:out value='${book}'/>
            </str:nestedString>
        </td></i>
    </tr>
    <tr>
        <td>Average Review:</td>
        <td><i>
            <%-- Show the average review --%>
            <str:replace replace='-' with='.'>
                <str:nestedString open='stars-' close='.gif'>
                    <c:out value='${book}'/>
                </str:nestedString> stars
            </str:replace>
        </td></i>
    </tr>
    <tr>
        <td>Date and Time:</td>
        <td><i>
            <c:out value='${now}'/>
        </td></i>
    </tr>
</table>
</body>
</html>
```

The preceding JSP page uses <c:import> to import content from Amazon.com with the URL specified by the `bookUrl` request parameter. The `var` attribute is specified for the <c:import> actions so that the imported content is stored in a string that is referenced by a page-scoped variable named `book`. Subsequently, the preceding JSP page uses <jsp:useBean> to create a date representing the current date and time. Finally, the JSP page uses the <str:nestedString> action from the Jakarta String Tag Library—which extracts a substring specified with strings that precede and follow the substring—to extract the book's title, sales rank, and average review from the string stored in the `book` page-scoped variable. The preceding JSP page also displays the current date and time with the scoped variable created by the <jsp:useBean> action at the top of the page.

Disclaimer: Scraping information from webpages is inherently risky business, because it relies on the absolute position of static text in a webpage's HTML; if the HTML is modified, you may have to change the code that scrapes information. As this book went to press, the example discussed in this section worked as advertised, but if Amazon.com modifies their webpage format, it may break that example.

5.7 Accessing Resources in Foreign Contexts

As websites grow, it's often convenient to encapsulate distinct functionality in separate Web applications. For example, if you develop open-source software, you may find it convenient to implement a Web application that documents your product and another Web application that provides examples that potential customers can try. From the perspective of a single Web application, other Web applications in the same website are known as foreign contexts.

Websites that have multiple Web applications often need to share resources between those applications. This section shows you how to use <c:import> to access resources in a foreign context. Before we proceed with the example, however, you should know that not all JSP containers support accessing resources that reside in foreign contexts. The example discussed in this section was tested with Tomcat 4.1, which lets you enable cross-context access with a special attribute that you specify when you declare your Web applications. Other JSP containers, such as Resin, do not support cross-context access.

Core Warning

Not all JSP containers support accessing resources in foreign contexts .

Two Web applications are used in the following example. Those Web applications and their pertinent JSP files are depicted in Figure 5–4.

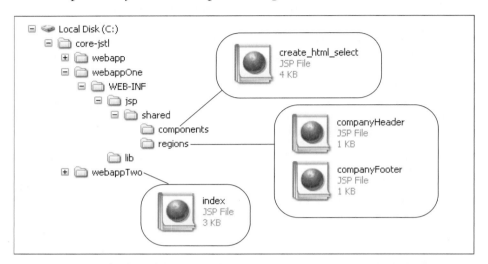

Figure 5–4   Two Web Applications and Their Contents

In the following example, `index.jsp` from the `webappTwo` application accesses `companyHeader.jsp`, `companyFooter.jsp`, and `create_html_select.jsp` from the `webappOne` application. Tomcat 4.1 requires you to specify those contexts with a `crossContext` attribute in the `Context` element in `server.xml`. Here is an excerpt from `server.xml` for the Web applications shown in Figure 5–4:

```
...
<Context path="/core-jstl/url/webappOne"
      docBase="C:/core-jstl/webappOne"
 crossContext="true"/>

<Context path="/core-jstl/url/webappTwo"
      docBase="C:/core-jstl/webappTwo"
 crossContext="true"/>
...
```

The `webappTwo` application, which consists of a single JSP page— `index.jsp`—is shown in Figure 5–5. That application lets you make a donation by filling out a form, as shown in the top picture in Figure 5–5. If you specify less than $1000 for your donation, the JSP page is redisplayed with the original information that you entered and you are asked to increase your donation, as you can see from the bottom picture in Figure 5–5.

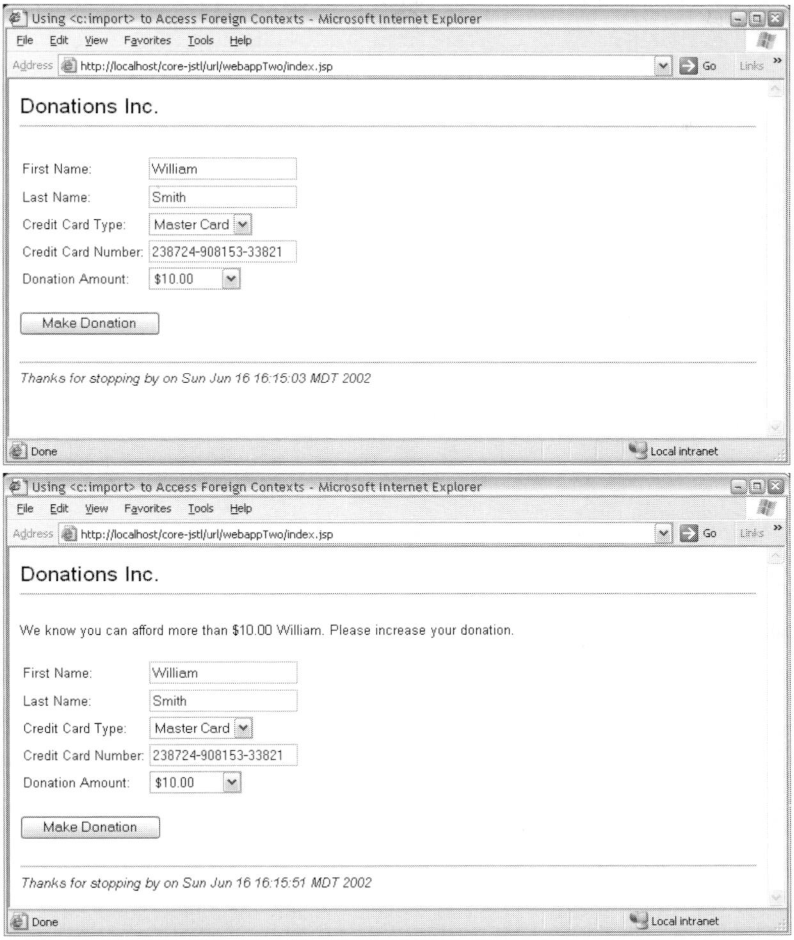

Figure 5–5   Accessing Resources in a Foreign Context with <c:import> and <c:param>

The JSP page shown in Figure 5–5 is listed in Listing 5.6.

There are three points of interest in the preceding JSP page. First, that JSP page uses <c:import> to import a header and a footer from the webappOne application. Second, the JSP page also uses <c:import> to import a JSP page from webappOne that creates HTML select elements. Finally, the JSP page uses <fmt:formatNumber> to format the donation amount as currency; we discuss formatting actions in "Formatting Actions" on page 308.

The header and footer imported from webappOne are simple JSP pages that are listed in Listing 5.7 and Listing 5.8, respectively.

Listing 5.6   *Accessing Foreign Contexts*

```
<!DOCTYPE HTML PUBLIC "-//W3C//DTD HTML 4.0 Transitional//EN">
<html>
    <head>
        <title>
            Using &lt;c:import&gt; to Access Foreign Contexts
        </title>
    </head>

    <body>
        <%@ taglib uri='http://java.sun.com/jstl/core' prefix='c' %>
        <%@ taglib uri='http://java.sun.com/jstl/fmt'  pre-
fix='fmt'%>

        <%-- Import a header shared among Web applications for this
             Web site --%>
        <c:import url='/WEB-INF/jsp/shared/regions/company-
Header.jsp'
             context='/core-jstl/url/webappOne'/>
        <p>

        <%-- If the user didn't give enough, ask for more --%>
        <c:if test='${param.amount < 1000}'>
           We know you can afford more than
           <fmt:formatNumber value='${param.amount}'
                             type='currency'/>
           <c:out value='${param.first}'/>. Please increase
           your donation.
        </c:if>

    <%-- Create a page-scoped variable -- for readability only --
             that represents the context-relative URL for
             create_html_select.jsp, which resides in the
             /core-jstl/url/webappOne context --%>
    <c:set var='create_html_component'>
        /WEB-INF/jsp/shared/components/create_html_select.jsp
    </c:set>

    <%-- This form does not specify an action, so this JSP page
         is reloaded when the submit button is activated --%>
    <form method='post'>
        <table>
          <tr>
            <td>First Name:</td>
            <td><input type='text' name='first'
                    value='<c:out value="${param.first}"/>'/>
            </td>
          </tr>
```

Listing 5.6 *Accessing Foreign Contexts (cont.)*

```
            <tr>
                <td>Last Name:</td>
                <td><input type='text' name='last'
                        value='<c:out value="${param.last}"/>'/>
                </td>
            </tr>
            <tr>
                <td>Credit Card Type:</td>
                <td>
                    <c:import url='${create_html_component}'
                        context='/core-jstl/url/webappOne'>
                      <c:param name='selectName' value='cardType'/>
                      <c:param name='items'
                            value='Visa, Master Card, Discover'/>
                    </c:import>
                </td>
            </tr>
            <tr>
                <td>Credit Card Number:</td>
                <td><input type='text' name='cardNumber'
                      value='<c:out value="${param.cardNumber}"/>'/>
                </td>
            </tr>
            <tr>
                <td>Donation Amount:</td>
                <td>
                    <c:import url='${create_html_component}'
                        context='/core-jstl/url/webappOne'>
                      <c:param name='selectName' value='amount'/>
                      <c:param name='items'
                            value='10,100,1000,10000'/>

                      <c:param name='formatDisplay'
                            value='currency'/>
                    </c:import>
                </td>
            </tr>
        </table>
        <p><input type='submit' value='Make Donation'/>
    </form>

    <%-- Import a footer shared among Web applications for this
        Web site --%>
    <c:import url='/WEB-INF/jsp/shared/regions/company-
Footer.jsp'
        context='/core-jstl/url/webappOne'/>
  </body>
</html>
```

Listing 5.7	/WEB-INF/jsp/shared/regions/companyHeader.jsp (from /core-jstl/url/webappOne context)

```
<font size='5'>
  Donations Inc.
</font>
<hr>
```

Listing 5.8	/WEB-INF/jsp/shared/regions/companyFooter.jsp (from /core-jstl/url/webappOne context)

```
<%@ taglib uri='http://java.sun.com/jstl/core' prefix='c' %>

<hr>
<jsp:useBean id='now' class='java.util.Date'/>
<i>Thanks for stopping by on <c:out value='${now}'/></i>
```

As you can see from Figure 5–5 on page 217, the HTML select elements created by that JSP page retain their values when the page is reloaded. As discussed in "Retaining Values for HTML Option Elements" on page 129, that behavior can be implemented with the <c:if> and <c:out> actions; for example, you could implement the donation amount element like this:

```
<%-- Create the HTML select element for the donation amount --%>
<select name ='amount'>

   <%-- For each item displayed by this select element, ... --%>
   <c:forEach var='item' items='10,100,1000,10000'>

      <%-- Create the starting option element--%>
      <option

      <%-- If the current item is the same as the last amount
           specified, generate a "select" string contained in the
           option start tag --%>
      <c:if test='${param.amount == item}'>
        selected
      </c:if>

      <%-- Generate the value for the option element --%>
      value='<c:out value="${item}"/>'

      <%-- Close off the option element start tag --%>
      >
```

```
      <%-- Generate the display value as currency for the
           option element body --%>
      <fmt:formatNumber value='${item}' type='currency'/>

      <%-- Generate the option element end tag --%>
      </option>
   </c:forEach>
</select>
```

The preceding code fragment creates an HTML select element for donation amounts. That select element retains the previously entered donation amount and formats the displayed amount as currency. It's not overly difficult to create that HTML select element with the preceding code, but nonetheless, you must remember the algorithm and know how to use the <c:forEach>, <c:out>, <c:if> and <fmt:formatNumber> actions. It would be beneficial if you could encapsulate that algorithm in a JSP page so you don't have to recall the algorithm every time you need to create an HTML select element that retains its values. The JSP page listed in Listing 5.6 on page 218 uses <c:import> and <c:param> to import a JSP page that creates HTML select elements. Here's how the JSP page listed in Listing 5.6 on page 218 imports that JSP page:

```
<html>
   ...
   <body>
      ...
      <%-- Create a page-scoped variable -- for readability only --
           that represents the context-relative URL for
           create_html_select.jsp, which resides in the
           /core-jstl/url/webappOne context --%>

      <c:set var='create_html_component'>
         /WEB-INF/jsp/shared/components/create_html_select.jsp
      </c:set>

      <%-- This form does not specify an action, so this JSP page
           is reloaded when the submit button is activated --%>
      <form method='post'>
         <table>
            ...
            <tr>
               <td>Donation Amount:</td>
               <td>
                  <c:import url='${create_html_component}'
                       context='/core-jstl/url/webappOne'>
                    <c:param name='selectName' value='amount'/>
                    <c:param name='items'
```

```
                        value='10,100,1000,10000'/>
                </c:import>
            </td>
        </tr>
        ...
    </table>
    ...
    </form>
    ...
    </body>
</html>
```

The preceding code fragment creates a scoped variable, solely for readability, that contains a string representing the URL of the JSP page—create_html_select.jsp—that creates HTML select elements that retain their values. That URL is a context-relative path, out of necessity because the JSP page that it references resides in a foreign context. The scoped variable is subsequently used to specify the url attribute for the <c:import> action, which also specifies the foreign context with its context attribute. The <c:import> action contains two <c:param> actions that specify a selectName request parameter whose value is amount and an items request parameter whose value is the comma-separated string 10,100,1000,10000.

The create_html_select.jsp JSP page is listed in Listing 5.9.

Listing 5.9	/WEB-INF/jsp/shared/components/create_html_select.jsp (from /core-jstl/url/webappOne context)

```
<%-- This handy JSTL component creates an HTML select
     element that retains its value if its page is reloaded.

     This component can be passed the following request
     parameters:

     selectName:    The name of the select element
     items:         The option values
     formatValue:   How option values should be formatted
     formatDisplay: How option display values should be formatted

     The items parameter must be a comma-separated string, and
     the formatValue and formatDisplay parameters must be one
     of the following: number, percent, or currency.

     Here's an example of how you'd use this component:
```

```
    <form>
       <table>
          <tr>
             <td>Select a value:</td>
             <td>
                <c:import url='create_html_select.jsp'>
                   <c:param name='selectName' value='amount'/>
                   <c:param name='items'      value='1,2,3,4,5'/>

                   <c:param name='formatValue'
                           value='currency'/>

                   <c:param name='formatDisplay'
                           value='currency'/>
                </c:import>
             </td>
          </tr>
       </table>
       <p><input type='submit'/>
    </form>

    The preceding code creates an HTML select element with
    the values 1-5. Those values are formatted as currency, so
    they look like this for the US English locale: $1.00,
    $2.00, ... $5.00.
--%>

<%@ taglib uri='http://java.sun.com/jstl/core' prefix='c'  %>
<%@ taglib uri='http://java.sun.com/jstl/fmt'  prefix='fmt'%>

<%-- Set a page-scoped variable representing the last value
     selected for the HTML select element generated by this
     component --%>
<c:set var='lastValue' value='${param[param.selectName]}'/>

<%-- Create the HTML select element --%>
<select name='<c:out value="${param.selectName}"/>'>
   <c:forEach var='item' items='${param.items}'>
      <%-- Start the option starting tag --%>
      <option

      <%-- If this item was the last item selected, add the
           string selected to the option starting tag --%>
      <c:if test='${item == lastValue}'>
         selected
```

Listing 5.9	/WEB-INF/jsp/shared/components/create_html_select.jsp (from /core-jstl/url/webappOne context) (cont.)

```
        </c:if>

        <%-- If the option's value should be formatted, format
             it with the formatting type (number, percent, or
             currency) specified with the formatValue parameter --%>
        <c:choose>
            <c:when test='${not empty param.formatValue}'>
                <fmt:formatNumber var='value' value='${item}'
                                  type='${param.formatValue}'/>
                    <c:out escapeXml='false' value='value=${value}'/>
            </c:when>

            <c:otherwise>
                value='<c:out value="${item}"/>'
            </c:otherwise>
        </c:choose>

        <%-- Close off the <option> starting tag --%>
        >

        <%-- If the option's display value should be formatted,
             format it with the formatting type (number, percent,
             or currency) specified with the formatDisplay
             parameter --%>
        <c:choose>
            <c:when test='${not empty param.formatDisplay}'>
                <fmt:formatNumber var='value' value='${item}'
                                  type='${param.formatDisplay}'/>
                <c:out value='${value}'/>
            </c:when>

            <c:otherwise>
                <c:out value='${item}'/>
            </c:otherwise>
        </c:choose>

        <%-- Add the <option> end tag --%>
        </option>
    </c:forEach>
</select>
```

The preceding JSP page encapsulates the creation of HTML select elements that retain their values. That JSP page can be passed four request parameters that represent the name of the select element, the items it displays, and how the element's values and display values should be formatted. *That JSP page represents a reusable component that can be used by multiple Web applications*; therefore, the example in this section shows how to access that component from a foreign context. If your JSP container does not support accessing resources in foreign contexts, you can still take advantage of components like the preceding JSP page by accessing them with an absolute URL.

5.8 Redirecting a Response

Before JSTL, the only way to redirect an HTTP response in a Java-based Web application was to use the `HttpServletResponse.sendRedirect` method. JSTL makes redirecting HTTP responses much easier with the <c:redirect> action, as illustrated by the application shown in Figure 5–6.

The application shown in Figure 5–6 logs access to external resources, which are JavaWorld articles that discuss Java design patterns. The application consists of two JSP pages. One of those JSP pages, shown in the top picture in Figure 5–6, uses the <c:url> and <c:param> JSTL actions, in conjunction with HTML anchor element, to provide links to five JavaWorld articles. Instead of pointing directly to the articles, those links point to a second JSP page that's passed the article's URL as a request parameter. The second JSP page, which is not shown in Figure 5–6, logs information about the links that were selected in the first JSP page and redirects the HTTP response to the JavaWorld article in question. The bottom pictures in Figure 5–6 show two of those articles.

The second JSP page sends information to the standard servlet log; that information looks like this:

```
Remote host 127.0.0.1 accessed Decorator Design Pattern article on
Wed Jun 12 13:31:09 MDT 2002
...
Remote host 127.0.0.1 accessed Composite Design Pattern article on
Wed Jun 12 13:31:44 MDT 2002
```

The information stored in the log file provides information about the remote host that accessed the article, the name of the article, and the date and time when the access occurred.

The JSP page shown in the top picture in Figure 5–6 is listed in Listing 5.10.

For readability, the preceding JSP page uses <c:set> actions to create scoped variables that reference the JavaWorld article URLs. Subsequently, the JSP page uses <c:url> with enclosed <c:param> actions to create five URLs that all point to a JSP page named `log_access.jsp`. Those URLs all contain a request parameter named `page` whose value represents the JavaWorld article's URL and a request

Figure 5–6   Use <c:redirect> to Log Access to External Resources

Listing 5.10   *Creating Article URLs*

```
<!DOCTYPE HTML PUBLIC "-//W3C//DTD HTML 4.0 Transitional//EN">
<html>
    <head>
       <title>Using &lt;c:redirect&gt;</title>
    </head>

    <body>
       <%@ taglib uri='http://java.sun.com/jstl/core' prefix='c' %>

       <%-- Define a prefix variable for readability --%>
       <c:set var='prefix'
          value='http://www.javaworld.com/javaworld/'/>

       <%-- The base URL for the overview article --%>
       <c:set var='overview'
        value='${prefix}jw-10-2001/jw-1012-designpatterns_p.html'/>

       <%-- The base URL for the strategy article --%>
       <c:set var='strategy'
        value='${prefix}jw-04-2002/jw-0426-designpatterns_p.html'/>

       <%-- The base URL for the decorator article --%>
       <c:set var='decorator'
        value='${prefix}jw-12-2001/jw-1214-designpatterns_p.html'/>

       <%-- The base URL for the proxy article --%>
       <c:set var='proxy'
        value='${prefix}jw-02-2002/jw-0222-designpatterns_p.html'/>

       <%-- The base URL for the composite article --%>
       <c:set var='composite'
        value='${prefix}jw-12-2001/jw-1228-jsptemplate_p.html'/>

       <%-- The encoded URL for the overview article --%>
       <c:url var='overviewUrl' value='log_access.jsp'>
          <c:param name='page' value='${overview}'/>
          <c:param name='name' value='Design Patterns Overview'/>
       </c:url>

       <%-- The encoded URL for the strategy article --%>
       <c:url var='strategyUrl' value='log_access.jsp'>
          <c:param name='page' value='${strategy}'/>
          <c:param name='name' value='Strategy Design Pattern'/>
       </c:url>
```

Listing 5.10   *Creating Article URLs (cont.)*

```
<%-- The encoded URL for the decorator article --%>
<c:url var='decoratorUrl' value='log_access.jsp'>
    <c:param name='page' value='${decorator}'/>
    <c:param name='name' value='Decorator Design Pattern'/>
</c:url>

<%-- The encoded URL for the proxy article --%>
<c:url var='proxyUrl' value='log_access.jsp'>
    <c:param name='page' value='${proxy}'/>
    <c:param name='name' value='Proxy Design Pattern'/>
</c:url>

<%-- The encoded URL for the composite article --%>
<c:url var='compositeUrl' value='log_access.jsp'>
    <c:param name='page' value='${composite}'/>
    <c:param name='name' value='Composite Design Pattern'/>
</c:url>

<font size='5'>
    Here are some JavaWorld articles on Java Design Patterns:
</font><p>

<%-- Links to articles with URLs created above --%>
<a href='<c:out value="${overviewUrl}"/>'>
    Java Design Patterns Overview
</a><p>
<a href='<c:out value="${strategyUrl}"/>'>
    The Strategy Design Pattern
</a><p>
<a href='<c:out value="${decoratorUrl}"/>'>
    The Decorator Design Pattern
</a><p>
<a href='<c:out value="${proxyUrl}"/>'>
    The Proxy Design Pattern
</a><p>
<a href='<c:out value="${compositeUrl}"/>'>
    J2EE Composite View Pattern
</a>
    </body>
</html>
```

parameter named name that represents the name of the article. Finally, the JSP page creates five HTML anchor elements that reference the URLs that point to `log_access.jsp`. That JSP page is listed in Listing 5.11.

Listing 5.11 *log_access.jsp*

```
<%@ taglib uri='http://java.sun.com/jstl/core' prefix='c' %>

<%-- Log a message in the log file --%>
<% application.log("Remote host " + request.getRemoteHost() +
                   " accessed " + request.getParameter("name") +
                   " article on " + new java.util.Date()); %>

<%-- Redirect the response to the specified page --%>
<c:redirect url='${param.page}'/>
```

The preceding JSP page uses a scriptlet to write a message to the application log file and subsequently uses <c:redirect> to redirect the response to the JavaWorld article.

CONFIGURATION
SETTINGS

Topics in This Chapter

- Overview
- The Config Class
- Accessing Configuration Settings in Servlets
- Accessing Configuration Settings in Life-Cycle Listeners
- Accessing Configuration Settings in Custom Actions

Chapter 6

Most of the JSTL actions discussed in the following chapters use configuration settings to create or access resources such as SQL data sources or resource bundles; for example, the following code prints a localized message:

```
<fmt:setLocale value='fr-CA' scope='request'/>
<fmt:message key='introduction-page-title'/>
```

In the preceding code fragment, the <fmt:setLocale> action assigns a value to a configuration setting known as FMT_LOCALE.[1] The <fmt:message> action uses that configuration setting to retrieve a localized message from an appropriate resource bundle. To effectively use JSTL's internationalization (I18N), formatting, or SQL actions, you must understand how configuration settings work.

You can also separate business and presentation logic by assigning a value to a configuration setting in a business component such as a servlet; for example, you can specify an SQL data source in a servlet, like this:[2]

```
public class InitializationServlet extends HttpServlet {
   public void init() throws ServletException {
      // Create the data source and store it as a configuration
      // variable in application scope
```

---

1. See "I18N Actions" on page 248 for more information about the internationalization actions.
2. See "Database Actions" on page 356 for more information about the SQL actions.

```
    Config.set(getServletContext(), Config.SQL_DATA_SOURCE,
            new MyDataSource());
  }
  public void destroy() {
   Config.remove(getServletContext(), Config.SQL_DATA_SOURCE);
  }
}
```

JSTL provides a `Config` class that implements a number of `static` methods that let you manipulate configuration settings. In the preceding code fragment, the servlet uses `Config.set` and `Config.remove`, respectively, to set the `SQL_DATA_SOURCE` configuration setting in application scope when the servlet is created and to remove it when the servlet is destroyed.

You can also specify an SQL data source with the <sql:setDataSource> action, but specifying it in a business component, such as the servlet in the preceding code fragment, is often preferable because you have complete control over how your data source is created and because keeping that logic out of JSP pages separates your business logic from your presentation logic.

Because it's important to understand JSTL configuration settings to effectively use the I18N, formatting, and SQL actions and because configuration settings let you separate business and presentation logic, this short chapter discusses configuration settings exclusively. If you're not interested in the I18N, formatting, or SQL actions, you can safely skip this chapter for JSTL 1.0; otherwise, let's enter the fascinating world of JSTL configuration settings.

6.1 Overview

In a servlet-based Web application, you can specify application-wide initialization parameters—known as *context initialization parameters*—for your application in the deployment descriptor; for example, the following code fragment stores the value `es-MX` in a context initialization parameter:

```
<!-- Specifying a default locale in WEB-INF/web.xml -->
<web-app>
   <context-param>
      <param-name>
         javax.servlet.jsp.jstl.fmt.locale
      </param-name>

      <param-value>
         es-MX
      </param-value>
```

```
    </context-param>

    ...

</web-app>
```

You might suspect that the parameter name `javax.servlet.jsp.jstl.fmt.locale` serves some official purpose, and you'd be right—if you add that context initialization parameter to your deployment descriptor (`WEB-INF/web.xml`), as in the preceding code fragment, you will set the default locale for JSTL I18N and formatting actions. In the preceding code fragment, that locale is set to Mexican Spanish.

It's often desirable to override settings for a particular scope; for example, you might want to temporarily override the `javax.servlet.jsp.jstl.fmt.locale` context initialization parameter for a page, request, or session, so JSTL lets you create scoped variables that override context initialization parameters. Those scoped variables are known as *configuration variables*, and they are most often created by JSTL actions; for example, you can use the <fmt:setLocale> action like this:

```
<fmt:setLocale value='fr-CA' scope='request'/>
```

The <fmt:setLocale> action in the preceding code fragment creates a French Canadian locale and stores it in a configuration variable in request scope. During the request, that configuration variable will take precedence over the context initialization parameter named `javax.servlet.jsp.jstl.fmt.locale`. When the request is over, the configuration variable is removed, and the default locale returns to the value specified in the context initialization parameter, assuming no other configuration variables of the same name exist in other scopes.

The combination of context initialization parameter and configuration variable is defined by the JSTL specification as a *configuration setting*. Configuration settings let you specify default values with context initialization parameters and subsequently override those defaults with configuration variables with a JSTL action or a business component. Configuration settings are defined by `static` constants in the `javax.servlet.jsp.jstl.core.Config` class and a name that corresponds to that constant; for example, the configuration setting named `javax.servlet.jsp.jstl.locale` is defined by the `FMT_LOCALE` constant in the `Config` class.

You use a configuration setting's *name* in deployment descriptors, but you use the static *constants* in business components, such as servlets or life-cycle listeners. Throughout this book, configuration settings are referred to by their constants; for example, the configuration setting named `javax.servlet.jsp.jstl.fmt.locale` is referred to as the `FMT_LOCALE` configuration setting.

The `FMT_LOCALE` configuration setting discussed in this section is one of six configuration settings in JSTL 1.0. All of the JSTL 1.0 configuration settings are listed in Table 6.1.

Table 6.1   JSTL 1.0 Configuration Settings

Constant[a]	Name[b]
`FMT_LOCALE`	`j.s.j.j.fmt.locale`
`FMT_FALLBACK_LOCALE`	`j.s.j.j.fmt.fallbackLocale`
`FMT_LOCALIZATION_CONTEXT`	`j.s.j.j.fmt.localizationContext`
`FMT_TIME_ZONE`	`j.s.j.j.fmt.timeZone`
`SQL_DATA_SOURCE`	`j.s.j.j.sql.dataSource`
`SQL_MAX_ROWS`	`j.s.j.j.sql.maxRows`

a. The constants are defined by the `javax.servlet.jsp.jstl.core.Config` class.
b. `j.s.j.j = javax.servlet.jsp.jstl`

The first three configuration settings listed in Table 6.1 are used by JSTL I18N and formatting tags. The fourth, which lets you specify a time zone, is used only by formatting actions. The last two let you specify an SQL data source and a limit for database queries.

In JSTL 1.0, four actions change configuration settings. Table 6.2 lists those actions and the configuration settings they modify.

Table 6.2   JSTL 1.0 Actions That Modify Configuration Settings

Action	Configuration Setting
`<fmt:setLocale>`	`FMT_LOCALE`
`<fmt:setBundle>`	`FMT_LOCALIZATION_CONTEXT`
`<fmt:setTimeZone>`	`FMT_TIME_ZONE`
`<sql:setDataSource>`	`SQL_DATA_SOURCE`

Notice that all of the actions in Table 6.2 are named `setXXX`, where `XXX` represents a configuration setting. The `FMT_FALLBACK_LOCALE` and `SQL_MAX_ROWS` configuration settings are not set by any JSTL actions; if you want to set them, you can specify them as context initialization parameters or you can set them in a business component.

Configuration settings all work the same way, so we will focus mostly on one configuration setting—FMT_LOCALE—throughout the rest of this chapter. Learning about that configuration setting will help you understand how all configuration settings work.

The **FMT_LOCALE** Configuration Setting

This book documents JSTL configuration settings with tables like Table 6.3, which documents the FMT_LOCALE configuration setting.

Table 6.3 The FMT_LOCALE Configuration Setting

Config Constant	FMT_LOCALE
Name	javax.servlet.jsp.jstl.fmt.locale
Type	java.lang.String or java.util.Locale
Set by	<fmt:setLocale>, Deployment Descriptor, Config class
Used by	<fmt:bundle>, <fmt:setBundle>, <fmt:message>, <fmt:formatNumber>, <fmt:parseNumber>, <fmt:formatDate>, <fmt:parseDate>

Each configuration setting has a type. All JSTL configuration settings can be specified with a string or an object; for example, you can specify the FMT_LOCALE configuration setting as a string, such as en-US or fr-CA, or as an instance of java.util.Locale.

Table 6.3 also tells you which JSTL actions set the FMT_LOCALE configuration setting (only <fmt:setLocale>) and which actions use it (quite a few).

Temporarily Overriding Configuration Settings

Figure 6–1 shows a simple Web application that illustrates how the FMT_LOCALE configuration setting works. There are two JSP pages in the application. The first page, referred to as Page 1, is shown at startup (shown on the left in Figure 6–1). That page has a submit button that takes you to the second page, referred to as Page 2 (shown on the right in Figure 6–1).

The first thing you need to know to make sense of the application shown in Figure 6–1 is that French is specified as the default locale with a context initialization parameter in the deployment descriptor. That deployment descriptor is listed in Listing 6.1.

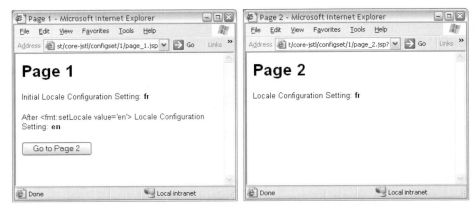

Figure 6–1   Using the `FMT_LOCALE` Configuration Setting

Listing 6.1 *WEB-INF/web.xml*

```xml
<?xml version="1.0" encoding="ISO-8859-1"?>

<!DOCTYPE web-app
   PUBLIC "-//Sun Microsystems, Inc.//DTD Web Application 2.3//EN"
   "http://java.sun.com/j2ee/dtds/web-app_2.3.dtd">

<web-app>
   <context-param>
      <param-name>javax.servlet.jsp.jstl.fmt.locale</param-name>
      <param-value>fr</param-value>
   </context-param>

   <welcome-file-list>
      <welcome-file>page_1.jsp</welcome-file>
   </welcome-file-list>
</web-app>
```

When the application shown in Figure 6–1 starts up, it displays Page 1 (`page_1.jsp`), which is designated as a welcome file in the deployment descriptor. That page uses a scriptlet to print the value of the `FMT_LOCALE` configuration setting, which is initially French (`fr`) because that's what was specified in the deployment descriptor. Listing 6.2 shows how that JSP page is implemented.

The scriptlet that prints the value of the `FMT_LOCALE` configuration setting uses the `static find` method from the JSTL `Config` class to find the value of the

Listing 6.2 *page_1.jsp*

```
<!DOCTYPE HTML PUBLIC "-//W3C//DTD HTML 4.0 Transitional//EN">
<html>
   <head>
      <title>Page 1</title>
   </head>

   <body>
      <%@ taglib uri='http://java.sun.com/jstl/fmt' prefix='fmt'%>
      <%@ page import='javax.servlet.jsp.jstl.core.*' %>

      <h1>Page 1</h1>
      <%-- The following scriptlet prints the value of the
           FMT_LOCALE configuration setting --%>
      <% Object o = Config.find(pageContext, Config.FMT_LOCALE);
         out.print("Initial Locale Configuration Setting: <b>");
         out.print(o + "</b><br>");
      %>

      <fmt:setLocale value='en' scope='page'/>

      <p>
      <% o = Config.find(pageContext, Config.FMT_LOCALE);
         out.print("After &lt;fmt:setLocale value='en'&gt;");
         out.print(" Locale Configuration Setting: <b>" +
                   o + "</b><br>");
      %>

      <form action='page_2.jsp'>
         <input type='submit' value='Go to Page 2'/>
      </form>
   </body>
</html>
```

FMT_LOCALE configuration setting. That method searches for a configuration variable in page, request, session, and application scopes, in that order; if it finds the configuration variable, it returns that variable's value. If the method does not find the configuration variable, it checks to see if a corresponding context initialization parameter exists; if so, it returns that parameter's value. In that way, scoped variables override context initialization parameters for configuration settings.[3]

---

3. See "The Config Class" on page 239 for more information about the Config class.

After it prints the FMT_LOCALE configuration setting, the preceding JSP page uses the <fmt:setLocale> action to override that setting with English for page scope, like this:

```
<fmt:setLocale value='en' scope='page'/>
```

Subsequently, the JSP page prints the FMT_LOCALE configuration setting again, to verify that for Page 1, the default locale has changed from French to English.

When you click on the submit button in Page 1, the browser loads Page 2, which is listed in Listing 6.3.

Listing 6.3	*page_2.jsp*

```
<!DOCTYPE HTML PUBLIC "-//W3C//DTD HTML 4.0 Transitional//EN">
<html>
    <head>
        <title>Page 2</title>
    </head>

    <body>
        <%@ page import='javax.servlet.jsp.jstl.core.*' %>

        <h1>Page 2</h1>
        <% Object o = Config.find(pageContext, Config.FMT_LOCALE);
            out.print("Locale Configuration Setting: <b>" +
                        o + "</b><br>");
        %>
    </body>
</html>
```

Page 2 (page_2.jsp), listed above, prints the FMT_LOCALE configuration setting with the same scriptlet used in Page 1.

Clicking on the submit button in Page 1 generates a new request, so the English override of the context initialization parameter in Page 1—which was specified for *page* scope—goes out of scope. Because that override goes out of scope, the FMT_LOCALE configuration setting for Page 2 returns to French.

What would happen if you changed this line of code from Page 1:

```
<fmt:setLocale value='en' scope='page'/>
```

to this:

```
<fmt:setLocale value='en' scope='request'/>
```

Will the output be different? No, because clicking on the Go to Page 2 button generates a *new request*, and the <fmt:setLocale> action in Page 1 sets the FMT_LOCALE configuration setting for the *current request*, so the setting once again goes out of scope. If you want to change the FMT_LOCALE configuration setting for Page 2, you can specify session or application scope for <fmt:setLocale>, like this:

```
<fmt:setLocale value='en' scope='session'/>
```

With the <fmt:setLocale> scope attribute set to session, as in the preceding code fragment, the FMT_LOCALE configuration setting will hold for Page 2, as shown in Figure 6–2.

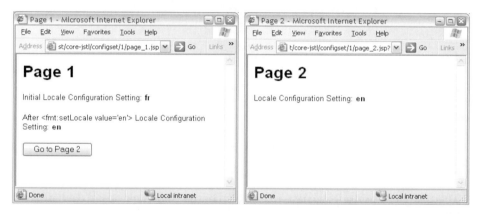

Figure 6–2   Overriding the FMT_LOCALE Configuration Setting in Session Scope

6.2 The Config Class

The Config class, which resides in the javax.servlet.jsp.jstl.core package, defines the following static methods:

```
Object find(PageContext pc, String name);

Object get(PageContext pc, String name, int scope);
Object get(ServletRequest request, String name);
Object get(HttpSession session, String name);
Object get(ServletContext context, String name);

void set(PageContext pc, String name, Object value,
         int scope);
void set(ServletRequest request, String name, Object value);
```

```
void set(HttpSession session, String name, Object value);
void set(ServletContext context, String name, Object value);

void remove(PageContext pc, String name, int scope);
void remove(ServletRequest request, String name);
void remove(HttpSession session, String name);
void remove(ServletContext context, String name);
```

The `find` method searches all four scopes: page, request, session, and application, in that order, for a scoped variable with the specified name. When it finds a scoped variable, the search is over, and the method returns the scoped variable's value. If the method does not find a scoped variable, it returns the value of the context initialization parameter of the same name. If the method does not find a scoped variable and no context initialization parameter was specified, the method returns `null`.

The `get`, `set`, and `remove` methods let you manipulate configuration settings for various scopes from JSP pages, servlets, life-cycle listeners, servlet filters, and custom tags; for example, `Config.set(PageContext, String name, Object value, int scope)` lets you set a configuration setting, in a *scope that you specify*, from a JSP page or a custom action, whereas `Config.set(HttpSession, String name, Object value)` lets you set a configuration setting for a *session*. The latter method can be called from a servlet or life-cycle listener, whereas the former, which requires a page context, can only be called from a scriptlet or custom action because it requires a `PageContext`.

The `Config` class also defines a `static` constant for each of the configuration settings. Those constants are listed in Table 6.1 on page 234; how they are used is discussed in the rest of this chapter, which explores accessing configuration settings in servlets, life-cycle listeners, and custom actions.

Accessing Configuration Settings in Servlets

JSTL actions let you do lots of interesting things in JSP pages, but there's still a place for servlets in most JSP-based Web applications because servlets are excellent for encapsulating business and controller logic. Because of their utility and ubiquity, you may wish to access configuration settings from servlets, like the servlet listed in Listing 6.4.

The servlet listed in Listing 6.4 uses the `Config` class to set the `FMT_LOCALE` configuration setting for application scope when the servlet starts and rescinds that setting when the servlet is destroyed. That servlet is functionally equivalent to the deployment descriptor listed in Listing 6.1 on page 236; both the servlet and the deployment descriptor set the `FMT_LOCALE` configuration setting when their respective applications are loaded.

| Listing 6.4 | *WEB-INF/classes/InitializationServlet.java* |

```
import javax.servlet.*;
import javax.servlet.http.*;
import javax.servlet.jsp.jstl.core.Config;

public class InitializationServlet extends HttpServlet {
   public void init() throws ServletException {
      Config.set(getServletContext(), Config.FMT_LOCALE, "fr");
   }
   public void destroy() {
      Config.remove(getServletContext(), Config.FMT_LOCALE);
   }
}
```

Notice that the servlet listed in Listing 6.4 specifies a French locale with the string fr, but it could have specified that locale with an instance of java.util.Locale, like this:

```
Config.set(getServletContext(), Config.FMT_LOCALE,
         java.util.Locale.FRENCH);
```

The servlet listed in Listing 6.4 must be loaded when the Web application is loaded, to ensure that the FMT_LOCALE configuration setting is in effect when the application runs. You specify that load-on-startup behavior in your deployment descriptor; for example, Listing 6.5 lists the deployment descriptor that declares the servlet listed in Listing 6.4.

The <load-on-startup> element specifies that the servlet must be loaded when the Web server starts.

Before we move on to life-cycle listeners, here's something to consider: Is the servlet discussed in this section equivalent to setting a context initialization parameter for the default locale, as we did in "Overview" on page 232?

The servlet discussed in this section is functionally equivalent to setting the FMT_LOCALE configuration setting in a deployment descriptor. Both approaches specify the FMT_LOCALE configuration setting for your application, and both can be temporarily overridden if you set the FMT_LOCALE configuration setting for page, request, or session scope. There is one small distinction, however. The servlet creates a *configuration variable* that's stored in application scope, whereas the deployment descriptor declares a *context initialization parameter*. The only practical difference between the two is that the configuration variable can be removed or replaced, whereas the context initialization parameter cannot, but the net effect is the same:

Listing 6.5	*WEB-INF/web.xml*

```
<?xml version="1.0" encoding="ISO-8859-1"?>

<!DOCTYPE web-app
    PUBLIC "-//Sun Microsystems, Inc.//DTD Web Application 2.3//EN"
    "http://java.sun.com/j2ee/dtds/web-app_2.3.dtd">

<web-app>
   <servlet>
      <servlet-name>initServlet</servlet-name>
      <servlet-class>InitializationServlet</servlet-class>
      <load-on-startup/>
   </servlet>

   <welcome-file-list>
      <welcome-file>page_1.jsp</welcome-file>
   </welcome-file-list>
</web-app>
```

`Config.find` will find the configuration setting in both cases, as long as they have not been temporarily overridden in another scope.[4]

Accessing Configuration Settings in Life-Cycle Listeners

You can also manipulate JSTL configuration settings with life-cycle listeners; for example, you might have a listener that sets the `FMT_LOCALE` configuration setting in accordance with a user's preferences whenever a session is activated for that user.

Listing 6.6 lists a simple life-cycle listener that is functionally equivalent to the servlet listed in Listing 6.4.

The preceding life-cycle listener is functionally equivalent to the deployment descriptor listed in Listing 6.1 on page 236 and the servlet listed in Listing 6.4; the listener, servlet, and deployment descriptor all set the `FMT_LOCALE` configuration setting in application scope when their respective applications are loaded.

Life-cycle listeners must be declared in a deployment descriptor. Listing 6.7 lists the deployment descriptor that declares the preceding life-cycle listener.

Because JSP containers use introspection on listener classes to discover the listener's type, you only have to declare a listener's class in your deployment descriptor. That type dictates when the listener's methods are invoked; for example, the listener listed in Listing 6.6 extends `ServletContextListener`, and

---

4. See "Temporarily Overriding Configuration Settings" on page 235 for more information about overriding configuration settings.

Listing 6.6 *WEB-INF/classes/listeners/LocaleListener.java*

```java
package listeners;

import javax.servlet.*;
import javax.servlet.jsp.jstl.core.Config;

public class LocaleListener implements ServletContextListener {
    public void contextInitialized(ServletContextEvent e) {
        Config.set(e.getServletContext(), Config.FMT_LOCALE, "fr");
    }
    public void contextDestroyed(ServletContextEvent e) {
        Config.remove(e.getServletContext(), Config.FMT_LOCALE);
    }
}
```

Listing 6.7 *WEB-INF/web.xml*

```xml
<?xml version="1.0" encoding="ISO-8859-1"?>

<!DOCTYPE web-app
  PUBLIC "-//Sun Microsystems, Inc.//DTD Web Application 2.3//EN"
  "http://java.sun.com/j2ee/dtds/web-app_2.3.dtd">

<web-app>
   <listener>
      <listener-class>
         listeners.DataSourceListener
      </listener-class>
   </listener>

   <welcome-file-list>
      <welcome-file>page_1.jsp</welcome-file>
   </welcome-file-list>
</web-app>
```

therefore its `contextInitialized` and `contextDestroyed` methods are called when its servlet context is initialized and destroyed, respectively.

Accessing Configuration Settings in Custom Actions

This section rounds out our discussion of configuration settings by showing you how to access all of them in a custom action. Figure 6–3 shows a JSP page that uses that custom action.

The JSP page shown in Figure 6–3 is listed in Listing 6.8.

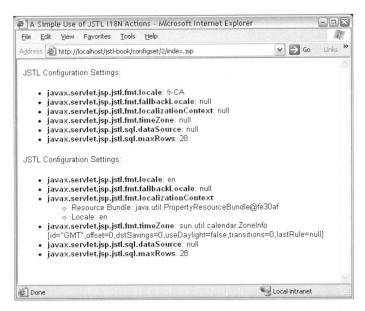

Figure 6–3   Using a Custom Action That Prints Configuration Settings

Listing 6.8   *index.jsp*

```
<!DOCTYPE HTML PUBLIC "-//W3C//DTD HTML 4.0 Transitional//EN">
<html>
   <head>
      <title>A Simple Use of JSTL I18N Actions</title>
   </head>

   <body>
      <%@ taglib uri='WEB-INF/core-jstl.tld 'prefix='core-jstl'%>
      <%@ taglib uri='http://java.sun.com/jstl/fmt' prefix='fmt'%>

      <core-jstl:showConfigSettings/>

      <fmt:setLocale value='en'/>
      <fmt:setBundle basename='company'/>
      <fmt:setTimeZone value='GMT'/>

      <core-jstl:showConfigSettings/>
   </body>
</html>
```

The preceding JSP page uses the custom action <core-jstl:showConfigSettings> to display all of the JSTL configuration settings, before and after setting the locale, bundle, and time zone configuration settings. Initially, the FMT_LOCALE and

SQL_MAX_ROWS configuration settings are set to fr-CA and 28, respectively, in the application's deployment descriptor. That deployment descriptor is listed in Listing 6.9.

Listing 6.9 *WEB-INF/web.xml*

```xml
<?xml version="1.0" encoding="ISO-8859-1"?>

<!DOCTYPE web-app
   PUBLIC "-//Sun Microsystems, Inc.//DTD Web Application 2.3//EN"
   "http://java.sun.com/j2ee/dtds/web-app_2.3.dtd">

<web-app>
   <context-param>
      <param-name>javax.servlet.jsp.jstl.fmt.locale</param-name>
      <param-value>fr-CA</param-value>
   </context-param>

   <context-param>
      <param-name>javax.servlet.jsp.jstl.sql.maxRows</param-name>
      <param-value>28</param-value>
   </context-param>

   <welcome-file-list>
      <welcome-file>
         index.jsp
      </welcome-file>
   </welcome-file-list>
</web-app>
```

The preceding deployment descriptor also specifies a welcome file. The Tag Library Descriptor (TLD) for the tag library is listed in Listing 6.10.

The preceding Tag Library Descriptor (TLD) specifies the tag library and its lone custom action. The tag handler for that custom action is listed in Listing 6.11.

Like the servlet and life-cycle listener discussed in Listing 6.4 on page 241 and Listing 6.6 on page 243, respectively, the tag handler listed above uses the Config class to access configuration settings. That tag handler prints all of the configuration settings, with special handling of the localization context setting, which specifies two things: a resource bundle and a locale.[5] Notice that the FMT_LOCALIZATION_CONTEXT configuration setting, like all JSTL configuration settings, can be specified with a string.[6] The tag handler listed in Listing 6.11 takes that possibility into account.

---

5. See "Localization Contexts" on page 263 for more information about localization contexts.
6. If you specify the FMT_LOCALIZATION_CONTEXT as a string, that string represents a resource bundle base name. See "Resource Bundles" on page 259 for more information about resource bundles.

Listing 6.10 *WEB-INF/core-jstl.tld*

```
<?xml version="1.0" encoding="ISO-8859-1"?>
<!DOCTYPE taglib PUBLIC
  "-//Sun Microsystems, Inc.//DTD JSP Tag Library 1.2//EN"
  "http://java.sun.com/j2ee/dtds/web-jsptaglibrary_1_2.dtd">

<taglib>
   <tlib-version>1.0</tlib-version>
   <jsp-version>1.2</jsp-version>
   <short-name>Core JSTL Example</short-name>
   <description>
      Show Configuration Settings with a Custom Action
   </description>

   <tag>
      <name>showConfigSettings</name>
      <tag-class>tags.ShowConfigSettingsTag</tag-class>
      <body-content>empty</body-content>
      <description>Shows configuration settings</description>
   </tag>
</taglib>
```

Listing 6.11 *WEB-INF/classes/tags/ShowConfigSettingsTag.java*

```
package tags;

import java.io.*;
import javax.servlet.jsp.*;
import javax.servlet.jsp.tagext.*;
import javax.servlet.http.*;

import javax.servlet.jsp.jstl.core.Config;
import javax.servlet.jsp.jstl.fmt.LocalizationContext;

public class ShowConfigSettingsTag extends TagSupport {
   private static String[] settings = {
      Config.FMT_LOCALE,                Config.FMT_FALLBACK_LOCALE,
      Config.FMT_LOCALIZATION_CONTEXT,Config.FMT_TIME_ZONE,
      Config.SQL_DATA_SOURCE,        Config.SQL_MAX_ROWS
   };

   public int doStartTag() throws JspException {
      try {
         JspWriter out = pageContext.getOut();

         out.print("JSTL Configuration Settings:<p><ul>");
```

Listing 6.11 *WEB-INF/classes/tags/ShowConfigSettingsTag.java (cont.)*

```java
        for(int i=0; i < settings.length; ++i) {
            String name = settings[i];
            Object o = Config.find(pageContext, name);
            out.print("<li><b>" + name + "</b>: ");

            if(o == null)
                out.print("null<br>");
            else {
                if(name.equals(Config.FMT_LOCALIZATION_CONTEXT)) {
                    // Like all JSTL configuration settings, the
                    // FMT_LOCALIZATION_CONTEXT setting can be
                    // specified with a string...
                    if(o instanceof java.lang.String)
                        out.println(o);
                    else {
                        LocalizationContext lc =
                                            (LocalizationContext)o;
                        out.print("<ul><li>Resource Bundle: ");
                        out.println(lc.getResourceBundle());
                        out.print("<li>Locale: ");
                        out.println(lc.getLocale() + "</ul>");
                    }
                }
                else {
                    out.print(o);
                }
            }
        }
        out.print("</ul></ul>");
    }
    catch(java.io.IOException ex) {
        throw new JspException(ex.getMessage());
    }
    return SKIP_BODY;
    }
}
```

In addition to illustrating how to access configuration settings from a custom action, you may also find the custom action discussed in this section useful as a debugging tool when you use the JSTL I18N, formatting, or SQL actions.

Now that you have a good understanding of JSTL configuration settings, you are ready to move on to the more advanced JSTL actions that let you internationalize your website, access a database, and use XML.

I18N ACTIONS

Topics in This Chapter

- Overview
- I18N and L10N
- Localization Contexts
- An Overview of the I18N Actions
- Use of <fmt:message>
- Request EncodingRequest Encoding
- I18N Custom Actions

Chapter 7

At the end of the 20th century, with the World Wide Web in its infancy, most Web sites were implemented for a single language, but that's starting to change as more Web sites offer content in multiple languages. Web sites that adapt to a reader's native language and customs have an obvious competitive advantage over those that do not.

JSTL provides a number of actions that help you internationalize your Web sites:

- <fmt:setLocale>
- <fmt:setBundle>
- <fmt:bundle>
- <fmt:message>
- <fmt:param>
- <fmt:requestEncoding>

JSTL also provides a handful of actions for formatting and parsing numbers, currencies, percents, and dates in a locale-dependent manner; those actions are discussed in "Formatting Actions" on page 308.

This chapter begins with an overview of the first five actions listed above, followed by an introduction to internationalization concepts, including locales, resource bundles, Unicode, and charsets. Subsequently, we discuss how you can make the most of the JSTL actions listed above.

If you don't know anything about the JSTL internationalization (I18N) actions or if you need to brush up on internationalization, you should read this entire chapter. If you're already familiar with the <fmt:message> action but you're not entirely comfortable with locales, resource bundles, charsets and Unicode, you can probably start reading at "I18N and L10N" on page 258.[1] If you've already used the <fmt:message> action and you understand the basics of internationalization, you can begin reading at "Localization Contexts" on page 263.

7.1 Overview

Before we begin, you should understand two basic concepts: *locales* and *resource bundles*. A locale is an identifier for a language and, optionally, a country; for example, the locale en specifies the English language, and the locale en-US specifies United States English. Resource bundles store locale-sensitive information in key/value pairs; for example, you might find the key/value pair greeting=hello in an English resource bundle, and the corresponding greeting=bonjour in a French resource bundle.

Resource bundles are defined by properties files or Java classes. Resource bundles are named with a base name and a locale; for example, you could define a resource in a properties file named errorMessages_en.properties. In that case, the *resource bundle base name* is errorMessages and the locale is en, for English. A corresponding properties file representing the French version (locale fr) of that resource bundle would be named errorMessages_fr.properties.

You typically internationalize Web applications in one of two ways:

* You implement multiple JSP pages, one for each locale that you support. Typically, a controller servlet will select which JSP page to display depending upon a user's preferred locales.

* You store locale-sensitive information in resource bundles, and JSP pages retrieve and display that information.

The first option listed above is labor intensive—you must duplicate every JSP page for each locale that you support. Because of the labor-intensive nature of that option, it is usually only viable when different locales require programmatic differences, such as different page layouts.

---

1. The abbreviations I18N and L10N represent the first and last characters and the number of characters in between the words internationalization and localization, respectively.

Most of the time, the second option listed above is preferred because it's easier to implement and maintain. Instead of multiple JSP pages for each supported locale, you implement a single JSP page that extracts locale-sensitive information from resource bundles.

For the most part, JSTL supports only the second option listed above, although you can use JSTL formatting tags to produce localized output for locale-specific JSP pages. Because JSTL actions are mainly intended for the second option listed above, this book discusses only that option.

Localizing Messages

Let's start our examination of the JSTL internationalization actions with a very simple internationalized Web application, shown in Figure 7–1.

Figure 7–1   A Simple Internationalized Web Application. The left picture shows the English version; the right picture shows the French version.

The Web application shown in Figure 7–1 consists of one JSP page and two resource bundles, one for English and another for French; that JSP page is listed in Listing 7.1.

The preceding JSP page uses <fmt:message> actions to display localized messages from a resource bundle. That resource bundle is defined by a locale and a resource bundle base name, which are specified with the <fmt:setLocale> and <fmt:setBundle> actions, respectively.

Using <fmt:message> is easy: you specify a key, and the action displays the key's value, which it extracts from a resource bundle; for example, in the preceding JSP page, the first <fmt:message> action prints the value—Widgets, Inc.—for the key company.name. That key/value pair is defined in the properties file listed in Listing 7.2.

Listing 7.1   *A JSP Page That Displays Localized Messages*

```
<!DOCTYPE HTML PUBLIC "-//W3C//DTD HTML 4.0 Transitional//EN">
<html>
   <head>
      <%@ taglib uri='http://java.sun.com/jstl/fmt' prefix='fmt'%>

      <%-- Specify a locale and a resource bundle base name for
           the <fmt:message> actions in this page --%>
      <fmt:setLocale value='en'/>
      <fmt:setBundle basename='messages'/>

      <%-- Use <fmt:message> to display the page title --%>
      <title><fmt:message key='page.title'/></title>
   </head>

   <body>
      <%-- Use <fmt:message> to display localized messages
           from the messages resource bundle --%>
      <font size='5'>
         <fmt:message key='company.name'/>
      </font>

      <p><fmt:message key='company.slogan'/>
      <hr>
   </body>
</html>
```

Listing 7.2   *WEB-INF/classes/messages_en.properties*

```
# English properties file

page.title=Localizing Messages
company.name=Widgets, Inc.
company.slogan=We Make the World's Best Widget
```

All <fmt:message> actions extract localized messages from a resource bundle. That resource bundle's name is the concatenation of a resource bundle base name with a locale, separated by an underscore; in this case, the appropriate resource bundle is messages_en.properties.[2]

---

2. The actual algorithm for locating a resource bundle is more complex; see "The Resource Bundle Lookup Algorithm" on page 276 for a complete description of that algorithm.

Switching locales is easy for the JSP page listed in Listing 7.1—you just change the value specified for the <fmt:setLocale> action; for example, to switch the JSP page shown in Figure 7–1 to French, you specify the locale as `fr`, like this:

```
...
<html>
   <head>
      ...
      <fmt:setLocale value='fr'/>
      ...
   </head>
   ...
</html>
```

Of course, you must have a corresponding French resource bundle; the properties file representing that resource bundle—`messages_fr.properties`—is listed in Listing 7.3.

Listing 7.3   *WEB-INF/classes/messages_fr.properties*

```
# French properties file

page.title=Localiser les Messages
company.name=Widgets, Inc.
company.slogan=Nous Faisons le Meilleur Widget du Monde
```

As you can tell from the Listing 7.2 and Listing 7.3 titles, the properties files for the Web application shown in Figure 7–1 reside in the `WEB-INF/classes` directory. That directory is where JSP containers look for Web application components, such as servlets, JavaBeans components (beans), custom JSP tags, and properties files. For complex Web applications, that directory can get cluttered in a hurry, so developers often put Web application components in `WEB-INF/classes` *subdirectories* that are typically qualified by company names; for example, if you worked for Acme Inc., you might put your properties files in a `WEB-INF/classes/com/acme` directory.

If you put your properties files in a `WEB-INF/classes` subdirectory, the resource bundle base name that you specify with <fmt:setBundle> must reflect that subdirectory; for example, the JSP page listed in Listing 7.4 is identical to the JSP page listed in Listing 7.1, except that the former specifies a resource bundle that corresponds to a properties file in a `WEB-INF/classes/com/acme` subdirectory.

Notice that the resource bundle base name specified in Listing 7.4 is `com.acme.messages`. That resource bundle base name tells the servlet container

| Listing 7.4 | *Accessing Properties Files in a WEB-INF/classes Subdirectory* |

```
<!DOCTYPE HTML PUBLIC "-//W3C//DTD HTML 4.0 Transitional//EN">
<html>
   <head>
      <%@ taglib uri='http://java.sun.com/jstl/fmt' prefix='fmt'%>

      <%-- Specify a locale and a resource bundle base name for
           the <fmt:message> actions in this page --%>
      <fmt:setLocale value='en'/>
      <fmt:setBundle basename='com.acme.messages'/>

      <%-- Use <fmt:message> to display the page title --%>
      <title>
         <fmt:message key='page.title'/>
      </title>
   </head>

   <body>
      <%-- Use <fmt:message> to display localized messages
           from the com.acme.messages resource bundle --%>
      <font size='5'>
         <fmt:message key='company.name'/>
      </font>

      <p><fmt:message key='company.slogan'/>
      <hr>
   </body>
</html>
```

that your messages resource bundle corresponds to a properties file (or a Java class file) in the WEB-INF/classes/com/acme directory. Whenever you place properties files in a subdirectory of WEB-INF/classes, you must specify your resource bundle base name in the same manner; for example, if you have a myMessages_en.properties file in a WEB-INF/classes/com/myCompany/ resources directory, you must specify your resource bundle base name like this: com.myCompany.resources.myMessages.

Multiple Resource Bundles

The preceding example illustrates the fundamentals of JSTL I18N actions. Those actions are very flexible, and they let you localize messages in a number of different ways. For example, the JSP page shown in Figure 7–2 uses two resource bundles.

Figure 7–2   Using Multiple Resource Bundles

The JSP page shown in Figure 7–2 is identical to the application shown in Figure 7–1, except that it also accesses a localized error message from a second resource bundle. The JSP page shown in Figure 7–2 is listed in Listing 7.5.

The <fmt:bundle> action establishes a resource bundle that's only used by <fmt:message> actions in its body. In the preceding JSP page, the <fmt:bundle> action specifies an `errors` resource bundle base name. The corresponding properties file, `WEB-INF/classes/errors_en.properties`, represents the English resource bundle. The properties file has only one key/value pair that is listed below.

```
error.cantFindResource=Resource Not Found
```

The corresponding entry in the French properties file— `WEB-INF/classes/errors_fr.properties`—is listed below.

```
error.cantFindResource=Ne pas Trouvez le Resource
```

Compound Messages

You can also use <fmt:message> with compound messages. A compound message is a message that contains one or more parameters; for example, the application shown in Figure 7–3 specifies the name of a resource with a parameter.

The JSP page shown in Figure 7–3 is listed in Listing 7.6.

In the preceding JSP page, both the <fmt:bundle> and <fmt:message> actions have a body. As in Listing 7.5, the bundle base name specified for <fmt:bundle> applies only to <fmt:message> actions in the body of the <fmt:bundle> action. The body of the <fmt:message> action contains a <fmt:param> action that specifies a parameter for the message. Compound messages specify parameters in curly braces; for example, the English message for the preceding code fragment looks like this:

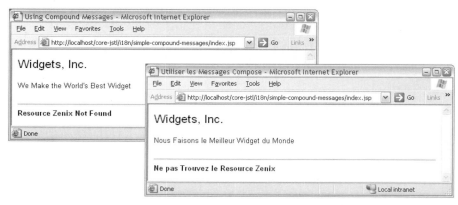

Figure 7–3   Compound Messages

Listing 7.5   *A JSP Page That Uses Multiple Resource Bundles*

```
<!DOCTYPE HTML PUBLIC "-//W3C//DTD HTML 4.0 Transitional//EN">
<html>
   <head>
      <%@ taglib uri='http://java.sun.com/jstl/fmt' prefix='fmt'%>

      <%-- Specify a locale and a resource bundle base name for
           the <fmt:message> actions in this page --%>
      <fmt:setLocale value='en'/>
      <fmt:setBundle basename='messages'/>

      <%-- Use <fmt:message> to display the page title --%>
      <title><fmt:message key='page.title'/></title>
   </head>

   <body>
      <%-- Use <fmt:message> to display localized messages
           from the messages resource bundle --%>
      <font size='5'><fmt:message key='company.name'/></font>
      <p><fmt:message key='company.slogan'/></p>

      <hr>

      <fmt:bundle basename='errors'>
         <%-- <fmt:message> actions in the body of the enclosing
              <fmt:bundle> action display localized messages from
              the errors resource bundle --%>
         <b><fmt:message key='error.cantFindResource'/></b>
      </fmt:bundle>
   </body>
</html>
```

Listing 7.6 *A JSP Page That Uses Compound Messages*

```
<!DOCTYPE HTML PUBLIC "-//W3C//DTD HTML 4.0 Transitional//EN">
<html>
    <head>
        <%@ taglib uri='http://java.sun.com/jstl/core' prefix='c'%>
        <%@ taglib uri='http://java.sun.com/jstl/fmt'  pre-
fix='fmt'%>

        <%-- Specify a locale and a resource bundle base name for
             the <fmt:message> actions in this page --%>
        <fmt:setLocale value='fr'/>
        <fmt:setBundle basename='messages'/>

        <%-- Use <fmt:message> to display the page title --%>
        <title><fmt:message key='page.title'/></title>
    </head>

    <body>
        <%-- Use <fmt:message> to display localized messages
             from the messages resource bundle --%>
        <font size='5'><fmt:message key='company.name'/></font>
        <p><fmt:message key='company.slogan'/></p>

        <hr>

        <%-- Normally, the scoped variable specified below would
             come from a data store or would be calculated. Here
             we create it with <c:set> for illustration. --%>
        <c:set var='resourceName' value='Zenix'/>

        <fmt:bundle basename='errors'>
            <%-- <fmt:message> actions in the body of the enclosing
                 <fmt:bundle> action display localized messages from
                 the errors resource bundle --%>
            <b><fmt:message key='error.cantFindResource'>
                <fmt:param value='${resourceName}'/>
            </fmt:message></b>
        </fmt:bundle>
    </body>
</html>
```

```
Resource {0} Not Found
```

And the French version is:

```
Ne pas Trouvez le Resource {0}
```

The parameter specified for the <fmt:param> action is substituted for {0} in the compound message. Messages can have any number of parameters, specified with

{0} through {n-1}, where n represents the number of parameters. For every parameter specified in a message, you should specify a corresponding <fmt:param> action in the body of the <fmt:message> action.

JSTL I18N actions have other features that we examine throughout the rest of this chapter; but first we need to discuss the basics of internationalization and localization. If you are already familiar with locales, resource bundles, Unicode, and charsets, you can skip the next section and start reading "An Overview of the I18N Actions" on page 264.

7.2 I18N and L10N

Internationalization, often abbreviated as I18N, is the process of implementing applications that support multiple locales. With JSTL, internationalization is performed with the actions introduced in "Overview" on page 250.

Localization, often abbreviated as L10N, is the process of adapting an internationalized application to support a specific locale. For the most part, with JSTL, that means creating a set of resource bundles for specific locales.

To develop internationalized Web applications that you can subsequently localize, you must have a basic understanding of locales, resource bundles, Unicode, and charsets, all of which are discussed in the following sections.

Locales

The most basic localization task is identifying geographical, political, or cultural regions, known as locales. Locale constants for countries and languages are defined by the International Standards Organization (ISO). Table 7.1 lists some examples of locale constants for selected countries.

Table 7.1   Examples of ISO Country Locale Constants

Country	Code
Canada	CA
China	CN
Germany	DE
Iceland	IS
Italy	IT
Mexico	MX
United States	US

For a complete list of country locale constants, see the following URL:

```
http://www.iso.org/iso/en/prods-services/iso3166ma/
02iso-3166-code-lists/list-en1.html
```

Table 7.2 lists some examples of language locale constants.

Table 7.2   Examples of Language Locale Constants

Language	Code
French	`fr`
Chinese	`zh`
German	`de`
Icelandic	`is`
Italian	`it`
Spanish	`es`
English	`en`

For a complete list of language locale constants, see the following URL:

```
http://www-old.ics.uci.edu/pub/ietf/http/related/
iso639.txt
```

When you specify a locale with <fmt:setLocale> or by specifying the FMT_LOCALE configuration setting directly,[3] you can specify a language, such as `fr` for French, or a language-country combination, such as `fr-CA`, for Canadian French. If you specify a language-country combination, you can use either a hyphen or an underscore to separate the language and country, so you can write Canadian French as `fr-CA` or `fr_CA`. The language code must always precede the country code.

You can also specify a variant for a locale. Variants are vendor- and browser-specific. For example, you can specify the variants `WIN` for Microsoft Windows or `MAC` for Macintosh. You can specify a locale variant with the <fmt:setLocale> action's `variant` attribute; for example, you could specify the Macintosh variant for France French like this: `<fmt:setLocale value='fr-FR' variant='MAC'/>`. In practice, locale variants are rarely used.

Resource Bundles

As we discussed in "Overview" on page 250, a resource bundle is a collection of key/value pairs. You can specify resource bundles with a properties file or with a Java class.

---

   3. See "Configuration Settings" on page 230 for more information about specifying
       configuration settings directly with servlets and life-cycle listeners.

Properties files are by far the most popular way to specify resource bundles, even though a resource bundle specified as a Java class is more flexible than one specified as a properties file. The reasons for that popularity are simple—properties files are easier to create than Java classes, and they do not need to be compiled.

Resource bundles, whether they are specified with a properties file or implemented as a Java class, must reside in either the `WEB-INF/classes` directory or a subdirectory of `WEB-INF/classes`.

Resource Bundles as Properties Files

Listing 7.7 lists a simple properties file that specifies localized messages in English for a login page.

Listing 7.7	*A Properties File That Represents a Resource Bundle*

```
# Application Properties -- English Version

login.window-title=Localized Error Messages
login.first-name=First Name
login.last-name=Last Name
login.email-address=Email Address
```

In a properties file, lines beginning with the # character are comments. Key/value pairs are specified with this syntax: *key=value*. In a properties file, both keys and values are always strings.

Resource Bundles as Java Classes

Listing 7.8 lists a Java class that specifies a resource bundle equivalent to the one represented by the properties file listed in Listing 7.7.

The Java class in the preceding listing extends `java.util.ListResource Bundle`, which defines one abstract method: `getContents`. That method returns a two-dimensional array of objects containing key/value pairs.

Specifying a resource bundle with a Java class is more flexible than using a properties file because values are not limited to strings, as is the case for properties files. Also, if you specify a resource bundle with a Java class, you can calculate values, which you cannot do in a properties file. In practice, those features are rarely used, and as a result properties files are the preferred method of specifying resource bundles.

Unicode and Charsets

Internally, the Java programming language uses Unicode to store characters. Unicode is a character coding system that assigns unique numbers for every character for every major language in the world.

Listing 7.8 *A Java Class That Represents a Resource Bundle*

```
import java.util.ListResourceBundle;

// Application Properties -- English Version

public class app_en extends ListResourceBundle {
    private static final Object[][] contents = {
        { "login.window-title",  "Localized Error Messages" },
        { "login.first-name",    "First Name" },
        { "login.last-name",     "Last Name" },
        { "login.email-address", "Email Address" },
    };
    public Object[][] getContents() {
        return contents;
    }
}
```

Java's use of Unicode means that JSP pages can store and display strings containing all characters found in all of the commonly used written languages. It also means that you can use Unicode escape sequences to represent characters that you may not find on your keyboard; Table 7.3 lists some of those characters.

Table 7.3 Unicode Escape Sequence Examples

UnicodeEscape	Symbol	Description
\u00C0	Á	Capital A, accent grave
\u00C9	È	Capital E, accent acute
\u00C9	Â	Capital A, accent circumflex
\u00A9	©	Copyright symbol
\u0099	™	Trademark
\u00B6	¶	Paragraph Sign
\u0086	†	Dagger Symbol

At their most fundamental level, browsers map bytes to characters or glyphs; for example, browsers will map \u00A9 to the copyright symbol. Those mappings are facilitated by a *charset*, which is defined as *a method of converting a sequence of bytes into a sequence of characters*.[4] The default charset for JSP pages is

---

4. That definition comes from RFC 2278—see http://www.faqs.org/rfcs/rfc2278.html.

ISO-8859-1, which maps bytes to characters for Latin-based languages. Table 7.4 lists charsets for a few languages.

Table 7.4   Charset Examples

Language	Language Code	Charset(s)
Chinese (Simplified/Mainland)	zh	GB2312
Chinese (Traditional/Taiwan)	zh	Big5
English	en	ISO-8859-1
French	fr	ISO-8859-15
German	de	ISO-8859-15
Icelandic	is	ISO-8859-1
Italian	it	ISO-8859-15
Japanese	ja	Shift_JIS, ISO-2022-JP, EUC-JP
Korean	ko	EUC-KR
Russian	ru	ISO-8859-5, KO18-R
Spanish	es	ISO-8859-15

There is also a single charset that can be used for all languages—the Universal Character Set (UCS), defined in 1993 by the ISO and the IEC.

The UCS can encode all of the characters and symbols for all of the written languages of the world, with room to spare. With 31 bits to represent each character or symbol, the UCS has room for a whopping 2 billion of them. That's the bad news, though, because most applications can only handle 16-bit encodings. The good news for the UCS is that it's Unicode compatible.

The majority of applications can't handle the UCS encoding, but because of its usefulness and compatibility with Unicode, a few transform encodings were developed, the most popular of which is UTF-8 (UCS Transformation Format 8). The UTF-8 charset transforms UCS into 1-, 2-, or 3-byte encodings, and because it preserves the US ASCII range, UTF-8 can transmit US ASCII as single bytes, which is much more efficient than the UCS. Those properties make UTF-8 the most widely used format for displaying multiple languages. In addition, many of the newer specifications from W3C and IETF use UTF-8 as a default character set. Internally, the Java programming language uses UTF-8 in .class files and for Java serialization.

See Listing 7.9 on page 280 for an example of a Web application that uses the UTF-8 charset.

7.3 **Localization Contexts**

As "Localizing Messages" on page 251 illustrated, <fmt:message> actions retrieve localized messages from a resource bundle. That resource bundle and the locale that was used to locate it are stored in a *localization context*, which is a simple bean that maintains a reference to a resource bundle and a locale. The <fmt:message> actions use the localization context's resource bundle, and the JSTL formatting actions use its locale.[5]

All of the examples in "Localizing Messages" on page 251 establish a localization context with a combination of <fmt:setLocale> and <fmt:setBundle> actions, for example:

```
<fmt:setLocale value='en-US'/>
<fmt:setBundle basename='messages'/>
...
<fmt:message key='someKey'/>
```

In the preceding code fragment, the <fmt:setLocale> action stores the U.S. English locale in a configuration setting named FMT_LOCALE.[6] Subsequently, the <fmt:setBundle> action performs a resource bundle lookup—see "Resource Bundle Lookup" on page 274 for the exact details of that lookup—using the locale stored in the FMT_LOCALE configuration setting and the resource bundle base name specified with the basename attribute. If that lookup was successful, <fmt:setBundle> stores the resource bundle and the locale that was used to locate it in a localization context and stores that localization context in a configuration setting named FMT_LOCALIZATION_CONTEXT. Subsequently, the <fmt:message> action uses the resource bundle stored in the localization context that <fmt:setBundle> stored in the FMT_LOCALIZATION_CONTEXT configuration setting.

All <fmt:message> actions use the (resource bundle stored in the) localization context stored in the FMT_LOCALIZATION_CONTEXT configuration setting to retrieve localized messages, except for <fmt:message> actions that are nested in <fmt:bundle> actions, like this:

```
<fmt:bundle basename='app'>
   <%-- The following <fmt:message> action uses the localization
   context created by the enclosing <fmt:bundle> action --%>
   <fmt:message key='someKey'/>
</fmt:bundle>
```

---

5. See "Formatting Actions" on page 308 for more information about formatting actions.
6. See "Configuration Settings" on page 230 for more information about configuration settings.

The <fmt:bundle> action creates a localization context that is used exclusively by <fmt:message> actions and formatting actions that are nested in the <fmt:bundle> action. That localization context temporarily overrides the localization context stored in the FMT_LOCALIZATION_CONTEXT configuration setting.

Now that we understand what a localization context is and how it's created and used by the I18N actions, let's take a closer look at those actions.

7.4 An Overview of the I18N Actions

The JSTL internationalization actions, which were listed at the beginning of this chapter and introduced in "Overview" on page 250, are listed in Table 7.5.

Table 7.5 JSTL Internationalization Actions

Action	Description
<fmt:setLocale>	Stores a locale in the FMT_LOCALE configuration setting. That configuration setting is used by <fmt:bundle> and <fmt:setBundle> actions to establish a localization context. The FMT_LOCALE configuration setting is also used by JSTL formatting actions. See "Formatting Actions" on page 308 for more information about formatting actions.
<fmt:setBundle>	Finds a resource bundle corresponding to the mandatory basename attribute and stores that resource bundle, along with the locale that was used to locate it, in a localization context stored in the FMT_LOCALIZATION_CONTEXT configuration setting. That resource bundle is only used by subsequent <fmt:message> actions, and the locale is only used by formatting actions.
<fmt:bundle>	Loads a resource bundle specified with the mandatory basename attribute and stores that resource bundle, along with the locale that was used to locate it, in a localization context. The resource bundle stored in the localization context is used by <fmt:message> actions in the body of the <fmt:bundle> action, and the locale stored in the localization context is used by formatting actions in the body of the <fmt:bundle> action.
<fmt:message>	Retrieves a localized message that corresponds to a key from a resource bundle. The <fmt:message> action sends that message to the current JspWriter or stores it in a scoped variable if the var attribute was specified.

Table 7.5   JSTL Internationalization Actions *(cont.)*

Action	Description
<fmt:param>	Specifies a single parameter for a compound message. That parameter is used by an enclosing <fmt:message> action.
<fmt:requestEncoding>	Sets the character encoding for an HTTP request. This action is used to properly decode request parameters that were encoded in a charset other than ISO-8859-1.[a]

a. See "Request Encoding" on page 287 for more information about <fmt:requestEncoding>.

JSTL uses three configuration settings for internationalization. Those configuration settings are listed in Table 7.6.

Table 7.6   JSTL Internationalization Configuration Settings[a]

Setting	Description
FMT_LOCALE (j.s.j.j.fmt.locale)	Specifies a default locale for <fmt:message>. If you specify this configuration setting, you disable the preferred locales set for your browser. You can set this configuration setting with <fmt:setLocale>.
FMT_FALLBACK_LOCALE (j.s.j.j.fmt. fallbacklocale)	Specifies a fallback locale that <fmt:bundle> and <fmt:setBundle> use to find a resource bundle.
FMT_LOCALIZATION_CONTEXT (j.s.j.j.fmt. localizationContext)	This configuration setting specifies a localization context used by I18N and formatting actions. A localization context is a bean with two properties: a resource bundle and locale.[b]

a. j.s.j.j = javax.servlet.jsp.jstl
b. See "Localization Contexts" on page 263.

The JSTL actions and configuration settings listed in the preceding tables are discussed in more detail throughout the rest of this chapter.

7.5 Use of <fmt:message>

The JSTL I18N actions all work together for one purpose: *to retrieve localized messages from resource bundles.*[7] The <fmt:message> action is responsible for that specific task, so nearly all the other I18N actions—<fmt:setLocale>,

<fmt:setBundle>, <fmt:bundle>, and <fmt:param>—exist, in one way or another, to support <fmt:message>. The <fmt:message> action extracts localized messages from a resource bundle with this syntax:[8]

<fmt:message key [bundle] [var] [scope]/>

The `key` attribute, which is mandatory in the preceding syntax, specifies a key in a resource bundle. Usually, <fmt:message> actions search for a localization context (that contains a resource bundle) themselves, but you can also specify a localization context with the optional `bundle` attribute.

<fmt:message> actions send their localized message to the current `JspWriter` or, if you specify the `var` and `scope` attributes, to a scoped variable. Here are three examples of how you can use <fmt:message> with the preceding syntax:

```
<fmt:message key='greeting'/>
<fmt:message key='greeting' var='msg' scope='request'/>
<fmt:message key='greeting' bundle='${aLocalizationContext}'/>
```

The first line of the preceding code fragment shows the simplest use of <fmt:message>: you only specify the `key` attribute. This is by far the most popular way to use <fmt:message>—you don't have to come up with a localization context on your own, and <fmt:message> prints to the current `JspWriter`. In most cases, that `JspWriter` prints to the browser, which is usually what you want.

The second line of the preceding code fragment shows how you can use <fmt:message> to store a localized message in a scoped variable. In that line of code, the <fmt:message> action stores a localized message in a scoped variable named `msg` in request scope. If you don't specify the `scope` attribute, for example, `<fmt:message key='greeting' var='msg'/>`, <fmt:message> will store the scoped variable in page scope. Later on, you can access that scoped variable with `<c:out value='${msg}'/>`, which will print the localized message that you stored in the `msg` scoped variable.

The third line of the preceding code fragment shows how you can use the `bundle` attribute to specify an explicit localization context for <fmt:message>.[9] A localization context—see "Localization Contexts" on page 263—is a simple bean that contains a resource bundle and a locale; if you specify a localization context with the `bundle` attribute, the corresponding <fmt:message> action will use that localization context's resource bundle to retrieve a localized message. This use of <fmt:message>

---

7. An exception is <fmt:requestEncoding>; see "Request Encoding" on page 287

8. Items in brackets are optional. See "<fmt:message" on page 502 for a complete description of <fmt:message> syntax.

9. The word bundle is a misnomer. The <fmt:message> `bundle` attribute used to refer to a resource bundle, but now it refers to a localization context.

is not very popular, because it's cumbersome to specify a localization context every time you use <fmt:message>.

You can also localize compound messages with <fmt:message>, with this syntax:

<fmt:message key [bundle] [var] [scope]>
      <fmt:param> actions
</fmt:message>

A compound message contains parameters; for example, at the bottom of your website you might show the current date with a compound message that looks like this: Today is: {0}, where {0} is a parameter that specifies the current date. You could do that like this:

```
<jsp:useBean id='now' class='java.util.Date'/>

<fmt:message key='footer.messages.todaysDate'>
   <fmt:param value='${now}'/>
</fmt:message>
```

The preceding code fragment uses <jsp:useBean> to create a Java bean—an instance of java.util.Date. A <fmt:param> action specifies that bean as a parameter for its enclosing <fmt:message> action. That <fmt:message> action substitutes the bean's value for {0} in the compound message. In a resource bundle, you would specify that compound message like this:

```
footer.messages.todaysDate=Today is: {0}
```

See "Compound Messages and <fmt:param>" on page 283 for more information about compound messages and message parameters. Also, see Listing 7.16 on page 285 for an alternative to <jsp:useBean> in the preceding code fragment by using the fmt_rt tag library.

The <fmt:message> action also lets you specify the message key in the body of the action, with this syntax:

<fmt:message [var] [scope] [bundle]>
      key
      optional <fmt:param> actions
</fmt:message>

Long message keys and message keys produced by custom actions are two reasons for the preceding syntax; for example, you might store categories for user preferences as message keys, and you might access those categories with custom actions, so you could do this:

```
<fmt:message>
  <acme:preference category='SESSION_TIMEOUT'/>
</fmt:message>
```

In the preceding code fragment, the <acme:preference> custom action returns the message key associated with a user's session timeout; e.g., `preferences.session.timeout`. That key is used by <fmt:message> to display a localized message; for example, `User Session Timeout`, for an English locale. That technique essentially lets you create constant values for message keys, so that you can change the keys without changing your JSP pages.

If you specify a `null` value or an empty string for the <fmt:message> key attribute, that <fmt:message> action will produce this message: `??????`. If a <fmt:message> action cannot locate a localization context or if the specified key is not defined in the resource bundle stored in the localization context, <fmt:message> will produce output that looks like this: `???<key>???`, where <key> represents the value that you specified for the action's `key` attribute.

Localization Context Lookup

As we saw in "Use of <fmt:message>" on page 265, <fmt:message> actions use a resource bundle stored in a localization context to turn message keys into localized messages. To locate a localization context, all <fmt:message> actions perform a *localization context lookup*; once they find a localization context, they use its resource bundle to localize their messages. That lookup works like this:

1. If the <fmt:message> *bundle attribute* is specified, use it.
2. If the <fmt:message> action is *nested in a <fmt:bundle> action*, use the enclosing <fmt:bundle> action's localization context.
3. Use the `FMT_LOCALIZATION_CONTEXT` *configuration setting*.

Core Approach

It's easy to remember how <fmt:message> actions search for a localization context if you realize that <fmt:message> searches *from within itself* (the `bundle` attribute) *outward* to its enclosing <fmt:bundle> action, if any, and then to the `FMT_LOCALIZATION_CONTEXT` configuration setting, which applies to a specific scope.

Let's discuss each of the steps listed above.

1. If the <fmt:message> *bundle attribute* is specified, use it.

First, <fmt:message> checks to see if you specified its `bundle` attribute, for example:

```
<fmt:message key='footer.messages.title' bundle='${messages}'/>
```

If you specify the `bundle` attribute, <fmt:message> assumes that the `bundle` attribute's value (`${messages}` in the preceding code fragment) is a localization context, and it uses that localization context's resource bundle to localize its message. That localization context is most often created by business components, but you can easily create one in a scriptlet, like this:[10]

```
<%@ page import='javax.servlet.jsp.jstl.fmt.LocalizationContext'%>
<%@ page import='java.util.*'%>

<% ResourceBundle rb =
    ResourceBundle.getBundle("messages", Locale.FRENCH);

    LocalizationContext lc = new LocalizationContext(rb);
    pageContext.setAttribute("messages", lc);
%>

<fmt:message key='company.slogan' bundle='${messages}'/>
```

The preceding code fragment retrieves a French resource bundle, which is used to create a localization context. The scriptlet stores the localization context in page scope by using `PageContext.setAttribute`. Subsequently, a <fmt:message> action accesses that localization context by specifying it with the action's `bundle` attribute.

Specifying a localization context with the <fmt:message> `bundle` attribute is cumbersome because you have to specify that localization context for every <fmt:message> action. It would be better if you could group <fmt:message> actions that use the same localization context; in fact, you can do just that with the <fmt:bundle> action, which is discussed next.

2. If the <fmt:message> action is *nested in a <fmt:bundle>*, use the enclosing <fmt:bundle> action's localization context.

If you don't specify the `bundle` attribute—as is usually the case—<fmt:message> actions check to see if they are nested in a <fmt:bundle> action. Here's the syntax for <fmt:bundle>:[11]

---

10. The scriptlet approach is not recommended; it's shown here for illustration only.
11. Items in brackets are optional. See "<fmt:bundle>" on page 500 for a complete description of <fmt:bundle> syntax, including the `prefix` attribute.

<fmt:bundle basename [prefix]>

> *body content, presumably with I18N or formatting actions, or both*

</fmt:bundle>

All <fmt:message> actions in the body of a <fmt:bundle> action implicitly access the localization context of their enclosing <fmt:bundle> action; for example, in the following code fragment, the first two <fmt:message> actions use the localization context established by their enclosing <fmt:bundle> action.

```
<fmt:bundle basename='messages'>
    <%-- The two <fmt:message> actions that follow use the resource
        bundle associated with the bundle base name "messages" --%>
    <fmt:message key='login.title'/>

    <fmt:message key='login.welcome'/>


    <%-- This <fmt:message> action uses a different
        localization context --%>
    <fmt:message key='login.footer' bundle='${footers}'/>
</fmt:bundle>
```

The third <fmt:message> action in the preceding code fragment uses a localization context that contains a resource bundle whose base name is footers. Because <fmt:message> actions check their bundle attribute first, that attribute overrides the localization context established by an enclosing <fmt:bundle>; so, in the preceding code fragment, the footers localization context overrides the messages localization context for the third <fmt:message> action.

The <fmt:bundle> action has a mandatory basename attribute that specifies a resource bundle base name. That attribute is a string that <fmt:bundle> actions use to search for a resource bundle, which is subsequently stored in the <fmt:bundle> action's localization context. See "The Resource Bundle Lookup Algorithm" on page 276 for more information about that resource bundle search.

The <fmt:bundle> action is great for grouping <fmt:message> actions that use the same localization context, so you don't have to specify a localization context for every <fmt:message> action. But <fmt:bundle> cannot span JSP pages; it would be nice if you could specify a localization context for all <fmt:message> actions in a particular scope, say, request or session. You can do that with the <fmt:setBundle> action, which is discussed below.

3. Use the FMT_LOCALIZATION_CONTEXT configuration setting.

If a <fmt:message> action is free-standing (meaning it's not enclosed in a <fmt:bundle> action) and its `bundle` attribute is not specified, then the <fmt:message> action looks for a localization context in the FMT_LOCALIZATION_CONTEXT configuration setting; for example:

```
<%-- The following <fmt:message> action is not nested in
<fmt:bundle> and does not specify the bundle attribute, so it uses
the FMT_LOCALIZATION_CONTEXT configuration setting --%>

<fmt:message key='footer.messages.title'/>
```

The FMT_LOCALIZATION_CONTEXT configuration setting is listed in Table 7.7.

Table 7.7   `FMT_LOCALIZATION_CONTEXT` Configuration Setting

Config Constant	FMT_LOCALIZATION_CONTEXT
Name	`javax.servlet.jsp.jstl.fmt.localizationContext`
Type	`java.lang.String` or `javax.servlet.jsp.jstl.fmt.LocalizationContext`
Set by	<fmt:setBundle>, Deployment Descriptor, `Config` class
Used by	<fmt:message>, <fmt:formatNumber>, <fmt:parseNumber>, <fmt:formatDate>, <fmt:parseDate>

In a nutshell, a JSTL configuration setting is a combination of a context initialization parameter and a scoped variable, where the latter can override the former. Configuration settings are searched for in this order: page scope, request scope, session scope, application scope, context initialization parameter.[12]

Because you can specify a configuration setting as a string, you can specify the FMT_LOCALIZATION_CONTEXT configuration setting as a context initialization parameter in a deployment descriptor, like this:

```
<web-app>
   ...
   <context-param>
```

---

12. See "Configuration Settings" on page 230 for more information about configuration settings.

```
        <param-name>
            javax.servlet.jsp.jstl.fmt.localizationContext
        </param-name>

        <param-value>
            messages
        </param-value>
    </context-param>
    ...
</web-app>
```

The preceding fragment of a deployment descriptor (WEB-INF/web.xml) declares a context initialization parameter named javax.servlet.jsp.jstl. localizationContext, which is the name of the FMT_LOCALIZATION_ CONTEXT configuration setting (see Table 7.7).

In a JSP page, you can override that context initialization parameter with the <fmt:setBundle> action—which, as you can see from Table 7.7, is the only JSTL action that sets the FMT_LOCALIZATION_CONTEXT configuration setting. Here's the <fmt:setBundle> syntax:[13]

<fmt:setBundle basename [var] [scope]/>

Like <fmt:bundle>, <fmt:setBundle> has a mandatory basename attribute that specifies a resource bundle basename; for example:

```
<fmt:setBundle basename='messages' scope='request'/>
```

The <fmt:setBundle> action in the preceding line of code locates a resource bundle based on the action's mandatory basename attribute (messages), and stores that resource bundle in the localization context stored in the FMT_LOCALIZATION_CONTEXT configuration setting. Instead of storing the localization context in that configuration setting, <fmt:setBundle> will store it in a scoped variable if you specify the var, and optionally the scope, attribute.

Whether you specify the FMT_LOCALIZATION_CONTEXT configuration setting in a deployment descriptor or with the <fmt:setBundle> action, you specify a resource bundle base name. That base name, combined with a locale, specifies a resource bundle; for example, an English resource bundle for error messages might be named errors_en.properties, where errors is the resource bundle base name.[14]

You can also specify the FMT_LOCALIZATION_CONTEXT configuration setting in a business component, such as a servlet like the one listed below:[15]

---

13. Items in brackets are optional. See "<fmt:setBundle>" on page 498 for a complete description of <fmt:setBundle> syntax.

14. See "Resource Bundles" on page 259 for more information about resource bundles and resource bundle base names.

```
...
import javax.servlet.jsp.jstl.core.Config;

public class InitializationServlet extends HttpServlet {
    public void init() throws ServletException {
        // Create a localization context and store it in
        // the FMT_LOCALIZATION_CONTEXT configuration setting

        Config.set(getServletContext(),
                Config.FMT_LOCALIZATION_CONTEXT,
                "messages"); // resource bundle base name
    }
}
```

When the servlet in the preceding code fragment starts, it sets the
FMT_LOCALIZATION_CONTEXT configuration setting with the string messages,
which represents a resource bundle base name. The preceding servlet uses the
Config class from the javax.servlet.jsp.jstl.core package to set the
FMT_LOCALIZATION_CONTEXT configuration setting. See "The Config Class" on
page 239 for more information about how you use the Config class.

You can also specify the FMT_LOCALIZATION_CONTEXT configuration setting
with an instance of javax.servlet.jsp.jstl.LocalizationContext; for
example, the preceding servlet could be modified as follows:

```
...
import java.util.Locale;
import java.util.ResourceBundle;
import javax.servlet.jsp.jstl.core.Config;
import javax.servlet.jsp.jstl.fmt.LocalizationContext;

public class InitializationServlet extends HttpServlet {
    public void init() throws ServletException {
        ...
        Locale l = Locale.US;
        ResourceBundle rb = ResourceBundle.getBundle("basename", l);

        Config.set(getServletContext(),
                Config.FMT_LOCALIZATION_CONTEXT,
                new LocalizationContext(rb, l));
        ...
    }
}
```

---

15. See "The Config Class" on page 239 for more information about the Config class.

This section discussed the localization context lookup. The next section discusses how a localization context's resource bundle, if not explicitly specified, is determined.

Resource Bundle Lookup

We've covered some ground since we started discussing <fmt:message> at "Use of <fmt:message>" on page 265; here are the highlights:

- <fmt:message> retrieves localized messages from resource bundles stored in localization contexts.

- <fmt:message> performs a localization context lookup by searching in the following locations:

  1. The <fmt:message> `bundle` attribute
  2. An enclosing <fmt:bundle> action
  3. The `FMT_LOCALIZATION_CONTEXT` configuration setting

- <fmt:bundle> lets you specify a single localization context for a group of <fmt:message> actions nested in the <fmt:bundle> action.

- <fmt:setBundle> lets you specify a localization context for a given scope. That localization context is shared by <fmt:message> actions in that scope.

<fmt:message> actions perform a *localization context lookup* to find a localization context they can use to localize messages. Those localization contexts are, for the most part, created by <fmt:bundle> or <fmt:setBundle>, both of which perform a *resource bundle lookup*, given a resource bundle base name. If you specify a string for the `FMT_LOCALIZATION_CONTEXT` configuration setting, <fmt:message> actions will also perform a resource bundle lookup, using that string as a resource bundle base name. We've already discussed localization context lookups in "Localization Context Lookup" on page 268, so this section focuses on the resource bundle lookup performed by <fmt:bundle>, <fmt:setBundle>, and <fmt:message>.

The resource bundle lookup performed by <fmt:bundle>, <fmt:setBundle>, and <fmt:message> requires two pieces of information: a resource bundle base name and one or more locales. You specify a resource bundle base name with the <fmt:bundle> and <fmt:setBundle> mandatory `bundle` attributes. The next section shows you how to specify the locale.

Locales

You can specify the locale(s) that the <fmt:bundle>, <fmt:setBundle>, and <fmt:message> actions use to find a resource bundle in one of two ways:

- The set of preferred locales that you specify in your browser
- The `FMT_LOCALE` configuration setting

By default, the resource bundle lookup uses your browser's preferred locales, but you can override that default with the `FMT_LOCALE` configuration setting. There are many ways to set the `FMT_LOCALE` configuration setting; for example, with a servlet, life-cycle listener, or custom action—"Configuration Settings" on page 230 shows you how to do all those things. The `FMT_LOCALE` configuration setting is listed in Table 7.8.

Table 7.8   The FMT_LOCALE Configuration Setting

Config Constant	FMT_LOCALE
Name	`javax.servlet.jsp.jstl.fmt.locale`
Type	`java.lang.String` or `java.util.Locale`
Set by	<fmt:setLocale>, Deployment Descriptor, `Config` class
Used by	<fmt:bundle>, <fmt:setBundle>, <fmt:message>, <fmt:formatNumber>, <fmt:parseNumber>, <fmt:formatDate>, <fmt:parseDate>

You can also set the `FMT_LOCALE` configuration setting with the <fmt:setLocale> action. That action has the following syntax:[16]

<fmt:setLocale value [variant] [scope]/>

The <fmt:setLocale> `value` attribute specifies a locale as either a language or a language-country combination, such as `fr` or `fr-CA`. The `variant` attribute specifies a browser- or vendor-specific value, such as `WIN` for Windows or `MAC` for Macintosh. See "Locales" on page 258 for more information about locales and variants. In practice, variants are seldom used.

The `scope` attribute, which can be `page`, `request`, `session`, or `application`, specifies the scope to which the locale applies. For example, if you specify application scope, the locale specified with the `value` attribute will apply to all JSP pages in your application. The default scope is `page`.

---

16. Items in brackets are optional. See "<fmt:setLocale>" on page 496 for a more complete description of <fmt:setLocale> syntax.

The Resource Bundle Lookup Algorithm

The resource bundle lookup algorithm performed by <fmt:message>, <fmt:bundle>, and <fmt:setBundle> starts with a resource bundle base name and a list of preferred locales. If you've set the FMT_LOCALE configuration setting, then your list of preferred locales consists of the single locale. If you haven't set the FMT_LOCALE configuration setting, then your browser's list of preferred locales will be used.

For each preferred locale in order of preference, JSTL searches for resource bundles in WEB-INF/classes—or a subdirectory of WEB-INF/classes—with the following names:

> basename + "_" + language + "_" + country + "_" + variant + "." + class
> basename + "_" + language + "_" + country + "_" + variant + "." + properties
> basename + "_" + language + "_" + country + "." + class
> basename + "_" + language + "_" + country + "." + properties
> basename + "_" + language + "." + class
> basename + "_" + language + "." + properties

For the preceding names, *basename* represents a bundle base name, and *language*, *country*, and *variant* are specified by a locale. As soon as a match is found, the algorithm selects that resource bundle and stops.

If the set of available resource bundles changes during the execution of a page, the resulting behavior is undefined; leaving that behavior undefined allows implementations to cache resource bundles to improve performance.

If no resource bundle is found for any of the preferred locales, the resource bundle lookup is applied to the *fallback* locale, which you can set with the FMT_FALLBACK_LOCALE configuration variable.[17]

If <fmt:bundle>, <fmt:setBundle>, or <fmt:message> cannot find a resource bundle with the preferred locales or the fallback locale, they try to find a resource bundle with only the base name.

To help clarify the resource bundle search algorithm, here are some examples that illustrate how the algorithm works:

Example 1:

- *Bundle base name*: Resources
- *Preferred locales*: en_GB, fr_CA

---

17. None of the JSTL actions set the FMT_FALLBACK_LOCALE configuration setting, so it's most often set in the deployment descriptor with a context initialization parameter.

- *Fallback locale:* `fr_CA`
- *Application resource bundles*:
  `/WEB-INF/classes/Resources_en.class`,
  `/WEB-INF/classes/Resources_fr_CA.properties`

The algorithm matches the `en_GB` locale with this Java class: `/WEB-INF/classes/Resources_en.class`.

Example 2:

- *Bundle base name*: Resources
- *Preferred locales*: `de, fr`
- *Fallback locale:* `en`
- *Application resource bundles*:
  `/WEB-INF/classes/Resources_en.properties`

The algorithm does not find a match for the `de` or `fr` locales, but it does find a match for the fallback locale; therefore, the selected resource bundle is specified with this properties file: `/WEB-INF/classes/Resources_en.properties`.

Example 3:

- *Bundle base name*: Resources
- *Preferred locales*: `fr, sv, en`
- *Fallback locale:* `de`
- *Application resource bundles*:
  `/WEB-INF/classes/Resources_fr_CA.properties`,
  `/WEB-INF/classes/Resources_sv.properties`,
  `/WEB-INF/classes/Resources_en.properties`,
  `/WEB-INF/classes/Resources_de.class`

The algorithm does not find a match for the `fr` locale, because that locale specifies French, not *Canadian* French. The algorithm does find a match for the `sv` locale (Swedish), and therefore selects the resource bundle specified with the properties file `/WEB-INF/classes/Resources_sv.properties`.

In this case, even though the user prefers French over Swedish and has a French resource bundle, that resource bundle will not be selected, because it is Canadian French. This example illustrates that resource bundles for a specific language and country should be backed up with a resource bundle covering just the language. If the country-specific differences for a language are too significant for a language-only bundle, users should specify two locales with both language and country in their list of preferred locales.

An Example of Dynamically Switching Locales

This section discusses a Web application, shown in Figure 7–4, that lets users change their locale by clicking on an image of a flag. Changing the locale initiates the resource bundle search algorithm discussed in "The Resource Bundle Lookup Algorithm" on page 276, which changes the current resource bundle. The Login button does not initiate a login; for the sake of illustration, it simply reloads the login page.

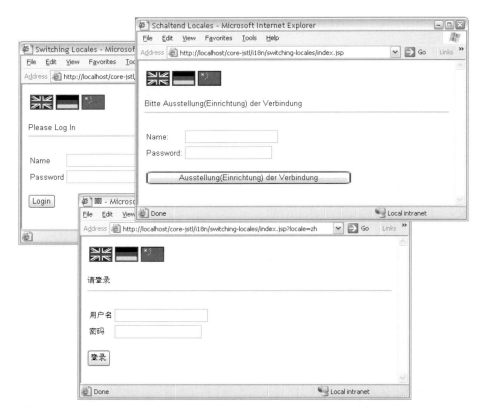

Figure 7–4   Using <fmt:setLocale>—Clicking on a Flag Switches Locales

The application shown in Figure 7–4 consists of three JSP pages: index.jsp, flags.jsp, and set_locale.jsp. Figure 7–4 only shows index.jsp, localized for English, German, and Chinese. The application also has three properties files in the WEB-INF/classes directory that represent resource bundles for English, German, and Chinese: app_en.properties, app_de.properties, and app_zh.properties, respectively.

As an aside, notice that the window title for the Chinese version of the application is not properly displayed. That's because the window uses the system charset and the application was run under Windows English. Because that charset does not support Chinese, the window itself cannot properly display characters in Chinese. The window title would be properly displayed if the application were run on an operating system that used the Chinese charset.

The JSP page shown in Figure 7–4 is listed in Listing 7.9, and the associated properties files are shown in Listings 7.10, 7.11, and 7.12.

The preceding JSP page sets its charset to `UTF-8` to support multiple locales; see "Unicode and Charsets" on page 260 for more information about charsets and `UTF-8`. The preceding JSP page uses <fmt:setBundle> to specify a bundle base name for the JSP page. The application's properties files are listed below.

The Chinese properties file—`app_zh.properties`—specifies messages with Unicode escape sequences; see "Unicode and Charsets" on page 260 for more information about Unicode.

The JSP page listed in Listing 7.9 also imports `flags.jsp` and `set_locale.jsp`. The former displays the flags, and the latter sets the locale, depending on which flag was last selected.

When the application is started, no flags have been selected, so the locale is determined from the `javax.servlet.jsp.jstl.fmt.locale` context initialization parameter, which is specified in `WEB-INF/web.xml`. Listing 7.13 lists an excerpt from that deployment descriptor.

In the preceding listing, the `FMT_LOCALE` configuration variable (whose value is `javax.servlet.jsp.jstl.fmt.locale`) is set to `de`, so the application shown in Figure 7–4 is initially displayed in German.

`flags.jsp` is listed in Listing 7.14.

The preceding JSP page displays the flags shown in Figure 7–4 on page 278. When you click on one of those flags, the current page in which `flags.jsp` resides is reloaded with the corresponding `locale` request parameter.

Note that the preceding JSP page uses the rather unusual HTML construct `<a href='?XXX'>`. That construct causes the current HTML (or JSP) page to be reloaded with `XXX` appended to the page's URL as a request parameter. That construct comes in handy for developing reusable HTML or JSP components, such as the JSP page listed in Listing 7.14. You can read about that construct in section 4.0 (Resolving Relative URLs) of RFC 1808; that RFC is available online at this URL: `http://www.ietf.org/rfc/rfc1808.txt`.

The JSP page `set_locale.jsp`, which sets the locale according to the last flag selected, is listed in Listing 7.15.

The preceding JSP page sets the locale for the user's session with <fmt:setLocale>, depending on the value of the `locale` request parameter. If that request parameter has not been set, the preceding JSP page does nothing.

Listing 7.9   *index.jsp*

```
<!DOCTYPE HTML PUBLIC "-//W3C//DTD HTML 4.0 Transitional//EN">
<html>
   <head>
      <%-- Set the charset to UTF-8 for multiple language
           support --%>
      <%@ page contentType='text/html; charset=UTF-8' %>

      <%@ taglib uri='http://java.sun.com/jstl/fmt'  prefix='fmt'%>
      <%@ taglib uri='http://java.sun.com/jstl/core' prefix='c'%>

      <%-- set_locale.jsp sets the locale according to the locale
           request parameter that is set by flags.jsp, which is
           imported below. set_locale.jsp uses <fmt:setLocale>--%>
      <c:import url='set_locale.jsp'/>

      <%-- Establish a localization context (based on the locale
           set by set_locale.jsp and the bundle base name specified
           for <fmt:setBundle>) used by subsequent <fmt:message>
           actions. Because the locale set by set_locale.jsp is
           used to establish that localization context,
           set_locale.jsp must be imported before
           <fmt:setBundle> is used. --%>
      <fmt:setBundle basename='app'/>

      <%-- Use <fmt:message> to show the page title --%>
      <title><fmt:message key='login.page.title'/></title>
   </head>

   <body>
      <%-- flags.jsp shows the flags --%>
      <c:import url='flags.jsp'/><br>

      <%-- All of the <fmt:message> actions that follow will
           use the resource bundle determined by the 'app'
           bundle base name and the locale that was last selected
           by a user clicking on a flag. Initially, that locale is
           set by the javax.servlet.jsp.jstl.fmt.locale
           context init param in WEB-INF/web.xml. --%>

      <fmt:message key='login.form.title'/><hr/>

      <form method='post'>
         <table>
            <tr><td><fmt:message key='login.textfield.name'/></td>
                <td><input type='text' name='userName'/></td>
```

Listing 7.9   *index.jsp (cont.)*

```
            </tr>
            <tr>
                <td><fmt:message key='login.textfield.pwd'/></td>
                <td><input type='password' name='password'/></td>
            </tr>
        </table><br>

        <input type='submit'
               value='<fmt:message key="login.button.submit"/>'/>
    </form>
  </body>
</html>
```

Listing 7.10   *WEB-INF/classes/app_en.properties*

```
login.page.title=Switching Locales
login.form.title=Please Log In
login.textfield.name=Name
login.textfield.pwd=Password
login.button.submit=Login
```

Listing 7.11   *WEB-INF/classes/app_de.properties*

```
login.page.title=Schaltend Locales
login.form.title=Bitte Ausstellung(Einrichtung) der Verbindung
login.textfield.name=Name:
login.textfield.pwd=Password:
login.button.submit=Ausstellung(Einrichtung) der Verbindung
```

Listing 7.12   *WEB-INF/classes/app_zh.properties*

```
login.page.title=\u8bf7\u767b\u5f55
login.form.title=\u8bf7\u767b\u5f55
login.textfield.name=\u7528\u6237\u540d
login.textfield.pwd=\u5bc6\u7801
login.button.submit=\u767b\u5f55
```

Listing 7.13 *WEB-INF/web.xml (Excerpt)*

```xml
<?xml version="1.0" encoding="ISO-8859-1"?>

<!DOCTYPE web-app
  PUBLIC "-//Sun Microsystems, Inc.//DTD Web Application 2.3//EN"
  "http://java.sun.com/j2ee/dtds/web-app_2.3.dtd">

<web-app>
   ...
   <context-param>
      <param-name>
         javax.servlet.jsp.jstl.fmt.locale
      </param-name>
      <param-value>
         de
      </param-value>
   </context-param>
   ...
</web-app>
```

Listing 7.14 *flags.jsp*

```jsp
<table>
   <tr><td>
      <a href='?locale=en'>
         <img src='graphics/flags/britain_flag.gif'/></a>

      <a href='?locale=de'>
         <img src='graphics/flags/german_flag.gif'/></a>

      <a href='?locale=zh'>
         <img src='graphics/flags/chinese_flag.gif'/></a>
   </td></tr>
</table>
```

The <fmt:setLocale> action calls ServletResponse.setLocale(), which is required by the servlet specification, to set the response charset to match the specified locale. Because of that requirement, index.jsp, listed in Listing 7.9 on page 280, should not have to specify the UTF-8 charset; however, some servlet containers do not properly implement that requirement, so the contentType page directive in Listing 7.9 on page 280 is necessary to ensure that the example works with all servlet containers.

Listing 7.15	*set_locale.jsp*

```
<%@ taglib uri='http://java.sun.com/jstl/fmt'  prefix='fmt'%>
<%@ taglib uri='http://java.sun.com/jstl/core' prefix='c'%>

<c:choose>
   <c:when test='${param.locale == "de"}'>
      <fmt:setLocale value='de' scope='session'/>
   </c:when>
   <c:when test='${param.locale == "zh"}'>
      <fmt:setLocale value='zh' scope='session'/>
   </c:when>
   <c:when test='${param.locale == "en"}'>
      <fmt:setLocale value='en' scope='session'/>
   </c:when>
</c:choose>
```

Also, notice that `flags.jsp` and `set_locale.jsp` can be used in any JSP page to switch locales. In fact, those JSP pages, modified to display different flags, are used in the Web applications discussed below and in "Validation with JSP Pages" on page 296.

Compound Messages and <fmt:param>

When you go to the store, you might say, "I'm going to {0}," where {0} represents the name of the store; after all, there are only so many ways to say that you're going to the store. Sometimes you might say, "I'm going to {0} to get {1}."

This phenomenon, known as parameterized text, is commonplace; in fact, you can find many occurrences of "The JSP page shown in {0} is listed in {1}" scattered throughout this book.

You can parameterize text by specifying *compound messages* in your resource bundles. Compound messages specify parameters with {0} to {n-1}, where n represents the number of parameters. <fmt:param> actions, contained within the body of <fmt:message> actions, specify values for those parameters; each <fmt:param> action specifies one parameter for the message displayed by its enclosing <fmt:message> action. The first <fmt:param> action contained within a <fmt:message> action specifies a value for the first parameter, the second <fmt:param> action specifies the second parameter, and so on.

You can use <fmt:param> by specifying a parameter with the `value` attribute, with this syntax:[18]

---

18. See "<fmt:param>" on page 504 for a more complete description of <fmt:param> syntax.

<fmt:param value/>

You can also specify a parameter within the body of a <fmt:param> action, with this syntax:

<fmt:param>
*　　value*
</fmt:param>

Figure 7–5 shows a Web application that uses both <fmt:param> syntaxes.

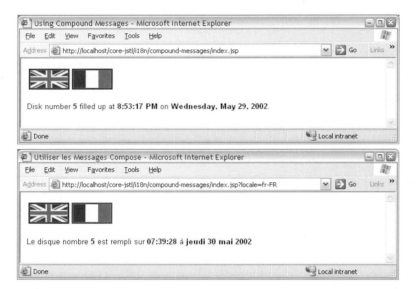

Figure 7–5　　Localizing Compound Messages with <fmt:param> Actions

The Web application shown in Figure 7–5 provides parameters for a disk number and date. The top picture in Figure 7–5 shows the English version of the message, and the bottom picture shows the French version.

The JSP page shown in Figure 7–5 is listed in Listing 7.16.

Like the JSP page shown in Figure 7–4 on page 278, the preceding JSP page imports `set_locale.jsp` and `flags.jsp` so the user can switch locales and sets the bundle base name to `app` for page scope.

The preceding JSP page uses both syntaxes of <fmt:param> to specify parameters for a message specified with the `message.diskFull` key. The <fmt:param> action specifies its value in its body, whereas the <fmt_rt:param> action specifies its value with the `value` attribute. Notice that the second `param` tag uses the runtime expression library version of the `param` action (<fmt_rt:param>) because it creates a

Listing 7.16 *index.jsp*

```
<!DOCTYPE HTML PUBLIC "-//W3C//DTD HTML 4.0 Transitional//EN">
<html>
   <head>
      <%@ taglib uri='http://java.sun.com/jstl/core' prefix='c' %>
      <%@ taglib uri='http://java.sun.com/jstl/fmt'  prefix='fmt'%>
      <%@ taglib uri='http://java.sun.com/jstl/fmt_rt'
              prefix='fmt_rt' %>

      <%-- set_locale.jsp sets the locale according to the locale
           request parameter that is set by flags.jsp, which is
           imported below. set_locale.jsp uses <fmt:setLocale> --%>
      <c:import url='set_locale.jsp'/>

      <%-- Establish a localization context (based on the locale
           set by set_locale.jsp and the bundle base name specified
           for <fmt:setBundle>) used by subsequent <fmt:message>
           actions. Because the locale set by set_locale.jsp is
           used to establish that localization context,
           set_locale.jsp must be imported before
           <fmt:setBundle> is used. --%>
      <fmt:setBundle basename='app'/>

      <title><fmt:message key='page.title'/></title>
   </head>

   <body>
      <c:import url='flags.jsp'/><br/>

      <%-- All of the <fmt:message> actions that follow will
           use the resource bundle determined by the 'app'
           bundle base name and the locale that was last selected
           by the user clicking on a flag. --%>

      <fmt:message key='message.diskFull'>
         <%-- Specify the parameter for the disk number
              in the body of the <fmt:param> action --%>
         <fmt:param>
            5
         </fmt:param>

         <%-- Specify the parameter for the date
              with the <fmt_rt:param> action's value
              attribute --%>
         <fmt_rt:param value='<%= new java.util.Date() %>'/>
      </fmt:message>
   </body>
</html>
```

Java object for its value, which is something you cannot do with the expression language equivalent action (<fmt:param>).[19]

The English and French properties files used by the application shown in Figure 7–5 are listed below.

Listing 7.17 *WEB-INF/classes/app_en.properties*

```
# application properties -- English Version

page.title=Using Compound Messages
message.diskFull=Disk number <b>{0}</b> filled up at \
<b>{1, time}</b> on <b>{1, date, full}</b>.
```

Listing 7.18 *WEB-INF/classes/app_fr.properties*

```
# application properties -- French Version

page.title=Utiliser les Messages Compose
message.diskFull=Le disque nombre <b>{0}</b> est rempli sur \
<b>{1, time}</b>  <b>{1, date, full}</b>
```

The messages in the preceding properties files identify parameters with {0} and {1}. Those parameters are supplied by the <fmt:param> and <fmt_rt:param> actions, respectively.

The preceding properties files also specify *styles* to format the date supplied by <fmt:param>; for example, {1, **time**} specifies the time portion of the date, and {1, **date**, **full**} specifies the full date without the time. You can use other styles, such as {n, percent}, to specify a number as a percent. See the Java documentation for the java.text.MessageFormat class for more information about those styles.

The flags.jsp and set_locale.jsp JSP pages imported by the preceding JSP page are nearly identical to the JSP pages of the same name discussed in "An Example of Dynamically Switching Locales" on page 278, except for the flags and locales they support. Those files are listed in Listing 7.19 and Listing 7.20 for completeness.

---

19. But you can use <fmt:param> in combination with <jsp:useBean>; see "Use of <fmt:message>" on page 265.

Listing 7.19   *flags.jsp*

```
<table>
   <tr><td>
      <a href='?locale=en-GB'>
         <img src='graphics/flags/united-kingdom-flag.gif'/></a>

      <a href='?locale=fr-FR'>
         <img src='graphics/flags/french-flag.gif'/></a>
   </td></tr>
</table>
```

Listing 7.20   *set_locale.jsp*

```
<%@ taglib uri='http://java.sun.com/jstl/core'prefix='c' %>
<%@ taglib uri='http://java.sun.com/jstl/fmt' prefix='fmt'%>

<c:choose>
   <c:when test='${param.locale == "fr-FR"}'>
      <fmt:setLocale value='fr-FR' scope='request'/>
   </c:when>
   <c:when test='${param.locale == "en-GB"}'>
      <fmt:setLocale value='en-GB' scope='request'/>
   </c:when>
</c:choose>
```

7.6 Request Encoding

If you have a Web application with HTML forms and your form data are encoded with a charset other than the default charset (ISO-8859-1), odds are that your form data will not be properly decoded when they are accessed as request parameters. The reason for this encoding/decoding mismatch is that most browsers do not properly handle the Content-Type header.

The HTTP specification defines a Content-Type request header that browsers can use to specify request encodings, but most browsers never set this request header. Because of this oversight, a page specified as a form's action will assume that the form's request parameters were encoded with the default charset (ISO-8859-1) and attempt to decode the request parameters with that encoding. If the request parameters were encoded with a charset other than ISO-8859-1, they will not be properly decoded by the form's action.

Let's examine the Web application shown in Figure 7–6 to see how Internet Explorer 6.0 fails to properly decode request parameters generated by forms with a charset other than ISO-8859-1.

Figure 7–6   Reading Request Parameters from Forms with a Chinese Charset

The Web application shown in Figure 7–6, localized for Chinese, consists of two JSP pages, one containing a simple form that asks for a user's name and another that tries to display the name that was entered in the form.

The JSP page containing the form is listed in Listing 7.21.

The preceding JSP page uses the JSP page directive to set the Content-Type header, specifying Mainland Chinese (GB2312) for the response charset. This is verified by the <c:out> action at the bottom of the page, which prints the character encoding for the page's response. As you can see from Figure 7–6, the response charset for the preceding JSP pages is indeed GB2312.

The action for the form in the preceding JSP page is show_parameters.jsp, which is listed in Listing 7.22.

The preceding JSP page sets its *response* charset to Mainland Chinese (GB2312) and tries to display the name request parameter, but as you can see from Figure 7–6,

Listing 7.21   *index.jsp*

```
<!DOCTYPE HTML PUBLIC "-//W3C//DTD HTML 4.0 Transitional//EN">
<html>
    <head>
        <title>Broken Request Decoding</title>
    </head>

    <body>
        <%@ taglib uri='http://java.sun.com/jstl/core' prefix='c'%>
        <%@ taglib uri='http://java.sun.com/jstl/fmt' prefix='fmt'%>

        <%-- Set the charset for this page's response to
             GB2312 (Chinese) --%>
        <%@ page contentType='text/html; charset=GB2312' %>

        <%-- Set the locale for <fmt:message> actions to zh
             (Chinese) --%>
        <fmt:setLocale value='zh'/>

        <%-- Set the bundle basename for <fmt:message> actions --%>
        <fmt:setBundle basename='app'/>
        <fmt:message key='login.form.title'/><hr>

        <form action='show_parameters.jsp'>
            <table><tr>
                <td><fmt:message key='login.textfield.name'/></td>

                <td><input type='text' name='name'
                     value=
                    '<fmt:message key="login.textfield.nameValue"/>'/>
                </td>
             </tr></table>
            <br>
            <input type='submit'
                   value='<fmt:message key="login.button.submit"/>'/>
        </form>

        <%-- Show the response's charset --%>
        Response Charset:
          <c:out value='${pageContext.response.characterEncoding}'/>
    </body>
</html>
```

Listing 7.22   *show_parameters.jsp*

```
<!DOCTYPE HTML PUBLIC "-//W3C//DTD HTML 4.0 Transitional//EN">
<html>
   <head>
      <title>Broken Request Decoding</title>
   </head>

   <body>
      <%@ taglib uri='http://java.sun.com/jstl/core'prefix='c'%>

      <%-- Set the charset for this page's response to
           GB2312 (Chinese) --%>
      <%@ page contentType='text/html; charset=GB2312' %>

      <p>Name: <c:out value='${param.name}'/>

      <%-- Show the request charset --%>
      Request Charset:
        <c:out value='${pageContext.request.characterEncoding}'/>
   </body>
</html>
```

---

that request parameter is not properly decoded. Subsequently, the preceding JSP page prints its *request* encoding, which is `null`, and therefore the <c:out> action displays nothing.

Because the JSP page containing the form specified its response charset as GB2312, and because that form invoked the preceding JSP page, the request charset for the preceding page should also be GB2312. But as you can see from Figure 7–6, that's not the case.

Servlet developers have long been aware of this problem, and they have come up with a workaround: they store the response charset for the JSP page containing the form in a session attribute. Before it decodes request parameters, the JSP page specified as the form's action sets its request charset to the value of that session attribute; for the preceding example, it would work like this:

```
<%-- This is from the JSP page containing the form --%>
...
<%-- Store the request charset in a session attribute--%>
<c:set var='requestCharset' value='GB2312' scope='session'/>
...
<form action='show_parameters.jsp'>
   ...
</form>
...
```

```
<%-- This is from the JSP page specified as the form's action --%>

<%
  <%-- Retrieve the request charset from the session attribute--%>
  String charset = (String)
                    pageContext.getAttribute("requestCharset",
                    PageContext.SESSION_SCOPE);

  <%-- Set the request character encoding with the value of the
       session attribute--%>
  request.setCharacterEncoding(charset);
%>
...
<%-- Now the request parameters will be decoded properly --%>
...
```

To save you the trouble of implementing the workaround listed in the preceding code fragment, JSTL does it for you. Whenever JSTL locates a resource bundle, it stores the charset corresponding to that resource bundle's locale in a configuration variable named `javax.servlet.jsp.jstl.fmt.request.charset` in session scope. You can use the <fmt:requestEncoding> action to set the request encoding for your JSP page to the value of that session attribute. Here is the syntax of that action:[20]

<fmt:requestEncoding [value]/>

If you don't specify a value for <fmt:requestEncoding>, the action works as described above, by setting the request encoding to the value of the `javax.servlet.jsp.jstl.fmt.request.charset` session attribute. Alternatively, you can explicitly specify the charset value with the `value` attribute.

Figure 7–7 shows the same application shown in Figure 7–6 on page 288, except that `show_parameters.jsp` uses the <fmt:requestEncoding> action to set its request encoding.

---

20. Items in brackets are optional; see "<fmt:requestEncoding>" on page 506 for a more complete description of <fmt:requestEncoding> syntax.

Figure 7–7 Using <fmt:requestEncoding>

Listing 7.23 lists show_parameters.jsp, revised to use the <fmt:requestEncoding> action.

Listing 7.23 *show_parameters.jsp (revised)*

```
<!DOCTYPE HTML PUBLIC "-//W3C//DTD HTML 4.0 Transitional//EN">
<html>
   <head>
      <title>Using &lt;fmt:requestEncoding&gt;</title>
   </head>

   <body>
      <%@ taglib uri='http://java.sun.com/jstl/core'prefix='c'%>
      <%@ taglib uri='http://java.sun.com/jstl/fmt' prefix='fmt'%>

      <%-- Set the charset for this page's response to
           GB2312 (Chinese) --%>
```

Listing 7.23	*show_parameters.jsp (revised) (cont.)*

```
   <%@ page contentType='text/html; charset=GB2312' %>

   <%-- The <fmt:requestEncoding> action sets the incoming
        request's charset to match the response charset
        of the referring page. Since we know the charset
        is GB2312, we could have specified it with the value
        attribute, like this:

        <fmt:requestEncoding value='GB2312'/>
   --%>
   <fmt:requestEncoding/>

   <p>Name: <c:out value='${param.name}'/>

   <%-- Show the request and response charsets --%>
   <p>Request Charset:
     <c:out value='${pageContext.request.characterEncoding}'/>
  </body>
</html>
```

7.7 I18N Custom Actions

The `javax.servlet.jsp.jstl.fmt.LocaleSupport` class provides support for looking up resource bundles and mapping message keys to their corresponding localized messages. That class defines four `static` methods, all named `getLocalizedMessage`, that take the following arguments:[21]

- `PageContext, String key`
- `PageContext, String key, String basename`
- `PageContext, String key, Object args[]`
- `PageContext, String key, Object args[], String basename`

Each of the `LocaleSupport.getLocalizedMessage` methods returns a localized string. You must specify a key, and optionally you can also specify a bundle base name or an array of parameters for compound message, or both; see "Compound Messages" on page 255 for more information about compound messages.

---

21. See page 508 for more information about the `LocaleSupport` class.

Because the `LocaleSupport` class resides in the `javax.servlet.jsp.`
`jstl.fmt` package, you can use its methods to retrieve localized messages from
resource bundles. This section discusses how to use those methods in the context of
form validation. First, we discuss how to perform form validation without using the
`LocaleSupport` methods; subsequently, in "Validation with a Custom Action That
Uses javax.servlet.jsp.jstl.fmt.LocaleSupport" on page 304, we see how to use those
methods in a custom action, which substantially reduces the amount of code page
authors have to write.

Figure 7–8 shows an internationalized Web application localized for English and
French. The top picture in Figure 7–8 shows a form that's validated by a servlet;
when the form is not filled out correctly, the application displays localized error
messages, as shown in the bottom picture in Figure 7–8.

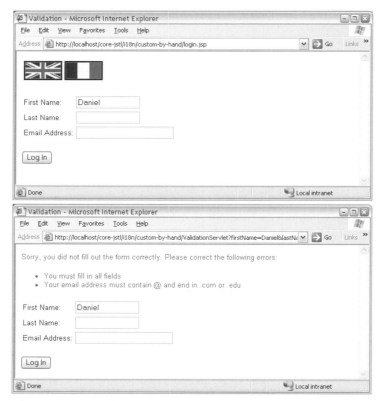

Figure 7–8   Form Validation—English Version

Like the Web application discussed in "An Example of Dynamically Switching
Locales" on page 278, the Web application shown in Figure 7–8 lets users switch

locales by clicking on an image of a flag. The flags and the corresponding mechanism for switching locales are discussed in "An Example of Dynamically Switching Locales", so that discussion is not repeated here.

Figure 7–9 shows the French version of the application, which also displays localized error messages when the form is not filled out correctly.

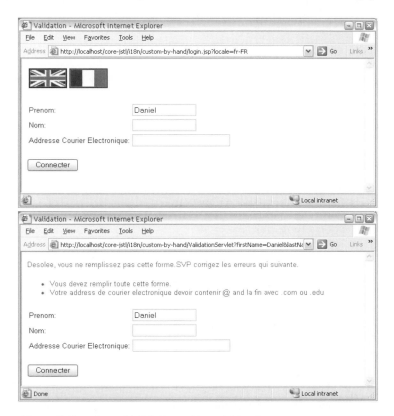

Figure 7–9   Form Validation—French Version

The JSP page shown in the top picture in Figure 7–9 is listed in Listing 7.24.

The preceding JSP page imports `set_locale.jsp`, which sets the locale according to which flag was last selected and subsequently creates a localization context for a resource bundle whose base name is `app`, and stores it in session scope with <fmt:setBundle>. See Listing 7.20 on page 287 for a listing of `set_locale.jsp`.

As you can see from Figure 7–9, the flags are only shown before a user submits the form. Once the form is submitted, the Web application assumes that the user has

Listing 7.24 *login.jsp*

```
<!DOCTYPE HTML PUBLIC "-//W3C//DTD HTML 4.0 Transitional//EN">
<html>
   <head>
      <%@ taglib uri='http://java.sun.com/jstl/core' prefix='c' %>
      <%@ taglib uri='http://java.sun.com/jstl/fmt' prefix='fmt'%>

      <%-- If a locale was specified as a request parameter,
           set_locale.jsp sets the locale for this session --%>
      <c:import url='set_locale.jsp'/>

      <fmt:setBundle basename='app' scope='session'/>

      <%-- Localize the window title --%>
      <title><fmt:message key='login.window-title'/></title>
   </head>

   <body>
      <%-- If there's no firstName request parameter ... --%>
      <c:if test='${param.firstName == null}'>
         <%-- Show the flags so the user can change locale --%>
         <c:import url='flags.jsp'/><br/>
      </c:if>

      <%-- process_validation_errors.jsp validates form fields--%>
      <c:import url='process_validation_errors.jsp'/>

      <%-- Import a JSP page that creates the login form --%>
      <c:import url='login_form.jsp'/>
   </body>
</html>
```

selected an appropriate locale, so the flags are not subsequently shown. The preceding JSP page implements that functionality by importing flags.jsp only if there is no firstName request parameter. See Listing 7.19 on page 287 for a listing of flags.jsp.

The preceding JSP page also imports two other JSP pages: process_validation_errors.jsp and login_form.jsp. The former displays localized error messages, and the latter displays the login form. Those JSP pages are discussed in the next section.

Validation with JSP Pages

This section, which continues the discussion of the application shown in Figure 7–9 on page 295, shows you how to retrieve and display localized error messages in a JSP page. In "Validation with a Custom Action That Uses javax.servlet.jsp.jstl.fmt.Locale-Support" on page 304, we discuss how to do that validation with a custom action.

Listing 7.25 lists `login_form.jsp`, which is imported by the JSP page listed in Listing 7.24.

The preceding JSP page uses a bean that stores form field values, so the user does not have to retype those values when validation errors occur. That bean is not

Listing 7.25 *login_form.jsp*

```
<%@ taglib uri='http://java.sun.com/jstl/core' prefix='c' %>
<%@ taglib uri='http://java.sun.com/jstl/fmt' prefix='fmt'%>

<jsp:useBean id='form' scope='request' class='beans.Form'>
   <jsp:setProperty name='form' property='*'/>
</jsp:useBean>

<%-- Store the name of the page that imports this page in a
     session attribute. That attribute is used by the validation
     servlet. --%>
<c:set var='failurePage'
     value='${pageContext.request.servletPath}'
     scope='session'/>

<%-- Store the name of the successful login page in a session
     attribute. That attribute is also used by the validation
     servlet. --%>
<c:set var='successPage'
     value='/loginComplete.jsp'
     scope='session'/>

<p><form action='ValidationServlet'/>
   <table><tr>
      <td><fmt:message key='login.first-name'/>:</td>
      <td><input type='text' size=15 name='firstName'
              value='<%= form.getFirstName() %>'/></td></tr><tr>

      <td><fmt:message key='login.last-name'/>:</td>
      <td><input type='text' size=15 name='lastName'
              value='<%= form.getLastName() %>'/></td></tr><tr>

      <td><fmt:message key='login.email-address'/>:</td>
      <td><input type='text' size=25 name='emailAddress'
              value='<%= form.getEmailAddress() %>'/></td></tr>
   </table>
   <p><input type=submit
         value='<fmt:message key="login.login-button"/>'/>
</form>
```

pertinent to our discussion here, and therefore it's not listed or discussed; however, you can download it from this book's Web site;[22] also, form beans are discussed in *Advanced JavaServer Pages*.[23]

There are two things to note about the JSP page listed in Listing 7.25. First, the form's action is a servlet. Second, two values are stored in session scope and are subsequently accessed by that servlet: the name of a JSP page to which the servlet forwards when form validation fails, and the name of another JSP page to which the servlet forwards when the form is filled out correctly. The former is the page that imports `login_form.jsp` (`login.jsp`), and the latter is `/loginComplete.jsp`.

The JSP page `/loginComplete.jsp`, which displays a localized greeting after a successful login, is listed in Listing 7.26.

Listing 7.26 */loginComplete.jsp*

```
<!DOCTYPE HTML PUBLIC "-//W3C//DTD HTML 4.0 Transitional//EN">
<html>
   <head>
      <%@ taglib uri='http://java.sun.com/jstl/core' prefix='c' %>
      <%@ taglib uri='http://java.sun.com/jstl/fmt' prefix='fmt'%>

      <%-- Localize the window title --%>
      <title><fmt:message key='login.thanks.window-title'/></title>
   </head>

   <body>
      <fmt:message key='login.thanks'/>
   </body>
</html>
```

The validation servlet referenced in Listing 7.25 is listed in Listing 7.27.

The validation servlet listed above overrides the `doGet` method and retrieves the value of a context initialization parameter named `app.validation.bundle. basename`, which specifies the base name of a bundle containing localized validation error messages. That base name is specified as a context initialization parameter so that you can change it without recompiling the servlet.

---

22. See "The Book's Web Site" on page xiv to find out more about this book's Web site.
23. David Geary, *Advanced JavaServer Pages*. Sun Microsystems Press, 2001.

Listing 7.27   *WEB-INF/classes/ValidationServlet.java*

```java
import java.io.IOException;
import java.util.Vector;

import javax.servlet.*;
import javax.servlet.http.*;

import beans.ValidationError;

public class ValidationServlet extends HttpServlet {
    public void doGet(HttpServletRequest req,
                      HttpServletResponse res)
                      throws IOException, ServletException {
        // Obtain a reference to the application
        ServletContext app = getServletContext();

        // Use the application to get the value of the
        // initialization parameter that specifies the bundle
        // basename
        String bundleBasename =
            app.getInitParameter("app.validation.bundle.basename");

        // Validate the form data
        boolean errorDetected = validate(req, bundleBasename,
                              req.getParameter("firstName"),
                              req.getParameter("lastName"),
                              req.getParameter("emailAddress"));

        // If the form data was invalid ...
        if(errorDetected) {
            // Retrieve the failure page from a session attribute
            String page = (String)req.getSession().
                      getAttribute("failurePage");

            // Forward to the failure page
            RequestDispatcher rd = app.getRequestDispatcher(page);
            rd.forward(req, res);
        }
        // If the form data was valid ...
        else {
            // Retrieve the success page from a session attribute
            String page = (String)req.getSession().
                      getAttribute("successPage");

            // Forward to the success page
            RequestDispatcher rd = app.getRequestDispatcher(page);
            rd.forward(req, res);
```

| Listing 7.27 | *WEB-INF/classes/ValidationServlet.java (cont.)* |

```
      }
   }
   private boolean validate(HttpServletRequest req,
                            String bundleBasename, String first,
                            String last, String email){
      boolean errorDetected = false;
      Vector errorKeys = new Vector();

      // If any of the fields were not filled in...
      if(first.equals("") || last.equals("") || email.equals("")){
         errorKeys.add("login.fill-in-all-fields");
         errorDetected = true;
      }
      // If email address is invalid...
      if(email.indexOf("@") == -1 ||
        (!email.endsWith(".com") && !email.endsWith(".edu"))) {
         errorKeys.add("login.bad-email-address");
         errorDetected = true;
      }
      // If the form parameters were invalid...
      if(errorDetected) {
         // Add message indicating invalid parameters
         errorKeys.add(0, "login.error-detected");

         // Store the validation error in a request attribute
         req.setAttribute("validateError",
               new ValidationError(bundleBasename, errorKeys));
      }
      return errorDetected;
   }
}
```

The preceding servlet passes the resource bundle base name, along with a reference to the HTTP request and the values filled out in the form, to a `validate` method. The `validate` method checks to see whether the form was filled out correctly; if not, it creates an instance of `ValidationError`, whose constructor is passed the bundle base name and an array of error message keys specified by the `validate` method. That validation error is subsequently stored in a request attribute, which is accessed by `process_validation_errors.jsp`.

After the `validate` method returns, the servlet listed above forwards to one of two JSP pages, depending on whether the validation succeeded or failed. The names of those JSP pages are retrieved from session attributes that are set in `login_form.jsp`, which is listed in Listing 7.25 on page 297.

Listing 7.28 lists the application's deployment descriptor.

Listing 7.28 *WEB-INF/web.xml*

```
<?xml version="1.0" encoding="ISO-8859-1"?>
<!DOCTYPE web-app
  PUBLIC "-//Sun Microsystems, Inc.//DTD Web Application 2.3//EN"
  "http://java.sun.com/j2ee/dtds/web-app_2.3.dtd">

<web-app>
   <context-param>
      <param-name>javax.servlet.jsp.jstl.fmt.locale</param-name>
      <param-value>en-US</param-value>
   </context-param>

   <context-param>
      <param-name>app.validation.bundle.basename</param-name>
      <param-value>validationErrors</param-value>
   </context-param>

   <servlet>
       <servlet-name>ValidationServlet</servlet-name>
      <servlet-class>ValidationServlet</servlet-class>
   </servlet>

   <servlet-mapping>
      <servlet-name>ValidationServlet</servlet-name>
      <url-pattern>/ValidationServlet</url-pattern>
   </servlet-mapping>

   <welcome-file-list>
      <welcome-file>login.jsp</welcome-file>
   </welcome-file-list>
 </web-app>
```

The deployment descriptor listed in Listing 7.28 defines a context initialization parameter named `javax.servlet.jsp.jstl.fmt.locale`, which corresponds to the FMT_LOCALE configuration setting. That context initialization parameter's value is set to `en-US`, so when the login page is first displayed, it will be localized for U.S. English. See "An Overview of the I18N Actions" on page 264 for more information about the FMT_LOCALE configuration setting.

The preceding deployment descriptor also defines a context initialization parameter named `app.validation.bundle.basename`, which defines the resource bundle base name for validation error messages. That context initialization parameter is used by the validation servlet listed in Listing 7.27.

The preceding deployment descriptor also defines a servlet mapping for the validation servlet listed in Listing 7.27 and specifies `login.jsp` as a welcome file so that the JSP page is displayed when the application is accessed in the browser.

The `ValidationError` class is listed in Listing 7.29.

Listing 7.29   *WEB-INF/classes/beans/ValidationError.java*

```
package beans;

import java.util.Vector;

// This class is immutable
public class ValidationError {
   private final String bundleBasename;
   private final Vector errorKeys;

   public ValidationError(String bundleBasename,
                          Vector errorKeys) {
      this.errorKeys = errorKeys;
      this.bundleBasename = bundleBasename;
   }
   public Vector getErrorKeys() {
      return errorKeys;
   }
   public String getBundleBasename() {
      return bundleBasename;
   }
}
```

`ValidationError` instances are simple immutable beans that store a bundle base name and a set of error keys. That base name and those error keys are accessed by `process_validation_errors.jsp`, which is listed in Listing 7.30.

The preceding JSP page checks to see if a validation error has been stored in a request attribute. If that request attribute does not exist, the JSP page does nothing.

If one or more errors were detected by the validation servlet listed in Listing 7.27 on page 299, then the preceding JSP page uses a scriptlet to retrieve a bundle base name and a set of error keys from the validation error stored in request scope. Subsequently, the preceding JSP page uses <fmt:bundle> to establish a localization context for its nested <fmt:message> actions. The JSP page then iterates over the error keys, extracting localized messages from the (resource bundle stored in) the localization context created by the <fmt:bundle> action.

As you can see from the preceding listing, displaying localized error messages can be fairly complicated. You can reduce that complexity to one line of code by

Listing 7.30   *process_validation_errors.jsp*

```jsp
<%@ taglib uri='http://java.sun.com/jstl/core' prefix='c' %>
<%@ taglib uri='http://java.sun.com/jstl/fmt' prefix='fmt'%>

<%-- If the request attribute "validateError" exists --%>
<c:if test='${requestScope.validateError != null}'>

   <%-- The following scriptlet performs these steps:
   1. Obtain a reference to the validation error.
   2. Store the error keys in page scope.
   3. Store the error's bundle base name in page scope. --%>

   <% beans.ValidationError error = (beans.ValidationError)
                      request.getAttribute("validateError");

      pageContext.setAttribute("errors", error.getErrorKeys());
      pageContext.setAttribute("bundleBasename",
                          error.getBundleBasename());
   %>

   <%-- Set the bundle base name for all <fmt:message> actions
        within the body of the <fmt:bundle> action --%>
   <fmt:bundle basename='${bundleBasename}'>
      <%-- For each error key...--%>
      <c:forEach var='key' items='${errors}'
          varStatus='status'>

        <c:choose>
           <%-- If it's the first key...--%>
           <c:when test='${status.first}'>
              <font color='red'>
                 <fmt:message key='${key}'/>
                 <ul>
           </c:when>

           <%-- If it's the last key ...--%>
           <c:when test='${status.last}'>
                  <li><fmt:message key='${key}'/></li>
                 </ul>
              </font>
           </c:when>

           <%-- If it's not the first or last key ...--%>
           <c:otherwise>
                  <li><fmt:message key='${key}'/></li>
           </c:otherwise>
        </c:choose>
     </c:forEach>
   </fmt:bundle>
</c:if>
```

implementing a custom action that displays those error messages. "Validation with a Custom Action That Uses javax.servlet.jsp.jstl.fmt.LocaleSupport" on page 304 shows you how to implement such a custom action, which uses the `javax.servlet.jsp.jstl.fmt.LocaleSupport` class to extract localized validation error messages from a resource bundle. Before we discuss that custom action, let's look at the English and French properties files that contain the localized validation errors, as listed in Listing 7.31 and Listing 7.32, respectively.

Listing 7.31 *WEB-INF/classes/validationErrors_en.properties*

```
# validation error messages -- English Version

login.error-detected=Sorry, you did not fill out the form \
correctly. Please correct the following errors:

login.fill-in-all-fields=You must fill in all fields

login.bad-email-address=Your email address must contain @ \
and end in .com or .edu
```

Listing 7.32 *WEB-INF/classes/validationErrors_fr.properties*

```
# validation error messages -- French Version

login.error-detected=Desolee, vous ne remplissez pas cette forme.\
 SVP corrigez les erreurs qui suivante.
login.fill-in-all-fields=Vous devez remplir toute cette forme.

login.bad-email-address=Votre address de courier electronique \
devoir contenir @ and la fin avec .com ou .edu
```

Validation with a Custom Action That Uses javax.servlet.jsp.jstl.fmt.LocaleSupport

Instead of retrieving localized error messages from a resource bundle and subsequently displaying them with a JSP page, as is the case for the JSP page listed in Listing 7.30 on page 303, we can encapsulate that functionality in a custom action. Listing 7.33 lists a revision of the `login.jsp` JSP page listed in Listing 7.24 on page 296. That revised JSP page uses a custom action to display validation error messages.

Implementing the <core-jstl:showValidateError> custom action is a two-step process: create a tag library descriptor in `WEB-INF`, and implement the tag handler class in `WEB-INF/classes/tags`. The tag library descriptor is listed in Listing 7.34.

Listing 7.33 *login.jsp (revised)*

```
<!DOCTYPE HTML PUBLIC "-//W3C//DTD HTML 4.0 Transitional//EN">
<html>
   <head>
      <%@ taglib uri='http://java.sun.com/jstl/core' prefix='c' %>
      <%@ taglib uri='http://java.sun.com/jstl/fmt' prefix='fmt'%>
      <%@ taglib uri='WEB-INF/core-jstl.tld' prefix='core-jstl' %>

      <%-- If a locale was specified as a request parameter,
           set_locale.jsp sets the locale for this session --%>
      <c:import url='set_locale.jsp'/>

      <fmt:setBundle basename='app' scope='session'/>

      <%-- Localize the window title --%>
      <title><fmt:message key='login.window-title'/></title>
   </head>

   <body>
      <%-- If there's no firstName request parameter ... --%>
      <c:if test='${param.firstName == null}'>
         <%-- Show the flags so the user can change locale --%>
         <c:import url='flags.jsp'/><br/>
      </c:if>

      <%-- This custom action takes the place of
           process_validation_errors.jsp from the previous
           example --%>
      <core-jstl:showValidateError/>

      <%-- Import a JSP page that creates the login form --%>
      <c:import url='login_form.jsp'/>
   </body>
</html>
```

The tag library descriptor listed above describes a tag library that contains the showValidateError tag with the <taglib> directive, specifying the version of the library, the JSP version required for the library, and a short name for the library. The tag library descriptor also describes the tag itself with the <tag> directive, specifying the tag name, Java class, and the type of body content the tag requires.

The tag handler for the <core-jstl:showValidateError> custom action is listed in Listing 7.35.

The tag handler listed above implements the same functionality as the JSP page listed in Listing 7.30 on page 303. That tag handler overrides the doEndTag method (because the tag has no body, the tag handler could have overridden doStartTag with identical results) and uses one of the getLocalizedMessage methods from

Listing 7.34 *WEB-INF/core-jstl.tld*

```
<?xml version="1.0" encoding="ISO-8859-1" ?>
<!DOCTYPE taglib PUBLIC
   "-//Sun Microsystems, Inc.//DTD JSP Tag Library 1.2//EN"
   "http://java.sun.com/j2ee/dtds/web-jsptaglibrary_1_2.dtd">

<taglib>
   <tlib-version>1.0</tlib-version>
   <jsp-version>1.2</jsp-version>
   <short-name>Core JSTL Validation Example Tag</short-name>

   <tag>
      <name>showValidateError</name>
      <tag-class>tags.ShowValidateErrorTag</tag-class>
      <body-content>none</body-content>
   </tag>
</taglib>
```

Listing 7.35 *WEB-INF/classes/tags/ShowValidateErrorTag.java*

```
package tags;

import java.util.Vector;

import javax.servlet.jsp.JspException;
import javax.servlet.jsp.tagext.TagSupport;
import javax.servlet.jsp.JspWriter;

import javax.servlet.jsp.jstl.fmt.LocaleSupport;

import beans.ValidationError;

public class ShowValidateErrorTag extends TagSupport {
   public int doEndTag() throws JspException {
      // Retrieve the validate-error scoped variable, which
      // is an instance of ValidationError
      ValidationError err =
                  (ValidationError)pageContext.getRequest().
                   getAttribute("validateError");
      if(err != null) {
         // Get error keys from the ValidationError
         Vector errorKeys = err.getErrorKeys();

         // Get the size of the errorKeys vector
         int numberOfKeys = errorKeys.size();

         // Get the bundle basename from the ValidationError
         String bundleBasename = err.getBundleBasename();
```

Listing 7.35   *WEB-INF/classes/tags/ShowValidateErrorTag.java (cont.)*

```java
        // Write output to this JspWriter
        JspWriter out = pageContext.getOut();

        // For each error key ...
        for(int i=0; i < errorKeys.size(); ++i) {
            try {
                // Retrieve the localized message
                String msg = LocaleSupport.getLocalizedMessage(
                            pageContext, (String)errorKeys.get(i),
                            bundleBasename);

                // If it's the first key...
                if(i == 0) {
                    out.print("<font color='red'>");
                    out.print(msg + "<br/><ul>");
                }
                else { // All but the first key...
                    out.print("<li>" + msg + "</li>");
                }

                // If it's the last key...
                if(i == numberOfKeys-1) {
                    pageContext.getOut().print("</font></ul>");
                }
            }
            catch(java.io.IOException ex) {
                throw new JspException(ex.getMessage());
            }
        }
    }
    return EVAL_PAGE;
    }
}
```

the `LocaleSupport` class to extract localized messages from the English and French validation error properties files listed in Listing 7.31 on page 304 and Listing 7.32 on page 304, respectively. Because JSTL exposes the `LocaleSupport` class by placing it in the `javax.servlet.jsp.jstl.fmt` package, custom actions like the one in the previous listing can extract localized messages in exactly the same manner as the JSTL <fmt:message> action.

FORMATTING ACTIONS

Topics in This Chapter

- Formatting and Parsing Numbers
- Formatting and Parsing Dates and Times
- Using Time Zones
- Determining a Formatting Locale

Chapter 8

If you want your website to be accessible to as many people as possible, it's crucial to localize text, as discussed in "I18N Actions" on page 248. But it's just as important to localize numbers, dates, and currencies; for example, if you publicized an event on your website and you specified the date as 06/12/2004, Americans would arrive on June 12th, whereas most Europeans would arrive on December 6th. Fortunately, JSTL provides six actions that you can use to format and parse numbers, currencies, percents, and dates:

- <fmt:formatNumber>
- <fmt:parseNumber>
- <fmt:formatDate>
- <fmt:parseDate>
- <fmt:timeZone>
- <fmt:setTimeZone>

The first two actions listed above—<fmt:formatNumber> and <fmt:parseNumber>—are the inverse of one another. The <fmt:formatNumber> action formats a numeric value, which you can specify as either a string or an instance of `java.lang.Number`, and outputs that numeric value as a string. The <fmt:parseNumber> action accepts a string representing a formatted number and parses that string into an unformatted numeric value (an instance of `java.lang.Number`).

The <fmt:formatDate> and <fmt:parseDate> actions are also the inverse of one another. The <fmt:formatDate> action formats an instance of `java.util.Date` and outputs a string, whereas <fmt:parseDate> accepts a string representing a formatted date and parses that string into an instance of `java.util.Date`.

You can use the formatting and parsing actions together to manipulate numeric values; for example, you could:

1. Parse a formatted number
2. Perform an arithmetic operation on the numeric value
3. Reformat the result of that operation as a currency

The last two actions listed above—<fmt:timeZone> and <fmt:setTimeZone>—let you establish a time zone for the <fmt:formatDate> and <fmt:parseDate> actions. See "Using Time Zones" on page 343 for more information about time zones and the time zone actions.

8.1 Formatting and Parsing Numbers

Numbers are formatted differently for different locales; for example, the number 234,682.155 (formatted for U.S. English) is formatted as 234.682,155 in French and German. The <fmt:formatNumber> action lets you format numbers according to a specified locale; for example, the following code formats the number 234682.155 as 234,682.155 for U.S. English:

```
<fmt:setLocale value='en-US'/>

Number Formatted for U.S. English:
<fmt:formatNumber value='234682.155'/>
```

Notice that the preceding code uses the <fmt:setLocale> action to establish a locale for the <fmt:formatNumber> action because <fmt:formatNumber> does not have an attribute that lets you specify a locale. There are other ways to establish a locale for JSTL formatting actions; for example, you can nest formatting actions in a <fmt:bundle> action or set the FMT_LOCALE configuration setting in a business component.[1] We can modify the preceding code fragment to format the specified numeric value for the German locale by changing the value of the <fmt:setLocale> action, like this:

---

1. See "Determining a Formatting Locale" on page 352 for more information about how the JSTL formatting actions determine their locales.

```
<fmt:setLocale value='de-DE'/>

Number Formatted for German:
<fmt:formatNumber value='234682.155'/>
```

Besides numbers, <fmt:formatNumber> can also format currencies and percents. The following <fmt:formatNumber> attributes control how numbers, currencies, and percents are formatted: `minIntegerDigits`, `maxIntegerDigits`, `minFractionDigits`, `maxFractionDigits`, and `groupingUsed`; for example:

```
<fmt:setLocale value='en-US'/>

<fmt:formatNumber value='234682.155'
        maxIntegerDigits='4'
      maxFractionDigits='2'
           groupingUsed='false'/>
```

The output for the preceding code fragment is `4682.16`. Notice that <fmt:formatNumber> handles rounding automatically. That rounding is carried out in *half-even mode* by rounding to the nearest even number when the number is equidistant between two numbers; for example, 0.154 will round to 0.15 and 0.156 will round to 0.16, but 0.155, which is equidistant from 0.15 and 0.16, rounds to the *nearest even number*, which is 0.16.

Every locale has a default pattern for numbers, currencies, and percents; for example, for U.S. English, numbers are formatted with this pattern: `#,###.` where # represents a digit, the comma represents a grouping separator, and the period represents a decimal separator. You can also specify custom patterns with the <fmt:formatNumber> `pattern` attribute, like this:

```
<fmt:setLocale value='en-US'/>

<fmt:formatNumber value='234682.155'
               pattern='#,####.00000'/>
```

The output of the preceding code fragment is `23,4682.15500` because the pattern specifies a grouping of four integer digits and five fraction digits. See "Custom Number Patterns" on page 319 for more information about custom formatting patterns for numbers.

The <fmt:formatNumber> action has a `type` attribute that lets you specify how <fmt:formatNumber> formats a number: as a number (the default), currency, or percent. For example, you can format a number as currency, like this:

```
<fmt:formatNumber value='234682.155' type='currency'/>
```

The preceding line of code formats the number 234682.155 as currency. If you set the locale to U.S. English, the output will be $234,682.16. The <fmt:formatNumber> action also has currencyCode and currencySymbol attributes that control the currency symbol that <fmt:formatNumber> uses to format currencies. See "Currencies" on page 326 for more information about formatting currencies.

You can also parse numbers, currencies, and percents with the <fmt:parseNumber> action; the following code fragment parses a number:

```
<fmt:setLocale value='en-US'/>

<fmt:formatNumber value='234682.155' var='formattedNumber'/>
<fmt:parseNumber value='${formattedNumber}'/>
```

By default, <fmt:formatNumber> sends its output to the current JspWriter, but if you specify the var attribute, <fmt:formatNumber> stores its output in a scoped variable whose name is specified with the var attribute. The <fmt:formatNumber> action stores scoped variables in page scope by default, but you can specify a different scope with the scope attribute.

In the preceding code fragment, <fmt:formatNumber> stores the string 234,682.155 in a scoped variable named formattedNumber in page scope. Subsequently, <fmt:parseNumber> parses that string by specifying the formattedNumber scoped variable for its value attribute. The resulting output is the original numeric value: 234682.155.

Like <fmt:formatNumber>, <fmt:parseNumber> has a type attribute that specifies the type of value that it parses. Just like the type attribute for <fmt:formatNumber>, the <fmt:parseNumber> action's type attribute can be specified as number (the default), currency, or percent. For example, the following code fragment uses <fmt:parseNumber> to parse a currency:

```
<c:set var='originalMonetaryAmount' value='$10,000'/>

<fmt:parseNumber value='${originalMonetaryAmount}'
                 var='parsedAmount'
            type='currency'
        parseLocale='en-US'/>

<c:set var='result' value='${parsedAmount - 1000}'/>

<fmt:setLocale value='en-US'/>
<fmt:formatNumber value='${result}' type='currency'/>
```

In the preceding code fragment, <fmt:parseNumber> parses a scoped variable as currency and stores the resulting numeric value in a scoped variable named parsedAmount. Subsequently, the <c:set> action subtracts 1000 from that amount and stores the resulting value in a scoped variable named result. Finally, <fmt:formatNumber> formats the value of the result scoped variable as U.S. currency. The resulting output of the preceding code fragment is $9,000.

In the preceding code fragment, the locale used by <fmt:parseNumber> is specified as U.S. English (en-US) because that's how the originalMonetaryAmount scoped variable is formatted. Unlike <fmt:formatNumber>, <fmt:parseNumber> provides an attribute—parseLocale—that lets you explicitly specify the locale that <fmt:parseNumber> uses to parse its value.[2]

The locale that <fmt:parseNumber> uses must have the same formatting pattern and formatting symbols as the value that <fmt:parseNumber> parses; for example, if you change the parse locale in the preceding code fragment to fr-FR, <fmt:parseNumber> will throw an exception because the formatting pattern and symbols for the French locale don't match the value that <fmt:parseNumber> tries to parse.

Like <fmt:formatNumber>, <fmt:parseNumber> has a pattern attribute that specifies a parsing pattern. Typically, that attribute is only used when a numeric value has been formatted with a custom pattern; for example, consider the following code fragment:

```
<fmt:setLocale value='en-US'/>
<c:set var='originalAmount' value='1,0,0,0.00'/>

<fmt:parseNumber value='${originalAmount}'
                 var='parsedAmount'
          pattern='#,#.##'/>

<c:set var='result' value='${parsedAmount - 100}'/>

<fmt:formatNumber value='${result}'/>
```

The preceding code fragment will print the value 900. You can specify a wide variety of formatting and parsing patterns; see "Custom Number Patterns" on page 319 for more information about custom patterns.

Figure 8–1 shows a JSP page that displays a numeric value formatted with <fmt:formatNumber>. That JSP page lets you modify most of the <fmt:formatNumber> action's attributes. In addition to illustrating how <fmt:formatNumber> works, the JSP page shown in Figure 8–1 represents

---

2. The JSTL expert group felt that <fmt:formatNumber> had enough attributes, so in the interest of simplicity, <fmt:formatNumber> does not have an attribute for a locale.

somewhat of a lab for <fmt:formatNumber>; you can modify parameters to discover how <fmt:formatNumber> works for various combinations of attributes.

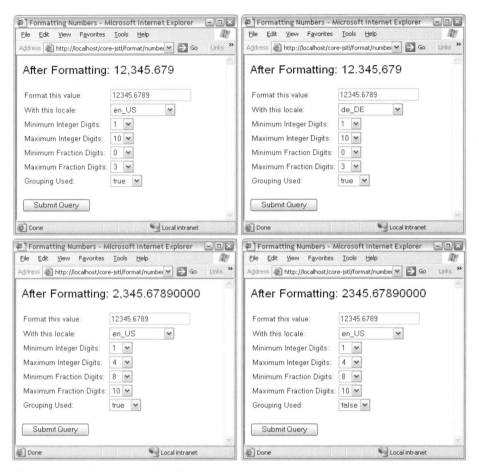

Figure 8–1   Formatting Numbers

The JSP page shown in Figure 8–1 lets you modify the value that <fmt:formatNumber> formats and the locale that it uses. You can also modify the following <fmt:formatNumber> attributes: `minIntegerDigits`, `maxIntegerDigits`, `minFractionDigits`, `maxFractionDigits`, and `groupingUsed`. In the upper-left picture, those attributes are set to 1, 10, 0, 3, and `true`, respectively. That picture shows a number formatted for the U.S. English (en-US) locale.

In the upper-right picture in Figure 8–1, the German locale (de-DE) is used to format the numeric value with the same attribute settings as the upper-left picture.

Notice that the formatting pattern for the German locale uses a period as the grouping separator and a comma as the decimal separator, which is the opposite of the U.S. English locale.

The bottom pictures in Figure 8–1 set the minimum fraction digits to 8, which causes the fractional component of the formatted value to be zero-padded to eight places. In the lower-left picture, the groupingUsed attribute for <fmt:formatNumber> is true, whereas that attribute is false in the lower-right picture. When the groupingUsed attribute is set to false, the grouping separator, which for the U.S. English locale is a comma, is not used.

The JSP page shown in Figure 8–1 is listed in Listing 8.1.

Listing 8.1 *Formatting Numbers*

```
<!DOCTYPE HTML PUBLIC "-//W3C//DTD HTML 4.0 Transitional//EN">
<html>
   <head>
      <title>Formatting Numbers</title>
   </head>

   <body>
      <%@ taglib uri='http://java.sun.com/jstl/core' prefix='c' %>
      <%@ taglib uri='http://java.sun.com/jstl/core_rt'
              prefix='c_rt' %>
      <%@ taglib uri='http://java.sun.com/jstl/fmt' prefix='fmt'%>

      <%-- Check locale and value request parameters --%>
      <c:choose>
         <c:when test='${not empty param.locale}'>
            <c:set var='locale' value='${param.locale}'/>
         </c:when>
         <c:otherwise>
            <c_rt:set var='locale'
                   value='<%= java.util.Locale.getDefault() %>'/>
         </c:otherwise>
      </c:choose>

      <c:choose>
         <c:when test='${not empty param.value}'>
            <c:set var='value' value='${param.value}'/>
         </c:when>
         <c:otherwise>
            <c:set var='value' value='12345.6789'/>
         </c:otherwise>
      </c:choose>
```

Listing 8.1   *Formatting Numbers (cont.)*

```
<%-- <fmt:formatNumber> doesn't have a formatLocale
     attribute, so the locale is specified with
     <fmt:setLocale> --%>
<fmt:setLocale value='${locale}'/>

<%-- Format the number --%>
<font size='5'>
   After Formatting:
   <fmt:formatNumber value='${value}'
          minIntegerDigits='${param.minIntDig}'
          maxIntegerDigits='${param.maxIntDig}'
         minFractionDigits='${param.minFrDig}'
         maxFractionDigits='${param.maxFrDig}'
             groupingUsed='${param.groupingUsed}'/>
</font>

<%-- Because this form does not specify an action, this
     JSP page will be reloaded when the form's submit
     button is activated --%>
<form>
   <table>
      <tr>
         <td>Format this value:</td>
         <td><input type='text'
                  value='<c:out value="${value}"/>'
                   name='value'/>
         </td>
      </tr>
      <tr>
         <td>With this locale:</td>
         <td>
         <select name='locale'>
            <c_rt:forEach var='formatLocale'
                       items='<%= java.text.NumberFormat.
                               getAvailableLocales()%>'>
              <option
              <c:if test='${locale == formatLocale}'>
                 selected
              </c:if>

              ><c:out value='${formatLocale}'/>
              </option>
            </c_rt:forEach>
         </select>
         </td>
      </tr>
```

Listing 8.1   *Formatting Numbers (cont.)*

```
<tr>
   <td>Minimum Integer Digits:</td>
   <td>
   <select name='minIntDig'>
      <c:forEach items='0,1,2,3,4,5,6,7,8,9,10'
                 var='minIntDig'>
         <option
         <c:if test='${param.minIntDig == minIntDig}'>
            selected
         </c:if>

         ><c:out value='${minIntDig}'/>
         </option>
      </c:forEach>
      </select>
   </td>
</tr>
<tr>
   <td>Maximum Integer Digits:</td>
   <td>
   <select name='maxIntDig'>
      <c:forEach items='0,1,2,3,4,5,6,7,8,9,10,40'
                 var='maxIntDig'>
         <option
         <c:if test='${param.maxIntDig == maxIntDig}'>
            selected
         </c:if>

         ><c:out value='${maxIntDig}'/>
         </option>
      </c:forEach>
      </select>
   </td>
</tr>
<tr>
   <td>Minimum Fraction Digits:</td>
   <td>
   <select name='minFrDig'>
      <c:forEach items='0,1,2,3,4,5,6,7,8,9,10'
                 var='minFrDig'>
         <option
         <c:if test='${param.minFrDig == minFrDig}'>
            selected
         </c:if>
```

Listing 8.1   *Formatting Numbers (cont.)*

```
                        ><c:out value='${minFrDig}'/>
                        </option>
                    </c:forEach>
                    </select>
                </td>
            </tr>
            <tr>
                <td>Maximum Fraction Digits:</td>
                <td>
                <select name='maxFrDig'>
                    <c:forEach items='0,1,2,3,4,5,6,7,8,9,10,40'
                                 var='maxFrDig'>
                        <option
                        <c:if test='${param.maxFrDig == maxFrDig}'>
                            selected
                        </c:if>

                        ><c:out value='${maxFrDig}'/>
                        </option>
                    </c:forEach>
                    </select>
                </td>
            </tr>
            <tr>
                <td>Grouping Used:</td>
                <td>
                <select name='groupingUsed'>
                  <c:forEach items='true,false' var='groupingUsed'>
                        <option
                        <c:if
                        test='${param.groupingUsed == groupingUsed}'>
                            selected
                        </c:if>

                        ><c:out value='${groupingUsed}'/>
                        </option>
                    </c:forEach>
                    </select>
                </td>
            </tr>
        </table>
        <p><input type='submit'/>
    </form>
  </body>
</html>
```

The preceding JSP page begins by checking the `locale` and `value` request parameters, which are generated by the page's form. If those values have not been specified, they are set to default values: the JSP container's default locale for the `locale` parameter and `12345.6789` for the `value` parameter.

Subsequently, the preceding JSP page sets the locale with the <fmt:setLocale> action and uses <fmt:formatNumber>, with the attributes specified in the form, to format the numeric value.

The rest of the JSP page creates the form. The `locale` HTML `select` element is populated with the available locales for number formatting. Also, all of the `select` elements display their previously selected values by testing whether the currently enumerated option value is equal to the previously selected value for that element.

Custom Number Patterns

As illustrated in "Formatting and Parsing Numbers" on page 310, you can format numeric values as numbers, currencies, or percents by specifying the <fmt:formatNumber> `type` attribute. When you specify that attribute, you are actually requesting a formatting pattern for a specific locale; for example, if you specify the `type` attribute as `number` for the U.S. English locale, you are requesting the pattern `#,###.`, which is the default number formatting pattern for that locale. You can further refine that locale-specific pattern with other <fmt:formatNumber> attributes, such as `minIntegerDigits` or `maxFractionDigits`. This section shows you how to specify custom formatting patterns that are *independent of any locale*. Because custom formatting patterns are independent of any locale, it's usually preferable to use the <fmt:formatNumber> `type` attribute in concert with the other formatting attributes, such as `minIntegerDigits` or `maxFractionDigits`, instead of custom patterns because the former uses locale-specific patterns automatically.

Note: This section provides an overview of custom number patterns; see the Java documentation for the `java.text.DecimalFormat` class for a more in-depth treatment of this subject.

Custom formatting patterns are defined like this:[3]

> *Pattern:*
> > *PositivePattern*
> > *PositivePattern ; NegativePattern*
> *PositivePattern:*

---

3. That definition comes from the Java documentation for the `java.text.DecimalFormat` class, which uses the same syntax as the Java Language Specification. The subscript *opt* means optional.

$Prefix_{opt}$ Number $Suffix_{opt}$

NegativePattern:
$Prefix_{opt}$ Number $Suffix_{opt}$

Prefix:
any Unicode characters except \uFFFE, \uFFFF, and special characters

Suffix:
any Unicode characters except \uFFFE, \uFFFF, and special characters

Number:
Integer $Exponent_{opt}$
Integer . Fraction $Exponent_{opt}$

Integer:
MinimumInteger
#
Integer
, Integer

MinimumInteger:
0
0 MinimumInteger
0 , MinimumInteger

Fraction:
$MinimumFraction_{opt}$ $OptionalFraction_{opt}$

MinimumFraction:
0 $MinimumFraction_{opt}$

OptionalFraction:
$OptionalFraction_{opt}$

Exponent:
E MinimumExponent

MinimumExponent:
0 $MinimumExponent_{opt}$

Formatting patterns consist of a subpattern for positive numbers and an optional subpattern for negative numbers. Those subpatterns consist of an *integer* value that can contain one or more # or 0 characters, in addition to an optional *prefix*, *fraction pattern*, and a *suffix*. A comma can appear within the *integer* portion of the pattern.

Table 8.1 lists the symbols that you can use within a formatting pattern.

From the preceding table, the most frequently used characters in custom formatting patterns are #, 0, the comma, and the period. Both the # and 0 characters represent digits, but the 0 character will fill with zeros if there is no corresponding digit for a given column, whereas nothing will be generated for a # character if there

Table 8.1 Number Pattern Symbols

Symbol	Location	Description
#	Number	A digit
0	Number	A digit; pads with zeros if there is no digit in the specified column
E	Number	Separator between mantissa and exponent for exponential formats
¤ (\u00A4)	Prefix/Suffix	Currency sign, replaced in the output by a currency symbol
%	Prefix/Suffix	Multiply by 100 and show as a percent
\u2030	Prefix/Suffix	Multiply by 1000 and show as per mille
;	Subpattern boundary	Format separator
.	Number	Placeholder for decimal or monetary separator
,	Number	Placeholder for grouping separator
'	Number	Quotes characters to avoid interpretation
–	Number	Default negative prefix

is no corresponding digit. For example, for the number 1.23, the pattern #.#### will generate 1.23, whereas the pattern 0.0000 will generate 1.2300.

You can use the # (or 0) character and a comma to specify how digits should be grouped within a number; for example, for the number 123456789, the pattern #,### will generate 123,456,789. Only the rightmost group of # characters specify grouping; for example, the pattern #,## is equivalent to #,####,## and #,##########,##. For the number 123456789, all three of the preceding patterns will generate 1,23,45,67,89.

You can also use the # (or 0) character and a period to specify how the fractional portion of a number is formatted; for example, the pattern #.## specifies two digits after the decimal point, so if the number 123.456 is formatted with that pattern, the result will be 123.46. Notice that rounding is automatically handled by the <fmt:formatNumber> action. Rounding mode is half-even; see "Formatting and Parsing Numbers" on page 310 for an explanation of that mode.

Figure 8–2 shows a JSP page that lets you specify a numeric value, a locale, and a formatting pattern. That JSP page uses <fmt:formatNumber>, with the specified locale and formatting pattern to format the specified value. The top two pictures illustrate the difference between the # and 0 characters, and the bottom picture shows what happens when you change locales.

As the top and bottom pictures in Figure 8–2 illustrate, the comma and period characters only specify *placeholders* for a locale's grouping separator and decimal separator, respectively. The same *patterns* are specified in the top and bottom pictures in Figure 8–2, but the *formatting* is different because the grouping and decimal separators for U.S. English and German are different.

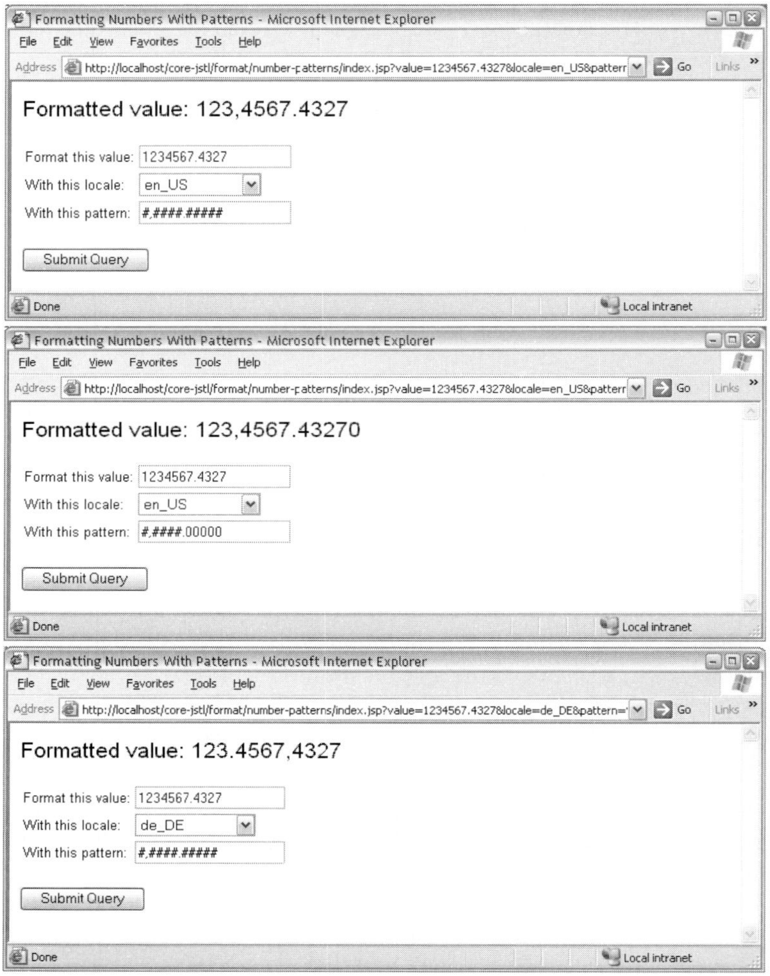

Figure 8–2   Formatting Numbers with Custom Patterns

The JSP page shown in Figure 8–2 is listed in Listing 8.2.

The preceding JSP page begins by checking the `locale` and `value` request parameters, which are generated by the page's form. If those parameters were not

Listing 8.2	*Formatting Numbers with Custom Patterns*

```
<!DOCTYPE HTML PUBLIC "-//W3C//DTD HTML 4.0 Transitional//EN">
<html>
   <head>
      <title>Formatting Numbers With Patterns</title>
   </head>

   <body>
      <%@ taglib uri='http://java.sun.com/jstl/core' prefix='c' %>
      <%@ taglib uri='http://java.sun.com/jstl/core_rt'
              prefix='c_rt' %>
      <%@ taglib uri='http://java.sun.com/jstl/fmt' prefix='fmt'%>

      <%-- Set values based on request parameters --%>
      <c:choose>
         <c:when test='${empty param.value}'>
            <c:set var='value' value='1234567.4327'/>
         </c:when>
         <c:otherwise>
            <c:set var='value' value='${param.value}'/>
         </c:otherwise>
      </c:choose>

      <c:choose>
         <c:when test='${empty param.locale}'>
            <c_rt:set var='locale'
                  value='<%= java.util.Locale.getDefault() %>'/>
         </c:when>
         <c:otherwise>
            <c:set var='locale' value='${param.locale}'/>
         </c:otherwise>
      </c:choose>

      <%-- Set the Locale --%>
      <fmt:setLocale value='${locale}'/>

      <%-- Show formatted number --%>
      <font size='5'>
         Formatted value:
         <fmt:formatNumber value='${value}'
                        pattern='${param.pattern}'/>
      </font>

      <%-- Because this form does not specify an action, this
           JSP page will be reloaded when the form's submit
           button is activated --%>
      <form>
```

Listing 8.2	*Formatting Numbers with Custom Patterns (cont.)*

```
<table>
   <tr>
      <td>Format this value:</td>
      <td><input type='text' name='value'
                 value='<c:out value="${value}"/>'/>
      </td>
   </tr>

   <tr>
      <td>With this locale:</td>
      <td>
      <select name='locale'>
         <c_rt:forEach var='thisLocale'
                       items='<%= java.text.NumberFormat.
                                  getAvailableLocales()%>'>
            <option
            <c:if test='${locale == thisLocale}'>
               selected
            </c:if>

            <c:out value='>${thisLocale}'
               escapeXml='false'/>
            </option>
         </c_rt:forEach>
      </select>
      </td>
   </tr>

   <tr>
      <td>With this pattern:</td>
      <td><input type='text' name='pattern'
                 value='<c:out value="${param.pattern}"/>'/>
      </td>
   </tr>
</table>
<p><input type='submit'/>
</form>
   </body>
</html>
```

specified, scoped variables representing those parameters are set to default values: the JSP container's default locale for the `locale` parameter, and `1234567.4327` for the `value` parameter.

The preceding JSP page subsequently sets the locale for the <fmt:formatNumber> action and uses that action, with the specified formatting pattern, to format the specified value. The rest of the JSP page creates the form.

You can use the preceding JSP page to experiment with formatting patterns and locales for various numeric values.

Percents

The <fmt:formatNumber> action lets you format percents in addition to numbers and currencies by specifying percent for the <fmt:formatNumber> action's type attribute, like this:

```
<fmt:setLocale value='en-US'/>
<fmt:formatNumber value='0.234778' type='percent'/>
```

When formatting percents, <fmt:formatNumber> *multiplies the specified value by 100* and adds a locale-sensitive percent symbol; for example, the preceding code fragment produces this output: 23%.[4]

By default, <fmt:formatNumber> does not show any fraction digits for percents, as you can see from the output of the preceding code fragment; however, you can force <fmt:formatNumber> to display those digits if you specify the minFractionDigits attribute, like this:

```
<fmt:formatNumber value='0.234778' type='percent'
     minFractionDigits='3'/>
```

The output of the preceding code fragment is 23.478%.

You can also specify any of the other <fmt:formatNumber> attributes when you format percents;[5] for example, you could do this:

```
<fmt:setLocale value='en-US'/>
<fmt:formatNumber value='0.234778' type='percent'
      minIntegerDigits='6'
     minFractionDigits='7'/>
```

The output of the preceding code fragment is 000,023.4778000%. If you change the locale to German (de-DE), <fmt:formatNumber> will use the grouping and decimal separators for that locale; for example, for the preceding use of <fmt:formatNumber> with the de-DE locale, you will get this output:

```
000.023,4778000%
```

---

4. The percent symbol—%—is nearly universal and is usually displayed after the number.
5. The exception is the pattern attribute, because the pattern and type attributes are mutually exclusive.

Additionally, you can also specify the <fmt:formatNumber> action's `groupingUsed` attribute to control whether the grouping separator symbol is used, although it's rarely specified in practice.

Currencies

You can format currencies in a locale-dependent manner by setting the <fmt:formatNumber> `type` attribute to `currency`; for example, here's a code fragment that formats currency for the United States:

```
<fmt:setLocale value='en-US'/>
<fmt:formatNumber value='0.234778' type='currency'/>
```

The preceding code fragment will produce this output: `$0.23`. By simply changing the locale used by <fmt:formatNumber>, you can format currencies for a different locale; for example, you can format currency for the euro, like this:[6]

```
<fmt:setLocale value='fr-FR'/>
<fmt:formatNumber value='0.234778' type='currency'/>
```

The preceding code fragment will only display the euro currency symbol if you are using JDK 1.4 (or higher). If you are using an older version of the Java Development Kit (JDK), you can specify the `EURO` locale variant, like this:

```
<fmt:setLocale value='fr-FR' variant='EURO'/>
<fmt:formatNumber value='0.234778' type='currency'/>
```

The <fmt:formatNumber> action provides two attributes that you can use to explicitly control the currency symbol: `currencySymbol` and `currencyCode`; for example, you can override the default currency symbol for France, like this:

```
<fmt:setLocale value='fr-FR'/>
<fmt:formatNumber value='0.234778'
                  type='currency'
    currencySymbol='$'/>
```

Instead of displaying the euro symbol, the preceding code fragment produces this output: `0,23 $`. Notice that we formatted the currency symbol for the preceding code fragment for the French locale by placing it after the number; however the default currency symbol for that locale is overridden with the $ character.

---

6. You must use the ISO-8859-15 or UTF-8 charsets to display the euro. On Windows, the windows-1252 charset should also correctly display the euro symbol.

As you can see from the preceding code fragment, the <fmt:formatNumber> `currencySymbol` attribute lets you specify the currency symbol *directly*. You can also use the <fmt:formatNumber> `currencyCode` attribute to *indirectly* specify the currency symbol; for example, the following code fragment uses the `currencyCode` attribute to specify the Australian dollar symbol for Australian currency:

```
<fmt:setLocale value='en-AU'/>
<fmt:formatNumber value='0.234778'
                  type='currency'
        currencyCode='AUD'/>
```

The output of the preceding code fragment is $0.23. The <fmt:formatNumber> action uses the JDK to translate the currency code to the proper currency symbol; for the preceding code fragment, the JDK translates the currency code AUD—for the en-AU locale—to the $ currency symbol.

When you specify a currency code, the actual currency symbol displayed can vary, depending upon the formatting locale; for example, the preceding code fragment uses the $ currency symbol for Australian dollars when the locale is en-AU (Australian English), but consider the following code fragment:

```
<fmt:setLocale value='en-US'/>
<fmt:formatNumber value='0.234778'
                  type='currency'
        currencyCode='AUD'/>
```

The preceding code fragment is identical to the previous code fragment, except for the formatting locale, which in this case is en-US (U.S. English). If the currency symbol displayed for the preceding code fragment was the same as the currency symbol displayed for the Australian locale ($), there would be no way to distinguish between U.S. and Australian currency, so the preceding code fragment uses the currency code AUD to make that distinction. The output of the preceding code fragment is AUD0.23.

Currency codes are a new addition to the 1.4 version of the JDK, so the <fmt:formatNumber> currencyCode attribute is only supported if you are using JDK 1.4 (or a later version). If you specify both the currencySymbol and currencyCode attributes, currencyCode will take precedence over currencySymbol if you are using JDK 1.4 (or later); however, if you are using JDK 1.3 (or an earlier version), the currencySymbol attribute will take precedence over the currencyCode attribute.

Currency codes are preferable to currency symbols because the JDK produces a currency symbol that's correct for the formatting locale, as the two preceding code fragments illustrate. For example, in the preceding code fragment, because the currency symbol for Australian dollars is $, you might be tempted to specify that *currency symbol* instead of the AUD *currency code*. But because the formatting locale is U.S. English, that currency symbol would be ambiguous, so it's better to specify a currency code (in this case AUD) and let the JDK select an unambiguous currency symbol for the formatting locale. Finally, the JDK currently has few localized currency symbols, but it may provide more in the future.

Currency codes are defined by ISO 4217; Table 8.2 lists some examples of those currency codes.

Table 8.2 Examples of Currency Codes[a]

Country	Currency	Code
France	French Franc	FRF
France	Euro	EUR
Germany	Deutsche Mark	DEM
Germany	Euro	EUR
Great Britain	Pound Sterling	GBP
Israel	New Israel Sheqel	ILS
Japan	Yen	JPY
Poland	Zloty	PLN
United States	US Dollar	USD

a. The French franc and German deutsche mark have been replaced by the euro.

For a complete list of ISO 4217 currency codes, see the following URL:

```
http://www.bsi-global.com/Technical+Information/Publicat
ions/_Publications/tig90x.doc
```

The JSP page shown in Figure 8–3 uses the <fmt:formatNumber> currencyCode to display formatted currencies for the countries listed in Table 8.2.[7]

The JSP page shown in Figure 8–3 is listed in Listing 8.3.

The preceding JSP page uses the UTF-8 charset to properly display all of the currency symbols.[8] If you don't use a charset that can display the currency symbol for a given locale, that currency symbol will not be properly displayed; for example, if

---

7. The grouping separator for the fr-FR locale is a period, but that character is a space in Figure 8–3 and Figure 8–4 because of a JDK 1.4 bug.

8. See "Unicode and Charsets" on page 260 for more information about the UTF-8 charset.

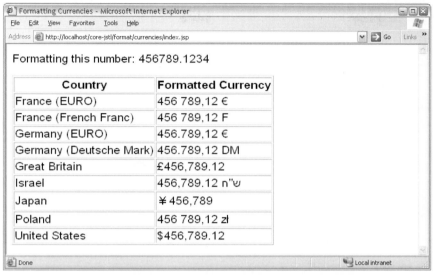

Figure 8–3   Formatting Currencies (font is enlarged to clearly show currency symbols)

Listing 8.3   *Formatting Currencies with <fmt:formatNumber>*

```
<!DOCTYPE HTML PUBLIC "-//W3C//DTD HTML 4.0 Transitional//EN">
<html>
   <head>
      <title>Formatting Currencies</title>
   </head>

   <body>
      <%-- Use the UTF-8 charset for multiple languages--%>
      <%@ page contentType='text/html; charset=UTF-8' %>

      <%@ taglib uri='http://java.sun.com/jstl/core' prefix='c' %>
      <%@ taglib uri='http://java.sun.com/jstl/fmt'  prefix='fmt'%>

      <c:set var='number' value='456789.1234'/>

      <font size='5'>
         <c:out value='Formatting this number: ${number}'/>
      </font>
```

Listing 8.3   *Formatting Currencies with <fmt:formatNumber> (cont.)*

```
<p><table border='1'>
   <tr>
      <th><font size='5'>Country</font></th>
      <th><font size='5'>Formatted Currency</font></th>
   </tr>

   <tr><td><font size='5'>France (EURO)</font></td>
      <fmt:setLocale value='fr-FR'/>
      <td><font size='5'>
         <fmt:formatNumber value='${number}'
                           type='currency'
                    currencyCode='EUR'/></font></td>
   </tr>

   <tr><td><font size='5'>France (French Franc)</font></td>
      <fmt:setLocale value='fr-FR'/>
      <td><font size='5'>
         <fmt:formatNumber value='${number}'
                           type='currency'
                    currencyCode='FRF'/></font></td></tr>

   <tr><td><font size='5'>Germany (EURO)</font></td>
      <fmt:setLocale value='de-DE'/>
      <td><font size='5'>
         <fmt:formatNumber value='${number}'
                           type='currency'
                    currencyCode='EUR'/></font></td></tr>

   <tr><td><font size='5'>Germany (Deutsche
Mark)</font></td>
      <fmt:setLocale value='de-DE'/>
      <td><font size='5'>
         <fmt:formatNumber value='${number}'
                           type='currency'
                    currencyCode='DEM'/></font></td></tr>

   <tr><td><font size='5'>Great Britain</font></td>
      <fmt:setLocale value='en-GB'/>
      <td><font size='5'>
         <fmt:formatNumber value='${number}'
                           type='currency'
                    currencyCode='GBP'/></font></td></tr>

   <tr><td><font size='5'>Israel</font></td>
      <fmt:setLocale value='he-IL'/>
      <td><font size='5'>
```

Listing 8.3	*Formatting Currencies with <fmt:formatNumber> (cont.)*

```
            <fmt:formatNumber value='${number}'
                              type='currency'
                     currencyCode='ILS'/></font></td></tr>

      <tr><td><font size='5'>Japan</font></td>
         <fmt:setLocale value='ja-JP'/>
         <td><font size='5'>
            <fmt:formatNumber value='${number}'
                              type='currency'
                     currencyCode='JPY'/></font></td></tr>

      <tr><td><font size='5'>Poland</font></td>
         <fmt:setLocale value='pl-PL'/>
         <td><font size='5'>
            <fmt:formatNumber value='${number}'
                              type='currency'
                     currencyCode='PLN'/></font></td></tr>

      <tr><td><font size='5'>United States</font></td>
         <fmt:setLocale value='en-US'/>
         <td><font size='5'>
            <fmt:formatNumber value='${number}'
                              type='currency'
                     currencyCode='USD'/></font></td></tr>
   </table>
  </body>
</html>
```

you don't specify the UTF-8 charset for the preceding JSP page, you will get the
result shown in Figure 8–4.[9]

If you don't use the UTF-8 charset, you must specify a charset that corresponds to
the currency symbol that you are trying to display; for example, if you want to display
the New Israel Sheqel currency symbol, you can use the ISO-8859-8 charset, and
if you want to display the euro currency symbol, you can use the ISO-8859-15
charset. Table 8.3 lists some example currency symbols and their corresponding
charsets.

For a complete list of Latin charsets and their corresponding countries, see the
following URL:

```
http://wwwbs.cs.tu-berlin.de/user/czyborra/charsets
```

---

9. Figure 8–4 shows the JSP page displayed by Tomcat 4.0.3; results may vary for other servlet
    containers.

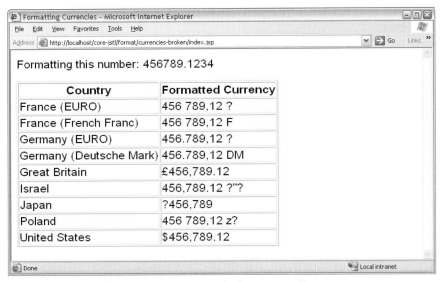

Figure 8–4   Formatting Currencies with the Wrong Charset

Table 8.3   Examples of Currency Symbols and Corresponding Charsets

Currency Symbol	Charset
Euro	ISO-8859-15
New Israel Sheqel	ISO-8859-8
Polish Zloty	ISO-8859-2

Core Warning

If you don't get the expected result when you display a currency symbol, make sure that you are using a charset that can display that currency symbol; for example, if you want to display the euro currency symbol, you can use the ISO-8859-15 charset. You can also use the UTF-8 charset, which should properly display all currency symbols.

8.2 Formatting and Parsing Dates and Times

Like numbers, dates are formatted differently for different locales; for example, the date May 9, 2002 is formatted (in short form) as 5/9/02 for the U.S. English (en-US) locale and as 09/05/02 for the France French (fr-FR) locale. JSTL provides two actions, <fmt:formatDate> and <fmt:parseDate>, that format and parse dates, respectively.

The <fmt:formatDate> action formats an instance of java.util.Date and outputs a string representation of that date. The three most common ways to create a date for <fmt:formatDate> are with <jsp:useBean>, <fmt_rt:formatDate>, or <fmt:parseDate>; for example, you can create a date with <jsp:useBean> like this:

```
<fmt:setLocale value='en-US'/>
<jsp:useBean id='today' class='java.util.Date'/>
<fmt:formatDate value='${today}'/>
```

In the preceding code fragment, the <jsp:useBean> action stores an instance of java.util.Date (which represents the current date) in a scoped variable named today in page scope. Subsequently, the <fmt:formatDate> action accesses that scoped variable and formats it according to the U.S. English locale. If the current date is the 9th of May in the year 2002, the output of the preceding code fragment will be May 9, 2002. If you change the locale specified with the <fmt:setLocale> action in the preceding code fragment to fr-FR, the output of the preceding code fragment will be 9 mai 2002.

You can also use the <fmt_rt:formatNumber> action to format an instance of java.util.Date that's created with a JSP expression, like this:

```
<fmt:setLocale value='en-US'/>
<fmt_rt:formatDate value='<%= new java.util.Date() %>'/>
```

The preceding code fragment is functionally identical to the code fragment listed above that uses the <jsp:useBean> action.

The <fmt:parseDate> action parses a string into an instance of java.util.Date, so you can use <fmt:parseDate> in concert with <fmt:formatDate> to format a string representation of a date, like this:

```
<fmt:setLocale value='en-US'/>
<fmt:parseDate value='May 9, 2002' var='date'/>
<fmt:formatDate value='${date}' dateStyle='short'/>
```

In the preceding code fragment, <fmt:parseDate> parses the string May 9, 2002 and stores the resulting java.util.Date instance in a scoped variable named date in page scope. Subsequently, the <fmt:formatDate> action accesses that scoped variable and formats the date with the short date style as 5/9/02.

The <fmt:formatDate> and <fmt:parseDate> actions can format and parse, respectively, a date, a time, or both. By default, those actions format and parse a date, but you can specify just the time or both the date and the time with the <fmt:formatDate> and <fmt:parseDate> type attributes; for example, you can format both the date and time like this:

```
<fmt:setLocale value='en-US'/>
<jsp:useBean id='today' class='java.util.Date'/>
<fmt:formatDate value='${today}' type='both'/>
```

Assuming a current date and time of May 9, 2002 at 2:36:53 P.M., the preceding code produces the following output for the U.S. English locale: May 9, 2002 2:36:53 PM. If you set the <fmt:formatDate> type attribute to time, the preceding code fragment will produce this output for the U.S. English locale: 2:36:53 PM.

Dates and times can be formatted (and parsed) with predefined formats, which are specified with the <fmt:formatDate> (and <fmt:parseDate>) dateStyle and timeStyle attributes. Valid values for those attributes are default, short, medium, long, and full, where default is the same as medium. The default value is used if the dateStyle and timeStyle attributes are not specified.

Examples of those predefined formats are shown in Table 8.4.

Table 8.4   Predefined Date and Time Formats

Value	Description	Example Date and Time for U.S. Locale
short	Numeric	10/19/00 6:07 PM
medium	Longer than short	Oct 19, 2000 6:07:01 PM
long	Longer than medium	October 19, 2000 6:07:01 PM MDT
full	Completely specified	Thursday, October 19, 2000 6:07:01 PM MDT

It's also easy to format dates and times for non-Latin languages; for example, here's how you'd format the current date and time for Chinese, Arabic, and Thai, all in the same JSP page:

```
<%-- Use UTF-8 to display multiple languages --%>
<%@ page contentType='text/html; charset=UTF-8' %>
<%@ taglib uri='http://java.sun.com/jstl/fmt' prefix='fmt' %>
```

```
<%-- Chinese, Taiwan --%>
<fmt:setLocale value='zh-TW'/>
<fmt_rt:formatDate value='<%= new java.util.Date() %>'
                   type='both'
            dateStyle='full'
            timeStyle='full'/>
<p>

<%-- Arabic, Saudi Arabia --%>
<fmt:setLocale value='ar-SA'/>
<fmt_rt:formatDate value='<%= new java.util.Date() %>'
                   type='both'
            dateStyle='full'
            timeStyle='full'/>
</p><p>

<%-- Thai, Thailand --%>
<fmt:setLocale value='th-TH'/>
<fmt_rt:formatDate value='<%= new java.util.Date() %>'
                   type='both'
            dateStyle='full'
            timeStyle='full'/>
</p>
```

Here's what the preceding code fragment produces for the 25th of May, 2002 at 2:17:17 PM, EDT:

2002年5月25日 下午02時17分17秒 EDT

25 2002 , مايو‎ EDT 02:17:17 م

วันเสาร์ที่ 25 พฤษภาคม พ.ศ. 2545, 14 นาฬิกา 17 นาที 17 วินาที

If the predefined formats listed in Table 8.4 are not sufficient, you can specify custom formatting patterns for both the <fmt:formatDate> and <fmt:parseDate> actions. Those custom formatting patterns are discussed in "Custom Patterns for Dates and Times" on page 336.

You can also specify a time zone for <fmt:formatDate> and <fmt:parseDate> with the timeZone attribute. That attribute comes in handy when a Web server resides in one time zone and clients reside in another; for example, the following code fragment formats the current date and time for the America/Denver time zone:

```
<fmt:setLocale value='en-US'/>
<jsp:useBean id='today' class='java.util.Date'/>
<fmt:formatDate value='${today}'
                type='both'
          timeZone='America/Denver'
          timeStyle='full'/>
```

In the preceding code fragment, the `timeStyle` attribute for the `<fmt:formatDate>` action is specified as `full`, so the time zone will be displayed. If the current date and time is May 9, 2002 at 3:16:13 PM, the output of the preceding code fragment will be:

```
May 9, 2002 3:16:13 PM MDT
```

In addition to the `<fmt:formatDate>` and `<fmt:parseDate>` `timeZone` attributes, you can also specify time zones with the `<fmt:timeZone>` and `<fmt:setTimeZone>` actions, which are discussed in "Using Time Zones" on page 343.

Custom Patterns for Dates and Times

If the predefined date and time patterns—see Table 8.4—are not sufficient for your needs, you can specify custom date and time patterns; for example, the following code fragment formats the current date and time according to a custom pattern:

```
<jsp:useBean id='now' class='java.util.Date'/>

<fmt:formatDate value='${now}'
                type='both'
            pattern="MM/dd/yyyy' at: 'hh:mm:ss"/>
```

The preceding code fragment formats the current date and time using the pattern `MM/dd/yyyy' at: 'hh:mm:ss`. Assuming a current date and time of May 11, 2002 at 10:43:53, the preceding code fragment will produce the following output: `05/11/2002 at: 10:40:53`. All characters within a custom date pattern are interpreted by the `<fmt:formatDate>` and `<fmt:parseDate>` actions, except for characters enclosed in single quotes. In the preceding code fragment, the quoted string `' at: '` is not interpreted.

You can also use custom date patterns to parse a string representation of a date with `<fmt:parseDate>`, like this:

```
<fmt:parseDate value='6/20/1957'
               var='parsedDate'
            pattern='MM/dd/yyyy'/>

<fmt:formatDate value='${parsedDate}'
               pattern="MMMM dd'th, 'yyyy' was a 'EEEE"/>
```

In the preceding code fragment, <fmt:parseDate> parses the string 6/20/1957 using the pattern MM/dd/yyyy and stores the resulting instance of java.util.Date in a scoped variable named parsedDate. Subsequently, <fmt:formatDate> formats that date with another custom date pattern. The output of the preceding code fragment is June 20th, 1957 was a Thursday.

You should note that patterns specified for <fmt:parseDate> must match the string that <fmt:parseDate> parses; for example, consider the following code fragment:

```
<fmt:parseDate value='20/6/1957'
          pattern='MM/dd/yyyy'/>
```

In the preceding code fragment, <fmt:parseDate> will throw an exception because 20 is not a valid numeric value for a month, even though the pattern MM/dd/yyyy is valid for many locales.

Table 8.5 lists the characters you can use in a custom date pattern.

Table 8.5   Characters Used in Date and Time Patterns [a]

Letter	DateorTimeComponent	Presentation	Examples
G	Era designator	Text	AD
y	Year	Year	2002 02
M	Month in year	Month	August Aug 08
w	Week in year	Number	50
W	Week in month	Number	3
D	Day in year	Number	224
d	Day in month	Number	20
F	Day of week in month	Number	6
E	Day in week	Text	Wednesday Wed
a	Am/pm marker	Text	AM PM
H	Hour in day (0-23)	Number	0
k	Hour in day (1-24)	Number	24
K	Hour in am/pm (0-11)	Number	0
h	Hour in am/pm (1-12)	Number	12
m	Minute in hour	Number	50
s	Second in minute	Number	55

Table 8.5   Characters Used in Date and Time Patterns [a] *(cont.)*

Letter	DateorTimeComponent	Presentation	Examples
S	Millisecond	Number	960
z	Time zone	General time zone	Pacific Standard Time PST GMT-08:00
Z	Time zone	RFC 822 time zone	0800

a. This table and the related discussion that follows is derived from the Java documentation for the `java.text.SimpleDateFormat` class.

The letters listed in the preceding table are usually specified in multiples; the number of times a letter is repeated determines presentation as follows, where each heading (such as ***Text***, ***Number***, etc.) corresponds to the `Presentation` column from the preceding table:[10]

- ***Text***:

  - *Formatting*: If you specify 4 or more letters, a full format is used; otherwise, an abbreviated form is used if available. For example, for Sunday, the patterns E, EE, and EEE will display `Sun`, whereas the pattern EEEE will display `Sunday`.
  - *Parsing*: Both the full and abbreviated forms are accepted, independently of the number of pattern letters.

- ***Number***:

  - *Formatting*: No matter how many letters you specify, the minimum number of digits is always shown; for example, if the day of the year is 125, that value will be displayed for D, DD, and DDD. If you specify more letters than the minimum number of digits, the number is zero-padded; for example, if the day of the year is 125 and you specify DDDD, then `0125` will be displayed.
  - *Parsing*: The number of letters is ignored unless it's needed to separate adjacent fields.

- ***Month***:

  - *Formatting*: If the number of letters is less than 3, the month is interpreted as a *Number*; otherwise, it's interpreted as *Text*. For

---

10. All of the following examples assume an `en-US` locale.

example, for the month of May, M and MM will display 5 and 05, respectively, whereas MMM will display May.

- *Parsing*: Same as formatting.

- **Year**:

  - *Formatting*: If the number of letters is less than 4, the year is truncated to two digits; for example, for the year 2002, y, yy, and yyy will all display 02, whereas yyyy will display 2002.
  - *Parsing*: If the number of letters is more than 2, the year is interpreted literally; for example, for the pattern MM/dd/yyyy, the string 01/11/12 will be parsed as January 11, 12 AD. For an abbreviated year pattern—y or yy—the year is interpreted relative to the time span into which it falls. A 100-year time span is split into two parts arranged around the *current date* as follows: one part spans the past 80 years, and the other spans the next 20 years. Given an abbreviated year, the time span into which the year falls is determined, and the century information is taken from that time span. For example, *for a parsing action used on* January 1, 1997, the string 01/11/12 would be parsed as January 11, 2012, because 2012 falls into the time span 1997 + 20 years and 1912 does not fall into the time span 1997 − 80 years; and the string "05/04/64" would be parsed as May 4, 1964 because 1964 falls into the time span 1997 − 80 years and 2064 does not fall into the time span 1997 + 20 years.

- **General time zone**:

  - *Formatting*: Time zones specified with a name, such as America/Denver, are interpreted as Text. You can also specify a time zone as a GMT offset, such as GMT-02:00 or GMT+03:30.
  - *Parsing*: Same as formatting, except RFC 822 time zones are also accepted.

- **RFC 822 time zone**:[11]

  - *Formatting*: A 4-digit time zone format, such as 0700.
  - *Parsing*: Same as formatting, except general time zones are also accepted.

---

11. See http://www.ietf.org/rfc/rfc0822.txt?number=822 for more information about RFC 822.

Table 8.6 lists some example date and time patterns for the U.S. English locale.

Table 8.6 Date and Time Pattern Examples for U.S. English

Pattern	Result
MM/dd/yyyy	05/06/2002
h 'o"clock and' mm 'minutes'	2 o'clock and 36 minutes
'Today is: 'EEEE, MMM dd	Today is Monday, May 06
h:mm a, z	2:36 AM, MST
E, MMM d'th at precisely:' hh:mm:ss:SS	Mon, May 6th at precisely: 02:36:27:497
'It"s' yyyy G	It's 2002 AD
k:m:s, dd/MM ''yy Z	14:36:27, 06/05 '02 -0600

The example patterns in the preceding table use a wide range of the characters listed in Table 8.5, including the characters for time zones and milliseconds. Notice that two consecutive single quotes in a row produce one single quote in the output.

Figure 8–5 shows a JSP page that you can use to specify a locale and a custom date pattern to format the current date. The top picture in Figure 8–5 shows a pattern that generates a fairly complete date format, and the bottom picture shows a pattern that generates a short date format with the year fully specified.

The JSP page shown in Figure 8–5 is listed in Listing 8.4.

The preceding JSP page lets you select a locale from any of the available locales that the JDK uses to format dates, by calling `java.text.DateFormat.getAvailableLocales()`. Because you can select from so many different locales, the preceding JSP page uses the `UTF-8` charset. See "Unicode and Charsets" on page 260 for more information about that charset.

After setting the charset, the preceding JSP page creates a scoped variable for the previously selected locale. If no locale was selected, the JSP page sets that scoped variable to the default locale. The JSP page uses that scoped variable to set the locale with <fmt:setLocale> and also to select the previously selected locale for the HTML `select` element that displays available locales for date formatting. Subsequently, the JSP page creates a scoped variable named `now` with <jsp:useBean> and uses <fmt:formatDate> to format that date with the specified pattern. The rest of the JSP page creates the form.

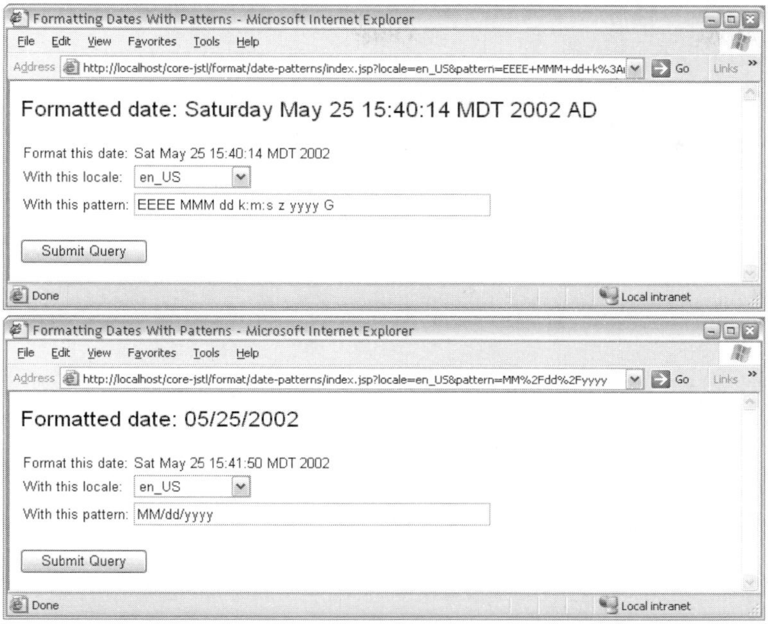

Figure 8–5   Formatting Dates with Custom Patterns

Listing 8.4   *Formatting Dates with Custom Patterns*

```
<!DOCTYPE HTML PUBLIC "-//W3C//DTD HTML 4.0 Transitional//EN">
<html>
   <head>
      <title>Formatting Dates With Patterns</title>
   </head>

   <body>
      <%@ page contentType='text/html; charset=UTF-8' %>

      <%@ taglib uri='http://java.sun.com/jstl/core' prefix='c' %>
      <%@ taglib uri='http://java.sun.com/jstl/fmt'  prefix='fmt'%>
      <%@ taglib uri='http://java.sun.com/jstl/core_rt'
            prefix='c_rt' %>

      <%-- Create a scoped variable based on the locale
           request parameter --%>
```

Listing 8.4   *Formatting Dates with Custom Patterns (cont.)*

```
<c:choose>
   <c:when test='${empty param.locale}'>
      <c_rt:set var='locale'
              value='<%= java.util.Locale.getDefault() %>'/>
   </c:when>
   <c:otherwise>
      <c:set var='locale' value='${param.locale}'/>
   </c:otherwise>
</c:choose>

<%-- Set the locale according to the locale request
     parameter --%>
<fmt:setLocale value='${locale}'/>

<%-- Create a scoped variable that contains the current
     date --%>
<jsp:useBean id='now' class='java.util.Date'/>

<%-- Show formatted number --%>
<font size='5'>Formatted date:
   <c:choose>
      <c:when test='${not empty param.pattern}'>
         <fmt:formatDate value='${now}'
                         pattern='${param.pattern}'/>
      </c:when>
      <c:otherwise>
         <fmt:formatDate value='${now}'/>
      </c:otherwise>
   </c:choose>
</font>

<%-- Because this form does not specify an action, this
     JSP page will be reloaded when the submit button
     is activated --%>
<form>
   <table>
      <tr>
         <td>Format this date:</td>
         <td><c:out value='${now}'/></td>
      </tr>

      <tr>
         <td>With this locale:</td>
         <td>
         <select name='locale'>
            <c_rt:forEach var='thisLocale'
```

Listing 8.4   *Formatting Dates with Custom Patterns (cont.)*

```
                              items='<%= java.text.DateFormat.
                                        getAvailableLocales()%>'>
                    <option>
                    <c:if test='${locale == thisLocale}'>
                       selected
                    </c:if>

                    <c:out value='>${thisLocale}'
                       escapeXml='false'/>
                    </option>
                 </c_rt:forEach>
              </select>
              </td>
           </tr>

           <tr>
              <td>With this pattern:</td>
              <td><input type='text' name='pattern' size='50'
                     value='<c:out value="${param.pattern}"/>'/>
              </td>
           </tr>
        </table>
        <p><input type='submit'/>
     </form>
   </body>
</html>
```

8.3 Using Time Zones

The <fmt:formatDate> and <fmt:parseDate> actions use a time zone to format and parse dates, respectively. Both of those actions have a timeZone attribute that lets you explicitly specify a time zone; for example:

```
<fmt:parseDate value='6/20/1957 14:00'
          timeZone='America/Los_Angeles'
             var='parsedDate'
          pattern='MM/dd/yyyy kk:mm'/>


Date in Eastern Time Zone:
<fmt:formatDate value='${parsedDate}'
          timeZone='America/New_York'
```

```
          type='both'
     timeStyle='full'/>
```

In the preceding code fragment, <fmt:parseDate> parses a string and stores the resulting date in a scoped variable named `parsedDate`.[12] The `timeZone` attribute tells <fmt:parseDate> that the date it parses is relative to the America/Los_Angeles time zone. Subsequently, the <fmt:formatDate> action formats the date stored in the `parsedDate` scoped variable. The `timeZone` attribute tells <fmt:formatDate> that it should interpret the date it formats relative to the America/New_York time zone. Here's the output for the preceding code fragment:

```
Date in Eastern Time Zone: Jun 20, 1957 5:00:00 PM EDT
```

Notice that the <fmt:formatDate> action in the preceding code fragment adjusts the time from the America/Los_Angeles time zone to the America/New_York time zone, taking into account Standard Daylight Time.

If you don't specify a `timeZone` attribute for <fmt:formatDate> or <fmt:parseDate>, those actions search for a time zone like this:

1. If the <fmt:formatDate> or <fmt:parseDate> actions are nested in a <fmt:timeZone> action, they use the time zone specified by that <fmt:timeZone> action; if those actions are not nested in a <fmt:timeZone> action, go to step 2.

2. If the `FMT_TIME_ZONE` configuration setting has been set, <fmt:formatDate> and <fmt:parseDate> will use the time zone specified by that configuration setting; if the `FMT_TIME_ZONE` configuration setting has not been set, go to step 3.

3. The <fmt:formatDate> and <fmt:parseDate> actions use the JSP container's time zone.

The <fmt:timeZone> action, mentioned in step 1 listed above, has a simple syntax:[13]

<fmt:timeZone value>
     body content, presumably with <fmt:formatDate> and <fmt:parseDate>
     actions
</fmt:timeZone>

Instead of using the `timeZone` attributes for <fmt:formatDate> and <fmt:parseDate>, you can use the <fmt:timeZone> action to specify a time zone for

---

12. That date is an instance of `java.util.Date`; see "Formatting and Parsing Dates and Times" on page 333 for more information about <fmt:parseDate>.
13. See "<fmt:timeZone>" on page 525 for a complete description of <fmt:timeZone>.

those actions; for example, the code fragment listed at the beginning of this section could be rewritten like this:

```
<fmt:timeZone value='America/Los_Angeles'>
   <fmt:parseDate value='6/20/1957 14:00'
                    var='parsedDate'
                pattern='MM/dd/yyyy kk:mm'/>
</fmt:timeZone>

Date in Eastern Time Zone:
<fmt:timeZone value='America/New_York'>
   <fmt:formatDate value='${parsedDate}'
                    type='both'
                timeStyle='full'/>
</fmt:timeZone>
```

The preceding code fragment is functionally identical to the code fragment listed at the beginning of this section. The <fmt:timeZone> action is preferable to the timeZone attribute for <fmt:parseDate> and <fmt:formatDate> when a number of <fmt:parseDate> and <fmt:formatDate> actions share a time zone.

If you don't specify the timeZone attribute for <fmt:parseDate> and <fmt:formatDate> actions and if those actions are not nested in a <fmt:timeZone> action, they will use the time zone stored in the FMT_TIME_ZONE configuration setting. You can set that configuration setting in a number of ways;[14] for example, you can set the FMT_TIME_ZONE configuration setting in a deployment descriptor, like this:

```
<web-app>
...
   <context-param>
      <param-name>javax.servlet.jsp.jstl.fmt.timeZone</param-name>
      <param-value>America/New_York</param-value>
   </context-param>
...
<web-app>
```

The preceding code fragment, from WEB-INF/web.xml, specifies a time zone of America/New_York for the FMT_TIME_ZONE configuration setting. Notice that the preceding code fragment specifies a parameter name of javax.servlet.jsp.jstl.fmt.timeZone, which is the name of the FMT_TIME_ZONE configuration setting.[15] If you set the FMT_TIME_ZONE

---

14. See "Configuration Settings" on page 230 for more information about configuration settings.
15. See "JSTL Formatting Configuration Settings" on page 510 for more information about the FMT_TIME_ZONE configuration setting.

configuration setting to America/New_York, as in the preceding code fragment, the following code fragment is equivalent to the code fragment listed at the beginning of this section:

```
<fmt:parseDate value='6/20/1957 14:00'
            timeZone='America/Los_Angeles'
                var='parsedDate'
            pattern='MM/dd/yyyy kk:mm'/>


Date in Eastern Time Zone:
<fmt:formatDate value='${parsedDate}'
                type='both'
            timeStyle='full'/>
```

In the preceding code fragment, the <fmt:formatDate> action will use the time zone specified with the FMT_TIME_ZONE configuration setting. You can also set the FMT_TIME_ZONE configuration setting with the <fmt:setTimeZone> action. That action has the following syntax:[16]

<fmt:setTimeZone value [var] [scope]/>

You could use the <fmt:setTimeZone> action to rewrite the code fragment listed at the beginning of this section, like this:

```
<fmt:setTimeZone value='America/Los_Angeles'/>
<fmt:parseDate value='6/20/1957 14:00'
                var='parsedDate'
            pattern='MM/dd/yyyy kk:mm'/>


Date in Eastern Time Zone:
<fmt:setTimeZone value='America/New_York'/>
<fmt:formatDate value='${parsedDate}'
                type='both'
            timeStyle='full'/>
```

In the preceding code fragment, the <fmt:setTimeZone> actions store a time zone in the FMT_TIME_ZONE configuration setting. Because the timeZone attribute is not set for the <fmt:parseDate> and <fmt:formatDate> actions in the preceding code fragment and because those actions are not nested in a <fmt:timeZone> action, they will use the time zone stored in the FMT_TIME_ZONE configuration setting.

---

16. Items in brackets are optional. See "<fmt:setTimeZone>" on page 527 for a complete description of <fmt:setTimeZone> syntax.

You can also use the <fmt:setTimeZone> `var` attribute to store a time zone in a scoped variable instead of the `FMT_TIME_ZONE` configuration setting, like this:

```
<fmt:setTimeZone value='America/Los_Angeles' var='parseTimeZone'/>
<fmt:parseDate value='6/20/1957 14:00'
                    var='parsedDate'
          timeZone='${parseTimeZone}'
          pattern='MM/dd/yyyy kk:mm'/>


Date in Eastern Time Zone:
<fmt:setTimeZone value='America/New_York' var='formatTimeZone'/>
<fmt:formatDate value='${parsedDate}'
             timeZone='${formatTimeZone}'
                 type='both'
          timeStyle='full'/>
```

In the preceding code fragment—which is functionally identical to the code fragment listed at the beginning of this section—the <fmt:setTimeZone> action is used to store the `America/Los_Angeles` time zone in a scoped variable named `parseTimeZone` and the `America/New_York` time zone in a scoped variable named `formatTimeZone`. Those scoped variables are used by the <fmt:parseDate> and <fmt:formatDate> actions, respectively. When you need to temporarily set a time zone that spans multiple pages—for example, if you need to set a time zone for a particular HTTP request—the <fmt:setTimeZone> action with the `var` attribute specified is preferable to the `timeZone` attribute for <fmt:parseDate> and <fmt:formatDate> and the `FMT_TIME_ZONE` configuration setting.

Finally, if you do not specify the `timeZone` attribute for <fmt:parseDate> and <fmt:formatDate> actions, those actions are not nested in a <fmt:timeZone> action, and if the `FMT_TIME_ZONE` configuration setting has not been set, those actions will use your JSP container's default time zone.

You must always specify time zones with time zone Standard IDs, which are of the form *Continent/City*, such as America/New_York; *Ocean/City*, such as Pacific/Honolulu; or *Continent/Region/City*, such as America/Indiana/Knox. Table 8.7 lists some examples of time zone Standard IDs.

Many time zones have abbreviations; for example America/Los_Angeles is often abbreviated as PST or PDT, for Pacific Standard Time and Pacific Daylight Time, respectively. But *you must not use time zone abbreviations when you specify time zones in your JSP code*, because abbreviations are highly ambiguous; for example, IST can mean either Irish Summer Time or India Standard Time.

For a complete list of time zone Standard IDs, see the following URL:

```
http://www.timezoneconverter.com/cgi-bin/zonehelp.tzc
```

Table 8.7   Time Zone Standard ID Examples

Standard ID	Comment
America/Adak	Aleutian Islands
America/Chicago	Central Time
America/Dawson	Pacific Time - North Yukon
America/Denver	Mountain Time
America/Detroit	Eastern Time, Michigan (most locations)
America/Los_Angeles	Pacific Time
America/Louisville	Eastern Time, Kentucky
America/New_York	Eastern Time
America/Noronha	Atlantic Islands
America/Yakutat	Alaska Time, Alaska panhandle neck
Pacific/Honolulu	Hawaii

In addition to providing a list of time zones, the preceding URL provides a link to a time zone converter. That converter lets you convert the current date and time from one time zone to another. Figure 8–6 shows a time zone converter that uses the JSTL formatting actions.

The first time the JSP page shown in Figure 8–6 is accessed, it selects the option in the HTML `select` element that represents the JSP container's time zone and displays the current date and time for that time zone. The top picture in Figure 8–6 shows the JSP page when it is first accessed.

After you select a time zone and activate the submit button, the JSP page shown in Figure 8–6 displays the current date and time for the JSP container's time zone and for the selected time zone. The bottom picture in Figure 8–6 shows the JSP page after the `America/Montreal` time zone has been selected.

The JSP page shown in Figure 8–6 is listed in Listing 8.5.

The preceding JSP page imports the `TimeZone`, `Date`, and `Locale` classes from the `java.util` package and creates a scoped variable named `now` that references a `Date` object representing the current date and time. Subsequently, the JSP page uses the `<c_rt:set>` action to store the default time zone, the name of the default time zone localized in U.S. English, and all of the available time zone Standard IDs in scoped variables, which are used later in the page. The preceding JSP page then creates its form. If no time zone was previously selected, the JSP page selects the option for the HTML `select` element that represents the JSP container's time zone; otherwise, the JSP page selects the previously selected time zone.

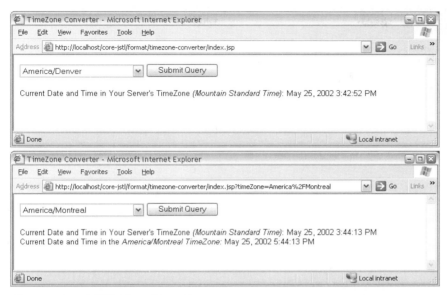

Figure 8–6   A JSTL Time Zone Converter

Listing 8.5   *A TimeZone Converter*

```html
<!DOCTYPE HTML PUBLIC "-//W3C//DTD HTML 4.0 Transitional//EN">
<html>
   <head>
      <title>TimeZone Converter</title>
   </head>

   <body>
      <%@ taglib uri='http://java.sun.com/jstl/core' prefix='c' %>
      <%@ taglib uri='http://java.sun.com/jstl/fmt'  pre-
fix='fmt'%>
      <%@ taglib uri='http://java.sun.com/jstl/core_rt'
             prefix='c_rt' %>

      <%-- These classes are needed below --%>
      <%@ page import='java.util.TimeZone' %>
      <%@ page import='java.util.Date' %>
      <%@ page import='java.util.Locale' %>
      <%@ page import='javax.servlet.jsp.jstl.core.Config' %>

      <%-- Set the locale to U.S. English --%>
      <fmt:setLocale value='en-US'/>
```

Listing 8.5   *A TimeZone Converter (cont.)*

```
<%-- Use this bean below --%>
<jsp:useBean id='now' class='java.util.Date'/>

<%-- Store the default time zone in a scoped variable --%>
<c_rt:set value='<%= TimeZone.getDefault() %>'
          var='defaultTimeZone'/>

<%-- Store the name of the default time zone in a
     scoped variable --%>
<c_rt:set value='<%= TimeZone.getDefault().
                     getDisplayName(Locale.US) %>'
          var='defaultTimeZoneName'/>

<%-- Store all available time zone Standard IDs in
     a scoped variable --%>
<c_rt:set value='<%= TimeZone.getAvailableIDs() %>'
          var='availableTimeZones'/>

<%-- Because this form does not specify an action, this
     JSP page will be reloaded when the form's submit
     button is activated --%>
<form>
   <%-- Create the HTML select element for selecting a
        time zone --%>
   <select name='timeZone'>
     <%-- For each available time zone --%>
     <c:forEach var='item' items='${availableTimeZones}'>
        <option
        <c:choose>
          <%-- If no time zone was previously selected --%>
           <c:when test='${empty param.timeZone}'>
              <%-- Select this option if it's equal to
                   the default time zone --%>
              <c_rt:if test='<%= TimeZone.getDefault().
                    equals(TimeZone.getTimeZone((String)
                    Config.find(pageContext, "item")))%>'>
                 selected
              </c_rt:if>
           </c:when>

           <%-- Select this option if it equals the last
                time zone selected --%>
           <c:when test='${param.timeZone == item}'>
             selected
           </c:when>
        </c:choose>
```

| Listing 8.5 | *A TimeZone Converter (cont.)* |

```
            ><c:out value='${item}'/></option>
        </c:forEach>
    </select>
    <input type='submit'/>
</form>

<%-- Display the current date and time in the JSP container's
     time zone --%>
Current Date and Time in Your Server's TimeZone<i>
(<c:out value='${defaultTimeZoneName}'/>)</i>:

<fmt:formatDate value='${now}' type='both'
            timeZone='${defaultTimeZone}'/><br>

<c:choose>
    <%-- If a time zone was previously selected, show
         the date and time for that time zone --%>
    <c:when test='${not empty param.timeZone}'>
        Current Date and Time in the
        <i><c:out value=' ${param.timeZone} TimeZone: '/></i>
        <fmt:timeZone value='${param.timeZone}'>
            <fmt:formatDate value='${now}' type='both'/>
        </fmt:timeZone>
    </c:when>
</c:choose>
    </body>
</html>
```

After the form has been created, the preceding JSP page displays the current date and time for the JSP container's time zone. If a time zone was previously selected, the JSP page also displays the current date and time for that time zone.

For the sake of illustration, the preceding JSP page formats the current date and time in two different ways. The date and time for the JSP container's time zone are formatted by specification of the timeZone attribute for the <fmt:formatDate> action. The date and time for the previously selected time zone are formatted by a <fmt:formatDate> action that is nested in a <fmt:timeZone> action. Specifying time zones in two different ways reinforces that there is more than one way to specify a time zone for <fmt:formatDate> and <fmt:parseDate> actions; see "Using Time Zones" on page 343 for more information about other ways to specify time zones.

8.4 Determining a Formatting Locale

So far in this chapter, all of the code examples have used <fmt:setLocale> to specify the locale used by the <fmt:formatNumber>, <fmt:parseNumber>, <fmt:formatDate>, and <fmt:parseDate> actions. But in practice, it's usually not necessary to use <fmt:setLocale> to establish a formatting locale because the formatting actions perform a rather elaborate search for a locale. This section discusses that search.

Before we discuss the search for a formatting locale, you must understand the concept of a localization context. You can read about localization contexts in "Localization Context Lookup" on page 268, but in a nutshell, a localization context is a simple JavaBeans component (bean) that maintains a resource bundle and a locale. For our purposes in this chapter, the resource bundle is immaterial, but the locale stored in a localization context is often used by formatting actions.

The search that formatting actions perform to locate a formatting locale proceeds as follows:

1. An Enclosing <fmt:bundle> Action

   All <fmt:bundle> actions establish a localization context, meaning they store a resource bundle and a locale in a localization context. If a formatting action is nested in a <fmt:bundle> action, it uses the locale stored in the localization context established by its enclosing <fmt:bundle> action.

2. The FMT_LOCALIZATION_CONTEXT Configuration Setting

   If a formatting action is not nested in a <fmt:bundle> action, it checks to see if the FMT_LOCALIZATION_CONTEXT configuration setting has been set; if so, the formatting action uses the locale stored in that configuration setting.

3. Formatting Locale Lookup

   If a formatting action is not nested in a <fmt:bundle> action and the FMT_LOCALIZATION_CONTEXT configuration setting has not been set, the formatting action performs a *formatting locale lookup*. That lookup is discussed in "Formatting Locale Lookup" on page 354.

Let's discuss each of the preceding steps in more detail.

1. An Enclosing <fmt:bundle> Action

Formatting actions that are nested in a <fmt:bundle> action use the locale stored in that <fmt:bundle> action's localization context; for example:

```
<%-- The following <fmt:bundle> action establishes a localization
     context that is only used in the body of the <fmt:bundle>
     action --%>
<fmt:bundle basename='messages'>
   <%-- The i18n and formatting actions nested in the enclosing
        <fmt:bundle> action use the localization context
        established by the enclosing <fmt:bundle> action --%>
   <fmt:message key='formatting.example.number'/>
   ...
   <fmt:formatNumber value='234682.155'/>
   ...
</fmt:bundle>
```

In the preceding code fragment, the <fmt:bundle> action tries to locate a resource bundle whose base name is messages; if it finds that resource bundle, it creates a localization context and stores the resource bundle and the locale that was used to locate that resource bundle in its localization context.[17] All of the <fmt:message> actions and all of the formatting actions nested in that <fmt:bundle> action use the same localization context; for example, in the preceding code fragment, the <fmt:message> action uses the resource bundle stored in the <fmt:bundle> action's localization context, and the <fmt:formatNumber> action uses the locale stored in the <fmt:bundle> action's localization context.

2. The FMT_LOCALIZATION_CONTEXT Configuration Setting

If a formatting action is not nested in a <fmt:bundle> action and the FMT_LOCALIZATION_CONTEXT configuration setting has been set, that formatting action uses the locale stored in the FMT_LOCALIZATION_CONTEXT configuration setting's localization context; for example:

```
<%-- This <fmt:setBundle> action establishes a localization context
     and stores it in the FMT_LOCALIZATION_CONTEXT configuration
     setting --%>
<fmt:setBundle basename='messages'/>

<%-- Because the following <fmt:formatNumber> action is not nested
     in a <fmt:bundle> action, it gets its locale from the
     localization context established by the preceding
     <fmt:setBundle> action --%>
<fmt:formatNumber value='234682.155'/>
```

In the preceding code fragment, the FMT_LOCALIZATION_CONTEXT configuration setting is set by the <fmt:setBundle> action.[18] The locale stored in the

---

17. See "Resource Bundle Lookup" on page 274 for more information about how
    <fmt:bundle> establishes a localization context.

FMT_LOCALIZATION_CONTEXT configuration setting is used by the <fmt:formatNumber> action.

If the localization context stored in the FMT_LOCALIZATION_CONTEXT configuration setting does not have a locale, formatting actions that do not reside in the body of a <fmt:bundle> action perform a formatting locale lookup, which is described in the next step.

3. Formatting Locale Lookup

If a formatting action is not nested in a <fmt:bundle> action and the FMT_LOCALIZATION_CONTEXT configuration setting has not been set, that formatting action performs a formatting locale lookup; for example:

```
<%-- If the FMT_LOCALIZATION_CONTEXT configuration setting has not
     been set, the following <fmt:formatNumber> action performs
     a formatting locale lookup to find a locale to use to
     format its value --%>
<fmt:formatNumber value='234682.155'/>
```

In the preceding code fragment, the <fmt:formatNumber> action is not nested in a <fmt:bundle> action. If the FMT_LOCALIZATION_CONTEXT configuration setting has not been set, that <fmt:formatNumber> action performs a formatting locale lookup, which is discussed in the next section.

Formatting Locale Lookup

Formatting actions that are not nested in a <fmt:bundle> action perform a formatting locale lookup if the FMT_LOCALIZATION_CONTEXT configuration setting has not been set or if that configuration setting does not contain a locale.

The formatting locale lookup tries to find an appropriate locale among a set of *available* locales. For <fmt:formatNumber> and <fmt:parseNumber>, the available locales are determined by a call to the getAvailableLocales method from java.text.NumberFormat. For <fmt:formatDate> and <fmt:parseDate>, the available locales are determined by a call to the getAvailableLocales method from java.text.DateFormat.

The formatting locale lookup proceeds as follows:

1.   Find a Matching Locale with the User's Preferred Locales

---

18. There are other ways to set the FMT_LOCALIZATION_CONTEXT configuration setting; see "Localization Context Lookup" on page 268 for more information.

First, the formatting actions compare each of the user's preferred locales against each of the available locales; when a match is found, the algorithm terminates and that locale is used by the formatting action.

There are two ways that you can specify your preferred locales: with your browser's language preferences or by setting the FMT_LOCALE configuration setting; the latter takes precedence over the former. You can set the FMT_LOCALE configuration setting in a number of ways; one way is with the <fmt:setLocale> action, which is how most of the code examples in this chapter establish a formatting locale.

2. Find a Matching Locale with the Fallback Locale

   If a formatting action cannot find a matching locale with a user's preferred locales, it will compare the fallback locale with each of the available locales.

   The fallback locale is specified with the FMT_FALLBACK_LOCALE configuration setting. There is no JSTL action that sets the FMT_FALLBACK_LOCALE configuration setting, so you must set that configuration setting in a deployment descriptor or a business component.

A preferred locale (or the fallback locale) matches an available locale if:

- They match exactly; that is, if the language, country, and variants all match, OR:
- The language and country match, OR:
- The language matches and the available locale does not specify a country.

DATABASE ACTIONS

Topics in This Chapter

Chapter 9

The vast majority of commercial websites are driven by relational databases. Because databases are so pervasive on the Web, JSTL provides a set of actions for database connectivity and access. The central theme of this chapter is how you can make the most of those actions.

First however, a cautionary note. Most often, it's desirable to separate presentation logic from business logic; for example, many Web applications are implemented with the Model-View-Controller (MVC) architecture, where business components manipulate a data model, and JSP pages present views of that data.[1] The JSTL SQL actions let you mix presentation and business logic as much as you want; for example, you can perform database updates with the <sql:update> action or execute database transactions with <sql:transaction>.

Ultimately, the extent to which you separate presentation and business logic is up to you. You may decide to limit database access to business components and therefore forbid the use of JSTL SQL actions in JSP pages.

Another approach is to allow database queries in JSP pages (with the <sql:query> action) and only allow database updates and transactions in business components. This approach provides a good degree of separation between presentation and business logic without requiring business components to encapsulate query results and make them available to JSP pages.

---

1. See David Geary, *Advanced JavaServer Pages*, Prentice Hall, 2001, for more information about separating presentation and business logic.

Finally, you can manipulate your database entirely in JSP pages by using all of the JSTL SQL actions. If you choose that approach, be aware that your Web application may be somewhat difficult to maintain and extend because you will be mixing presentation and business logic in JSP pages.

This chapter begins with an overview of the JSTL SQL actions, followed by a short discussion of a simple database used throughout this chapter. After those preliminaries, this chapter discusses the following actions: connecting to databases, querying databases, updating databases, executing database transactions, and implementing custom actions.

9.1 Overview

In this section we introduce the JSTL SQL actions and the configuration settings used in conjunction with those actions.

SQL Actions

JSTL provides six SQL actions that let you do the following:

- Connect to a database
- Query a database and access query results
- Perform database queries with prepared statements
- Update a database
- Execute database transactions

The JSTL SQL actions are listed in Table 9.1.

The <sql:setDataSource> action lets you specify a data source for your database. You can specify that data source as an instance of `javax.sql.DataSource`, or as a string representing either a Java Naming and Directory Interface (JNDI) relative path or JDBC parameters. You can store that data source in the `SQL_DATA_SOURCE` configuration setting or in a scoped variable.

The <sql:query> action queries a database and stores the result in a scoped variable. The <sql:query> action lets you use prepared statements with SQL query parameters and also lets you limit the number of rows in a query.

The <sql:update> action updates a database (by inserting, updating, or deleting rows) or modifies one (by creating, altering, or dropping tables) and lets you store the number of rows affected by the update in a scoped variable. Like <sql:query>, <sql:update> can execute prepared statements.

Table 9.1   JSTL Database Actions

Action	Description
<sql:setDataSource>	Stores a data source in a scoped variable or the SQL_DATA_SOURCE configuration setting.
<sql:query>	Queries a database and stores the query result in a scoped variable.
<sql:update>	Updates a database with a Data Manipulation Language (DML) command or a Data Definition Language (DDL) command.
<sql:param>	Sets SQL parameters for enclosing <sql:query> and <sql:update> actions.
<sql:dateParam>	Sets SQL date parameters for enclosing <sql:query> and <sql:update> actions.
<sql:transaction>	Establishes a transaction for enclosed <sql:query> and <sql:update> actions.

The <sql:transaction> action defines a database transaction with nested <sql:query> and <sql:update> actions. If one of the nested queries or updates fails, <sql:transaction> rolls back the entire transaction and throws an exception; otherwise, <sql:transaction> commits the transaction.

The <sql:param> and <sql:dateParam> actions supply SQL parameters for prepared statements to <sql:query> or <sql:update> actions.

Configuration Settings

JSTL uses two configuration settings in conjunction with the SQL actions: SQL_DATA_SOURCE and SQL_MAX_ROWS.[2] You can use the former to specify a data source, and the latter to limit the number of rows returned by database queries.

The SQL_DATA_SOURCE configuration setting is listed in Table 9.2.

The SQL_DATA_SOURCE configuration setting is used by the <sql:query>, <sql:update>, and <sql:transaction> actions. You can set that configuration setting in the deployment descriptor, in a business component with the Config class, or with the <sql:setDataSource> action. See "How JSTL Locates Data Sources" on page 363 for more information about how the SQL_DATA_SOURCE configuration setting is used, and see "Creating Data Sources" on page 365 for more information about how you can set that configuration setting.

---

2. See "Configuration Settings" on page 230 for more information about configuration settings.

Table 9.2   The `SQL_DATA_SOURCE` Configuration Setting

Config Constant	SQL_DATA_SOURCE
Name	`javax.servlet.jsp.jstl.sql.dataSource`
Type	`java.lang.String` or `javax.sql.DataSource`
Set by	<sql:setDataSource>, Deployment Descriptor, `Config` class
Used by	<sql:query>, <sql:update>, and <sql:transaction>

The `SQL_MAX_ROWS` configuration setting is listed in Table 9.3.

Table 9.3   The `SQL_MAX_ROWS` Configuration Setting

Config Constant	SQL_MAX_ROWS
Name	`javax.servlet.jsp.jstl.sql.maxRows`
Type	`java.lang.String` or `java.lang.Integer`
Set by	Deployment Descriptor, `Config` class
Used by	<sql:query>

The `SQL_MAX_ROWS` configuration setting is not set by any JSTL actions, but you can set that configuration setting in the deployment descriptor or in a business component with the `Config` class. See "Using <sql:query>" on page 378 for more information about the `SQL_MAX_ROWS` configuration setting.

9.2 A Simple Database

All of the examples in this chapter were tested with the MySQL database management system (DBMS).[3] "Setting Up the MySQL Database Used in This Book" on page 556 provides instructions on downloading and installing MySQL and an associated JDBC driver, in addition to showing you how to create and populate the database used in this chapter.

The examples in this chapter access a simple database with three tables: `Customers`, `Orders`, and `Accounts`. Figure 9–1 shows the data contained in the `Customers` table.

---

3. An exception is the example discussed in "Executing Database Transactions" on page 411, which uses the Cloudscape database because MySQL does not implement database constraints.

Cust_ID	Name	Phone_Number	Street_Address	City	State
1	William Dupont	(652)488-9931	801 Oak Street	Eugene	Nebraska
2	Anna Keeney	(716)834-8772	86 East Amherst Street	Buffalo	New York
3	Mariko Randor	(451)842-8933	923 Maple Street	Springfield	Tennessee
4	John Wilson	(758)955-5934	8122 Genessee Street	El Reno	Oklahoma
5	Lynn Seckinger	(552)767-1935	712 Kehr Street	Kent	Washington
6	Richard Tattersall	(455)282-2936	21 South Park Drive	Dallas	Texas
7	Gabriella Sarintia	(819)152-8937	81123 West Seneca Street	Denver	Colorado
8	Lisa Hartwig	(818)852-1937	6652 Sheridan Drive	Sheridan	Wyoming
9	Shirley Jones	(992)488-3931	2831 Main Street	Butte	Montana
10	Bill Sprague	(316)962-0632	1043 Cherry Street	Cheektowaga	New York
11	Greg Doench	(136)692-6023	99 Oak Street	Upper Saddle River	New Jersey
12	Solange Nadeau	(255)767-0935	177 Rue St. Catherine	Montreal	Quebec
13	Heather McGann	(554)282-0936	7192 913 West Park	Buloxie	Mississippi
14	Roy Martin	(918)888-0937	5571 North Olean Avenue	White River	Arkansas
15	Claude Loubier	(857)955-0934	1003 Rue de la Montagne	St. Marguerite de Lingwick	Quebec
16	Dan Woodard	(703)555-1212	2993 Tonawonda Street	Springfield	Missouri
17	Ron Dunlap	(761)678-4251	5579 East Seneca Street	Kansas City	Kansas
18	Keith Frankart	(602)152-6723	88124 Milpidas Lane	Springfield	Maryland
19	Andre Nadeau	(541)842-0933	94219 Rue Florence	St. Marguerite de Lingwick	Quebec
20	Horace Celestin	(914)843-6553	99423 Spruce Street	Ann Arbor	Michigan

Figure 9–1   The Customers Table

Initially, the database contains 20 customers. Each customer has a customer ID, name, phone number, and address. In the interest of simplicity, all of the (fictitious) customers reside in North America.

Figure 9–2 shows the `Orders` table and the `Accounts` table.

Each order in the database contains an order number, an order date, a customer ID, an amount, and a description. For the sake of brevity, only the first seven customers in the database have orders. All of the customers have accounts. The `Accounts` table is only used by the example in "Executing Database Transactions" on page 411.

For the sake of illustration, the tables shown in Figure 9–1 and Figure 9–2 use a simplified design; for example, the `Orders` table keeps track of orders for single items with no notion of quantity and directly stores order amounts and product names that are localized for English. A better design would include an additional `Products` table that listed product IDs and prices and a modified `Orders` table that stored product IDs instead of descriptions and quantities instead of amounts. Moreover, you should never store localized data in a database, because you will want to easily localize that data when you display it. In general, you should adhere to the following rules when storing data in a database:

Order_Number	Order_Date	Cust_ID	Amount	Description
1	2002-05-20	1	129.99	Wristwatch
2	2002-05-21	1	19.95	Coffee grinder
3	2002-05-24	1	29.76	Bath towel
4	2002-05-23	1	39.34	Deluxe cheese grater
5	2002-05-22	2	56.75	Champagne glass set
6	2002-05-20	2	28.11	Instamatic camera
7	2002-05-22	2	38.77	Walkman
8	2002-05-21	2	56.76	Coffee maker
9	2002-05-23	2	21.47	Car wax
10	2002-05-21	2	16.8	Tape recorder
11	2002-05-24	2	25.44	Art brush set
12	2002-05-22	3	47.63	Game software
13	2002-05-23	3	93.96	Furby collection
14	2002-05-20	4	81.27	CD Player
15	2002-05-21	4	66.83	Microphone
16	2002-05-23	4	75.91	Dish set
17	2002-05-22	4	32.67	Electric toothbrush
18	2002-05-24	5	17.45	Case of mouthwash
19	2002-05-20	5	88.81	Vacuum cleaner
20	2002-05-21	5	29.13	Fine chocolates
21	2002-05-21	5	77.02	Computer monitor arm
22	2002-05-22	6	119.11	Tennis shoes
23	2002-05-23	7	107.96	Beanie Baby collection
24	2002-05-22	7	101.97	Humidifier
25	2002-05-22	7	223.55	Exercise bike
27	2002-05-24	7	49.42	Coffee maker

Cust_ID	Balance
1	1245.97
2	130400.0
3	28745.9
4	125863.0
5	25.99
6	891.34
7	924.76
8	1578.22
9	1258.77
10	259876.0
11	125866.0
12	159.88
13	590886.0
14	678231.0
15	245.33
16	8999.06
17	1342.82
18	197312.0
19	907310.0
20	921345.0

Figure 9–2 The Orders Table (left) and the Accounts Table (right)

- Store *dates and times* according to ISO 8601, which defines locale-independent formats for dates and times.[4] The `Orders` table adheres to this rule by storing dates in the format YYYY-MM-DD, as defined by ISO 8601.
- Store *products* with numeric IDs instead of localized descriptions. You can map those IDs to descriptions with separate tables in the database or with resource bundles in your application. See "Resource Bundles" on page 259 for more information about resource bundles and how you can use them to localize text.

Store *prices* in a locale-independent manner in a fixed representation, such as the format defined by the `java.lang.Long.toString` or `java.lang.Double.toString` methods. The `Orders` and `Accounts` tables in Figure 9–2 store their currencies in that manner.

---

4. See `http://www.cl.cam.ac.uk/~mgk25/iso-time.html` for more information about ISO 8601.

Note that the examples in this chapter are not internationalized. The database design and the lack of internationalization in this chapter are intentional because proper database design and internationalization would obfuscate the concepts that this chapter illustrates, namely, how to use the JSTL SQL actions.

9.3 How JSTL Locates Data Sources

Three JSTL SQL actions access a database: <sql:query>, <sql:update>, and <sql:transaction>. Those actions use a data source to access a database, so they all have an optional `dataSource` attribute that specifies that data source. When you use those actions, JSTL locates a data source with this algorithm:

Locate a value:

1. If the `dataSource` attribute was specified for <sql:query>, <sql:update>, or <sql:transaction>, JSTL uses that attribute's value to access the data source, so go to step 3; otherwise, go to step 2.
2. If the `SQL_DATA_SOURCE` configuration setting exists, JSTL uses that setting's value to access the data source. Go to step 3.

Evaluate the value:

3. If step 1 or 2 yields no value or `null`, JSTL throws an exception.
4. If step 1 or 2 yields a data source, JSTL uses it; if not, go to step 5.
5. If step 1 or 2 yields a string, go to step 6.

Access the data source:

6. JSTL assumes that the string obtained from step 1 or 2 is a JNDI relative path, and tries to access that JNDI resource.
7. If step 6 failed, JSTL uses the string to create a JDBC connection.
8. If steps 6 and 7 failed, JSTL throws an exception.

Let's take a closer look at how the preceding steps work:

Locate a value:

You can specify a data source with the `dataSource` attribute for <sql:query>, <sql:update>, or <sql:transaction>; for example, you can execute a database query like this:

```
<sql:query var='customers' dataSource='${myDataSource}'>
   SELECT * FROM CUSTOMERS
</sql:query>
```

In the preceding code fragment, the scoped variable myDataSource can reference either a string or an instance of javax.sql.DataSource. If that attribute references an instance of javax.sql.DataSource, that data source is used by the query; if it references a string, JSTL interprets the string as either a JNDI resource or JDBC parameters.

You can also specify a string for the dataSource attribute directly, like this:

```
<sql:query var='customers'
   dataSource='aJNDIResourceOrJDBCParameters'>
   SELECT * FROM CUSTOMERS
</sql:query>
```

You don't have to specify the dataSource attribute for <sql:query>, <sql:update>, or <sql:transaction>; for example, you can execute a database query like this:

```
<sql:query var='customers'>
   SELECT * FROM CUSTOMERS
</sql:query>
```

If you omit the dataSource attribute, JSTL assumes that the value of the SQL_DATA_SOURCE configuration setting, if it exists, represents a data source. If the SQL_DATA_SOURCE, configuration setting does not exist and you don't specify the dataSource attribute, the <sql:query>, <sql:update>, and <sql:transaction> actions will throw an exception.

You can specify a value for the SQL_DATA_SOURCE configuration setting in the deployment descriptor, with a business component, or with the <sql:setDataSource> action. See "Creating Data Sources" on page 365 for more information about setting the SQL_DATA_SOURCE configuration setting.

Evaluate the value:

The value that you specify for a data source can be a string or an instance of javax.sql.DataSource. If it's the latter, JSTL uses it as is; if it's the former, continue to the next step.

Access the Data Source:

If you specify a data source as a string, JSTL first assumes that the string is a relative path to a JNDI resource and tries to retrieve that resource from the JSP container's

JNDI naming context. If the JNDI lookup fails, then <sql:query>, <sql:update>, and <sql:transaction> assume that the string represents JDBC parameters and try to create a JDBC connection.

If you specify a data source as a string and that string is not a valid JNDI relative path and does not represent valid JDBC parameters, then <sql:query>, <sql:update>, and <sql:transaction> will throw an exception.

Summary:

You can specify a data source *as*:

- an instance of `javax.sql.DataSource`
- a string representing a JNDI relative path that points to a data source
- a string representing a JDBC URL and, optionally, a driver, user name, and password

You can specify a data source *with*:

- <sql:query>, <sql:update>, <sql:transaction>, and <sql:setDataSource>
- the `SQL_DATA_SOURCE` configuration setting[5]

This section discussed how JSTL *locates* a data source; how you *create* a data source and make it available to JSTL is the topic of the next section.

9.4 Creating Data Sources

This section tells you how to create a data source. "How JSTL Locates Data Sources" on page 363 spells out the algorithm that JSTL uses to locate your data source.

Fundamentally, there are three ways, listed in Table 9.4, to create a data source.

You can specify data source characteristics with a context initialization parameter in your deployment descriptor and let JSTL create a new data source or access an existing one that fits those characteristics. You can specify those characteristics as a JNDI resource or as JDBC parameters. *This option is attractive because you don't have to write any code.* If you care about advanced database features such as connection pooling or distributed transactions, don't use this approach with JDBC

---

5. If you use <sql:setDataSource> without the `var` attribute, the specified data source is stored in the `SQL_DATA_SOURCE` configuration setting.

Table 9.4   Creating a Data Source with JSTL[a]

Create Data Source With[b]	Store Data Source In	Advantage
The deployment descriptor	A context initialization parameter	You don't have to write any code.
The <sql:setDataSource> action	The SQL_DATA_SOURCE configuration setting or a scoped variable	You can specify a data source for a particular scope.
A business component	The SQL_DATA_SOURCE configuration setting or a scoped variable	Separates business and presentation logic, so you have total control over the data source.

a. All of the approaches listed in this table can create JDBC or JNDI data sources.
b. A business component can be a servlet, servlet filter, life-cycle listener, Java bean, or custom action.

parameters, because JSTL will most likely create a data source that's a simplistic wrapper around a JDBC connection.

The <sql:setDataSource> action lets you specify a data source in a JSP page. You can specify that data source as an instance of javax.sql.DataSource or as a string that represents a JNDI resource or JDBC parameters. Because you can specify the scope of a data source with <sql:setDataSource>, *this option is attractive because you can temporarily set a data source for a particular scope.*

You can also create a data source in a business component, such as a servlet, servlet filter, life-cycle listener, custom action, or JavaBeans component. *This option lets you separate business and presentation logic and gives you total control over the data source that you create.* Those characteristics make it the best choice for more complex Web applications developed jointly by page authors and software developers.

The following sections discuss the options in Table 9.4:

- "Specify Your Data Source in the Deployment Descriptor" on page 366
- "Specify Your Data Source with <sql:setDataSource>" on page 369
- "Create Your Data Source in a Business Component" on page 372

Specify Your Data Source in the Deployment Descriptor

The easiest way to create a data source is to specify it in your deployment descriptor because you don't have to write any code; for example, Listing 9.1 shows an excerpt from a deployment descriptor that specifies a data source with a JDBC URL and driver.

Listing 9.1	*WEB-INF/web.xml (Excerpt—Specifying a Data Source)*

```xml
<?xml version="1.0" encoding="ISO-8859-1"?>

<!DOCTYPE web-app
  PUBLIC "-//Sun Microsystems, Inc.//DTD Web Application 2.3//EN"
  "http://java.sun.com/j2ee/dtds/web-app_2.3.dtd">

<web-app>
   <context-param>
      <param-name>
       javax.servlet.jsp.jstl.sql.dataSource
      </param-name>

      <param-value>
       jdbc:mysql://localhost/core-jstl,org.gjt.mm.mysql.Driver
      </param-value>
   </context-param>
   ...
</web-app>
```

The preceding deployment descriptor specifies a data source for the SQL_DATA_SOURCE configuration setting with a context initialization parameter. The name of that context initialization parameter is javax.servlet.jsp. jstl.sql.dataSource, which is the name of the SQL_DATA_SOURCE configuration setting—see Table 9.2 on page 360. Whenever you specify a configuration setting in the deployment descriptor, you must use the configuration setting's name (in this case, javax.servlet.jsp.jstl.sql.dataSource) instead of the Config constant by which the configuration setting is known (in this case, SQL_DATA_SOURCE). See "Configuration Settings" on page 230 for more information about configuration settings and how you can specify them in deployment descriptors and business components.

Note: If your JDBC URL contains a comma, you can escape the comma with a backslash, like this: \, . You can also escape the escape character, if necessary, like this: \\.

When you specify a JDBC data source with a context initialization parameter, that parameter's value must be a string that specifies a JDBC URL. Optionally, you can also specify a JDBC driver, user name, and password. All of those characteristics are specified in one string, separated by commas. The preceding code fragment specifies a JDBC URL (jdbc:mysql://localhost/core-jstl) and a JDBC driver (org.gjt.mm.mysql.Driver). That code fragment could have also specified a user name and password, like this:

```
<web-app>
   <context-param>
      <param-name>
       javax.servlet.jsp.jstl.sql.dataSource
      </param-name>

      <param-value>
       jdbc:mysql://local-
host/core-jstl,org.gjt.mm.mysql.Driver,royBoy,batonRouge
      </param-value>
   </context-param>
   ...
</web-app>
```

In the preceding code fragment, royBoy is the user name and batonRouge is the password.

If you specify JDBC parameters in your deployment descriptor, like the code fragment listed above, JSTL will create a data source wrapped around a JDBC connection. *Typically, that data source won't have advanced features* like connection pooling or distributed transactions. If you want those advanced features, you can specify a data source of your choosing as a JNDI resource instead of JDBC parameters, like this:

```
<web-app>
   <context-param>
      <param-name>
         javax.servlet.jsp.jstl.sql.dataSource
      </param-name>

      <param-value>
         jdbc/MyDataSource
      </param-value>
   </context-param>
   ...
</web-app>
```

In the preceding code fragment, jdbc/MyDataSource specifies a relative path to a JNDI resource. JSTL prepends the context used for Web application resources—which is standardized by the J2EE specification—to that relative path; for the preceding code fragment, JSTL will search for a JNDI resource, using the absolute path java:comp/env/jdbc/MyDataSource.

Realize that using JNDI does not guarantee that your data source will have advanced features such as connection pooling or distributed transactions; however, using JNDI lets you use a data source that you (or your system administrator) specify. That data source may or may not have advanced features. It's the data source—not JNDI, which is a directory service—that provides advanced database features. In contrast, if you specify JDBC parameters in the deployment descriptor or with <sql:setDataSource>, JSTL will create a data source for you, so you have no control over the actual data source. In all likelihood, that data source will not provide advanced features such as connection pooling or distributed transactions.

If you specify a data source in the deployment descriptor, that data source is stored in the SQL_DATA_SOURCE configuration setting *that's accessible to all the JSP pages in your application*, so you don't have to explicitly specify a data source for <sql:query>, <sql:update>, and <sql:transaction> actions; for example, you can execute a query like this:

```
<sql:query var='customers'>
   SELECT * FROM CUSTOMERS
</sql:query>
```

You can only specify strings for context initialization parameters, so you can only specify a string for the SQL_DATA_SOURCE configuration setting in the deployment descriptor. If you need to specify an object for your data source, you can do so in a business component or you can use the <sql:setDataSource> action, which is discussed next.

Specify Your Data Source with <sql:setDataSource>

The <sql:setDataSource> action lets you specify a data source in a JSP page with this syntax:[6]

> *<sql:setDataSource [var] [scope] {dataSource | url [driver] [user] [password]}/>*

The <sql:setDataSource> action creates (or accesses an existing) data source[7] and stores it in a scoped variable under the name that you specify with the var attribute. If you don't specify the var attribute, <sql:setDataSource> stores the data source in the SQL_DATA_SOURCE configuration setting.

You can specify a data source with the dataSource attribute of the <sql:setDataSource> action. The value that you specify for the dataSource

---

6. Items in brackets are optional. See "<sql:setDataSource>" on page 531 for a more complete description of <sql:setDataSource> syntax.
7. The existing data source must have the exact same characteristics as the specified data source.

attribute can be a comma-separated string or a scoped variable that references a string or an instance of `javax.sql.DataSource`. If that value is a string, it must specify a JNDI resource or JDBC parameters, just like the string that you specify for a data source in the deployment descriptor; for example:

```
<%-- Set values for JDBC url, driver, user name, and password --%>
<c:set var='url'    value='jdbc:mysql://localhost/core-jstl'/>
<c:set var='driver' value='org.gjt.mm.mysql.Driver'/>
<c:set var='user'   value='royBoy'/>
<c:set var='pwd'    value='batonRouge'/>

<%-- Set the data source for this JSP page --%>
<sql:setDataSource dataSource='${url},${driver},${user},${pwd}'/>
```

The preceding code fragment specifies a data source with a JDBC URL, a JDBC driver, and a user name and password. All of those characteristics are specified in a single string, separated by commas. Remember, the driver, user name, and password are all optional.

Instead of using the `dataSource` attribute to specify JDBC parameters with a comma-separated string, as in the preceding code fragment, you can use the `url` attribute and, optionally, the `driver`, `user`, and `password` *attributes*, to achieve the same effect, for example:

```
<%-- Set the data source for this JSP page --%>
<sql:setDataSource url='jdbc:mysql://localhost/core-jstl'
            driver='org.gjt.mm.mysql.Driver'
              user='royBoy'
          password='batonRouge'/>
```

The preceding code fragment is functionally identical to the code fragment that precedes it.

Like the code fragment in "Specify Your Data Source in the Deployment Descriptor" on page 366 that specified a data source in the deployment descriptor, the <sql:setDataSource> action in the preceding code fragment stores the resulting data source in the SQL_DATA_SOURCE configuration setting. Because the `scope` attribute was not specified for the <sql:setDataSource> action in that code fragment, that data source only applies to the current JSP page. You can specify a different scope, like this:

```
<sql:setDataSource dataSource='${url},${driver},${user},${pwd}'
                    scope='session'/>
```

In the preceding code fragment, the data source specified with JDBC parameters is also stored in the SQL_DATA_SOURCE configuration setting, but that data source applies to session scope, meaning that all <sql:query>, <sql:update>, and

<sql:transaction> actions in the current session (that don't specify a dataSource attribute of their own) will implicitly use that data source.

You can also specify a data source stored in a JNDI resource with <sql:setDataSource>, just like you can in the deployment descriptor, like this:

```
<sql:setDataSource dataSource='jdbc/MyDataSource'/>
```

In the preceding code fragment, jdbc/MyDataSource specifies a relative path to a JNDI resource. JSTL prepends the context used for Web application resources—which is standardized by the J2EE specification—to that relative path; for the preceding code fragment, JSTL will search for a JNDI resource, using the absolute path java:comp/env/jdbc/MyDataSource.

In all of the code fragments so far in this section, the <sql:setDataSource> action stores a data source in the SQL_DATA_SOURCE configuration setting, but you can also use <sql:setDataSource> to store a data source in a scoped variable, like this:

```
<sql:setDataSource dataSource='${url},${driver},${user},${pwd}'
                    var='myDataSource' scope='request'/>
```

In the preceding code fragment, the <sql:setDataSource> action stores a data source in a scoped variable named myDataSource. That scoped variable persists only for the current request, but you can change that by specifying a different value for the scope attribute, such as session or application. If you don't specify the scope variable, the scope will default to page and that data source will only be available to SQL actions in the current JSP page.

If you use <sql:setDataSource> to store a data source in a scoped variable, as in the preceding code fragment, you must explicitly access that data source in <sql:query>, <sql:update>, and <sql:transaction> actions, like this:

```
<sql:query var='customers' dataSource='${myDataSource}'>
   SELECT * FROM CUSTOMERS
</sql:query>
```

In the preceding code fragment, the <sql:query> action uses the data source specified above with the <sql:setDataSource> action. For the combination of the two preceding code fragments, that <sql:query> action must reside in the same request as the <sql:setDataSource> action.

Notice that, unlike specifying a data source in the deployment descriptor, you can specify a scope for a data source with the <sql:setDataSource> action. That feature lets you temporarily override a previously specified data source. For example, if you specify a data source in your deployment descriptor, that data source will apply to all JSP pages in your application. If you subsequently use <sql:setDataSource> (without specifying the var attribute) in a JSP page, the data source you specify with

<sql:setDataSource> will temporarily override the data source that you specified in your deployment descriptor.

Finally, if you specify JDBC parameters for the <sql:setDataSource> action's `dataSource` attribute, the data source specified by those parameters will be created by the JSTL implementation. In all likelihood, that data source will not provide advanced features such as connection pooling or distributed transactions.[8] If you need those advanced features, you can specify a data source of your choosing stored in a JNDI resource or you can create your data source in a business component; the latter is discussed in the next section.

Create Your Data Source in a Business Component

Besides specifying data sources in deployment descriptors or with the <sql:setDataSource> action, you can also create a data source in a business component, such as a servlet or a life-cycle listener. Of those three approaches, creating a data source in a business component is usually the best option for two reasons. First, you need not specify a data source in your JSP pages, and so you gain a degree of separation between business and presentation logic. Second, you have total control over the data source that you create, which is not the case if JSTL creates a data source for you.

The drawback to creating a data source in a business component is that you must write and compile Java code. Because of that requirement, creating a data source in a business component is most appropriate for more complex Web applications developed jointly by page authors and Java developers.

This section shows you how to create a data source with an initialization servlet.

A Simple Data Source

Before we can create a data source, we need a data source implementation. For illustration only, Listing 9.2 lists a simple data source that acts as a wrapper around a JDBC connection.

The data source listed in the preceding code is unremarkable; its only purpose is to provide a data source that we can create in a business component. In a production environment, data sources that you use will most likely be implemented by your database vendor and will probably offer amenities such as connection pooling or distributed transactions.

---

8. That restriction is the same for data sources specified with JDBC parameters in the deployment descriptor. See "Specify Your Data Source in the Deployment Descriptor" on page 366 for more information.

Listing 9.2   *WEB-INF/classes/beans/SimpleDataSource.java*

```
package beans;

import java.io.PrintWriter;
import java.sql.Connection;
import java.sql.DriverManager;
import java.sql.SQLException;
import javax.sql.DataSource;

public class SimpleDataSource implements DataSource {
   private String driver, url;
   private boolean driverLoaded = false;

   public SimpleDataSource(String driver, String url) {
      this.driver = driver;
      this.url    = url;
   }
   public synchronized Connection getConnection()
                                 throws SQLException {
      return getConnection(null, null);
   }
   public synchronized Connection getConnection(
                                 String user, String pwd)
                                 throws SQLException {
      Connection connection = null;

      if(!driverLoaded) {
         try {
            Class.forName(driver).newInstance();
            driverLoaded = true;
         }
         catch(ClassNotFoundException ex) {
            throw new SQLException("Can't find driver " + driver);
         }
      }
      if(user == null || pwd == null)
         connection = DriverManager.getConnection(url);
      else
         connection = DriverManager.getConnection(url, user, pwd);

      return connection;
   }
   public PrintWriter getLogWriter() throws SQLException {
      return null;
   }
   public void setLogWriter(PrintWriter logWriter)
                                        throws SQLException {
```

Listing 9.2 | *WEB-INF/classes/beans/SimpleDataSource.java (cont.)*

```
      throw new SQLException("Logging not supported");
   }
   public int getLoginTimeout() throws SQLException {
      return 0;
   }
   public void setLoginTimeout(int loginTimeout)
                                      throws SQLException {
      throw new SQLException("Login timeout not supported");
   }
}
```

Creating a Data Source in an Initialization Servlet

Implementing a servlet that creates a data source and makes it available to the JSTL SQL actions is a simple matter, as evidenced by the servlet listed in Listing 9.3.

Listing 9.3 | *WEB-INF/classes/InitializationServlet.java (Initialization Servlet That Creates a Data Source)*

```
import javax.servlet.*;
import javax.servlet.http.*;
import beans.SimpleDataSource;
import javax.servlet.jsp.jstl.core.Config;

public class InitializationServlet extends HttpServlet {
   private ServletContext app = null; // the application

   public void init() throws ServletException {
      // Create the data source
      SimpleDataSource dataSource = new SimpleDataSource(
            "org.gjt.mm.mysql.Driver", // db driver
            "jdbc:mysql://localhost/core-jstl"); // db URL

      // Store the data source in the SQL_DATA_SOURCE
      // configuration setting
      Config.set(getServletContext(), Config.SQL_DATA_SOURCE,
               dataSource);
   }
   public void destroy() {
      // Remove the SQL_DATA_SOURCE configuration setting
      Config.remove(getServletContext(), Config.SQL_DATA_SOURCE);
   }
}
```

The servlet listed above creates an instance of `SimpleDataSource`, specifying a JDBC URL and driver. The `SimpleDataSource` class is discussed in "A Simple Data Source" on page 372.

The servlet stores a data source in the `SQL_DATA_SOURCE` configuration setting by using the `Config.set` method. That `static` method stores an object in a configuration setting; see "The Config Class" on page 239 for more information about the `Config` class. Because the `Config.set` method is passed a reference to the servlet context (the application), the data source will be available to all JSP pages in the application. When the servlet is destroyed, it removes the data source from the `SQL_DATA_SOURCE` configuration setting with the `Config.remove` method.[9]

To ensure that the data source created by the preceding servlet is available to all of your JSP pages, you should load that servlet at startup, which you can do by specifying the <load-on-startup> element in your deployment descriptor. Listing 9.4 lists an excerpt from the deployment descriptor that shows you how to specify that element.

Listing 9.4	WEB-INF/web.xml (Excerpt—Specifying the <load-on-startup> Element)

```
<?xml version="1.0" encoding="ISO-8859-1"?>

<!DOCTYPE web-app
    PUBLIC "-//Sun Microsystems, Inc.//DTD Web Application 2.3//EN"
    "http://java.sun.com/j2ee/dtds/web-app_2.3.dtd">

<web-app>
   ...
   <servlet>
      <servlet-name>initServlet</servlet-name>
      <servlet-class>InitializationServlet</servlet-class>
      <load-on-startup/>
   </servlet>
   ...
</web-app>
```

Because the servlet listed in Listing 9.3 stores a data source in the `SQL_DATA_SOURCE` configuration setting, you do not need to explicitly specify that data source in your JSP pages, as discussed in "How JSTL Locates Data Sources" on page 363. If you prefer, you can store your data source in a scoped variable instead of the `SQL_DATA_SOURCE` configuration setting, like this:

---

9. See "Configuration Settings" on page 230 for more information about configuration settings and the `Config` class.

```
public class InitializationServlet extends HttpServlet {
   private String dsName = "myDataSource"; // the data source name

   public void init() throws ServletException {
      ...
      // Store the data source in application scope
      getServletContext().setAttribute(dsName, dataSource);
   }
   public void destroy() {
      // Remove the data source from application scope
      getServletContext().removeAttribute(dsName);
   }
}
```

If you store your data source in a scoped variable, as in the preceding code fragment, you must explicitly access that data source with <sql:query>, <sql:update>, and <sql:transaction> actions, as discussed in "How JSTL Locates Data Sources" on page 363.

Because the servlet listed in Listing 9.3 hardcodes the JDBC URL and driver, you will have to modify and recompile that servlet if you change your database management system. You can eliminate that dependency by specifying the names of your JDBC URL and driver in your deployment descriptor; for example, Listing 9.5 lists an excerpt from the deployment descriptor that does just that.

Listing 9.5	*WEB-INF/web.xml (Excerpt—Specifying JDBC URL and Driver)*

```
<?xml version="1.0" encoding="ISO-8859-1"?>

<!DOCTYPE web-app
   PUBLIC "-//Sun Microsystems, Inc.//DTD Web Application 2.3//EN"
   "http://java.sun.com/j2ee/dtds/web-app_2.3.dtd">

<web-app>
   ...
   <context-param>
      <param-name>
         application.sql.url
      </param-name>

      <param-value>
         jdbc:mysql://localhost/core-jstl
      </param-value>
   </context-param>

   <context-param>
      <param-name>
```

Listing 9.5	*WEB-INF/web.xml (Excerpt—Specifying JDBC URL and Driver) (cont.)*

```
            application.sql.driver
        </param-name>

        <param-value>
            org.gjt.mm.mysql.Driver
        </param-value>
    </context-param>

    <servlet>
        <servlet-name>initServlet</servlet-name>
        <servlet-class>InitializationServlet</servlet-class>
        <load-on-startup/>
    </servlet>
    ...
</web-app>
```

The preceding deployment descriptor specifies context initialization parameters for a JDBC URL and driver. Those context initialization parameters are used by the servlet listed in Listing 9.6.

Listing 9.6	*WEB-INF/classes/InitializationServlet.java (Using Context Initialization Parameters for JDBC URL and Driver)*

```
import javax.servlet.*;
import javax.servlet.http.*;
import beans.SimpleDataSource;
import javax.servlet.jsp.jstl.core.Config;

public class InitializationServlet extends HttpServlet {
    private String dsName = "myDataSource"; // the data source name

    public void init() throws ServletException{
        ServletContext app = getServletContext();

        // Retrieve the data source name, driver, and url from
        // initialization parameters
        String
            driver = app.getInitParameter("application.sql.driver"),
            url = app.getInitParameter("application.sql.url");

        // Create the data source
        SimpleDataSource dataSource = new SimpleDataSource(
                                        driver, url);
```

Listing 9.6	WEB-INF/classes/InitializationServlet.java (Using Context Initialization Parameters for JDBC URL and Driver) (cont.)

```
    // Store the data source in the SQL_DATA_SOURCE
    // configuration setting
    Config.set(app, Config.SQL_DATA_SOURCE, dataSource);
  }
  public void destroy() {
    // Remove the SQL_DATA_SOURCE configuration setting
    Config.remove(getServletContext(), Config.SQL_DATA_SOURCE);
  }
}
```

The preceding servlet uses the `ServletContext.getInitParameter` method to retrieve the values for the context initialization parameters specified in the deployment descriptor listed in Listing 9.5. Those values are subsequently used to create a data source, which the servlet stores in the `SQL_DATA_SOURCE` configuration setting.

Core Approach

The preferred way to expose a data source for the JSTL SQL actions is to specify data source characteristics with context initialization parameters and to create the data source with a business component that stores it in the `SQL_DATA_SOURCE` configuration setting. This approach has two benefits: JSP pages do not have to explicitly reference the data source, and business components do not have to be recompiled if any of the characteristics of the data source change.

9.5 Querying a Database

This chapter has already introduced simple database queries with <sql:query>. This section examines the use of that action in more detail, including accessing query results, limiting query size, and scrolling through large queries.

Using <sql:query>

The <sql:query> action lets you perform a database query. That action has the following syntax:[10]

<sql:query sql var [scope] [dataSource] [startRow] [maxRows]/>

The `sql` attribute specifies the SQL query. That query can optionally be specified in the body of the <sql:query> action, with this syntax:

<sql:query var [scope] [dataSource] [startRow] [maxRows]>
    SQL Query
</sql:query>

The <sql:query> action stores the query result in a scoped variable whose name is specified with the mandatory `var` attribute.

The <sql:query> action also has four optional attributes: `scope`, `dataSource`, `startRow`, and `maxRows`.

The `scope` attribute specifies the scope for the `var` scoped attribute; the default is page scope.

The `dataSource` attribute specifies a data source. You can specify that attribute as a string or a scoped variable that references a string or an instance of `javax.sql.DataSource`. See "How JSTL Locates Data Sources" on page 363 for examples of setting the `dataSource` attribute.

The `startRows` attribute lets you specify a zero-based starting row for a query. The default value—0—specifies the first row in a query. The last row is specified as *n-1*, where *n* is the number of rows in the query.

The `maxRows` attribute specifies the maximum number of rows in a query. That attribute lets you limit the size of your queries and thereby guard against so-called runaway queries and also lets you scroll through large queries. The latter is illustrated in "Scrolling Through Large Queries" on page 385. If you don't specify the `maxRows` attribute, database queries will not be limited.

If you want to limit the size of all queries for an application, you don't have to specify the `maxRows` attribute for all of your queries; instead, you can set the `SQL_MAX_ROWS` configuration setting, for example:

```
public class InitializationServlet extends HttpServlet {
   public void init() throws ServletException {
      // Limit the default size of all queries in your application
      Config.set(getServletContext(), Config.SQL_MAX_ROWS, 25);
   }
}
```

The preceding code fragment sets the `SQL_MAX_ROWS` configuration setting in a servlet that's presumably loaded at startup. It's more common, however, to set the `SQL_MAX_ROWS` configuration setting in the deployment descriptor, like this:

---

10. Items in brackets are optional. See "<sql:query>" on page 533 for a more complete description of <sql:query> syntax.

```
<web-app>
  ...
  <context-param>
    <param-name>javax.servlet.jsp.jstl.sql.maxRows</param-name>
    <param-value>25</param-value>
  </context-param>
  ...
</web-app>
```

It's more convenient to set the SQL_MAX_ROWS configuration setting in the deployment descriptor, because you don't have to write any code. If you set the SQL_MAX_ROWS setting in the deployment descriptor, as in the preceding code fragment, you must use that configuration setting's name, which is javax.servlet.jsp.jstl.sql.maxRows. See "Configuration Settings" on page 359 for more information about configuration settings that support the JSTL SQL actions, and see "Configuration Settings" on page 230 for more information about configuration settings in general.

You can also use <sql:query> with SQL parameters, with the following syntaxes:

<sql:query sql var [scope] [dataSource] [startRow] [maxRows]>
     <sql:param> and <sql:dateParam> actions
</sql:query>

<sql:query var [scope] [dataSource] [startRow] [maxRows]>
     SQL Query
     optional <sql:param> and <sql:dateParam> actions
</sql:query>

See "Prepared Statements and SQL Parameters" on page 389 for more information about SQL parameters and the <sql:param> and <sql:dateParam> actions.

Now that we have a good grasp of how to use <sql:query>, let's take a look at an example, shown in Figure 9–3, that queries a database, accesses the query result, and displays the result in an HTML table.

The JSP page shown in Figure 9–3—index.jsp—is listed in Listing 9.7.

The JSP page listed in Listing 9.7 performs a query that selects all customers from the Customers table—see "A Simple Database" on page 360 for more information about that table. That query uses a data source specified in the deployment descriptor (WEB-INF/web.xml) with the javax.servlet.jsp.jstl.sql.dataSource context initialization parameter, as discussed in "Specify Your Data Source in the Deployment Descriptor" on page 366. *All of the examples in the rest of this chapter create data sources in the same way.*

The result of the query is stored in page scope in a scoped variable named customers, and the HTML table is created by accessing three of that query's properties: rowCount, columnNames, and rowsByIndex. Those properties are discussed in the next section.

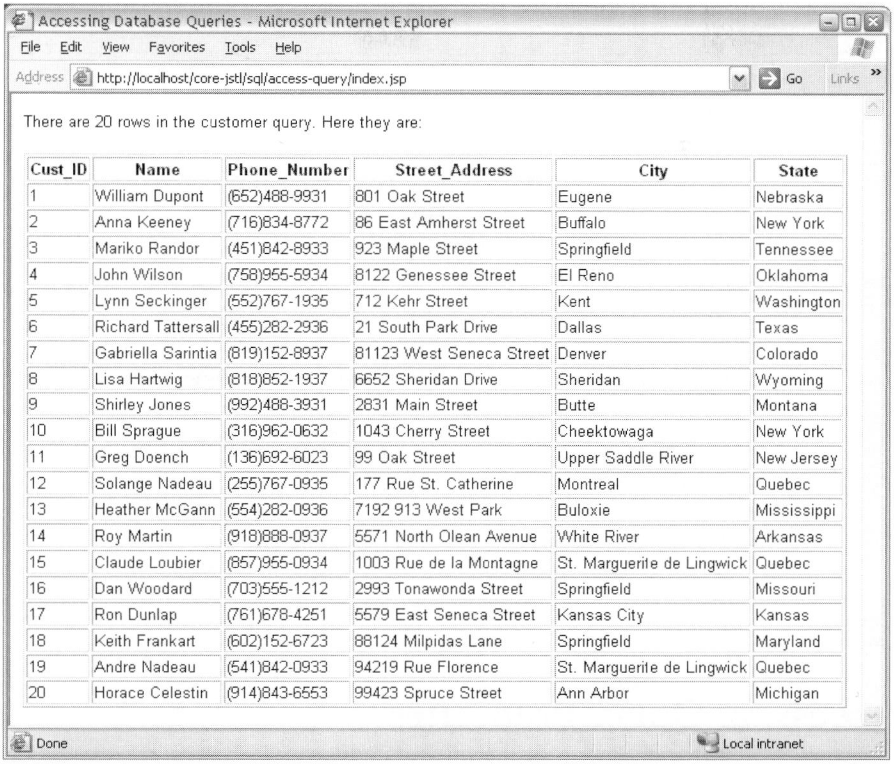

Figure 9–3   Querying a Database

Listing 9.7   *index.jsp (Querying)*

```
<!DOCTYPE HTML PUBLIC "-//W3C//DTD HTML 4.0 Transitional//EN">
<html>
    <head>
        <title>Accessing Database Queries</title>
    </head>

    <body>
        <%@ taglib uri='http://java.sun.com/jstl/core' prefix='c' %>
        <%@ taglib uri='http://java.sun.com/jstl/sql'  prefix='sql'%>

        <sql:query var='customers'>
            SELECT * FROM CUSTOMERS
        </sql:query>
        <%-- Access the rowCount property of the query --%>
        <p>There are <c:out value='${customers.rowCount}'/> rows
```

Listing 9.7	*index.jsp (Querying) (cont.)*

```
        in the customer query. Here they are:</p>

    <%-- Create a table with column names and row data --%>
    <p><table border='1'>
       <tr>
          <c:forEach var='columnName'
                   items='${customers.columnNames}'>
             <th><c:out value='${columnName}'/></th>
          </c:forEach>
       </tr>

       <c:forEach var='row' items='${customers.rowsByIndex}'>
          <tr>
             <c:forEach var='rowData' items='${row}'>
                   <td><c:out value='${rowData}'/></td>
             </c:forEach>
          </tr>
       </c:forEach>
    </table>
  </body>
</html>
```

Accessing Query Properties

Every time you execute a database query with <sql:query>, a query result is created and stored in a variable in one of the four scopes (page, request, session, or application). Queries have five properties that let you access their data; those properties are listed in Table 9.5.

It's easy to access a query's results with the properties listed in Table 9.5; for example, assume that you executed a database query, like this:

```
<sql:query var='customers'>
   SELECT * FROM CUSTOMERS
</sql:query>
```

You can iterate over the customers query column names like this:

```
<c:forEach var='columnName' items='${customers.columnNames}'>
   <c:out value='${columnName}'/><br>
</c:forEach>
```

The preceding code fragment prints each column name from the customer's query. It's more common, however, to generate an HTML table with a query's

Table 9.5 Query Properties

Property	Description
columnNames	An array of strings representing column names.
rows	An array of sorted maps. Each of those maps represents a row of data from the query.
rowsByIndex	A two-dimensional array of objects representing rows of data from the query.
rowCount	A count of the rows in the query.
limitedByMaxRows	A boolean value that indicates whether the number of rows in the query was limited.

properties—here's how you would generate such a table for the `customers` query with the `columnNames` and `rows` properties:

```
<table border='1'>
    <tr>
        <c:forEach var='columnName' items='${customers.columnNames}'>
            <th><c:out value='${columnName}'/></th>
        </c:forEach>
    </tr>

    <c:forEach var='row' items='${customers.rows}'>
        <tr>
            <%-- Access each entry in the row map --%>
            <td><c:out value='${row.Cust_ID}'/></td>
            <td><c:out value='${row.NAME}'/></td>
            <td><c:out value='${row.phone_number}'/></td>
            <td><c:out value='${row.StReEt_aDdReSs}'/></td>
            <td><c:out value='${row.City}'/></td>
            <td><c:out value='${row.StAtE}'/></td>
        </tr>
    </c:forEach>
</table>
```

The preceding code fragment iterates over the `customers.rows` property and places the corresponding data from each row in the table. The `customers.rows` property is an array of maps, so you access row data with column names, which are case insensitive, as you can probably tell from the preceding code fragment. Alternatively, you can use the `customers.rowsByIndex` property to generate the exact same table generated by the preceding code fragment, like this:

```
<table border='1'>
   <tr>
      <c:forEach var='columnName' items='${customers.columnNames}'>
         <th><c:out value='${columnName}'/></th>
      </c:forEach>
   </tr>

   <c:forEach var='row' items='${customers.rowsByIndex}'>
      <tr>
         <%-- Iterate over the row array --%>
         <c:forEach var='rowData' items='${row}'>
            <td><c:out value='${rowData}'/></td>
         </c:forEach>
      </tr>
   </c:forEach>
</table>
```

The customers.rowsByIndex property is an array of arrays, so you access row data by iterating over each array, as shown in the preceding code fragment.

If you use the rows property to access a query's row data, you only have to iterate once, but you must know the names of the query's columns. If you use the rowsByIndex property to access row data, you have to iterate twice, but you do not need to know the names of the query's columns.

In general, you will probably prefer the rowsByIndex property when you need to manipulate all of a query's row data in the order in which that data is stored. You will probably prefer the rows property when you need to manipulate a subset of a query's row data or when you need to reorder that data. For example, it's easy to change the order in which row data is displayed in the preceding code fragment that uses the customers.rows property, perhaps by displaying the Name column before the Cust_ID column. That would be much more difficult to do in the code fragment that uses the customers.rowsByIndex property.

The rowCount and limitedByMaxRows properties are simple scalar properties that you can access like this:[11]

```
There are <c:out value='${customers.rowCount}'/> rows in this
query.

<c:choose>
   <c:when test='${customers.limitedByMaxRows}'>
      This query was limited.
   </c:when>
   <c:otherwise>
      This query was not limited.
   </c:otherwise>
</c:choose>
```

---

11. A scalar property contains a single value.

Scrolling Through Large Queries

As discussed in "Using <sql:query>" on page 378, the <sql:query> action has two attributes—startRow and maxRows—that let you limit the rows contained in a query. You can also scroll through large queries by using those attributes together.

The startRow attribute is zero-based; for example, if you specify 0 for that attribute, the starting row will be the first row in the query. The maxRows attribute specifies the maximum number of rows returned by the query; for example, if you specify 3 for that attribute, a maximum of three rows will be returned.[12] Here are two examples of how the startRow and maxRows attributes work together: If a query potentially has 20 rows and you specify 0 for startRow and 3 for maxRows, the query result will contain three rows, starting with the first row in the query. If you specify 3 for the startRow attribute and 3 for the maxRows attribute, the query result will contain rows 4, 5, and 6.

Figure 9–4 shows a simple Web application that lets you scroll through the query shown in Figure 9–3 on page 381. The top picture in Figure 9–4 shows a JSP page that lets you select a scroll increment, which is subsequently passed to another JSP page as a request parameter. The second JSP page, shown in the middle and bottom pictures in Figure 9–4, lets you scroll forward and backward through the query.

The top picture shows a JSP page that lets you select a scrolling increment. The middle picture shows the first three customers in the query, and the bottom picture shows the two last customers in the query.

The JSP page shown in the top picture in Figure 9–4 is listed in Listing 9.8.

The preceding JSP page uses the <c:forEach> action to create options for an HTML select element. Those options represent a scroll increment. The action for the form in Listing 9.8 is scroll_query.jsp, which is passed the scroll increment as a request parameter. That JSP page is listed in Listing 9.9.

The preceding JSP page starts with a <c:choose> action that has three code segments. The first time that JSP page is executed, there is no scroll request parameter, so the code in the body of the first <c:when> action is invoked. That code executes a query that selects all customers from the database—solely to ascertain how many customers are currently in the database—and subsequently creates three session attributes: scrollStart, which is set to 0, scrollInc, which is set to the value of the scrollIncrement request parameter, and scrollMax, which is set to the number of rows in the query.

Next, the preceding JSP page executes another customer query bracketed by the scrollStart and scrollInc session attributes. The result of that second query is used to create an HTML table.

---

12. If you specify -1 for the maxRows attribute, all of the query rows will be included in the query result.

Figure 9–4   Scrolling through Large Database Queries.

After the table has been created, the preceding JSP page creates two HTML anchor elements that both reference the JSP page in which they reside. Those anchors pass a request parameter named scroll that indicates scrolling direction. Finally, the JSP page prints the values of the scrollStart, scrollInc, and scrollMax session attributes.

When the anchor elements are activated, the preceding JSP page is reloaded, and passed the scroll request parameter. The <c:choose> action at the top of the

---

Listing 9.8   *index.jsp (Scrolling)*

```
<!DOCTYPE HTML PUBLIC "-//W3C//DTD HTML 4.0 Transitional//EN">
<html>
   <head>
      <title>Scrolling Through Database Queries</title>
   </head>

   <body>
      <%@ taglib uri='http://java.sun.com/jstl/core' prefix='c' %>

      <form action='scroll_query.jsp'>
         By clicking the submit button, you will be transferred
         to a JSP page that scrolls through a database query
         with 20 rows.
         <p>Please select a Scroll Increment:
         <select name='scrollIncrement'>
            <c:forEach var='item' items='1,2,3,4,5'>
               <option value='<c:out value="${item}"/>'>
                  <c:out value='${item}'/>
               </option>
            </c:forEach>
         </select>
         <p><input type='submit'/>
      </form>
   </body>
</html>
```

Listing 9.9   *scroll_query.jsp*

```
<!DOCTYPE HTML PUBLIC "-//W3C//DTD HTML 4.0 Transitional//EN">
<html>
   <head>
      <title>Scrolling Through Database Queries</title>
   </head>

   <body>
      <%@ taglib uri='http://java.sun.com/jstl/core' prefix='c'%>
      <%@ taglib uri='http://java.sun.com/jstl/sql'  prefix='sql'%>

      <c:choose>
         <%-- When there is no scroll request parameter --%>
         <c:when test='${empty param.scroll}'>
            <%-- This query is executed solely to ascertain the
                 number of customers in the database, which is
                 used to set the scrollMax attribute below --%>
```

Listing 9.9   *scroll_query.jsp (cont.)*

```
<sql:query var='exploring'>
    SELECT * FROM CUSTOMERS
</sql:query>

<%-- Set scrollMax to the number of rows in the
     Customers table --%>
<c:set var='scrollMax'
    value='${exploring.rowCount}'
    scope='session'/>

<%-- Set scrollStart to 0 and scrollInc to the value
     of the request parameter scrollIncrement --%>
<c:set var='scrollStart'
    value='0' scope='session'/>
  <c:set var='scrollInc' value='${param.scrollIncrement}'
      scope='session'/>
</c:when>

<%-- When the scroll request parameter is forward --%>
<c:when test='${param.scroll == "forward"}'>
    <%-- If it's valid to increment scrollStart --%>
    <c:if test='${scrollStart + scrollInc < scrollMax}'>
        <%-- Increment scrollStart by scrollInc --%>
        <c:set var='scrollStart'
            value='${scrollStart + scrollInc}'
            scope='session'/>
    </c:if>
</c:when>

<%-- When the scroll request parameter is backward --%>
<c:when test='${param.scroll == "backward"}'>
    <%-- If it's valid to decrement scrollStart --%>
    <c:if test='${scrollStart - scrollInc >= 0}'>
        <%-- Decrement scrollStart by scrollInc --%>
        <c:set var='scrollStart'
            value='${scrollStart - scrollInc}'
            scope='session'/>
    </c:if>
</c:when>
</c:choose>

<%-- Perform a customer query limited by the scrollStart and
     scrollInc variables --%>
<sql:query var='customers' startRow='${scrollStart}'
                           maxRows='${scrollInc}'>
    SELECT * FROM CUSTOMERS
    ORDER BY CUST_ID
</sql:query>
```

Listing 9.9	*scroll_query.jsp (cont.)*

```
<%-- Create a table with column names and row data --%>
<p><table border='1'>
   <tr>
      <c:forEach var='columnName'
              items='${customers.columnNames}'>
         <th><c:out value='${columnName}'/></th>
      </c:forEach>
   </tr>

   <c:forEach var='row' items='${customers.rowsByIndex}'>
      <tr>
         <c:forEach var='rowData' items='${row}'>
            <td><c:out value='${rowData}'/></td>
         </c:forEach>
      </tr>
   </c:forEach>
</table>

<%-- Create anchors that point back to this page with a
      request parameter indicating scroll direction --%>
<p>
<a href='?scroll=forward'>Scroll Forward</a><br>
<a href='?scroll=backward'>Scroll Backward</a>

<%-- Show the values of the scrollStart, scrollInc, and
      scrollMax session attributes --%>
<p><c:out value='Scroll Start: ${scrollStart}'/>,
   <c:out value='Scroll Inc:   ${scrollInc}'/>,
   <c:out value='Scroll Max:   ${scrollMax}'/><br>
   </body>
</html>
```

page executes code that increments or decrements the `scrollStart` session attribute, depending on whether the `scroll` request parameter is "forward" or "backward." Subsequently, the JSP page executes a query limited by the values of the `scrollStart` and `scrollInc` session attributes and redisplays the results in a table, along with the anchors and the values of the `scrollStart`, `scrollInc`, and `scrollMax` session attributes.

Prepared Statements and SQL Parameters

Web applications often need to execute queries with parameters. For example, the Web application shown in Figure 9–5 accesses orders for a specified customer that are greater than a certain amount. Both the customer and the order amount are entered by a user and are, therefore, query parameters.

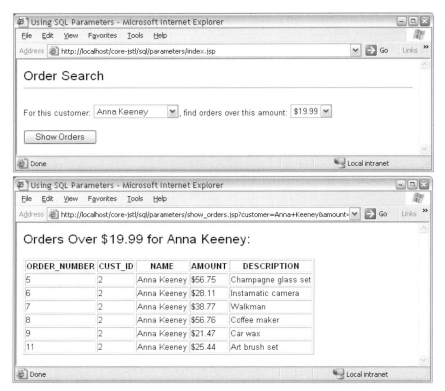

Figure 9–5   Using SQL Parameters to Select Customer/Order Amount.

The top picture shows a JSP page that lets users select a customer and an order amount. The bottom picture shows orders for that customer that are greater than $19.99.

The top picture in Figure 9–5 shows a JSP page that lets you select a customer and specify a minimum order amount. When the Show Orders button is activated, the JSP page shown in the bottom picture is loaded. That JSP page executes a query with the specified customer and order amount, and displays the result in an HTML table.

The JSP page shown in the top picture in Figure 9–5 is listed in Listing 9.10.

The preceding JSP page executes a query against all the customers in the database. That query is subsequently used to populate an HTML select element, which lets users select a customer. After a user selects a customer and a minimum order amount, clicking on the submit button takes the user to show_orders.jsp, which is listed in Listing 9.11.

The preceding JSP page executes a query, specifying the customer and minimum order amount with <sql:param> actions. That action has the following syntax:

<sql:param value/>

Listing 9.10	*index.jsp (Using SQL Parameters: 1)*

```
<!DOCTYPE HTML PUBLIC "-//W3C//DTD HTML 4.0 Transitional//EN">
<html>
    <head>
        <title>Using SQL Parameters</title>
    </head>

    <body>
        <%@ taglib uri='http://java.sun.com/jstl/core' prefix='c' %>
        <%@ taglib uri='http://java.sun.com/jstl/sql'  prefix='sql'%>

        <font size='5'>Order Search</font><hr>

        <%-- This query is used to populate the customer option --%>
        <sql:query var='customers'>
            SELECT * FROM CUSTOMERS
        </sql:query>

        <form action='show_orders.jsp'>
            For this customer:
            <select name='customer'>
                <c:forEach var='row' items='${customers.rows}'>
                    <option value="<c:out value='${row.NAME}'/>">
                        <c:out value='${row.NAME}'/>
                    </option>
                </c:forEach>
            </select>, find orders over this amount:

            <select name='amount'>
                <option value='1.99'>$1.99</option>
                <option value='19.99'>$19.99</option>
                <option value='49.99'>$49.99</option>
                <option value='75.99'>$75.99</option>
                <option value='99.99'>$99.99</option>
            </select>
            <p><input type='submit' value='Show Orders'>
        </form>
    </body>
</html>
```

You can also specify the value in the body of the <sql:param> action with this syntax:

<sql:param>
*   value*
</sql:param>

Listing 9.11   *show_orders.jsp (Selecting Orders)*

```
<!DOCTYPE HTML PUBLIC "-//W3C//DTD HTML 4.0 Transitional//EN">
<html>
    <head>
      <title>Using SQL Parameters</title>
    </head>

    <body>
      <%@ taglib uri='http://java.sun.com/jstl/core' prefix='c' %>
      <%@ taglib uri='http://java.sun.com/jstl/sql'  prefix='sql'%>
      <%@ taglib uri='http://java.sun.com/jstl/fmt'  prefix='fmt'%>

      <font size='5'>
        Orders Over
          <fmt:formatNumber type='currency'>
            <c:out value='${param.amount}'/>
          </fmt:formatNumber>
        for <c:out value='${param.customer}'/>:
      </font>

      <%-- Select orders over a specified amount for a
          specified customer --%>
      <sql:query var='orders'>
        SELECT * FROM Orders JOIN Customers
        WHERE Amount > ? AND Name = ? AND
        Customers.Cust_ID = Orders.Cust_ID

        <%-- Specify a parameter value with the value attr --%>
        <sql:param value='${param.amount}'/>

        <%-- Specify a parameter value in the body content --%>
        <sql:param>
          <c:out value='${param.customer}'/>
        </sql:param>
      </sql:query>

      <%-- Display the query results --%>
      <p><table border='1'>
        <tr>
          <th>ORDER_NUMBER</th>
          <th>CUST_ID</th>
          <th>NAME</th>
          <th>AMOUNT</th>
          <th>DESCRIPTION</th>
        </tr>
```

Listing 9.11	*show_orders.jsp (Selecting Orders) (cont.)*

```
            <c:forEach var='row' items='${orders.rows}'>
                <fmt:formatNumber var='amount' type='currency'>
                    <c:out value='${row.AMOUNT}'/>
                </fmt:formatNumber>
                <tr>
                    <td><c:out value='${row.Order_Number}'/></td>
                    <td><c:out value='${row.Cust_ID}'/></td>
                    <td><c:out value='${row.Name}'/></td>
                    <td><c:out value='${amount}'/></td>
                    <td><c:out value='${row.Description}'/></td>
                </tr>
            </c:forEach>
        </table>
    </body>
</html>
```

Notice that you must use <c:out> to specify SQL parameters in the body of an <sql:param> action—you *cannot* specify a JSTL EL expression directly in the body of an <sql:param> action, like this:

```
<%-- This code fragment will not work with JSP 1.2 --%>
<sql:param>
    ${param.someRequestParameter}
</sql:param>
```

JSTL EL expressions are not supported in JSP 1.2, so you cannot use them directly in the body of an action, but support for JSTL EL expressions is planned for JSP 2.0. In the meantime, you can use the <c:out> action, like this:

```
<%-- This code fragment will not work with JSP 1.2 --%>
<sql:param>
    <c:out value='${param.someRequestParameter}'/>
</sql:param>
```

As illustrated in Listing 9.11, specifying SQL query parameters is a two-step process:

1. In the query, specify dynamic values with a question mark.
2. In the body of the <sql:query> action, include an <sql:param> action for each of the query parameters.

The order of the question marks and the <sql:param> actions is significant: the value specified for the first <sql:param> action corresponds to the first question mark in the query, the second <sql:param> action's value corresponds to the second question mark, and so on.

Date Parameters

"Prepared Statements and SQL Parameters" on page 389 showed you how to use the <sql:param> action to specify parameters for <sql:query> and <sql:update> actions, but that approach will not work for parameters that are instances of java.util.Date. If you specify an instance of java.util.Date as a parameter representing an SQL date, time, or timestamp, that java.util.Date instance requires special handling. That special handling involves wrapping instances of java.util.Date in an instance of java.sql.Date (for dates), java.sql.Time (for times), and java.sql.Timestamp (for dates and times). Fortunately, you need not be concerned with those details, because JSTL provides an <sql:dateParam> action that makes instances of java.util.Date suitable for SQL dates, times, and timestamp parameters. That action has the following syntax:[13]

<sql:dateParam value [type]/>

The value attribute must be an instance of java.util.Date, and the type attribute must be either date, time, or timestamp, to indicate the type of SQL parameter that the value attribute represents. The default value for the type attribute is timestamp.

Figure 9–6 shows a Web application, similar to the Web application shown in Figure 9–5 on page 390, that searches for orders that match a certain criterion. For the Web application shown in Figure 9–6, that criterion is the date the orders were placed. The top picture in Figure 9–6 shows a JSP page that lets you select an order date, and the bottom picture in Figure 9–6 shows a JSP page that displays all of the orders placed on the date that you specified.

The top picture shows a JSP page that lets users select an order date. The bottom picture shows all orders for that date.

The JSP page shown in the top picture in Figure 9–6 is listed in Listing 9.12.

The preceding JSP page creates a simple HTML form that lets you select a date. That form's action is show_orders.jsp, which is listed in Listing 9.13.

The preceding JSP page creates an instance of java.util.Date by parsing the date request parameter, using the <fmt:parseDate> action. See "Formatting and Parsing Dates and Times" on page 333 for more information about <fmt:parseDate>. Subsequently, the JSP page executes a database query that joins the Orders and Customers tables, where the order date is specified with a

---

13. Items in brackets are optional. See "<sql:dateParam>" on page 540 for a more complete description of <sql:dateParam> syntax.

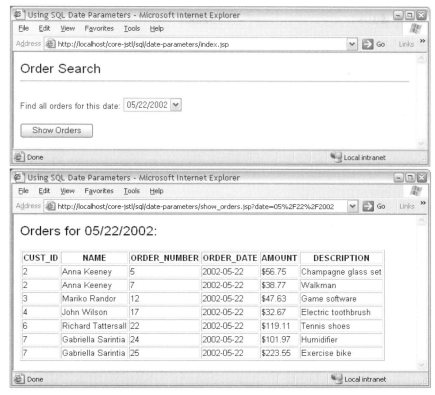

Figure 9–6   Using SQL Date Parameters to Select Order Date.

request parameter that's made available to the <sql:query> action with an <sql:dateParam> action. Notice that the <sql:param> action in that JSP page is commented; if you uncomment that action and comment the <sql:dateParam> action, the resulting query will contain no row data, which illustrates that you cannot use the <sql:param> action for parameters that are instances of java.util.Date. After the query has completed, the JSP page displays the result of that query in an HTML table.

Anytime you have user input that is used in a database query, as is the case for the Web application shown in Figure 9–5 on page 390 or Figure 9–6 on page 395, you will need to use the <sql:param> or <sql:dateParam> actions or a custom action— see "Implementing Database Custom Actions" on page 418 for more information on implementing custom actions that supply SQL parameters. In addition to using <sql:param> and <sql:dateParam> actions with <sql:query>, you can also use them with <sql:update>. The <sql:update> action is discussed in the next section.

Listing 9.12   *index.jsp (Using SQL Parameters: 2)*

```
<!DOCTYPE HTML PUBLIC "-//W3C//DTD HTML 4.0 Transitional//EN">
<html>
    <head>
        <title>Using SQL Date Parameters</title>
    </head>

    <body>
        <font size='5'>Order Search</font><hr>

        <%-- A form with an HTML select element and a
            submit button --%>
        <form action='show_orders.jsp'>
            Find all orders for this date:
            <select name='date'>
                <option value='05/20/2002'>05/20/2002</option>
                <option value='05/21/2002'>05/21/2002</option>
                <option value='05/22/2002'>05/22/2002</option>
                <option value='05/23/2002'>05/23/2002</option>
                <option value='05/24/2002'>05/24/2002</option>
            </select>
            <p><input type='submit' value='Show Orders'>
        </form>
    </body>
</html>
```

Listing 9.13   *show_orders.jsp (Selecting a Date)*

```
<!DOCTYPE HTML PUBLIC "-//W3C//DTD HTML 4.0 Transitional//EN">
<html>
    <head>
        <title>Using SQL Date Parameters</title>
    </head>

    <body>
        <%@ taglib uri='http://java.sun.com/jstl/core' prefix='c' %>
        <%@ taglib uri='http://java.sun.com/jstl/sql'  prefix='sql'%>
        <%@ taglib uri='http://java.sun.com/jstl/fmt'  prefix='fmt'%>

        <%-- Parse the date request parameter into a
            java.util.Date object and store it in a scoped
            variable in page scope --%>
        <fmt:parseDate var='javaDate' value='${param.date}'
                dateStyle='short'/>
```

Listing 9.13   *show_orders.jsp (Selecting a Date) (cont.)*

```
    <font size='5'>
       Orders for <c:out value='${param.date}'/>:
    </font>

    <%-- Select orders placed on the date specified by the
         request parameter --%>
    <sql:query var='orders'>
       SELECT * FROM Orders JOIN Customers
       WHERE Orders.Order_Date = ? AND
       Customers.Cust_ID = Orders.Cust_ID

       <%-- You can't just specify a Java date with <sql:param>,
            like this...
       <sql:param value='${javaDate}'/> --%>

       <%-- ...instead, you have to use <sql:dateParam>: --%>
       <sql:dateParam value='${javaDate}' type='date'/>
    </sql:query>

    <%-- Display the query results --%>
    <p><table border='1'>
       <tr>
          <th>CUST_ID</th>
          <th>NAME</th>
          <th>ORDER_NUMBER</th>
          <th>ORDER_DATE</th>
          <th>AMOUNT</th>
          <th>DESCRIPTION</th>
        </tr>

       <c:forEach var='row' items='${orders.rows}'>
          <fmt:formatNumber var='amount' type='currency'>
             <c:out value='${row.AMOUNT}'/>
          </fmt:formatNumber>
          <tr>
             <td><c:out value='${row.Cust_ID}'/></td>
             <td><c:out value='${row.Name}'/></td>
             <td><c:out value='${row.Order_Number}'/></td>
             <td><c:out value='${row.Order_Date}'/></td>
             <td><c:out value='${amount}'/></td>
             <td><c:out value='${row.Description}'/></td>
          </tr>
       </c:forEach>
    </table>
  </body>
</html>
```

9.6 Updating a Database

Besides supporting database queries with <sql:query>, JSTL also supports database updates with an <sql:update> action. The <sql:update> action supports both Data Manipulation Language (DML) commands and Data Definition Language (DDL) commands. The more common DML commands are:

- `INSERT`
- `UPDATE`
- `DELETE`

The `INSERT` command lets you insert a row in a table, `UPDATE` lets you update information in a row, and `DELETE` lets you delete rows. The more common DDL commands are:

- `CREATE TABLE`
- `DROP TABLE`
- `ALTER TABLE`

Both DML and DDL commands are executed with an SQL statement for the <sql:update> action. That action has the following syntax:[14]

> *<sql:update sql [var] [scope] [dataSource]/>*

The `sql` attribute specifies the SQL statement. Like <sql:query>, that statement can optionally be specified in the body of <sql:update>, like this:

> *<sql:update [var] [scope] [dataSource]>*
>   *SQL Statement*
> *</sql:update>*

Also, like <sql:query>, <sql:update> lets you specify a data source with the `dataSource` attribute.

The rest of this section shows you how to use <sql:update> to perform DML commands. DDL commands are executed in exactly the same manner, except for the SQL statement, so those are left as an exercise for the reader.

---

14. Items in brackets are optional. See "<sql:update>" on page 535 for a more complete
    description of <sql:update> syntax.

Database Inserts

Inserting rows in a database is easy with the <sql:update> action, as illustrated by the simple Web application shown in Figure 9–7 and Figure 9–8. That application consists of two JSP pages, one that collects information and another that performs the database insert.

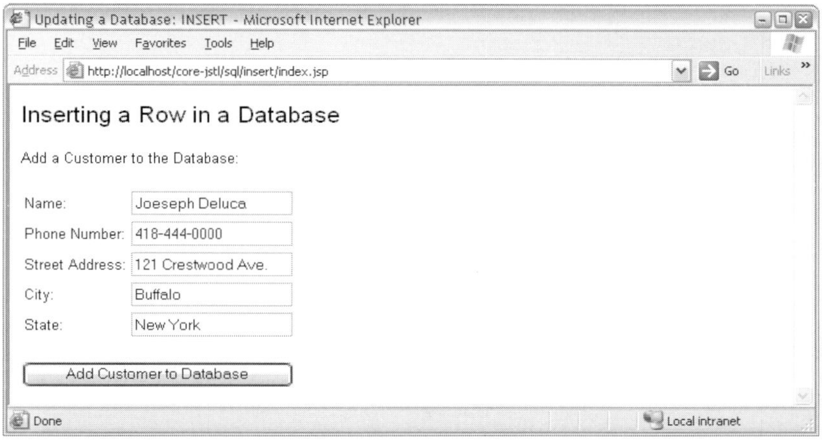

Figure 9–7 A JSP Page That Collects Customer Information

The JSP page shown in Figure 9–7 collects information about a customer that is subsequently inserted into the database; that insertion is performed by the JSP page shown in Figure 9–8.

The JSP page shown in Figure 9–7 is listed in Listing 9.14.

The preceding JSP page is unremarkable—it merely provides a form that lets users enter information for a new customer. The action for that form is `insert_customer.jsp`, which is shown in Figure 9–8 and listed in Listing 9.15.

The preceding JSP page performs two database queries that select all of the customers in the database. The first query is executed solely to ascertain how many customers are stored in the database so that the proper customer ID can be specified for the new customer. After the initial query, the preceding JSP page uses <sql:update> to perform the insert. Because all of the customer data is dynamically generated in a form, <sql:param> actions are used to specify customer parameters.

The <sql:update> action lets you specify an optional `var` attribute that stores the number of rows affected by the operation in a scoped variable. The preceding JSP page uses that attribute to show how many customers were inserted in the database.

Subsequently, the preceding JSP page performs a second query and displays the results of that query in an HTML table.

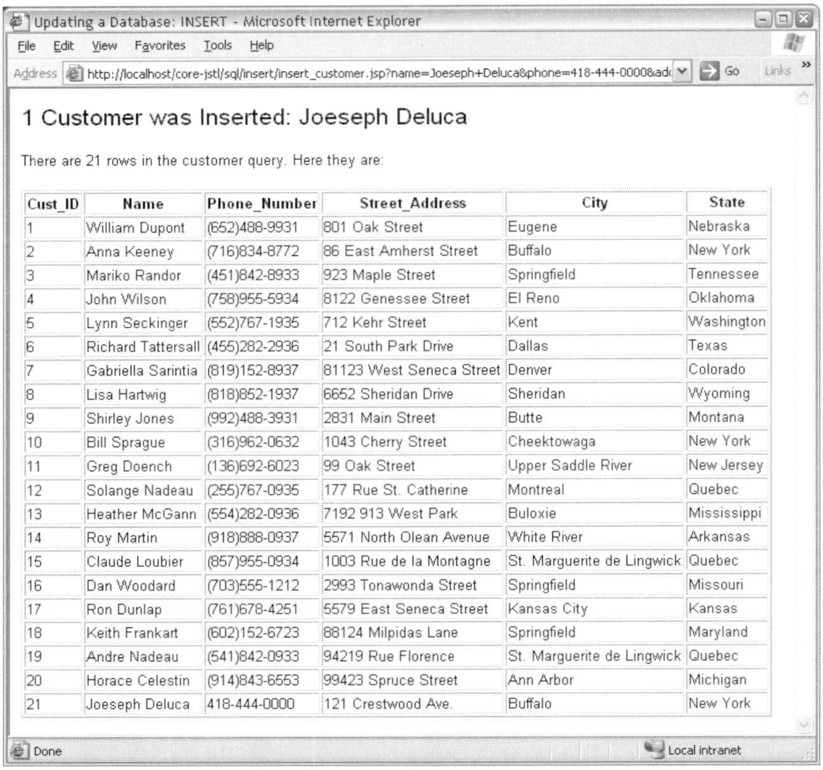

Cust_ID	Name	Phone_Number	Street_Address	City	State
1	William Dupont	(652)488-9931	801 Oak Street	Eugene	Nebraska
2	Anna Keeney	(716)834-8772	86 East Amherst Street	Buffalo	New York
3	Mariko Randor	(451)842-8933	923 Maple Street	Springfield	Tennessee
4	John Wilson	(758)955-5934	8122 Genessee Street	El Reno	Oklahoma
5	Lynn Seckinger	(552)767-1935	712 Kehr Street	Kent	Washington
6	Richard Tattersall	(455)282-2936	21 South Park Drive	Dallas	Texas
7	Gabriella Sarintia	(819)152-8937	81123 West Seneca Street	Denver	Colorado
8	Lisa Hartwig	(818)852-1937	6652 Sheridan Drive	Sheridan	Wyoming
9	Shirley Jones	(992)488-3931	2831 Main Street	Butte	Montana
10	Bill Sprague	(316)962-0632	1043 Cherry Street	Cheektowaga	New York
11	Greg Doench	(136)692-6023	99 Oak Street	Upper Saddle River	New Jersey
12	Solange Nadeau	(255)767-0935	177 Rue St. Catherine	Montreal	Quebec
13	Heather McGann	(554)282-0936	7192 913 West Park	Buloxie	Mississippi
14	Roy Martin	(918)888-0937	5571 North Olean Avenue	White River	Arkansas
15	Claude Loubier	(857)955-0934	1003 Rue de la Montagne	St. Marguerite de Lingwick	Quebec
16	Dan Woodard	(703)555-1212	2993 Tonawonda Street	Springfield	Missouri
17	Ron Dunlap	(761)678-4251	5579 East Seneca Street	Kansas City	Kansas
18	Keith Frankart	(602)152-6723	88124 Milpidas Lane	Springfield	Maryland
19	Andre Nadeau	(541)842-0933	94219 Rue Florence	St. Marguerite de Lingwick	Quebec
20	Horace Celestin	(914)843-6553	99423 Spruce Street	Ann Arbor	Michigan
21	Joeseph Deluca	418-444-0000	121 Crestwood Ave.	Buffalo	New York

Figure 9–8 Inserting a Row in a Database

Database Updates

Updating information in a database is also performed with the <sql:update> action. Figure 9–9 shows a Web application that lets you update information for a single customer in the database. That Web application consists of three JSP pages. The first JSP page, shown in the top picture in Figure 9–9, lets you select a customer to update. The second JSP page, shown in the two middle pictures, lets you modify the selected user's information. The third JSP page, shown in the bottom picture, shows the result of the update.

The top picture shows a JSP page that lets users select a customer to update. The two middle pictures show the original data (middle-top) and the modified data (middle-bottom). The bottom picture shows the result of the update.

The JSP page shown in the top picture in Figure 9–9 is listed in Listing 9.16.

Figure 9–9   Updating a Row in a Database.

The preceding JSP page uses a database query to populate an HTML `select` element with the names of all the customers in the database. When the form's submit button is activated, `collect_update_info.jsp` is loaded. That JSP page is listed in Listing 9.17.

The preceding JSP page performs a query against the selected customer to populate an HTML form. Because customer names are unique in our database, that

Listing 9.14   *index.jsp (Inserting a Row)*

```
<!DOCTYPE HTML PUBLIC "-//W3C//DTD HTML 4.0 Transitional//EN">
<html>
   <head>
      <title>Updating a Database: INSERT</title>
   </head>

   <body>
      <font size='5'>Inserting a Row in a Database</font>

      <form action='insert_customer.jsp'>
         Add a Customer to the Database:<p>
         <table>
            <tr><td>Name:</td>
               <td><input type='text' name='name'/></td></tr>
            <tr><td>Phone Number:</td>
               <td><input type='text' name='phone'/></td></tr>
            <tr><td>Street Address:</td>
               <td><input type='text' name='address'/></td></tr>
            <tr><td>City:</td>
               <td><input type='text' name='city'/></td></tr>
            <tr><td>State:</td>
               <td><input type='text' name='state'/></td></tr>
         </table>
         <p><input type='submit'
                value='Add Customer to Database'/>
      </form>
   </body>
</html>
```

Listing 9.15   *insert_customer.jsp*

```
<!DOCTYPE HTML PUBLIC "-//W3C//DTD HTML 4.0 Transitional//EN">
<html>
   <head>
      <%@ taglib uri='http://java.sun.com/jstl/core' prefix='c'%>
      <%@ taglib uri='http://java.sun.com/jstl/sql'  prefix='sql'%>
      <title>Updating a Database: INSERT</title>
   </head>

   <body>
      <%-- This query is made to find out how many customers
           are currently in the database --%>
      <sql:query var='customers'>
         SELECT * FROM CUSTOMERS
```

Listing 9.15   *insert_customer.jsp (cont.)*

```
    </sql:query>

    <%-- Perform the database update --%>
    <sql:update var='updateResult'>
       INSERT INTO CUSTOMERS VALUES (?, ?, ?, ?, ?, ?)
       <sql:param value='${customers.rowCount+1}'/>
       <sql:param value='${param.name}'/>
       <sql:param value='${param.phone}'/>
       <sql:param value='${param.address}'/>
       <sql:param value='${param.city}'/>
       <sql:param value='${param.state}'/>
    </sql:update>

    <%-- Show the result of the update --%>
    <font size='5'>
       <c:out value='${updateResult} Customer was Inserted:'/>
       <c:out value='${param.name}'/>
    </font>

    <%-- After adding a customer, perform another customer
         query --%>
    <sql:query var='customers'>
       SELECT * FROM CUSTOMERS
    </sql:query>

    <%-- Access the rowCount property of the query --%>
    <p><c:out value='There are ${customers.rowCount} rows'/>
     in the customer query. Here they are:</p>

    <%-- Create a table with column names and row data --%>
    <p><table border='1'>
       <tr>
         <c:forEach var='columnName'
                  items='${customers.columnNames}'>
           <th><c:out value='${columnName}'/></th>
         </c:forEach>
        </tr>

       <c:forEach var='row' items='${customers.rowsByIndex}'>
         <tr>
           <c:forEach var='rowData' items='${row}'>
             <td><c:out value='${rowData}'/></td>
           </c:forEach>
         </tr>
       </c:forEach>
    </table>
  </body>
</html>
```

Listing 9.16   *index.jsp (Updating a Row)*

```
<!DOCTYPE HTML PUBLIC "-//W3C//DTD HTML 4.0 Transitional//EN">
<html>
   <head>
      <title>Updating a Database: UPDATE</title>
   </head>

   <body>
      <%@ taglib uri='http://java.sun.com/jstl/core' prefix='c' %>
      <%@ taglib uri='http://java.sun.com/jstl/sql'  prefix='sql'%>

      <%-- This query is used to populate the customers option--%>
      <sql:query var='customers'>
         SELECT * FROM CUSTOMERS
      </sql:query>

      <form action='collect_update_info.jsp'>
         Select a Customer to Update:
         <select name='customer'>
            <c:forEach var='row' items='${customers.rows}'>
               <option value="<c:out value='${row.name}'/>">
                  <c:out value='${row.name}'/>
               </option>
            </c:forEach>
         </select>

         <p><input type='submit'
                   value='Update Selected Customer'/>
      </form>
   </body>
</html>
```

Listing 9.17   *collect_update_info.jsp*

```
<!DOCTYPE HTML PUBLIC "-//W3C//DTD HTML 4.0 Transitional//EN">
</html>
   </head>
      <title>Updating a Database: UPDATE</title>
   </head>

   <body>
      <%@ taglib uri='http://java.sun.com/jstl/core' prefix='c' %>
      <%@ taglib uri='http://java.sun.com/jstl/sql'  prefix='sql'%>
```

Listing 9.17   *collect_update_info.jsp (cont.)*

```
<%-- Perform a query against the selected customer --%>
<sql:query var='customers'>
    SELECT * FROM CUSTOMERS WHERE NAME = ?
    <sql:param value='${param.customer}'/>
</sql:query>

<%-- Set a variable for the row as a shorthand to be
     used below --%>
<c:set var='row' value='${customers.rows[0]}'/>

<%-- Populate a form with the query performed above --%>
<form action='update_customer.jsp'>
    <table>
        <tr><td>Name:</td>
            <td><c:out value='${row.NAME}'/></td></tr>

        <tr><td>Phone:</td>
            <td><input type='text'
                value='<c:out value="${row.PHONE_NUMBER}"/>'
                 name='phone'/></td></tr>

        <tr><td>Address:</td>
            <td><input type='text'
               value='<c:out value="${row.STREET_ADDRESS}"/>'
                name='address'
                size='35'/></td></tr>

        <tr><td>City:</td>
            <td><input type='text'
                    value='<c:out value="${row.CITY}"/>'
                    name='city'/></td></tr>

        <tr><td>State:</td>
            <td><input type='text'
                    value='<c:out value="${row.STATE}"/>'
                    name='state'/></td></tr>
    </table>
    <p>
    <input type='submit'
            value="Update <c:out value='${row.NAME}'/>">

    <input type='hidden' name='name'
            value='<c:out value="${row.NAME}"/>'/>
</form>
</body>
</html>
```

query always contains a single row of data. To make that single row of data more accessible, the JSP page stores that data in a page scope variable named row as a convenient shorthand for ${customers.rows[0]}.

The form in the preceding JSP page displays the user's name, but does not allow the name to be updated. Because of that restriction, the user's name will not be encoded as a request parameter when a user activates the form's submit button, so the form stores that name in a hidden field.

When a user activates the submit button, the JSP page update_customer.jsp is loaded in the browser. That JSP page is listed in Listing 9.18.

Listing 9.18   *update_customer.jsp*

```
<!DOCTYPE HTML PUBLIC "-//W3C//DTD HTML 4.0 Transitional//EN">
<html>
    <head>
        <title>Updating a Database: UPDATE</title>
    </head>

    <body>
        <%@ taglib uri='http://java.sun.com/jstl/core' prefix='c' %>
        <%@ taglib uri='http://java.sun.com/jstl/sql'  prefix='sql'%>

        <%-- Perform the database update --%>
        <sql:update var='updateResult'>
            UPDATE CUSTOMERS SET PHONE_NUMBER = ?,
            STREET_ADDRESS = ?, CITY = ?, STATE = ?
            WHERE NAME = ?
            <sql:param value='${param.phone}'/>
            <sql:param value='${param.address}'/>
            <sql:param value='${param.city}'/>
            <sql:param value='${param.state}'/>
            <sql:param value='${param.name}'/>
        </sql:update>

        <%-- Perform a query against the updated customer --%>
        <sql:query var='customers'>
            SELECT * FROM CUSTOMERS WHERE NAME = ?
            <sql:param value='${param.name}'/>
        </sql:query>
```

Listing 9.18 *update_customer.jsp (cont.)*

```
<%-- Show how many rows were updated --%>
<p><font size='4'>
  <c:out value='${updateResult} row updated '/>
  <c:out value='for ${param.name}:'/>
</font>

<%-- Display updated data with the query performed above--%>
<c:forEach var='row' items='${customers.rows}'>
   <p><table border='1'>
      <tr><td>Phone:</td>
         <td><c:out value='${row.PHONE_NUMBER}'/></td>
      </tr>

      <tr><td>Address:</td>
         <td><c:out value='${row.STREET_ADDRESS}'/></td>
      </tr>

      <tr><td>City:</td>
         <td><c:out value='${row.CITY}'/></td>
      </tr>

      <tr><td>State:</td>
         <td><c:out value='${row.STATE}'/></td>
      </tr>
   </table>
</c:forEach>
</body>
</html>
```

The preceding JSP page updates the selected user's information in the database with <sql:update> and <sql:param>, and executes a subsequent query against the user. That query is then used to populate an HTML table.

Database Deletes

Deleting rows from a database is also performed with the <sql:update> action. Figure 9–10 shows a Web application, consisting of two JSP pages, that deletes a selected customer from the database.

The top picture in Figure 9–10 shows a JSP page that lets you select a customer to delete from the database. That JSP page is listed in Listing 9.19.

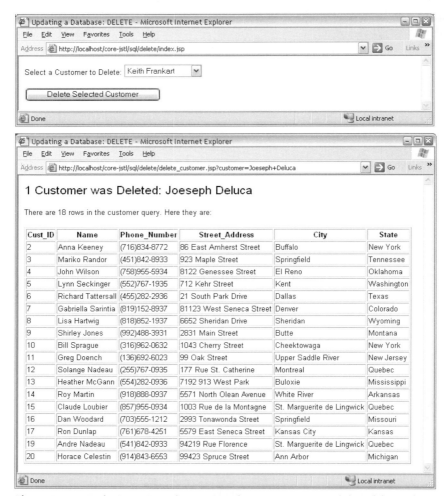

Figure 9–10 Deleting a Row from a Database. Row 18 was deleted from the Customers table, which originally had 20 customers.

When the submit button in the preceding JSP page's form is activated, `delete_customer.jsp` is loaded in the browser. That JSP page is listed in Listing 9.20.

The preceding JSP page uses <sql:update> and <sql:param> to delete the selected customer from the database. Subsequently, a query against all customers in the database is executed, and the result of that query is displayed in an HTML table.

Listing 9.19   *index.jsp (Deleting a Row)*

```
<!DOCTYPE HTML PUBLIC "-//W3C//DTD HTML 4.0 Transitional//EN">
<html>
   <head>
      <title>Updating a Database: DELETE</title>
   </head>

   <body>
      <%@ taglib uri='http://java.sun.com/jstl/core' prefix='c' %>
      <%@ taglib uri='http://java.sun.com/jstl/sql'  prefix='sql'%>

      <%-- This query is used to populate the customers option--%>
      <sql:query var='customers'>
         SELECT * FROM CUSTOMERS
      </sql:query>

      <form action='delete_customer.jsp'>
         Select a Customer to Delete:
         <select name='customer'>
            <c:forEach var='row' items='${customers.rows}'>
               <option value="<c:out value='${row.NAME}'/>">
                  <c:out value='${row.NAME}'/>
               </option>
            </c:forEach>
         </select>
         <p><input type='submit'
                 value='Delete Selected Customer'>
      </form>
   </body>
</html>
```

Listing 9.20   *delete_customer.jsp*

```
<!DOCTYPE HTML PUBLIC "-//W3C//DTD HTML 4.0 Transitional//EN">
<html>
   <head>
      <title>Updating a Database: DELETE</title>
   </head>

   <body>
      <%@ taglib uri='http://java.sun.com/jstl/core' prefix='c' %>
      <%@ taglib uri='http://java.sun.com/jstl/sql'  prefix='sql'%>
```

Listing 9.20   *delete_customer.jsp (cont.)*

```
<%-- Perform the database delete --%>
<sql:update var='updateResult'>
    DELETE FROM CUSTOMERS WHERE NAME = ?
    <sql:param value='${param.customer}'/>
</sql:update>

<%-- Show how many rows were deleted --%>
<font size='5'>
    <c:out value='${updateResult} Customer was Deleted:'/>
    <c:out value='${param.customer}'/>
</font>

<%-- Make a query of all customers in the database --%>
<sql:query var='customers'>
    SELECT * FROM CUSTOMERS
</sql:query>

<%-- Access the rowsCount property of the query --%>
<p><c:out value='There are ${customers.rowCount} rows'/>
 in the customer query. Here they are:

<%-- Create a table with column and row data --%>
<p><table border='1'>
    <tr>
        <c:forEach var='columnName'
                items='${customers.columnNames}'>
            <th><c:out value='${columnName}'/></th>
        </c:forEach>
    </tr>

    <c:forEach var='row' items='${customers.rowsByIndex}'>
        <tr>
            <c:forEach var='rowData' items='${row}'>
                <td><c:out value='${rowData}'/></td>
            </c:forEach>
        </tr>
    </c:forEach>
    </table>
</body>
</html>
```

9.7 Executing Database Transactions

It's often desirable to execute a group of SQL updates or queries atomically; for example, if you transfer funds from bank account A to bank account B, you don't want to deposit the money in account B if the withdrawal from account A failed. Database transactions let you treat any number of SQL updates atomically—if one of the updates fails, the entire transaction is rolled back. The transaction is committed only if all of the updates are successful.

JSTL supports database transactions with the <sql:transaction> action. That action has the following syntax:[15]

<sql:transaction [dataSource] [isolation]>
     <sql:query> and <sql:update> actions
<sql:transaction>

The <sql:transaction> action wraps enclosed <sql:update> and <sql:query> actions in a database transaction. As with <sql:query> and <sql:update>, you can specify a data source with <sql:transaction>. But because all queries and updates within a single transaction must be executed against a single data source, it is illegal to specify a data source for <sql:query> or <sql:update> actions within a <sql:transaction> action.

You can also specify a transaction isolation level with the isolation attribute; valid values for that attribute are:

- read_uncommitted
- read_committed
- repeatable_read
- serializable

Transaction isolation levels specify how database locks are set during a transaction; for example, read_uncommitted specifies that one user can read uncommitted changes from another user's transaction. The isolation levels listed above are listed from the least to the most restrictive. Normally, you will not need to set isolation levels for your transactions, because they are set by your database or your system

---

15. Items in brackets are optional. See "<sql:transaction>" on page 537 for a more complete
    description of <sql:transaction> syntax.

administrator. See *JDBC API Tutorial and Reference*[16] for more information about transaction isolation levels.

Figure 9–11 shows a Web application that lets you transfer money from one account to another. That transfer is implemented with two database updates, one that withdraws money from one account and another that subsequently deposits that money into another account. Those two database updates are encapsulated in a database transaction, like this:

```
<c:catch var='transactionException'>
   <sql:transaction>
      <sql:update>
         ... withdraw money from one account ...
      </sql:update>

      <sql:update>
         ... deposit that money in another account ...
      </sql:update>
   </sql:transaction>
</c:catch>
```

The database used by the Web application shown in Figure 9–11 specifies a constraint for account balances, like this:

```
ALTER TABLE ACCOUNTS ADD CONSTRAINT
CONSTRAINT_1 CHECK (Balance > 0)
```

The preceding constraint will not allow an account balance to be less than 0. If you try to transfer money from account A to account B, and account A does not have sufficient funds, that constraint will cause the transaction to fail and the <sql:transaction> action will throw an exception. That exception will be caught by the <c:catch> action listed in preceding code fragment.

Note: *Because MySQL does not fully support database constraints, the example in this section uses the Cloudscape database, which supports constraints.*

The top two pictures in Figure 9–11 illustrate a successful transaction, and the bottom pictures illustrate a rolled back transaction.

The top pictures show a successful transaction and the bottom pictures show a failed transaction.

The top pictures in Figure 9–11 show a transfer of $1000 from the first customer (William Dupont) to the second customer (Anna Keeney). That transaction is successful because William originally had $1145.97. If you look at the upper-right

16. White, Fisher, Cattell, Hamilton, Hapner,. *JDBC API Tutorial and Reference*, Addison-Wesley, 1999.

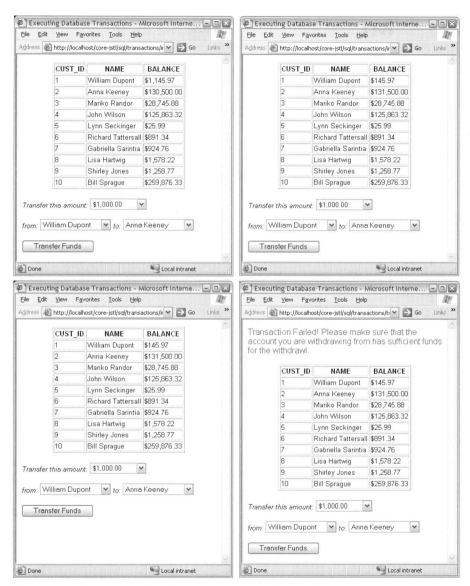

Figure 9–11 Executing Database Transactions with <sql:transaction>.

picture, you will see that William's balance has been reduced by $1000 and Anna's balance has increased by the same amount.

The bottom pictures in Figure 9–11 show a failed transaction. Once again, a transfer of $1000 is attempted from William to Anna, but this time, William does not have that much money, so the transaction fails. The lower-right picture shows the results of that failure—an error message states that the transaction failed.

The Web application shown in Figure 9–11 consists of two JSP pages, one that displays an HTML table and the form for transferring funds and another that executes the transaction. The former is listed in Listing 9.21.

Listing 9.21	*index.jsp (Displaying HTML Table)*

```
<!DOCTYPE HTML PUBLIC "-//W3C//DTD HTML 4.0 Transitional//EN">
<html>
   <head>
      <title>Executing Database Transactions</title>
   </head>

   <body>
      <%@ taglib uri='http://java.sun.com/jstl/core' prefix='c' %>
      <%@ taglib uri='http://java.sun.com/jstl/sql'  prefix='sql'%>
      <%@ taglib uri='http://java.sun.com/jstl/fmt'  prefix='fmt'%>

      <%-- Execute a query, limited to 10 rows, that joins the
           Customers and Accounts tables --%>
      <sql:query var='customers' maxRows='10'>
         SELECT CUST_ID, NAME, BALANCE
         FROM CUSTOMERS JOIN ACCOUNTS
         USING (Cust_ID)
      </sql:query>

      <%-- Create a table with column names and row data --%>
      <p><table align='center' border='1'>
      <tr>
         <%-- Create the table header --%>
         <c:forEach var='column' items='${customers.columnNames}'>
            <th><c:out value='${column}'/></th>
         </c:forEach>
      </tr>

      <%-- For each row in the query... --%>
      <c:forEach var='row' items='${customers.rowsByIndex}'>
         <tr>
            <%-- For the data in each row... --%>
            <c:forEach var='rowData' items='${row}'
                 varStatus='status'>
               <c:choose>
                  <%-- For the 3rd column, which represents
                       account balance... --%>
                  <c:when test='${status.count == 3}'>
                     <%-- Format the currency according to the
                          user's preferred locales --%>
                     <td><fmt:formatNumber value='${rowData}'
                                           type='currency'/></td>
```

Listing 9.21   *index.jsp (Displaying HTML Table) (cont.)*

```
            </c:when>
            <%-- For all other columns... --%>
            <c:otherwise>
                <%-- Put the data, as is, in the table --%>
                <td><c:out value='${rowData}'/></td>
            </c:otherwise>
          </c:choose>
        </c:forEach>
    </tr>
</c:forEach>
</table>

<%-- The form... --%>
<form action='transfer_funds.jsp'>
    <i>Transfer this amount:</i>
    <select name='amount'>
        <%-- For each of the monetary amounts... --%>
        <c:forEach var='amt' varStatus='status'
                items='100,1000,10000,100000,1000000'>

            <%-- Format the amount according to the user's
                 preferred locales --%>
            <fmt:formatNumber var='money' value='${amt}'
                                          type='currency'/>
            <%-- Create an HTML option element --%>
            <option
                <%-- If the amount previously selected is the
                     same as the current option, select it --%>
                <c:if test='${param.amount == amt}'>
                  selected
                </c:if>

                <%-- Output the amount and the closing '>' for
                     the option element --%>
                <c:out value='value=${amt}'/> >

                <%-- Output the value of the option element
                     as formatted currency --%>
                <c:out value='${money}'/>
            </option>
        </c:forEach>
    </select>
    <p><i>from:</i>
    <select name='fromCustomer'>
        <%-- For the "from" customer... --%>
        <c:forEach var='row' items='${customers.rows}'>
            <%-- Create an HTML option element --%>
            <option
```

Listing 9.21   *index.jsp (Displaying HTML Table) (cont.)*

```jsp
                            <%-- If the "from" customer previously selected
                                 is the same as the current customer,
                                 select it --%>
                            <c:if
                               test='${param.fromCustomer == row.cust_id}'>
                               selected
                            </c:if>

                            <%-- Output the "from" customer's ID for the
                                 option element's value and the option's
                                 closing '>' --%>
                            <c:out value='value=${row.cust_id}'/> >

                            <%-- Output the "from" customer's name --%>
                            <c:out value='${row.name}'/>
                      </option>
                   </c:forEach>
             </select>
             <i>to:</i>
             <select name='toCustomer'>
                <%-- For the "to" customer... --%>
                <c:forEach var='row' items='${customers.rows}'>
                   <%-- Create an HTML option element --%>
                   <option
                      <%-- If the "to" customer previously selected
                           is the same as the current customer,
                           select it --%>
                      <c:if test='${param.toCustomer == row.cust_id}'>
                         selected
                      </c:if>

                      <%-- Output the "to" customer's ID for the
                           option element's value and the option's
                           closing '>' --%>
                      <c:out value='value=${row.cust_id}'/> >

                      <%-- Output the "to" customer's name --%>
                      <c:out value='${row.name}'/>
                   </option>
                </c:forEach>
             </select>
             <p><input type='submit' value='Transfer Funds'>
          </form>
       </body>
</html>
```

The JSP page in the preceding listing executes a database query that joins the Customers and Accounts tables. Those tables are depicted in Figure 9–2 on page 362. The CUST_ID, NAME, and BALANCE columns are selected in the join, and the result of that query is used to build the table that you see in Figure 9–11 on page 413.

The preceding JSP page is notable for formatting currency stored in the database. That formatting is accomplished with the <fmt:formatNumber> action, which is discussed in "Formatting and Parsing Numbers" on page 310. Also note that the HTML option elements retain their previously selected values.

The form in the preceding JSP page transmits the following request parameters: fromCustomer, toCustomer, and amount. Those parameters are used by the form's action, transfer_funds.jsp, which is listed in Listing 9.22.

Listing 9.22 *transfer_funds.jsp*

```
<!DOCTYPE HTML PUBLIC "-//W3C//DTD HTML 4.0 Transitional//EN">
<html>
   <head>
      <title>Executing Database Transactions</title>
   </head>

   <body>
      <%@ taglib uri='http://java.sun.com/jstl/core' prefix='c'%>
      <%@ taglib uri='http://java.sun.com/jstl/sql'  prefix='sql'%>
      <%@ taglib uri='http://java.sun.com/jstl/fmt'  prefix='fmt'%>

      <%-- The transaction is enclosed in a <c:catch>
           action. If the transaction fails, the <sql:transaction>
           action will throw an exception, which <c:catch> stores
           in a scoped variable named transactionException --%>
      <c:catch var='transactionException'>
         <%-- The transaction... --%>
         <sql:transaction>
            <%-- Withdraw money from the "from" customer's
                 account --%>
            <sql:update>
               UPDATE ACCOUNTS SET BALANCE = BALANCE - ?
               WHERE CUST_ID = ?
                <sql:param value='${param.amount}'/>
                <sql:param value='${param.fromCustomer}'/>
            </sql:update>
            <%-- Deposit the money withdrawn from the "from"
                 customer's account in the "to" customer's
                 account --%>
```

Listing 9.22 *transfer_funds.jsp (cont.)*

```
        <sql:update>
            UPDATE ACCOUNTS SET BALANCE = BALANCE + ?
            WHERE CUST_ID = ?
            <sql:param value='${param.amount}'/>
            <sql:param value='${param.toCustomer}'/>
        </sql:update>
    </sql:transaction>
</c:catch>

<%-- If the transactionException scoped variable is not
        empty, the transaction failed --%>
<c:if test='${not empty transactionException}'>
    <%-- Display the error message --%>
    <font size='4' color='red'>
        Transaction Failed! Please make sure that the account
        you are withdrawing from has sufficient funds
        for the withdrawl.
    </font>
</c:if>

<%-- Import the JSP page with the form for transferring
        funds --%>
<c:import url='index.jsp'/>
    </body>
</html>
```

The preceding JSP page performs a transaction that consists of two updates. The first update withdraws money from fromCustomer's account, and the second deposits that money in the toCustomer's account. If either of those updates fails, the transaction is rolled back and the <sql:transaction> action throws an exception.

If <sql:transaction> throws an exception, that exception is caught by the <c:catch> action, which stores it in a scoped variable named transactionException. If the transaction failed, the preceding JSP page displays an error message. Subsequently, the preceding JSP page imports the JSP page that contains the form for transferring funds, in case the user wants to execute another transaction.

9.8 Implementing Database Custom Actions

The JSTL database actions are comprehensive enough to support most database scenarios in a production environment; however, on occasion you may need a custom action that gathers data from disparate sources, processes that data, and subsequently specifies it as a parameter to <sql:query> or <sql:update>. For example, in "Database Inserts" on page 399, one JSP page supplies request parameters representing information about a new customer to a second JSP page, and the second JSP page performs a database insert to add the customer to the database. Because both JSP pages were implemented by the same person, the request parameters generated by the first JSP page are exactly what's needed for the second JSP page to add a new customer to the database. Here's a code segment from the second JSP page that shows how those request parameters are used:

```
<sql:update var='updateResult'>
   INSERT INTO CUSTOMERS VALUES (?, ?, ?, ?, ?, ?)
   <sql:param value='${customers.rowsCount+1}'/>
   <sql:param value='${param.name}'/>
   <sql:param value='${param.phone}'/>
   <sql:param value='${param.address}'/>
   <sql:param value='${param.city}'/>
   <sql:param value='${param.state}'/>
</sql:update>
```

But what if the request parameters did not exactly match the SQL parameters needed to create a new customer in the database? For example, if the form in the first JSP page collected the user's name with two input fields, one for first name and one for last name, the corresponding request parameters would have to be coalesced into one name. That task could be performed by a scriptlet that stores the coalesced name in a scoped variable, or a custom action could perform that task,[17] like this:

```
<html>
   ...
   <body>
      ...
      <%@ taglib uri='WEB-INF/core-jstl.tld' prefix='core-jstl'%>

      <%-- Perform the database update --%>
      <sql:update var='updateResult'>
         INSERT INTO CUSTOMERS VALUES (?, ?, ?, ?, ?, ?)
         <sql:param value='${customers.rowCount+1}'/>

         <%-- The <core-jstl:nameParam> custom action coalesces
              the first and last names (which are request
              parameters) and passes them to its enclosing
              <sql:update> action --%>
         <core-jstl:nameParam/>

         <sql:param value='${param.phone}'/>
```

---

17. In general, custom actions are preferable to scriptlets because custom actions provide a degree of separation between business and presentation logic.

```
         <sql:param value='${param.address}'/>
         <sql:param value='${param.city}'/>
         <sql:param value='${param.state}'/>
      </sql:update>

      . . .

   </body>

   . . .

</html>
```

The code fragment listed above uses an application-specific custom action—<core-jstl:nameParam>—that coalesces first and last names stored in the request parameters and supplies the coalesced name as a parameter to its enclosing <sql:update>. That custom action behaves just like <sql:param> by sending a parameter to its enclosing <sql:update> action. Let's see how that custom action is implemented.

First, in WEB-INF/core-jstl.tld, we declare the tag library that contains <core-jstl:nameParam>, with a tag library descriptor, which is listed in Listing 9.23.

Listing 9.23   *WEB-INF/core-jstl.tld*

```
<?xml version="1.0" encoding="ISO-8859-1" ?>
<!DOCTYPE taglib
   PUBLIC "-//Sun Microsystems, Inc.//DTD JSP Tag Library 1.2//EN"
   "http://java.sun.com/dtd/web-jsptaglibrary_1_2.dtd">
<taglib>
   <tlib-version>1.0</tlib-version>
   <jsp-version>1.2</jsp-version>
   <short-name>app</short-name>
   <display-name>application tags</display-name>
   <description>
     A tag library with an action that passes a parameter to
     a query action
   </description>

   <tag>
     <name>nameParam</name>
     <tag-class>tags.NameParamTag</tag-class>
     <body-content>NONE</body-content>
     <description>
       Coalesces first and last names obtained from request
       parameters, and passes them as an SQL query parameter
       to an enclosing tag that implements
       javax.servlet.jsp.jstl.sql.SQLExcecutionTag
     </description>
   </tag>
</taglib>
```

Second, we implement the action itself, which is listed in Listing 9.24.

Listing 9.24 *WEB-INF/classes/tags/NameParamTag.java*

```
package tags;

import javax.servlet.ServletRequest;
import javax.servlet.jsp.JspException;
import javax.servlet.jsp.tagext.TagSupport;

import javax.servlet.jsp.jstl.sql.SQLExecutionTag;

public class NameParamTag extends TagSupport {
    public int doStartTag() throws JspException {
        Class klass =
            javax.servlet.jsp.jstl.sql.SQLExecutionTag.class;

        SQLExecutionTag ancestor = (SQLExecutionTag)
                            findAncestorWithClass(this, klass);
        if(ancestor != null) {
            ServletRequest request = pageContext.getRequest();

            ancestor.addSQLParameter(
              request.getParameter("firstName") + " " +
              request.getParameter("lastName"));
        }
        else {
            throw new JspException("This tag can only be in the " +
                "body of a tag that implements " +
                "javax.servlet.jsp.jstl.sql.SQLExecutionTag");
        }
        return SKIP_BODY;
    }
}
```

The tag handlers for <sql:query> and <sql:update> both implement the javax.servlet.jsp.jstl.sql.SQLExecutionTag interface, which defines a single method: addSQLParameter(Object). The custom action listed above checks to see whether it has an ancestor action that implements that interface; if so, it calls that action's addSQLParameter method, passing it the coalesced name. If the custom action does not have an ancestor that implements SQLExecutionTag, it throws an exception.

XML ACTIONS

Topics in This Chapter

Chapter 10

XML and the Java programming language—which represent portable data and portable code, respectively—are a powerful combination for developing portable Web applications that can freely share information.

XML, which stands for e**X**tensible **M**arkup **L**anguage, is a meta-language that can be used to define markup languages, such as XHTML. XML lets you define a document's structure with extensible markup, meaning tags that you define; for example, see "A Simple XML File" on page 424, which uses XML to define the structure of a simple Rolodex document. XML provides the following benefits:

- *Simplicity*: XML defines document structure with textual elements. That way, humans and computers alike can easily read and understand the document.

- *Extensibility*: Unlike other markup languages, for example, HTML, XML does not define a fixed set of tags for markup. You can define your own set of markup tags for different types of documents.

- *Separation of content from presentation*: Although you can certainly use XML to define a document's presentation, typically, XML is used to define document structure only. That lets you reuse the same XML document for multiple presentations, which are typically generated with XSL Transformation language (XSLT) stylesheets.

- *Openness and widespread industry adoption*: XML is not a proprietary language and can be freely used without restrictions. XML has been widely adopted by companies in the computer industry, including Sun and Microsoft.

JSTL provides a comprehensive set of XML actions that greatly facilitate the implementation of XML-based Web applications. Those actions, which are the focus of this chapter, support parsing and transforming XML and also provide additional features such as accessing XML documents with the XPath language, filtering XML, specifying transformation parameters, and accessing external entities. All of those features are discussed in the sections that follow.

10.1 A Simple XML File

For illustration, the examples discussed in this chapter use a single XML file, listed in Listing 10.1.[1]

| Listing 10.1 | *rolodex.xml (Simple Version)* |

```xml
<?xml version="1.0" encoding="ISO-8859-1"?>
<rolodex>
   <contact>
      <firstName>Anna</firstName>
      <lastName>Keeney</lastName>
      <company>BSC, Inc.</company>
      <email>anna.keeney@worldlink.net</email>
      <phone type="work">716-873-9644</phone>
      <phone type="home">716-834-8772</phone>
   </contact>
   <contact>
      <firstName>Lynn</firstName>
      <lastName>Seckinger</lastName>
      <company>Sabreware, Inc.</company>
      <email>lynn.seckinger@telecom.net</email>
      <phone type="work">716-219-2012</phone>
   </contact>
   <contact>
      <firstName>Ronald</firstName>
      <lastName>Dunlap</lastName>
      <company>World Traders, Inc.</company>
      <email>ron.dunlap@worldlink.net</email>
      <phone type="work">915-783-6494</phone>
      <phone type="home">915-843-8727</phone>
   </contact>
</rolodex>
```

---

1. "Accessing External Entities" on page 460 uses a modified version of `rolodex.xml`. The modified version includes a Document Type Definition (DTD).

The preceding XML file represents a Rolodex that contains business contacts composed of first and last names, company name, e-mail, and work and home phone numbers. Home phone numbers are optional, as you can see from the second contact listed above.

10.2 XML Actions Overview

The JSTL XML actions are listed in Table 10.1.

Table 10.1 XML Actions

Action	Description
<x:choose>	XML version of <c:choose>
<x:forEach>	XML version of <c:forEach>
<x:if>	XML version of <c:if>
<x:otherwise>	XML version of <c:otherwise>
<x:out>	XML version of <c:out>
<x:param>	XML version of <c:param>; specifies a transformation parameter for an <x:transform> action
<x:parse>	Parses an XML document
<x:set>	XML version of <c:set>
<x:transform>	Transforms an XML document
<x:when>	XML version of <c:when>

Many of the actions listed in Table 10.1 access information stored in XML files.[2] Those actions access that information with XPath expressions, all of which are specified with attributes named `select`; for example, the following code fragment displays all of the first and last names from the Rolodex XML file listed in Listing 10.1 on page 424:

---

2. Those actions are <x:forEach>, <x:if>, <x:out>, <x:set>, and <x:when>.

```
<x:forEach select='$document//contact'>
  <x:out select='lastName'/>, <x:out select='firstName'/>
  <br>
</x:forEach>
```

In the preceding code fragment, the <x:forEach> action iterates over all of the Rolodex contacts with the XPath expression `$document//contact`, where `$document` represents the parsed XML file. Inside the body of that <x:forEach> action, <x:out> actions access the first and last names for each contact with the XPath expressions `firstName` and `lastName`, respectively.

Notice that most of the actions listed in Table 10.1 are XML counterparts of the JSTL Core actions; for example, the <x:forEach> and <x:out> actions are counterparts of the <c:forEach> and <c:out> actions. The main difference between the XML actions and their Core counterparts are the XML actions' `select` attributes, which specify an XPath expression. The only JSTL XML actions that do not have Core counterparts are <x:parse>, which parses an XML document, and <x:transform>, which uses XSLT to transform XML documents.

The following section provides a brief overview of XPath. If you are already familiar with XPath, you can commence reading at "Parsing XML" on page 432.

10.3 XPath Overview

Because JSTL XML actions use XPath to access XML data, it helps to have at least a bird's-eye view of XPath. The discussion in this section is by no means a comprehensive examination of XPath, but if you are unfamiliar with XPath, it will get you started. There are many articles on the Web and books that discuss XPath in detail; *XSLT Programmer's Reference* is one such resource that covers XPath extensively.[3]

XPath is a language specifically designed to access information contained in XML documents. XPath grew out of a common need between two W3C initiatives—XSLT and XPointer—to access specific locations within XML documents.[4] XPath uses a tree model to represent XML documents; for example, Figure 10–1 shows the XPath tree model for the Rolodex XML file.

---

3. See Michael Kay, *XSLT Programmer's Reference*, Wrox Press Ltd., June 2000.
4. You can find the XSLT and XPointer specifications at `http://www.w3.org/TR/xslt` and `http://www.w3.org/TR/xptr`, respectively.

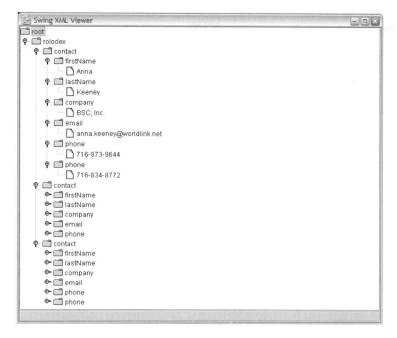

Figure 10–1 An XPath Tree Model of the Rolodex XML Document[5]

For brevity, Figure 10–1 shows child nodes only for the first contact in the Rolodex XML file and does not show attribute nodes for phone numbers.

XPath expressions operate on the XPath tree model of an XML document. The next section introduces XPath expressions.

XPath Expressions and Types

Unlike other XML-related technologies, such as XSLT, XPath does not use XML syntax; instead, it uses a syntax similar to that used for directory paths. That syntax is familiar to anyone who has used a command prompt for a file system or typed URLs in a browser; for example, the following XPath expression evaluates to a *node-set* that contains all of the nodes corresponding to the first names of all contacts in the Rolodex XML file:

```
/rolodex/contact/firstName
```

---

5. The code for the Swing XML Viewer is included with the code for this book; see "The Book's Web Site" on page xiv for more information about that code.

The preceding expression is known as a *location path*. Location paths always resolve to a `node-set`, which is an unordered collection of nodes without duplicates. There are two types of location paths: *absolute* and *relative*. Absolute location paths begin with a forward slash, whereas relative location paths do not. Notice that this convention is the same as the convention used for UNIX filesystems and URLs; for example, the path `/etc/profile` is relative to the filesystem root, whereas `etc/profile` is relative to the current working directory.

The preceding XPath expression is an absolute location path; here's a relative location path:

```
contact/firstName
```

The XPath expression shown above is relative to the node at which the expression was applied, known as the *context node*. If the context node for the preceding expression was `/rolodex`, that expression would produce the same result as the first XPath expression shown in this section.

Location paths are composed of *location steps* separated by forward slashes; for example, the location path `/rolodex/contact/firstName` is composed of three location steps. Each location step can be qualified with a *predicate*. A predicate is a boolean expression contained within square brackets at the end of a location step; for example, the following expression specifies a predicate:

```
/rolodex/contact[firstName = "Lynn"]
```

The preceding expression evaluates to a `node-set` of all contacts in the Rolodex XML file whose first names are equal to `Lynn`.

All XPath expressions resolve to one of four XPath types, listed below:

- `boolean` (`true` or `false`)
- `number` (floating-point)
- `node-set` (an unordered collection of nodes without duplicates)
- `string` (a sequence of Unicode characters)[6]

XPath Type Coercion

XPath performs type coercion as necessary; for example, for the expression `"2" = 2` the string is coerced to a number before the comparison is made. One of the most common coercions converts `node-sets` to one of the other three XPath types (`boolean`, `number`, or `string`).

---

6. See "Unicode and Charsets" on page 260 for more information about Unicode.

For example, in the XPath expression—

```
/rolodex/contact[1]/lastName = "Keeney"
```

—the location path `/rolodex/contact[1]/lastName` resolves to a `node-set` containing a single node that represents the last name of the first contact in the Rolodex XML file. That `node-set` is converted to a string, which is compared to the string `Keeney`, resulting in a `true` value for the XML file listed in Listing 10.1 on page 424.

Table 10.2 shows how each of the four XPath types is coerced to a `boolean`, `number`, or `string`.

Table 10.2   XPath Type Coercion

convert to —>	boolean	number	string
node-set	true if the node-set is not empty; false otherwise	The node-set is first coerced to a string, which is subsequently coerced to a number	The string value of the first node in the node-set
boolean	——	true is converted to 1; false to 0	true is converted to "true"; false to "false"
number	0 is converted to false; all other numbers are true	——	All numbers are converted to a string representation of the number
string	nonempty strings are true; empty strings are false	string representations of numbers are converted to numbers; otherwise, they are converted to NaN[a]	——

a.   NaN, defined by the IEEE 754 Floating-Point Specification, stands for Not a Number.

For each of its types, XPath defines a set of functions. Those functions are the topic of the next section.

XPath Functions

XPath expressions can contain function calls; for example, the following expression returns a number that represents the number of nodes in a `node-set`:

```
count(/rolodex/contact)
```

The preceding expression evaluates to a number that represents a count of the number of contacts—3—contained in the Rolodex XML file. The count function is one of seven node-set functions defined by XPath. Table 10.3 lists the XPath node-set functions.

Table 10.3 Node-set Functions[a]

Function Prototype	Description
number **count**(node-set)	Returns the number of nodes in a node-set
node-set **id**(object)	Selects a node with the specified id[b]
number **last**()	Returns the size of the current node-set
string **local-name**(node-set?)	Returns the local part of a node's qualified name
string **name**(node-set?)	Returns the node's qualified name
string **namespace-uri**(node-set?)	Returns the namespace URI associated with the specified node
number **position**()	Returns the position within the current node-set

    a.   ? = optional argument; if omitted, defaults to the context node
    b.   IDs are required to be unique

XPath also defines string functions; for example, you can use the string-length function to determine the length of a string, like this:

```
string-length(/rolodex/contact[1]/lastName)
```

The preceding XPath expression returns the string length of the first contact's last name in the Rolodex XML file listed in Listing 10.1 on page 424. Notice that type coercion takes place in that expression; the location path /rolodex/contact[1]/lastName is converted to a string according to the rules specified in Table 10.2 on page 429.

The XPath string functions are listed in Table 10.4.

XPath also defines a handful of boolean functions; for example, you can use the not function like this:

```
not(count(/rolodex/contact) = 0)
```

Table 10.4 String Functions[a]

Function Prototype	Description
string **concat**(string,string,string*)	Concatenates the specified strings
boolean **contains**(string,string)	Returns true if the first string contains the second; false otherwise
string **normalize-space**(string?)	Returns a string with leading and trailing whitespace stripped and multiple spaces collapsed into a single space
boolean **starts-with**(string,string)	Returns true if the first string starts with the second; false otherwise
number **string-length**(string?)	Returns the number of characters in the specified string
string **substring**(string,number,number?)	Returns a substring of the specified string, with the first and last numbers representing the start and end, respectively, of the substring; the numbers are 1-based, meaning the position of the first character is 1, not 0.
string **substring-after**(string,string)	Returns a substring of the first string, starting with the first character after the first occurrence of the second string
string **substring-before**(string,string)	Returns a substring of the first string that precedes the first occurrence of the second string
string **translate**(string,string,string)	Returns the first string with characters in the second string replaced with characters from the third string

a.   ? = optional; if omitted, defaults to the context node converted to a string. ° = one or more.

The previous expression evaluates to true if the number of contacts in the Rolodex is not equal to zero.[7]

The XPath boolean functions are listed in Table 10.5.

---

7.   That expression is equivalent to count(/rolodex/contact) != 0

Table 10.5 Boolean Functions

Function Prototype	Description
boolean **boolean**(object)	Converts the specified object to a boolean value; nonempty node-sets, nonzero numbers and strings with a length > 0 evaluate to true
boolean **false**()	Returns false
boolean **lang**(string)	Returns true if the xml:lang attribute of the context node matches the specified string
boolean **not**(boolean)	Returns true if the boolean argument is false; otherwise, returns true
boolean **true**()	Returns true

Finally, XPath also defines a handful of number functions, listed in Table 10.6.

Table 10.6 Number Functions

Function Prototype	Description
number **ceiling**(number)	Returns the smallest integer that is not less than the specified number
number **floor**(number)	Returns the largest integer that is not greater than the specified number
number **number**(object)	Converts the specified object to a number
number **round**(number)	Returns an integer that's closest to the specified number; if there are two such numbers, the larger is returned
number **sum**(node-set)	Returns the sum of each node, converted to a number, in the node-set

Now that we have a basic understanding of XPath, let's see how we can use the JSTL XML actions to manipulate XML documents.

10.4 Parsing XML

Before we can manipulate data in an XML document, we must first parse the document with the <x:parse> action, which has the following syntax:[8]

<x:parse xml [systemId] [filter] {var [scope] | varDom [scopeDom]}/>

The preceding syntax for the <x:parse> action has two required attributes: xml and either var or varDom, which represent the name of a scoped variable that references the parsed document. The xml attribute, which represents an XML document, can be a string or a reader.

If you specify the var attribute, the JSTL implementation is free to represent the parsed document with any data type. If you specify the varDom attribute instead, the JSTL implementation must make the parsed document available as a Document Object Model (DOM) object. If you specify the var attribute, you can set the scope for that variable with the scope attribute; likewise, you can specify the scopeDom attribute to set the scope for the variable specified with the varDom attribute.

The <x:parse> action also supports an alternative syntax that lets you specify the XML document in the body of the action:

<x:parse [systemId] [filter] {var [scope] | varDom [scopeDom]}
  xml
</x:parse>

The preceding syntax is the same as the first syntax, except that the xml attribute is replaced by the body of the action.

Both <x:parse> syntaxes support two additional attributes: systemId and filter. The systemId attribute specifies a URI used to resolve external entities. The use of that attribute is discussed in "Accessing External Entities" on page 460. The filter attribute specifies a Simple API for XML (SAX) filter that's used to filter the XML parsed by the <x:parse> action. The use of that attribute is discussed in "Filtering XML" on page 452.

The <x:parse> action does not perform validation against XML DTDs or Schemas.

Figure 10–2 shows a JSP page that parses the Rolodex XML file listed in Listing 10.1 on page 424 and displays the information contained in that file.

The JSP page shown in Figure 10–2 is listed in Listing 10.2.

Parsing an XML file with <x:parse> is typically a two-step process, as is the case for the preceding JSP page.[9] The first step, which is normally accomplished with the <c:import> action, imports the file and stores the contents of that file in a string or reader. In the preceding JSP page, the <c:import> action imports the file

---

8. Items in brackets are optional. See "<x:parse>" on page 543 for a complete description of <x:parse> syntax.

9. You can also parse XML in one step if you specify the XML in the body of the <x:parse> action; however, because the XML document typically resides in a separate file, the two-step approach is most often used.

Figure 10–2   Parsing XML

Listing 10.2   *index.jsp (Parsing XML)*

```
<!DOCTYPE HTML PUBLIC "-//W3C//DTD HTML 4.0 Transitional//EN">
<html>
   <head>
      <title>Parsing XML</title>
   </head>

   <body>
      <%@ taglib uri='http://java.sun.com/jstl/core' prefix='c' %>
      <%@ taglib uri='http://java.sun.com/jstl/xml'  prefix='x' %>

      <%-- Import the XML file --%>
      <c:import var='rolodex_xml' url='rolodex.xml'/>

      <%-- Parse the XML file --%>
      <x:parse var='document' xml='${rolodex_xml}'/>

      <p>There are
         <x:out select='count($document//contact)'/>
         contacts in the rolodex.<p>
      <x:out
         select='count($document//contact/phone[@type="work"])'/>
      of those contacts have a work phone number and
```

| Listing 10.2 | *index.jsp (Parsing XML) (cont.)* |

```
<x:out
    select='count($document//contact/phone[@type="home"])'/>
of those contacts have a home phone number.<p>

<%-- For each contact in the Rolodex... --%>
<x:forEach select='$document//contact'>
    <table>
        <tr>
            <td>First Name:</td>
            <td><x:out select='firstName'/></td>
        </tr>

        <tr>
            <td>Last Name:</td>
            <td><x:out select='lastName'/></td>
        </tr>

        <tr>
            <td>Email:</td>
            <td><x:out select='email'/></td>
        </tr>

        <tr>
            <td>Work Phone:</td>
            <td><x:out select='phone[@type="work"]'/></td>
        </tr>

        <%-- Home phone is optional, so we check to see
             if it exists before processing it --%>
        <x:if select='phone[@type="home"]'>
            <tr>
                <td>Home Phone:</td>
                <td><x:out select='phone[@type="home"]'/></td>
            </tr>
        </x:if>
    </table><p>
</x:forEach>
</body>
</html>
```

rolodex.xml and stores the contents of that file in a string that you can reference with a scoped variable named rolodex_xml. The second step parses the contents of the XML file with <x:parse>; in the preceding JSP page, the scoped variable named rolodex_xml is specified with the xml attribute and the parsed XML is stored in a page-scoped variable named document.

Once you've parsed XML with the <x:parse> action, you can use the scoped variable created by that action to access the parsed XML file. The preceding JSP page shows you how to do that with the <x:if>, <x:out>, and <x:forEach> actions. That JSP page uses the <x:out> action to display the number of contacts in the Rolodex and the number of contacts that have work and home phone numbers. The JSP page uses the <x:forEach> action to iterate over every contact in the Rolodex and uses <x:if> and <x:out> actions in the body of the <x:forEach> action to display the information associated with each contact.

Besides XML parsing, there are a few other points of interest in the preceding JSP page. First, the <x:forEach> action and the <x:out> actions that are not contained in the body of the <x:forEach> action establish a context node by specifying the name of the scoped variable—document—that references the parsed XML with this syntax: $document//... The <x:out> actions and the <x:if> action contained in the body of the <x:forEach> action do *not* specify a context node, because the context node—which represents each contact in the order in which it appears in the XML file—is established by the <x:forEach> action.

Second, the double slash is an XPath abbreviated syntax that means all of the nodes that are descendants of a specified node;[10] for example, the XPath expression `$document//contact` evaluates to a `node-set` that contains all of the contact nodes within the document, regardless of where they appear in the document; that expression is equivalent to `$document/rolodex/contact`, which also selects all of the document's contacts.

Third, notice the use of the <x:if> action. The body of that action is evaluated if the XPath expression specified with the `select` attribute evaluates to `true`. That expression—`phone[@type="home"]`—specifies a location path, `phone`—that selects all `phone` nodes that are children of the context node. That expression also specifies a predicate—`[@type="home"]`—which restricts that `node-set` to `phone` nodes that have a `type` attribute equal to `home`. The end result of that expression is a `node-set` of all `phone` nodes that are children of the context node and that have a `type` attribute whose value is `home`. That `node-set` is coerced to a `boolean` value according to the algorithm described in Table 10.2; if the `node-set` is not empty, the expression evaluates to `true` and the body of the <x:if> action is evaluated. Otherwise, it evaluates to `false` and the body of the <x:if> action is not evaluated.

The preceding JSP page specifies a scoped variable—document—in XPath expressions to establish a context node. JSTL XML actions let you access other JSP variables, including request parameters and cookies, as discussed in the next section.

---

10. The specified node is also included in the `node-set` if it matches the location path criteria.

10.5 Using Scoped Variables in XPath Expressions

As evidenced by the JSP page listed in Listing 10.2, you can access JSP scoped variables in XPath expressions as long as the Java type of those variables matches an expected XPath type. XPath data types and their corresponding Java types are listed in Table 10.7.

Table 10.7   XPath Data Types and Corresponding Java Types

XPath Type	Java Type
boolean	java.lang.Boolean
node-set	Implementation-specific, including the type of object exported by <x:parse>
number	java.lang.Number
string	java.lang.String

You can use scoped variables in XPath expressions as long as those scoped variables reference an object whose Java type is listed in Table 10.7. Furthermore, you can only use scoped variables where XPath expects a variable of the corresponding XPath type (boolean, number, string, or node-set). For example, you can do this—

```
<c:import var='rolodex_xml' url='rolodex.xml'/>
<x:parse var='document' xml='${rolodex_xml}'/>

<x:out select='count($document//contact)'/>
```

—but you can't do this:

```
<c:import var='rolodex_xml' url='rolodex.xml'/>
<x:parse var='document' xml='${rolodex_xml}'/>

<c:set var='doc' value='document'/>
<x:out select='count($doc//contact)'/>
```

The preceding code won't work because the doc scoped variable references a *string*; for the preceding <x:out> select attribute, XPath expects $doc to reference a *node-set*. However, you could do this:

```
<c:import var='rolodex_xml' url='rolodex.xml'/>
<x:parse var='document' xml='${rolodex_xml}'/>

<c:set var='doc' value='${document}'/>
<x:out select='count($doc//contact)'/>
```

The preceding code works because the doc scoped variable references a node-set, not a string. Realize that the preceding code, which adds a level of indirection to access the document scoped variable, does not provide any advantage over the initial code fragment discussed above. The preceding code is presented for illustration.

Table 10.8 shows the different types of expressions that you can use in XPath expressions to access cookies, request parameters and headers, context initialization parameters, and JSP scoped variables.

Table 10.8 XPath Variable Bindings

Expression	Interpretation
$identifier	pageContext.findAttribute("identifier")
$cookie:identifier	Returns the value of the cookie named identifier
$header:identifier	request.getHeader("identifier")
$initParam:identifier	application. getInitParameter("identifier")
$param:identifier	request.getParameter("identifier")
$pageScope:identifier	pageContext.getAttribute("identifier", PageContext.PAGE_SCOPE)
$requestScope:identifier	pageContext.getAttribute("identifier", PageContext.REQUEST_SCOPE)
$sessionScope:identifier	pageContext.getAttribute("identifier", PageContext.SESSION_SCOPE)
$applicationScope:identifier	pageContext.getAttribute("identifier", PageContext.APPLICATION_SCOPE)

So how does the syntax listed in Table 10.8 differ from the syntax used to access the same data with EL expressions, as listed in Table 2.5 on page 64? Here's an example:

```
<%-- Store a string in request scope --%>
<c:set value='hello' var='greeting' scope='request'/>

<%-- Access the greeting scoped variable with EL expressions --%>
<c:out value='${greeting}'/><br>
<c:out value='${requestScope.greeting}'/><p>

<%-- Access the greeting scoped variable with XPath expressions
--%>
<x:out select='$greeting'/><br>
<x:out select='$requestScope:greeting'/>
```

The preceding code uses <c:set> to store a string in a scoped variable in request scope. Subsequently, that code accesses the scoped variable with <c:out> and <x:out> actions. The first <c:out> action and the first <x:out> action access the greeting scoped variable without specifying its scope, whereas the second <c:out> action and the second <x:out> action specify that scope with the requestScope identifier. The output of the preceding code fragment looks like this:

```
hello
hello

hello
hello
```

Realize that the expression specified for the <x:out> action's select attribute must be a valid XPath expression; for example, the following code fragment is valid—

```
<c:set value='hello' var='greeting' scope='request'/>
<c:out value='${Greeting: requestScope.greeting}'/>
```

—because the expression specified for the <c:out> action's value attribute is a valid EL expression, but the following code fragment will throw an exception because Greeting: $requestScope:greeting is not a valid XPath expression—

```
<c:set value='hello' var='greeting' scope='request'/>
<x:out select='Greeting: $requestScope:greeting'/>
```

However, you can do this—

```
<c:set value='hello' var='greeting' scope='request'/>
<x:out select='string-length($requestScope:greeting)'/>
```

—because the value specified for the <x:out> select attribute is a valid XPath expression.

The Web application shown in Figure 10–3 illustrates how you can use request parameters in an XPath expression. That application consists of two JSP pages, one that lets you enter an area code, and another that displays all contacts in the Rolodex XML file that have work phone numbers with the specified area code.

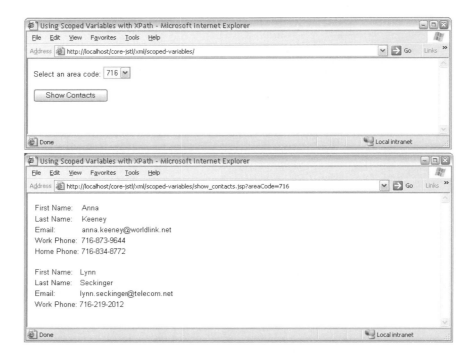

Figure 10–3   Accessing Request Parameters in XPath Expressions

The JSP page shown in the top picture in Figure 10–3 is listed in Listing 10.3.

The preceding JSP page contains a simple form that lets you select an area code. The action for the form is `show_contacts.jsp`, which is listed in Listing 10.4.

The preceding JSP page iterates over all the contacts in the Rolodex XML file and displays information associated with contacts whose work phone number corresponds to the selected area code. Those contacts are determined with an <x:if> action whose `select` attribute is `starts-with(phone[@type="work"], $param:areaCode)`. That XPath expression, which uses the XPath `starts-with` function listed in Table 10.4 on page 431, evaluates to `true` if the contact's phone number starts with the specified area code. The JSP page accesses that area code with the syntax for request parameters listed in Table 10.8 on page 438.

Listing 10.3   *index.jsp (Using Scoped Variables with XPath)*

```
<!DOCTYPE HTML PUBLIC "-//W3C//DTD HTML 4.0 Transitional//EN">
<html>
   <head>
      <title>Using Scoped Variables with XPath</title>
   </head>

   <body>
      <%-- A form that lets the user select an area code --%>
      <form action='show_contacts.jsp'>
         Select an area code:
         <select name='areaCode'>
            <option value='915'>915</option>
            <option value='716'>716</option>
         </select>

         <p><input type='submit' value='Show Contacts'/>
      </form>
   </body>
</html>
```

Listing 10.4   *show_contacts.jsp*

```
<!DOCTYPE HTML PUBLIC "-//W3C//DTD HTML 4.0 Transitional//EN">
<html>
   <head>
      <%@ taglib uri='http://java.sun.com/jstl/core' prefix='c' %>
      <%@ taglib uri='http://java.sun.com/jstl/xml'  prefix='x' %>
      <title>Using Scoped Variables with XPath</title>
   </head>

   <body>
      <%-- Import the phone book XML file --%>
      <c:import var='rolodex_xml' url='rolodex.xml'/>

      <%-- Parse the phone book XML file --%>
      <x:parse var='document' xml='${rolodex_xml}'/>

      <%-- For each address --%>
      <x:forEach select='$document//contact'>
         <%-- If this contact's work phone starts with the
              specified area code, show contact information --%>
         <x:if
        select='starts-with(phone[@type="work"],$param:areaCode)'>
```

Listing 10.4 *show_contacts.jsp (cont.)*

```
            <table>
                <tr>
                    <td>First Name:</td>
                     <td><x:out select='firstName'/></td>
                </tr>

                <tr>
                    <td>Last Name:</td>
                     <td><x:out select='lastName'/></td>
                </tr>

                <tr>
                    <td>Email:</td>
                     <td><x:out select='email'/></td>
                </tr>

                <tr>
                    <td>Work Phone:</td>
                     <td><x:out select='phone[@type="work"]'/></td>
                </tr>

                <%-- Home phone number is optional, so we check
                     to see if it exists before creating a table
                     row --%>
                <x:if select='phone[@type="home"]'>
                    <tr>
                         <td>Home Phone:</td>
                        <td><x:out select='phone[@type="home"]'/></td>
                    </tr>
                </x:if>
            </table><br>
        </x:if>
    </x:forEach>
  </body>
</html>
```

Now that we've seen how to parse XML, access the contents of the parsed XML, and access scoped variables and JSTL implicit objects in XPath expressions, let's move on to transforming XML with XSLT.

10.6 Transforming XML with XSLT

Sometimes XML documents are useful in and of themselves, but often those documents need to be transformed into some other format (for example, HTML or XML) that's a modification of the original document. Because transforming XML documents is commonplace, a language—the XSL Transformation language (XSLT)— has been developed explicitly for that purpose. XSLT's popularity is the impetus behind the JSTL <x:transform> action, which applies XSLT to an XML document.

A discussion of XSLT, which is a rather complex and powerful language, is beyond the scope of this book; however, the basic idea is that an XSLT stylesheet is applied to an XML document. That stylesheet transforms the XML document according to a set of XSLT template rules. How those rules are specified and how they work are discussed on page 444.

The <x:transform> action has three syntaxes; here's one of them:[11]

<x:transform xml xslt [xmlSystemId] [xsltSystemId] [{var [scope] | result}]/>

The `xml` attribute represents an XML document and, like the `xml` attribute for the <x:parse> action, can be a string or a reader. Additionally, the <x:transform> `xml` attribute can also be an instance of `javax.xml.transform.Source` or `org.w3c.dom.Document` or an object exported by <x:set> or <x:parse>. The `xslt` attribute, which represents an XSLT stylesheet, can be a string, reader, or an instance of `javax.xml.transform.Source`.

The `xmlSystemId` and `xsltSystemId` attributes specify URIs for resolving external entities for the XML document and XSLT stylesheet, respectively. See "Accessing External Entities" on page 460 for more information about accessing external entities.

By default, <x:transform> sends the transformed document to the current `JspWriter`. You can, however, capture that output in a scoped variable by specifying the `var` attribute (and, optionally, the `scope` attribute), or you can capture the output in an instance of `javax.xml.transform.Result` by specifying an object of that type for the `result` attribute.

You can also use the <x:transform> action with this syntax:

<x:transform xml xslt [xmlSystemId] [xsltSystemId] [{var [scope] | result}]>
  <x:param> actions
</x:transform>

---

11. Items in brackets are optional. See "<x:transform>" on page 553 for a complete description of <x:transform> syntax.

The preceding syntax lets you specify transformation parameters with <x:param> actions in the body of the <x:transform> action; see "Using Transformation Parameters" on page 446 for more information about using that syntax.

The third syntax lets you specify the XML document and, optionally, transformation parameters in the body of the <x:transform> action:

<x:transform xslt [xmlSystemId] [xsltSystemId] [{var [scope] | result}]>
    xml
    optional <x:param> actions
</x:transform>

Figure 10–4 shows a JSP page that uses <x:transform> to transform the Rolodex XML document listed in Listing 10.1 on page 424 to HTML.

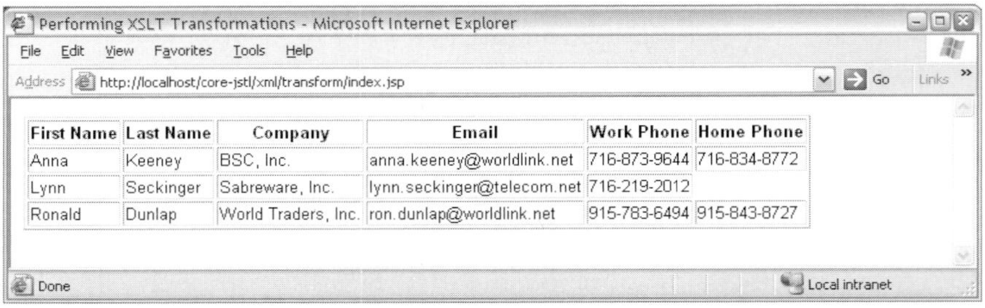

Figure 10–4 Transforming XML with XSLT

The JSP page shown in Figure 10–4 is listed in Listing 10.5.

The preceding JSP page is straightforward: the <c:import> action imports an XML document and an XSLT stylesheet. The resulting scoped variables, which reference string representations of the document and stylesheet, are specified for the <x:transform> action's xml and xslt attributes, respectively. Because neither the var attribute nor the result attribute is specified, the <x:transform> action sends its output to the current JspWriter.

As you can see from the preceding JSP page, the <x:transform> action is easy to use. Perhaps the most interesting aspect of that JSP page is the XSLT stylesheet it references, which is listed in Listing 10.6.

XSLT is a declarative language based on template rules. Each template rule consists of a *pattern* and an *action* and is specified with <xsl:template>; for example, in the preceding stylesheet there are three template rules:

```
<xsl:template match='/'>...</xsl:template>
<xsl:template match='contact'>...</xsl:template>
<xsl:template match='contact/*'>...</xsl:template>
```

Listing 10.5	*index.jsp (Transforming XML to HTML)*

```
<!DOCTYPE HTML PUBLIC "-//W3C//DTD HTML 4.0 Transitional//EN">
<html>
   <head>
      <title>Performing XSLT Transformations</title>
   </head>

   <body>
      <%@ taglib uri='http://java.sun.com/jstl/core' prefix='c' %>
      <%@ taglib uri='http://java.sun.com/jstl/xml'  prefix='x' %>

      <%-- Import the XML file and XSLT stylesheet --%>
      <c:import var='rolodex_xml' url='rolodex.xml'/>
      <c:import var='rolodex_xsl' url='rolodex.xsl'/>

      <%-- Perform the transformation --%>
      <x:transform xml='${rolodex_xml}' xslt='${rolodex_xsl}'/>
   </body>
</html>
```

The patterns for the rules are /, which matches the document's root element; contact, which matches contact elements; and contact/*, which matches all contact child elements.

The action for the rule matching the root element creates HTML that looks like this:

```
<table border='1'>
   <tr>
      <th>First Name</th>
      <th>Last Name</th>
      <th>Company</th>
      <th>Email</th>
      <th>Work Phone</th>
      <th>Home Phone</th>
   </tr>
</table>
```

The rule matching the root element has an <xsl:apply-templates> tag after the table header for Home Phone. That tag recursively applies matching rules to the root element's children. Those rules create a table row for each contact element and table data for each contact child element.

The preceding XSLT stylesheet is relatively simple, but XSLT stylesheets can be quite complex and often require parameters. Specifying and using transformation parameters is the topic of the next section.

Listing 10.6 *rolodex.xsl (Generating HTML)*

```
<xsl:stylesheet xmlns:xsl="http://www.w3.org/1999/XSL/Transform"
                version="1.0">
   <!-- Generate HTML for the document root -->
   <xsl:template match='/'>
      <table border='1'>
         <tr>
            <th>First Name</th>
            <th>Last Name</th>
            <th>Company</th>
            <th>Email</th>
            <th>Work Phone</th>
            <th>Home Phone</th>
         </tr>
         <xsl:apply-templates/>
      </table>
   </xsl:template>

   <!-- Create a table row for each item and apply templates -->
   <xsl:template match='contact'>
      <tr><xsl:apply-templates/></tr>
   </xsl:template>

   <!-- Create table data for each item and apply templates -->
   <xsl:template match='contact/*'>
      <td><xsl:apply-templates/></td>
   </xsl:template>
</xsl:stylesheet>
```

Using Transformation Parameters

It's often necessary to parameterize XSLT stylesheets with transformation parameters; for example, the Web application shown in Figure 10–5 uses a transformation parameter to specify a table column that is removed from the HTML table shown in the top picture.

The Web application shown in Figure 10–5 consists of three JSP pages and an XSLT stylesheet. The top picture shows the welcome page, which performs an initial transformation of the XML document to an HTML table. The bottom two pictures in Figure 10–5 show a second JSP page that performs a transformation with a transformation parameter that specifies a column that's removed from the table. The middle picture shows the Email column removed, and the bottom picture shows the Home Phone column removed.

The JSP page shown in the top picture in Figure 10–5 is listed in Listing 10.7.

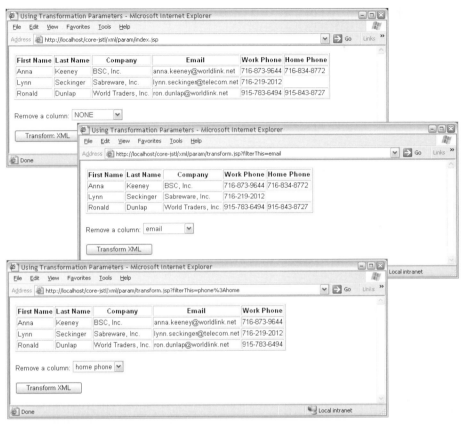

Figure 10–5 Using XSLT Parameters

The preceding JSP page, which is the Web application's welcome page, imports the XML document and XSLT stylesheet and stores the resulting scoped variables in session scope. Subsequently, the JSP page performs an initial transformation with the <x:transform> action and includes a JSP page that creates the form that lets you select a column to remove. That JSP page—form.jsp—is listed in Listing 10.8.

The preceding JSP page creates a form with an HTML select element that retains its value when the JSP page is reloaded.[12] That form's action is transform.jsp, which is listed in Listing 10.9.

---

12. See "Retaining Values for HTML Option Elements" on page 129 for more information about HTML select elements that retain their values.

Listing 10.7   *index.jsp (Using Transformation Parameters)*

```
<!DOCTYPE HTML PUBLIC "-//W3C//DTD HTML 4.0 Transitional//EN">
<html>
   <head>
      <title>Using Transformation Parameters</title>
   </head>

   <body>
      <%@ taglib uri='http://java.sun.com/jstl/core' prefix='c' %>
      <%@ taglib uri='http://java.sun.com/jstl/xml'  prefix='x' %>

      <%-- Import the XML file and XSLT stylesheet and store the
           result in session-scoped variables, which are accessed
           below and in transform.jsp --%>
      <c:import var='rolodex_xml' scope='session'
               url='rolodex.xml'/>
      <c:import var='rolodex_xsl' scope='session'
               url='rolodex.xsl'/>

      <%-- Transform the XML document with the XSLT stylesheet --%>
      <x:transform xml='${rolodex_xml}' xslt='${rolodex_xsl}'/>

      <c:import url='form.jsp'/>
   </body>
</html>
```

The preceding JSP page transforms the Rolodex XML document with the scoped variables representing the XML document and the XSLT stylesheet stored in session scope by the JSP page listed in Listing 10.7. The preceding JSP page specifies a transformation parameter with the <x:param> action. The name of that transformation parameter is `filteredColumn`, and its value is the value of the request parameter named `filterThis`, which is created by the JSP page listed in Listing 10.8. The XSLT stylesheet that's applied to the Rolodex XML document is `rolodex.xsl`, which is listed in Listing 10.10.

The preceding XSLT stylesheet first declares the `filteredColumn` transformation parameter. *XSLT stylesheets must declare all transformation parameters that they use.* If you do not declare transformation parameters in your stylesheets, they will not be available, even though you specify them with the <x:param> action, as is the case for the JSP page listed in Listing 10.9.

After declaring the `filteredColumn` transformation parameter, the preceding stylesheet specifies template rules for the document `root` element, the `contact` elements, the `contact` element's children, and `phone` elements. Each of those rules behaves differently, depending on the value of the `filteredColumn`

Listing 10.8 *form.jsp (Creating a Request Parameter)*

```
<%@ taglib uri='http://java.sun.com/jstl/core' prefix='c' %>

<form action='transform.jsp'>
    Remove a column:
    <select name='filterThis'>
        <option value='NONE'
            <c:if test='${param.filterThis == "NONE"}'>
                selected
            </c:if> >NONE
        </option>

        <option value='email'
            <c:if test='${param.filterThis == "email"}'>
                selected
            </c:if> >email
        </option>

        <option value='phone@home'
            <c:if test='${param.filterThis == "phone@home"}'>
                selected
            </c:if> >home phone
        </option>

        <option value='phone@work'
            <c:if test='${param.filterThis == "phone@work"}'>
                selected
            </c:if> >work phone
        </option>
    </select>

    <p><input type='submit' value='Transform XML'/>
</form>
```

transformation parameter. The rule that matches the document `root` element omits the table header for the appropriate column, depending on the `filteredColumn` transformation parameter; for example, if that parameter is `email`, the `Email` column is not generated.

There are a couple of points of interest in the preceding stylesheet. First, that stylesheet uses the <xsl:if> tag, which, like the JSTL <x:if> action, evaluates its body content if the corresponding XPath expression evaluates to `true`. For example, the rule that matches `contact` child elements generates table data if the value of the `filteredColumn` transformation parameter does not match the local name of the child element. Second, even though the rule for `contact` child elements will

Listing 10.9   *transform.jsp*

```
<!DOCTYPE HTML PUBLIC "-//W3C//DTD HTML 4.0 Transitional//EN">
<html>
   <head>
      <title>Using Transformation Parameters</title>
   </head>

   <body>
      <%@ taglib uri='http://java.sun.com/jstl/core' prefix='c' %>
      <%@ taglib uri='http://java.sun.com/jstl/xml'  prefix='x' %>

      <%-- Transform the XML document with the XSLT stylesheet --%>
      <x:transform xml='${rolodex_xml}' xslt='${rolodex_xsl}'>
          <x:param name='filteredColumn'
                   value='${param.filterThis}'/>
      </x:transform>

      <c:import url='form.jsp'/>
   </body>
</html>
```

Listing 10.10   *rolodex.xsl (Declaring a Parameter)*

```
<xsl:stylesheet xmlns:xsl="http://www.w3.org/1999/XSL/Transform"
                version="1.0">

   <!-- Declare the filteredColumn parameter-->
   <xsl:param name='filteredColumn'/>

   <!-- Generate HTML for the document root -->
   <xsl:template match='/'>
      <table border='1'>
         <tr>
            <th>First Name</th>
            <th>Last Name</th>
            <th>Company</th>

            <xsl:if test='$filteredColumn != "email"'>
               <th>Email</th>
            </xsl:if>

            <xsl:if test='$filteredColumn != "phone@work"'>
               <th>Work Phone</th>
            </xsl:if>
```

Listing 10.10	*rolodex.xsl (Declaring a Parameter) (cont.)*

```
            <xsl:if test='$filteredColumn != "phone@home"'>
               <th>Home Phone</th>
            </xsl:if>

            <xsl:apply-templates/>
         </tr>
      </table>
   </xsl:template>

   <!-- Create a table row for each item and apply templates -->
   <xsl:template match='contact'>
      <tr><xsl:apply-templates/></tr>
   </xsl:template>

   <!-- Create table data for all elements that are children
        of contact elements, except for home and work phone, which
        are processed below -->
   <xsl:template match='contact/*'>
      <xsl:if test='$filteredColumn != local-name()'>
         <td><xsl:apply-templates/></td>
      </xsl:if>
   </xsl:template>

   <!-- Create table data for the Work Phone element -->
   <xsl:template match='contact/phone[@type="work"]'>
      <xsl:if test='$filteredColumn != "phone@work"'>
         <td><xsl:apply-templates/></td>
      </xsl:if>
   </xsl:template>

   <!-- Create table data for the Home Phone element -->
   <xsl:template match='contact/phone[@type="home"]'>
      <xsl:if test='$filteredColumn != "phone@home"'>
         <td><xsl:apply-templates/></td>
      </xsl:if>
   </xsl:template>
</xsl:stylesheet>
```

match phone elements, separate rules are declared for those elements. Those rules are necessary because the filteredColumn transformation parameter specifies work phones with phone@work and home phones with phone@home, which do not match the local name of the phone elements, which is simply phone.

In effect, the stylesheet discussed in this section filters specified columns from the HTML table. Another approach is to filter the XML document itself when you parse the document. That approach is discussed in the next section.

10.7 Filtering XML

You can filter XML documents with a SAX filter.[13] SAX, which stands for Simple API for XML, is a language-independent, event-based API for parsing XML. SAX reports parsing events—such as the start and end of elements—through callback methods. For example, consider the following simple XML document:

```
<?xml version='1.0'?>
<document>
   <greeting>Welcome</greeting>
</document>
```

SAX represents the preceding XML document as a series of events, like this:

```
start document event
start element event: document
start element event: greeting
characters event: Welcome
end element event: greeting
end element event: document
end document event
```

SAX applications handle those events by registering an event handler and implementing methods that correspond to the events listed above.

As of SAX 2.0, you can filter XML documents by inserting a filter between the SAX parser and the application that handles SAX events. Using JSTL to filter XML documents with a SAX filter is a simple two-step process:

1. Implement a SAX filter.
2. Specify a reference to the filter implemented in step 1 as the value of the <x:parse> action's `filter` attribute.

Figure 10–6 shows a Web application that implements the steps listed above to filter specific elements in an XML document

---

13. You can read more about SAX at `http://www.saxproject.org`.

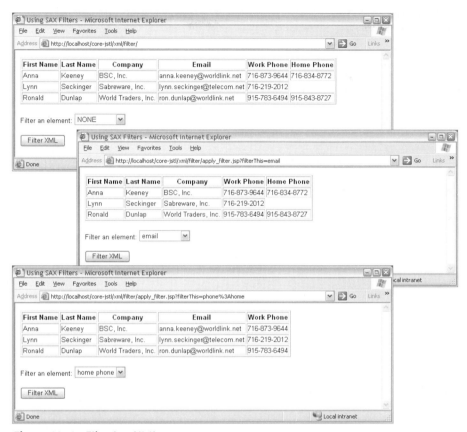

Figure 10–6   Filtering XML

The Web application shown in Figure 10–6 is similar to the Web application discussed in "Using Transformation Parameters" on page 446, except the former uses a SAX filter to filter elements in XML documents, whereas the latter removes columns from the HTML table with an XSLT stylesheet.

The top picture in Figure 10–6 shows the application's welcome page. The middle picture shows the XSLT-generated HTML table with `email` elements filtered, and the bottom picture shows the HTML table with home `phone` elements filtered.

Listing 10.11 lists the welcome page for the application shown in Figure 10–6.

Listing 10.11   *index.jsp (Using SAX Filters)*

```
<!DOCTYPE HTML PUBLIC "-//W3C//DTD HTML 4.0 Transitional//EN">
<html>
   <head>
      <title>Using SAX Filters</title>
   </head>

   <body>
      <%@ taglib uri='http://java.sun.com/jstl/core' prefix='c' %>
      <%@ taglib uri='http://java.sun.com/jstl/xml'  prefix='x' %>

      <%-- Import the XML document and XSLT stylesheet and store
           the result in session-scoped variables, which are
           accessed below and in apply_filter.jsp --%>
      <c:import var='rolodex_xml' scope='session'
                url='rolodex.xml'/>
      <c:import var='rolodex_xsl' scope='session'
                url='rolodex.xsl'/>

      <%-- Transform the XML document with the XSLT stylesheet --%>
      <x:transform xml='${rolodex_xml}' xslt='${rolodex_xsl}'/>

      <%-- Import the form --%>
      <c:import url='form.jsp'/>
   </body>
</html>
```

The preceding JSP page imports the XML document and XSLT stylesheet and stores the resulting scoped variables in session scope. Subsequently, that JSP page performs an initial transformation and imports the JSP page that creates the form. That JSP page—form.jsp—is listed in Listing 10.12.

The preceding JSP page creates a form with an HTML select element that retains its value when the JSP page is reloaded.[14] That form's action is apply_filter.jsp, which is listed in Listing 10.13.

The preceding JSP page uses <jsp:useBean> to create a SAX filter. A <c:set> action within the body of the <jsp:useBean> action specifies the type of element that the filter filters with the value of the filterThis request parameter. Subsequently, the JSP page parses the XML document, specifying the filter with the <x:parse> filter attribute. The JSP page then performs the transformation, specifying the name of the filtered element with a transformation parameter. Finally,

---

14. See "Retaining Values for HTML Option Elements" on page 129 for more information about HTML select elements that retain their values.

Listing 10.12	*form.jsp (Creating a Selection Form)*

```
<%@ taglib uri='http://java.sun.com/jstl/core' prefix='c' %>

<%-- Create a form that lets the user select an inventory
     column to filter --%>
<form action='apply_filter.jsp'>
   Filter an element:
   <select name='filterThis'>
      <option value='NONE'
         <c:if test='${param.filterThis == "NONE"}'>
            selected
         </c:if> >NONE
      </option>

      <option value='email'
         <c:if test='${param.filterThis == "email"}'>
            selected

         </c:if> >email
      </option>

      <option value='phone@home'
         <c:if test='${param.filterThis == "phone@home"}'>
            selected
         </c:if> >home phone
      </option>

      <option value='phone@work'
         <c:if test='${param.filterThis == "phone@work"}'>
            selected
         </c:if> >work phone
      </option>
   </select>

   <p><input type='submit' value='Filter XML'/>
</form>
```

the JSP page includes `form.jsp` so the user can subsequently select a different element to filter.

SAX filters are straightforward to implement. Although it's not strictly necessary, most SAX filters extend the `org.xml.sax.helpers.XMLFilterImpl` class, which implements the SAX handler interfaces. That base class simply forwards all handler events to an XML reader; implementing a SAX filter involves extending that class and selectively overriding those handler methods as desired.

Listing 10.13   *apply_filter.jsp*

```
<!DOCTYPE HTML PUBLIC "-//W3C//DTD HTML 4.0 Transitional//EN">
<html>
   <head>
      <title>Using SAX Filters</title>
   </head>

   <body>
      <%@ taglib uri='http://java.sun.com/jstl/core' prefix='c' %>
      <%@ taglib uri='http://java.sun.com/jstl/xml'  prefix='x' %>

      <%-- Create a filter -- an ElementFilter instance -- and
           set the name of the element that the filter filters --%>
      <jsp:useBean id='filter' class='filters.ElementFilter'>
         <c:set target='${filter}' property='elementToFilter'
                value='${param.filterThis}'/>
      </jsp:useBean>

      <%-- Parse the XML document with the filter --%>
      <x:parse var='document' xml='${rolodex_xml}'
           filter='${filter}'/>

      <%-- Transform the XML document with the XSLT stylesheet
--%>
      <x:transform xml='${document}' xslt='${rolodex_xsl}'>
         <x:param name='filteredColumn'
                value='${param.filterThis}'/>
      </x:transform>

      <%-- Import the form --%>
      <c:import url='form.jsp'/>
   </body>
</html>
```

The SAX filter created by the preceding JSP page is listed in Listing 10.14. That filter is a general-purpose filter that filters elements from an XML document. You can specify those elements in two ways: with the name of the element, which filters all elements with that name, or with an element/attribute combination specified with this syntax: *element@attribute*. Elements, and optionally attributes, are specified with the filter's `setElementToFilter` method. The filter overrides the `startElement`, `endElement`, and `characters` methods, which are defined by the `org.xml.sax.ContentHandler` interface.

After the JSP page listed in Listing 10.13 on page 456 parses the Rolodex XML file with the preceding SAX filter, that JSP page performs a transformation that

Listing 10.14   *WEB-INF/classes/filters/ElementFilter.java*

```
package filters;


import org.xml.sax.helpers.XMLFilterImpl;
import org.xml.sax.Attributes;
import org.xml.sax.SAXException;

// A filter that filters a specific element or an
// element/attribute combination

public class ElementFilter extends XMLFilterImpl {
   private String filterThisElement,
                  filterThisAttribute;

   private boolean filtering; // A flag that tracks filtering state

   public ElementFilter() {
      // The element and attribute are unspecified when the filter
      // is created, and the filtering flag is set to false
      filterThisElement = filterThisAttribute = null;
      filtering  = false;
   }
   public void setElementToFilter(String filterThis) {
      int position;

      // If there's an at-sign in the filterThis string...
      if((position = filterThis.indexOf("@")) != -1) {
         // Interpret the part of the string before the at-sign
         // as the element name
         filterThisElement = filterThis.substring(0, position);

         // Interpret the part of the string after the at-sign
         // as the attribute name
         filterThisAttribute = filterThis.substring(position+1);
      }
      else { // There's not an at-sign in the filterThis string
         filterThisElement = filterThis;
      }
   }
   public void characters(char[] chars, int start, int length)
            throws SAXException {
      // If we're not filtering, pass on the event
      if(!filtering)
         super.characters(chars, start, length);
   }
   public void startElement(String uri, String localName,
```

Listing 10.14 *WEB-INF/classes/filters/ElementFilter.java (cont.)*

```
                              String qName, Attributes attrs)
                              throws SAXException {
   // If this element matches the element we need to filter...
   if(localName.equals(filterThisElement)) {
      // If an attribute was specified...
      if(filterThisAttribute != null) {
         // Loop over attributes looking for a match...
         for(int i=0; i < attrs.getLength(); ++i) {
            // If this attribute matches the attribute we're
            // supposed to filter...
            if(attrs.getValue(i).equals(filterThisAttribute)) {
               // Set filtering to true and break out of loop
               filtering = true;
               break;
            }
         }
      }
      else { // If no attribute was specified
         filtering = true;
      }
   }

   // If we're not filtering this element, pass on the
   // event
   if(!filtering)
      super.startElement(uri, localName, qName, attrs);
}
public void endElement(String uri, String localName,
                       String qName)
                       throws SAXException {
   // If we're not filtering, pass on the event
   if(filtering == false)
      super.endElement(uri, localName, qName);

   // If we're filtering, stop
   if(filtering)
      filtering = false;
}
}
```

transforms the filtered XML document into an HTML table. The XSLT stylesheet that performs that transformation—rolodex.xsl—is listed in Listing 10.15.

The preceding stylesheet is passed a transformation parameter that specifies the table column that corresponds to the filtered element. That parameter is used to omit

Listing 10.15	*rolodex.xsl (Transforming a Filtered XML Document)*

```
<xsl:stylesheet xmlns:xsl="http://www.w3.org/1999/XSL/Transform"
                version="1.0">

    <!-- Declare the filteredColumn parameter-->
    <xsl:param name='filteredColumn'/>

    <!-- Generate HTML for the document root -->
    <xsl:template match='/'>
        <table border='1'>
            <tr>
                <th>First Name</th>
                <th>Last Name</th>
                <th>Company</th>

                <xsl:if test='$filteredColumn != "email"'>
                    <th>Email</th>
                </xsl:if>

                <xsl:if test='$filteredColumn != "phone@work"'>
                    <th>Work Phone</th>
                </xsl:if>

                <xsl:if test='$filteredColumn != "phone@home"'>
                    <th>Home Phone</th>
                </xsl:if>

                <xsl:apply-templates/>
            </tr>
        </table>
    </xsl:template>

    <!-- Create a table row for each item and apply templates -->
    <xsl:template match='contact'>
        <tr><xsl:apply-templates/></tr>
    </xsl:template>

    <!-- Create table data for each item's children and
         apply templates -->
    <xsl:template match='contact/*'>
        <td><xsl:apply-templates/></td>
    </xsl:template>
</xsl:stylesheet>
```

the specified table column. Additionally, the stylesheet creates a table row for each
`contact` element and table data for all of the `contact` element's child elements.

10.8 Accessing External Entities

XML documents often reference entities, which are typically text that is reused among one or more XML documents. Entities can be internal, meaning they are defined within the XML document that uses them, or external, meaning they are defined elsewhere. The JSTL <x:parse> and <x:transform> actions support external entities with attributes that specify URIs that point to an entity's file.

The Web application shown in Figure 10–7 references an external entity that specifies the owner of the Rolodex, which is defined in `rolodex.xml`.

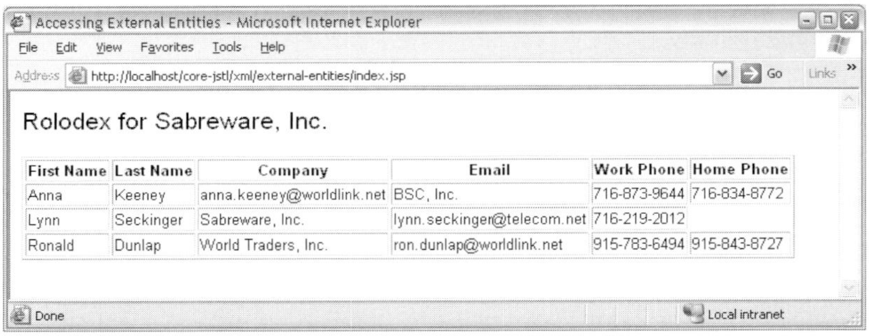

Figure 10–7   Accessing External Entities

External entities are specified with a Document Type Definition (DTD). Listing 10.16 lists a modification of the Rolodex XML file listed in Listing 10.1 on page 424 that specifies a DTD that references an external entity.

The external entity specified in the preceding DTD is named `owner` and is defined in the file `owner.xml`. That file is listed in Listing 10.17.

If you use the <x:parse> action to parse an XML document that contains external entities, you can specify the URI for those entities with the <x:parse> `systemId` attribute, as illustrated by the JSP page listed in Listing 10.18.

The `systemId` attribute specified in the preceding JSP page points to the URI of the Web application because the external entity's file—`owner.xml`—resides in the top-level directory of the Web application.

The XSLT stylesheet used by the preceding JSP page to transform the Rolodex XML document into an HTML table is listed in Listing 10.19.

The preceding stylesheet is nearly identical to the stylesheet listed in Listing 10.6 on page 446, except that the preceding stylesheet displays the owner of the Rolodex, which is specified with the `owner` external entity in the Rolodex XML document.

Listing 10.16   *rolodex.xml (Specifying a DTD)*

```
<?xml version="1.0" encoding="ISO-8859-1" ?>
<!DOCTYPE rolodex [

   <!ELEMENT rolodex
             (owner,contact,firstName,lastName,email,phone)>
   <!ELEMENT owner    (#PCDATA)>
   <!ELEMENT contact  (#PCDATA)>
   <!ELEMENT firstName (#PCDATA)>
   <!ELEMENT lastName (#PCDATA)>
   <!ELEMENT company  (#PCDATA)>
   <!ELEMENT email    (#PCDATA)>
   <!ELEMENT phone    (#PCDATA)>

   <!ATTLIST phone home CDATA #REQUIRED>
   <!ATTLIST phone work CDATA #IMPLIED>
   <!ENTITY owner SYSTEM "owner.xml">

]>

<rolodex>
   <owner>&owner;</owner>
   <contact>
      <firstName>Anna</firstName>
      <lastName>Keeney</lastName>
      <email>anna.keeney@worldlink.net</email>
      <company>BSC, Inc.</company>
      <phone type="work">716-873-9644</phone>
      <phone type="home">716-834-8772</phone>
   </contact>
   <contact>
      <firstName>Lynn</firstName>
      <lastName>Seckinger</lastName>
      <company>Sabreware, Inc.</company>
      <email>lynn.seckinger@telecom.net</email>
      <phone type="work">716-219-2012</phone>
   </contact>
   <contact>
      <firstName>Ronald</firstName>
      <lastName>Dunlap</lastName>
      <company>World Traders, Inc.</company>
      <email>ron.dunlap@worldlink.net</email>
      <phone type="work">915-783-6494</phone>
      <phone type="home">915-843-8727</phone>
   </contact>
</rolodex>
```

Listing 10.17   *owner.xml*

```
<!-- The name of the Rolodex owner -->
Sabreware, Inc.
```

Listing 10.18   *index.jsp (Accessing External Entities)*

```
<!DOCTYPE HTML PUBLIC "-//W3C//DTD HTML 4.0 Transitional//EN">
<html>
    <head>
        <title>Accessing External Entities</title>
    </head>

    <body>
        <%@ taglib uri='http://java.sun.com/jstl/core' prefix='c' %>
        <%@ taglib uri='http://java.sun.com/jstl/xml'  prefix='x' %>

        <%-- Import the XML file and XSLT stylesheet --%>
        <c:import var='rolodex_xml' url='rolodex.xml'/>
        <c:import var='rolodex_xsl' url='rolodex.xsl'/>

        <%-- Parse the XML File --%>
        <x:parse var='document' xml='${rolodex_xml}'
        systemId='http://localhost/core-jstl/xml/external-entities/'
        />

        <%-- Perform the transformation --%>
        <x:transform xml='${document}' xslt='${rolodex_xsl}'/>
    </body>
</html>
```

Listing 10.19   *rolodex.xsl (Generating HTML for Root Document)*

```
<xsl:stylesheet xmlns:xsl="http://www.w3.org/1999/XSL/Transform"
                version="1.0">
   <!-- Generate HTML for the document root -->
   <xsl:template match="/">
      <table border='1'>
         <tr>
            <th>First Name</th>
            <th>Last Name</th>
            <th>Company</th>
            <th>Email</th>
            <th>Work Phone</th>
            <th>Home Phone</th>
            <xsl:apply-templates/>
         </tr>
      </table>
   </xsl:template>

   <xsl:template match="owner">
      <p>
         <font size='5'>
            Rolodex for <xsl:value-of select='.'/>
         </font>
      </p>
   </xsl:template>

   <!-- Create a table row for each item and apply templates -->
   <xsl:template match="contact">
      <tr><xsl:apply-templates/></tr>
   </xsl:template>

   <!-- Create table data for each item and apply templates -->
   <xsl:template match="contact/*">
      <td><xsl:apply-templates/></td>
   </xsl:template>
</xsl:stylesheet>
```

JSTL REFERENCE

Topics in This Chapter

- Action Reference Index
- General-Purpose Actions
- Conditional Actions
- Iteration Actions
- URL Actions
- Internationalization Actions
- Formatting Actions
- Database Actions
- XML Core Actions
- XML Flow Control Actions
- XML Transform Actions

Chapter 11

JSTL 1.0 has 42 actions, each of which has an average of two syntaxes and four attributes. That's a lot of information, most of which will eventually become second nature to you the more you use JSTL. In the meantime, this chapter provides a handy reference that summarizes each action with brief discussions of the action's syntaxes, attributes, and error handling.

JSTL provides four tag libraries, which are listed in Table 11.1.

Table 11.1   JSTL Tag Libraries

Library	Actions	Description	See Page
Core	14	*Fundamentals*: If/then statements and switch constructs, creating output, creating and destroying scoped variables, accessing properties of JavaBeans components (beans), handling exceptions, iterating over collections, and constructing URLs and importing their content.	469
Formatting	12	*Internationalization and Formatting*: Setting locales and resource bundles, localizing text and compound messages, formatting numbers, percents, currencies, and dates.	492

Table 11.1 JSTL Tag Libraries *(cont.)*

Library	Actions	Description	See Page
SQL	6	*Database Access*: Specifying a data source, executing queries, updates, and transactions, iterating over query results.	529
XML	10	*XML Parsing and Transforming*: Parsing XML and transforming it with XSLT.	543

This chapter provides references for the actions contained in the tag libraries listed above, in the order in which they are listed.

11.1 Action Reference Index

This section lets you quickly locate an action in this chapter with an index of all of the JSTL actions. That index consists of four tables that list actions alphabetically for the Core, Formatting, SQL, and Database actions, in that order.

Core Actions

Table 11.2 Core Action Reference Index

Action	See Page	Action	See Page
<c:catch>	474	<c:out>	469
<c:choose>	476	<c:param>	491
<c:forEach>	480	<c:redirect>	489
<c:forTokens>	482	<c:remove>	473
<c:if>	475	<c:set>	471
<c:import>	486	<c:url>	490
<c:otherwise>	478	<c:when>	477

Formatting Actions

Table 11.3 Formatting Action Reference Index

Action	See Page	Action	See Page
<fmt:bundle>	500	<fmt:parseNumber>	515
<fmt:formatDate>	518	<fmt:requestEncoding>	506
<fmt:formatNumber>	511	<fmt:setBundle>	498
<fmt:message>	502	<fmt:setLocale>	496
<fmt:param>	504	<fmt:setTimeZone>	527
<fmt:parseDate>	522	<fmt:timeZone>	525

SQL Actions

Table 11.4 SQL Action Reference Index

Action	See Page	Action	See Page
<sql:dateParam>	540	<sql:setDataSource>	531
<sql:param>	539	<sql:transaction>	537
<sql:query>	533	<sql:update>	535

XML Actions

Table 11.5 XML Action Reference Index

Action	See Page	Action	See Page
<x:choose>	549	<x:param>	555
<x:forEach>	551	<x:parse>	543
<x:if>	548	<x:set>	546
<x:otherwise>	550	<x:transform>	553
<x:out>	545	<x:when>	549

Exposed Classes and Interfaces Index

Besides actions, JSTL also provides a number of classes and interfaces that Java developers can use to implement custom actions that behave similarly to, or work alongside of, JSTL actions. Discussions of those classes and interfaces are also provided in this chapter; the following tables provide an index to them.

Core Classes and Interfaces

Table 11.6   Core Classes and Interfaces Reference Index

Class or Interface	See Page
ConditionalTagSupport	479
LoopTagSupport	484
LoopTag	483
LoopTagStatus	484

Formatting Classes and Interfaces

Table 11.7   Formatting Classes and Interfaces Reference Index

Class or Interface	See Page
LocaleSupport	508
LocalizationContext	509

SQL Classes and Interfaces

Table 11.8   SQL Classes and Interfaces Reference Index

Class or Interface	See Page
SQLExecutionTag	542
Result	541
ResultSupport	542

11.2 General-Purpose Actions

JSTL provides a handful of general-purpose actions for manipulating scoped variables, beans and maps, and handling exceptions. Those actions are listed in Table 11.9.

Table 11.9   General-Purpose Actions

Action	Description
<c:out>	Evaluates an expression (either an EL expression for <c:out> or a JSP expression for <c_rt:out>) and sends the result of that evaluation to the current Jsp-Writer.
<c:set>	Sets the value of a scoped variable, a property of a bean, or an entry in a Java map.
<c:remove>	Deletes a scoped variable.
<c:catch>	Catches any exceptions of type java.lang.Throwable thrown in the body of the action and optionally stores that exception in a page-scoped variable.

Evaluates an expression and sends the result of that expression to the current JspWriter.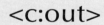

Syntax:[1]

Syntax #1: Without a body

```
<c:out value [escapeXml] [default]/>
```

Syntax #2: With a body that specifies the default value

```
<c:out value [escapeXml]>
    default
</c:out>
```

---

1. Items in brackets are optional.

Description:

The <c:out> action evaluates an expression—either an EL expression (<c:out>) or a JSP expression (<c_rt:out>)—and sends the result of that evaluation, coerced to a string, to the current JspWriter.

Attributes:

Attribute[a]	Type	Description
value	Object	The expression that is either an EL expression for <c:out> or a JSP expression for <c_rt:out>.
escapeXml	boolean	A value that specifies whether the following characters are converted to their corresponding character entity codes: < > & ' ". The default value is true.
default	Object	A default value that is used instead of the supplied expression if that expression is null or invalid.

    a.   static | *dynamic*

Constraints and Error Handling:

• If you specify an invalid value attribute such as null, <c:out> uses the default value instead.

• If the expression specified by the value attribute is null or invalid and no default value is specified, <c:out> emits an empty string.

In a Nutshell:

The <c:out> action replaces the syntax for JSP expressions—<%= *expr* %>—and is JSTL's most heavily used action; it's used in nearly every code example throughout this book. You can use <c:out> for JSTL Expression Language (EL) expressions and <c_rt:out> for JSP expressions. You specify those expressions with the value attribute.

You can optionally specify a default value that <c:out> sends to the current JspWriter if the specified value is null or is not a valid expression. You can specify the default value with the default attribute or in the body of the <c:out> action.

The escapeXml attribute specifies whether certain characters are converted to HTML character entity codes. Those characters and their corresponding entity codes are listed in Table 11.10. By default, the escapeXml attribute is true, meaning <c:out> converts the characters listed in Table 11.10 to their corresponding character entity codes. If you specify `false` for the `escapeXml` attribute, `<c:out>` will not convert those characters.

Table 11.10 `<c:out>` Default Character Conversions

Character	Character Entity Code
<	<
>	>
&	&
'	&#039
"	&#034

Stores a value in a scoped variable or a property of a target object   **`<c:set>`**

Syntax:[2]

Syntax #1: Without a body, sets the value of a scoped variable

```
<c:set value var [scope]/>
```

Syntax #2: With a body that specifies the value of a scoped variable

```
<c:set var [scope]>
    value
</c:set>
```

Syntax #3: Without a body, sets the value of a bean property or a key/value pair in a map

```
<c:set value target property/>
```

Syntax #4: With a body that specifies the value of a bean property or the value of a key/value pair in a map

```
<c:set target property>
    value
</c:set>
```

---

2. Items in brackets are optional.

Description:

The <c:set> action lets you store a value in a scoped variable or a bean property. You can also use <c:set> to add, modify, or remove a key/value pair in a map.

Attributes:

Attribute[a]	Type	Description
value	Object	The expression that is either an EL expression for <c:out> or a JSP expression for <c_rt:out>. That value represents a bean property value or the value of a map entry.
target	Object	An object whose property, specified with the property attribute, is set to the value specified with the value attribute. That object must be either a bean or an instance of java.util.Map.
property	String	The name of a bean property or the name of a key for a map entry.
var	String	The name of a scoped variable that contains the value specified by the value attribute. That scoped variable's type is whatever type the value evaluates to.
scope	String	The scope of the scoped variable whose name is specified by the var attribute; default is page scope.

a. static | *dynamic*

Constraints and Error Handling:

• For syntaxes 1 and 2, if the value attribute evaluates to null, <c:set> removes the scoped variable identified by the var and scope attributes.

• For syntaxes 3 and 4, if the value attribute evaluates to null and the target is a bean, <c:set> sets that bean's property to null.

• For syntaxes 3 and 4, if the value attribute evaluates to null and the target is an instance of java.util.Map, <c:set> removes the entry whose key corresponds to the property attribute.

• For syntaxes 3 and 4, <c:set> throws an exception if the value of the target attribute evaluates to null or if the value of the target attribute is not a bean or an instance of java.util.Map.

In a Nutshell:

For syntaxes 1 and 2, <c:set> sets the value of a scoped variable that you specify with the var attribute and, optionally, the scope attribute.

For syntaxes 3 and 4, <c:set> sets a property of a target object. If the target object is a bean, <c:set> sets that bean's property—which you specify with the `property` attribute—with the value that you specify with the `value` attribute.

If the target object is a Java map and that map has an entry whose key corresponds to the `property` attribute, <c:set> sets the value of that entry to the value you specify with the `value` attribute. If the map does not have an entry corresponding to the `property` attribute, <c:set> creates an entry, adds it to the map, and sets its value to the value that you specify with the `value` attribute.

Removes a scoped variable   # **<c:remove>**

Syntax:[3]

```
<c:remove var [scope]/>
```

Description:

The <c:remove> action removes a scoped variable that you specify with the `var` attribute and, optionally, the `scope` attribute.

Attributes:

Attribute[a]	Type	Description
var	String	The name of the scoped variable that <c:remove> removes.
scope	String	The scope of the scoped variable whose name is specified by the `var` attribute; default is page scope.

a.   static | *dynamic*

In a Nutshell:

If you don't specify the `scope` attribute, <c:remove> removes the scoped variable by calling `PageContext.removeAttribute(var)`. That method searches the page, request, session, and application scopes—in that order—and removes the first scoped variable that it finds with the name that you specified with the `var` attribute. If you do specify the `scope` attribute, <c:remove> removes the scoped variable by calling `PageContext.removeAttribute(var, scope)`, which removes the specified variable from the specified scope.

---

3. Items in brackets are optional.

<c:catch>	Catches an exception and optionally stores it in a page-scoped variable

Syntax:[4]

```
<c:catch [var]>
    body content
</c:catch>
```

Description:

The <c:catch> action catches the first exception thrown from its body content. If you specify the optional var attribute, <c:catch> stores the exception in a scoped variable with a name corresponding to the var attribute's value.

Attributes:

Attribute[a]	Type	Description
var	String	The name of a page-scoped variable that references the exception thrown from the body of the <c:set> action.

a. static | *dynamic*

In a Nutshell:

Most of the time, you will probably specify the var attribute for the <c:catch> action so that <c:catch> will store the exception that it catches in a scoped variable. If you don't specify that attribute, <c:catch> will catch the exception but it won't save it; essentially, that approach lets you ignore exceptions and is not recommended.

11.3 Conditional Actions

JSTL provides four actions that let you handle simple conditions or mutually exclusive conditions. Simple conditions execute some code based on whether a single condition is true, whereas mutually exclusive conditions execute some code based on

---

4. Items in brackets are optional.

whether one of many conditions is true. The JSTL conditional actions are listed in Table 11.11.

Table 11.11 Conditional Actions

Action	Description
<c:if>	Evaluates a boolean expression; if the expression is true, <c:if> evaluates its body content, if any. You can also store the result of the boolean expression in a scoped variable.
<c:choose>	The outermost action for mutually exclusive conditions. This action can only contain <c:when> actions and an optional <c:otherwise> action, in that order.
<c:when>	One or more <c:when> actions can be nested in a <c:choose> action. The body content of the first <c:when> action whose test attribute value evaluates to true is evaluated.
<c:otherwise>	One (and only one) <c:otherwise> action can reside—as the last action—in a <c:choose> action. The <c:otherwise> action represents a default in a switch statement.

One class—ConditionalTagSupport—is exposed for conditional custom actions.

JSTL Conditional Actions

Performs a simple conditional test	<c:if>

Syntax:[5]

Syntax #1: Without a body, stores the test result in a scoped variable

```
<c:if test var [scope]/>
```

Syntax #2: With a body that is evaluated if the test condition is true

```
<c:if test [var] [scope]>
    body content
</c:if>
```

---

5. Items in brackets are optional.

Description:

You can use <c:if> to do two things: conditionally execute some code contained in the body of the action and store the boolean result of the test condition in a scoped variable. You can do both of those things simultaneously with syntax 2.

Attributes:

Attribute[a]	Type	Description
test	boolean	A test condition.
var	String	The name of a scoped variable that references the boolean result of the value of the test attribute.
scope	String	The scope of the scoped variable whose name is specified by the var attribute; default is page scope.

    a.   static | *dynamic*

Constraints and Error Handling:

- If you specify the scope attribute, you must also specify the var attribute.

In a Nutshell:

The <c:if> action evaluates a boolean expression specified with the test attribute; if that expression is true and the <c:if> action has a body, the body is evaluated; otherwise it is ignored. If you specify the var attribute, <c:if> will store the result of the boolean expression in a scoped variable. You can also use <c:if> without a body, as illustrated by syntax 1, to store the result of a boolean expression in scoped variable; presumably, that scoped variable is referenced elsewhere to determine whether some functionality is performed.

<c:choose>   Encapsulates a mutually exclusive condition

Syntax:

```
<c:choose>
    nested <c:when> actions and an optional <c:otherwise> action
</c:choose>
```

Description:

The body of a <c:choose> action can contain one or more <c:when> actions and an optional <c:otherwise> action. The body content of the first <c:when> action whose condition evaluates to `true` is evaluated; otherwise, the body of the <c:otherwise> action, if present, is evaluated.

Attributes: none

Constraints and Error Handling:

- The body of a <c:choose> action can only contain whitespace, one or more <c:when> actions, and an optional <c:otherwise> action. If present, the <c:otherwise> action must be the last action nested in the <c:choose> action.

In a Nutshell:

The <c:choose> action is used in conjunction with <c:when> and <c:otherwise> to emulate if/else and switch statement constructs.[6]

An alternative in a <c:choose> action	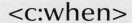

Syntax:

```
<c:when test>
    body content
</c:when>
```

Description:

A <c:when> action can only exist in the body of a <c:choose> action. The body content of the first <c:when> action whose test condition—specified with the `test` attribute—evaluates to `true` is evaluated.

Attributes:

Attribute[a]	Type	Description
test	boolean	A test condition.

a. static | *dynamic*

---

6. See "Conditional Actions" on page 127 for more information about implementing if/then statements and switch constructs.

Constraints and Error Handling:

- <c:when> actions can only exist in the body of a <c:choose> action.

- <c:when> actions must come before the <c:otherwise> action, if present, in the same <c:choose> action.

In a Nutshell:

The <c:when> action is similar to the <c:if> action; both actions have a test conditions specified with a `test` attribute. The difference is that <c:when> actions must appear within a <c:choose> action and represent one of several (two or more) alternatives.

<c:otherwise> The default alternative in a <c:choose> action

Syntax:

```
<c:otherwise>
    body content
</c:otherwise>
```

Description:

The <c:choose> action represents the last alternative in a <c:choose> action. The body content of a <c:otherwise> action is similar to the default in a Java switch statement.

Attributes: none

Constraints and Error Handling:

- <c:otherwise> actions must be the last action contained in a <c:choose> action.

Exposed Class

The JSTL conditional actions expose one class—ConditionalTagSupport—that you can use to implement conditional custom actions. That class is discussed below.

A class implemented by the
<c:forEach> and <c:forTokens>
tag handlers

ConditionalTagSupport

Definition:

```
class ConditionalTagSupport {
    public ConditionalTagSupport()
    public abstract boolean condition() throws JspTagException
    public void setVar(String var)
    public void setScope(String scope)
}
```

Description:

The `abstract condition` method returns a `boolean` value that determines whether the action's body is evaluated. If that method returns `true`, the body is evaluated; otherwise, it is ignored.

The `ConditionalTagSupport` class also provides setter methods for `var` and `scope` attributes. Those attributes are used in exactly the same manner as they are for the <c:if> action. See "Conditional Custom Actions" on page 145 for more information about how you can extend the `ConditionalTagSupport` class to implement custom conditional actions.

11.4 Iteration Actions

JSTL provides two actions that you can use to iterate over various types of data:

- <c:forEach>
- <c:forTokens>

An overview of the actions listed above is provided in the following pages. A more in-depth examination of those actions can be found in "Iteration Actions" on page 150.

JSTL also provides an interface and two classes that let you develop custom iteration actions and access an iteration's status:

- `LoopTag` (interface)
- `LoopTagSupport` (class)
- `LoopTagStatus` (class)

An overview of the interface and classes listed above can be found at "Exposed Classes and Interfaces" on page 483. You can also find an in-depth examination of accessing loop status at "Iteration Status" on page 171 and implementing custom iteration actions in "Custom Iteration Actions" on page 178.

JSTL Iteration Actions

| `<c:forEach>` Iterates over integer values or a data structure |

Syntax:[7]

Syntax #1: Iterates over a collection of objects

```
<c:forEach items [begin] [end] [step] [var] [varStatus]>
    body content
</c:forEach>
```

Syntax #2: Iterates over a set of integer values

```
<c:forEach begin end [step] [var] [varStatus]>
    body content
</c:forEach>
```

Description:

You can use the <c:forEach> action to iterate over a data structure, such as an array, map, or collection if you specify that data structure with the `items` attribute. You can also use <c:forEach> to iterate over integer values if you don't specify the `items` attribute.

---

7. Items in brackets are optional.

Attributes:

Attribute[a]	Type	Description
items	String, Array, Collection, Iterator, Enumeration, Map	The items that <c:forEach> iterates over. This attribute is not specified when you iterate over explicit integer values.
begin	int	If you iterate over explicit integer values, this attribute specifies the starting value. If you iterate over a data structure, this attribute specifies the index of the first item that's accessed in that data structure.
end	int	If you iterate over explicit integer values, this attribute specifies the ending value. If you iterate over a data structure, this attribute specifies the index of the last item that is potentially accessed in that data structure.
step	int	The amount that the loop index is incremented for every round of an iteration.
var	String	The name of a scoped variable that references the iteration's current item. If you iterate over explicit integer values, that scoped variable contains the current integer value; if you iterate over a data structure, it contains the current object from that data structure.
varStatus	String	The name of a scoped variable that references an object that has properties corresponding to the status of the iteration. That object's type is `LoopTagStatus`.

a.   static | *dynamic*

Constraints and Error Handling:

- If you specify the `begin` attribute, its value must be greater than or equal to zero.
- If you specify the `end` attribute, its value must be greater than or equal to the value that you specify for the `begin` attribute.
- If you specify the step attribute, its value must be greater than or equal to 1.

In a Nutshell:

The <c:forEach> action can iterate over integer values or a data structure that can be one of the following: map, collection, array, or a comma-separated string. The <c:forEach> action can also use an iterator or an enumeration to iterate over an underlying collection.

`<c:forTokens>`   Iterates over tokens in a string

Syntax:[8]

```
<c:forTokens items delims [begin] [end] [step] [var] [varStatus]>
    body content
</c:forTokens>
```

Description:

The `<c:forTokens>` action iterates over a string of tokens delimited by delimiters that you specify with the `delims` attribute.

Attributes:

Attribute[a]	Type	Description
items	String	A string that `<c:forTokens>` iterates over. Tokens in the string are delimited by the delimiters specified with the `delims` attribute.
begin	int	A zero-based index that represents the first token that `<c:forTokens>` iterates over.
end	int	A zero-based index that represents the last token that is potentially accessed in the string specified with the `items` attribute.
step	int	The amount that the loop index is incremented for every round of an iteration.
var	String	The name of a scoped variable that references the iteration's current item.
varStatus	String	The name of a scoped variable that references an object that has properties corresponding to the status of the iteration. That object's type is `LoopTagStatus`.

    a.   static | *dynamic*

Constraints and Error Handling:

- If you specify the `begin` attribute, its value must be greater than or equal to zero.

---

    8.   Items in brackets are optional.

- If you specify the end attribute, its value must be greater than or equal to the value that you specify for the begin attribute.
- If you specify the step attribute, its value must be greater than or equal to 1.

In a Nutshell:

The <c:forEach> action can iterate over tokens in a string as long as those tokens are delimited by commas. If you need to iterate over a string whose tokens are delimited by characters other than commas, you can use the <c:forTokens> action. The <c:forTokens> action is especially handy when you need to iterate over strings with multiple tokens that represent nested data; see "The <c:forTokens> Action" on page 166 for an example of that usage.

Exposed Classes and Interfaces

The JSTL iteration actions expose one interface and two classes:

- `javax.servlet.jsp.jstl.core.LoopTag` (interface)
- `javax.servlet.jsp.jstl.core.LoopTagSupport`(class)
- `javax.servlet.jsp.jstl.core.LoopTagStatus`(class)

The classes and interface listed above are discussed below.

An interface implemented by the <c:forEach> and <c:forTokens> tag handlers	**LoopTag**

Definition:

```
interface LoopTag {
    public Object getCurrent()
    public LoopTagStatus getLoopStatus()
}
```

Description:

The <c:forEach> and <c:forTokens> actions have tag handlers that implement the LoopTag interface. You can take advantage of that implementation to implement custom actions that collaborate with <c:forEach> and <c:forTokens> actions; see "Collaboration Custom Actions" on page 178 for more information about implementing collaboration custom actions.

LoopTagSupport
The superclass for <c:forEach> and <c:forTokens> tag handlers

Definition:

```
class LoopTagSupport {
    public LoopTagSupport()
    protected abstract Object next() throws JspTagException
    protected abstract boolean hasNext() throws JspTagException
    protected abstract void prepare() throws JspTagException
    protected void validateBegin() throws JspTagException
    protected void validateEnd() throws JspTagException
    protected void validateStep() throws JspTagException
    public Object getCurrent() throws JspTagException
    public LoopTagStatus getLoopStatus()
    public void setVar(String)
    public void setVarStatus(String)
}
```

Description:

To implement iteration custom actions, extend the `LoopTagSupport` class, which provides convenience methods for implementing those types of custom actions. The `LoopTagSupport` class is also the superclass of the <c:forEach> and <c:forTokens> tag handlers. See "Custom Iteration Actions" on page 178 for more information about developing iteration custom actions.

LoopTagStatus
A class that provides information about an iteration's status

Definition:

```
class LoopTagStatus {
    public Object getCurrent()
    public int getIndex()
    public int getCount()
    public boolean isFirst()
    public boolean isLast()
}
```

```
            public Integer getBegin()
            public Integer getEnd()
            public Integer getStep()
      }
```

Description:

The LoopTagStatus interface provides information about the status of an iteration. When you specify the varStatus attribute for <c:forEach> or <c:forTokens>,
an object that implements the LoopTagStatus interface is made available in the
body of those actions. You can use that object to obtain information about the current
iteration.

11.5 URL Actions

JSTL provides URL actions that let you import content from absolute and relative
URLs in addition to resources from foreign contexts. You can also redirect HTTP
responses and create URLs with automatic URL rewriting and request parameter
encoding, as necessary. The JSTL URL actions are listed in Table 11.12.

Table 11.12   URL Actions

Action	Description
<c:import>	Imports the content of a URL-based resource.
<c:redirect>	Redirects an HTTP response.
<c:url>	Creates a URL, applying URL rewriting as necessary.
<c:param>	Encodes a request parameter for <c:import>, <c:redirect>, or <c:url>.

The <c:import> and <c:redirect> actions import content from URLs and redirect
HTTP responses, respectively. Those actions provide the main functionality of the
JSTL URL actions. The <c:url> and <c:param> actions provide a support role by
creating URLs with URL rewriting incorporated as necessary and by encoding
request parameters, respectively.

The JSTL URL actions do not expose any classes or interfaces.

<c:import>   Imports the content of a URL-based resource

Syntax:[9]

Syntax #1: The content of the specified URL is sent to the current `JspWriter` or stored as a string in a scoped variable

```
<c:import url [context] [var] [scope] [charEncoding]>
    optional <c:param> actions
</c:import>
```

Syntax #2: The content of the specified URL is only available within the body of the action through a reader

```
<c:import url varReader [context] [charEncoding]>
    body content that presumably extracts information from varReader
</c:import>
```

Description:

The <c:import> action is similar to the <jsp:include> action, but it offers more features and flexibility. The <c:import> action can perform the following functions:

- Import content from a resource specified with a relative URL
- Import content from a resource in a foreign context[10]
- Import content from a resource specified with an absolute URL
- Store imported content in a string referenced by a scoped variable
- Provide access to imported content with a reader[11]
- Specify a character encoding for imported content
- Specify URLs, foreign contexts, and character encodings with the JSTL expression language

The <jsp:include> action can only perform the first function listed above.

---

9. Items in brackets are optional.
10. A foreign context is another Web application in the same website.
11. The reader option offers better performance than that obtained by storing content in a string.

Attributes:

Attribute[a]	Type	Description
url	String	The <c:import> action imports content from a resource. This attribute specifies a URL that points to that resource.
context	String	The <c:import> action can import content from a resource in a foreign context (meaning another Web application). This attribute specifies that foreign context.
charEncoding	String	This attribute specifies a character encoding, such as ISO-8859-1 or UTF-8, used to decode imported content.
var	String	The name of a scoped variable that references a string containing the imported content.
scope	String	The scope of the scoped variable whose name is specified by the var attribute; default is page scope.
varReader	String	Instead of storing content in a string referenced by a scoped variable, you can access that content through a reader, thereby improving performance. This attribute specifies the name of that reader.

a.   static | *dynamic*

Constraints and Error Handling:

• If you specify a null value, an empty string, or an invalid value for the url attribute, <c:import> will throw a JspException.

• If you specify a null value or an empty string for the charEncoding attribute, that attribute is ignored.

• If a request dispatcher cannot be found for an internal resource, <c:import> throws a JspException with the resource path included in the exception's message.

• If the request the dispatcher's include method throws an exception when trying to access an internal resource, <c:import> throws a JspException with the caught exception as the root cause.

• If accessing a resource results in a response status code outside the range of 200–299 (that range represents a successful operation), <c:import> throws a JspException with the resource path and status code in the exception's message.

• For external resources, if the URLConnection class throws an IOException or a RuntimeException, <c:import> throws a JspException that contains the original exception's message. That JspException also includes the original exception as the root cause.

In a Nutshell:

The <c:import> action provides the most features of any of the JSTL URL actions and is the most heavily used. By default, <c:import> writes its content to the current JspWriter, but if you specify the var attribute (and optionally the scope attribute), <c:import> will store its imported content in a string instead. You can access that string through a scoped variable whose name corresponds to the value that you specified for the var attribute.

Besides storing imported content in a string, you can also access that content directly with a reader whose name you specify with the varReader attribute. Accessing imported content with a reader is more efficient than storing it in a string, because the content is not buffered, so you may opt for the reader option when importing a resource that has a lot of content. Readers created by <c:import> are only available within the body of the <c:import> action because the <c:import> end tag is responsible for closing the reader. Because of that requirement, the reader must be available immediately after the <c:import> start tag; therefore, you cannot specify <c:param> actions in the body of the <c:import> action that was specified with a varReader attribute, as you can when content is imported directly or stored in a string.

If you specify a relative URL with the url attribute that points to a resource in the same context (Web application), <c:import> imports content in exactly the same manner as does <jsp:include>. In that case, you can specify a context-relative path, which starts with a forward slash and specifies a path to a resource from the application's top-level directory, or you can specify a page-relative path that does not begin with a forward slash and that specifies a path relative to the JSP page in which the <c:import> action resides. *When you import content from a relative URL in the same context, the entire environment of the importing JSP page is available to the imported resource*, including request attributes, session attributes, and request parameters of the importing page.

You can import resources from a foreign context by specifying the url and context attributes. In that case, the url attribute's value must be a context-relative path and the context attribute must be the context of the foreign context. Both of those attributes must start with a forward slash. *When you import the content of a resource in a foreign context, only the request environment of the importing page is available to that resource*. Note that not all JSP containers support accessing resources that reside in foreign contexts; if that is the case for your JSP container, you can use an absolute URL to access those resources.

Besides importing resources in the same context and resources in a foreign context, <c:import> can also import content from resources specified with absolute

URLs. *If you specify an absolute URL for the* url *attribute, none of the execution environment of the importing JSP page is available to that resource for security reasons, even if that absolute URL resolves to a resource in the same context.*

Finally, you can specify a character encoding, for example Shift_JIS or UTF-8, that <c:import> uses to decode characters from the imported resource. You specify that encoding with the charEncoding attribute.

Redirects an HTTP response to a specified URL

Syntax:[12]

> Syntax #1: Without a body
>
>> <c:redirect url [context]/>
>
> Syntax #2: With a body that specifies parameters
>
>> <c:redirect url [context]>
>>   <c:param> actions
>> </c:redirect>

Description:

The <c:redirect> action redirects an HTTP response to a specified URL and aborts processing of the JSP page in which the <c:redirect> action resides.

Attributes:

Attribute[a]	Type	Description
url	String	The <c:redirect> action redirects an HTTP response to a URL specified with this attribute.
context	String	If the url attribute specifies a url in a foreign context, this attribute specifies that foreign context.

a.   static | *dynamic*

In a Nutshell:

The url attribute must specify a relative URL or an absolute URL. If the URL points to a resource in a foreign context, you must specify the context attribute in

---

12. Items in brackets are optional.

addition to the url attribute, and the values for both of those attributes must start with a forward slash. Like <c:import>, <c:redirect> will rewrite the URL to maintain a session, as appropriate, when you redirect to a relative resource.

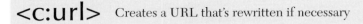

<c:url>   Creates a URL that's rewritten if necessary

Syntax:[13]

Syntax #1: Without a body

```
<c:url value [context] [var] [scope]/>
```

Syntax #2: With a body that specifies parameters

```
<c:url value [context] [var] [scope]>
    <c:param> actions
</c:url>
```

Description:

The <c:url> action processes a URL and rewrites relative URLs to maintain session information, as appropriate.

Attributes:

Attribute[a]	Type	Description
value	String	The URL that <c:url> processes.
context	String	If the URL specified with the value attribute represents a resource in a foreign context, you must also specify this attribute, which represents that foreign context.
var	String	The name of a scoped variable that references the processed URL.
scope	String	The scope of the scoped variable whose name is specified by the var attribute; default is page scope.

a.   static | *dynamic*

---

13. Items in brackets are optional.

In a Nutshell:

You specify a URL with the <c:url> action's value attribute (and the context attribute if the URL points to a resource in a foreign context); <c:url> modifies that URL so that it's suitable for submission to a browser. You can also specify request parameters with nested <c:param> actions.

The <c:url> action will apply URL rewriting, if necessary, to maintain session information *for relative URLs only*; for security reasons, <c:url> will not apply URL rewriting to absolute URLs.

You can specify a page-relative URL, context-relative URL, or an absolute URL for the value attribute. You can also specify a URL that points to a resource in a foreign context by specifying both the value and context attributes. If you specify a URL that points to a resource in a foreign context, the value that you specify for the value attribute must be a context-relative URL and the value that you specify for the context attribute must begin with a forward slash.

If you specify <c:param> actions inside the body of a <c:url> action, the request parameters that you specify with those <c:param> actions will be properly encoded; however, if the original URL that you specify with the value attribute contains characters, such as spaces, which should be encoded, you must make sure that they are encoded to begin with.

By default, the <c:url> action writes the processed URL to the current JspWriter, but <c:url> will store its URL in a scoped variable if you specify the var attribute (and optionally, the scope attribute). The name of that scoped variable is the value that you specify for the var attribute.

The <c:url> action prepends the context path of the current Web application to relative URLs that you specify with the value attribute. Because the <c:import> action also prepends the context path to relative URLs, *you must not use the URL created by <c:url> to specify a URL for <c:import> for relative URLs*. See "The <c:url> Action" on page 208 for more information about this restriction.

Encodes a request parameter and adds it to a URL   **<c:param>**

Syntax:

Syntax #1: Without a body, specifying a value with the value attribute

```
<c:param name value/>
```

Syntax #2: With a body, specifying a value in the body of the action

```
<c:param name>
    value
</c:param>
```

Description:

The <c:param> action encodes a request parameter that you specify with the name and value attributes. That encoded request parameter is added to a URL created by <c:import>, <c:url>, or <c:redirect>.

Attributes:

Attribute[a]	Type	Description
name	String	The name of the request parameter.
value	String	The value of the request parameter.

a. static | *dynamic*

Constraints and Error Handling:

• If you specify a null value or an empty string for the name attribute, the <c:param> action does nothing.

• If you specify a null value for the value attribute, <c:param> processes that value as an empty value.

In a Nutshell:

All <c:param> actions must be nested in <c:import>, <c:url>, or <c:redirect> actions. The <c:param> action is analogous to <jsp:param>, which specifies parameters for the <jsp:include> action.

11.6 Internationalization Actions

The JSTL internationalization (I18N) actions help you internationalize your Web applications. Three configuration settings support these actions.

Overview of JSTL Internationalization Actions

Table 11.13 lists the JSTL I18N actions.

Table 11.13   Internationalization Actions

Action	Description
<fmt:setLocale>	Sets the FMT_LOCALE configuration setting, which is used for resource bundle lookups; those resource bundles are used by <fmt:message> actions. The FMT_LOCALE configuration setting is also used by JSTL formatting actions; see page 509.
<fmt:setBundle>	Searches for a resource bundle identified with the required basename attribute. <fmt:setBundle> stores that resource bundle (and the locale used to locate that resource bundle) in the FMT_LOCALIZATION_CONTEXT configuration setting.
<fmt:bundle>	Searches for a resource bundle identified with the required basename attribute, using the same search algorithm used by <fmt:setBundle>. That resource bundle is only used by <fmt:message> actions and formatting actions in the body of the <fmt:bundle> action.
<fmt:message>	Retrieves a localized message from a resource bundle. That message is sent to the current JspWriter, or if the var attribute is specified, the message is stored in a scoped variable. <fmt:message> searches for a resource bundle in: 1. Its bundle attribute 2. Its enclosing <fmt:bundle> action 3. The FMT_LOCALIZATION_CONTEXT configuration setting
<fmt:param>	Specifies a single parameter for a compound message. That parameter is used by an enclosing <fmt:message> action.
<fmt:requestEncoding>	Sets the character encoding for an HTTP request. This action is necessary because most browsers do not specify the Content-Type header, making it impossible for applications to determine the encoding of request parameters that were encoded with a charset other than ISO-8859-1.

JSTL Internationalization Configuration Settings

The following configuration settings support JSTL internationalization:

- FMT_LOCALE
- FMT_FALLBACK_LOCALE
- FMT_LOCALIZATION_CONTEXT

FMT_LOCALE

The FMT_LOCALE configuration setting is listed in Table 11.14.

Table 11.14   FMT_LOCALE

Config Constant	FMT_LOCALE
Name	javax.servlet.jsp.jstl.fmt.locale
Type	java.lang.String or java.util.Locale
Set by	<fmt:setLocale>, Deployment Descriptor, Config class
Used by	<fmt:bundle>, <fmt:setBundle>, <fmt:message>, <fmt:formatNumber>, <fmt:parseNumber>, <fmt:formatDate>, <fmt:parseDate>

The FMT_LOCALE configuration setting specifies a locale for both internationalization and formatting actions. *If you set this configuration setting, internationalization and formatting actions will ignore your browser's locale preferences.* See "<fmt:setLocale>" on page 496 for more information about the <fmt:setLocale> action, which is the only JSTL action that directly sets the FMT_LOCALE configuration setting.

You can also set the FMT_LOCALE configuration setting with a context initialization parameter or in a business component. See "Configuration Settings" on page 230 for more information on how to do that.

FMT_FALLBACK_LOCALE

The FMT_FALLBACK_LOCALE configuration setting is listed in Table 11.15.

Table 11.15   FMT_FALLBACK_LOCALE

Config Constant	FMT_FALLBACK_LOCALE
Name	javax.servlet.jsp.jstl.fmt.fallbackLocale

Table 11.15   FMT_FALLBACK_LOCALE *(cont.)*

Type	`java.lang.String` or `java.util.Locale`
Set by	Deployment Descriptor, `Config` class
Used by	<fmt:bundle>, <fmt:setBundle>, <fmt:message>, <fmt:formatNumber>, <fmt:parseNumber>, <fmt:formatDate>, <fmt:parseDate>

In the quest for a resource bundle or a formatting locale, JSTL I18N and formatting actions will resort to the locale stored in the FMT_FALLBACK_LOCALE configuration setting if the user's preferred locales do not yield a resource bundle.

FMT_LOCALIZATION_CONTEXT

The FMT_LOCALIZATION_CONTEXT configuration setting is listed in Table 11.16.

Table 11.16   FMT_LOCALIZATION_CONTEXT

Config Constant	FMT_LOCALIZATION_CONTEXT
Name	`javax.servlet.jsp.jstl.fmt.localizationContext`
Type	`java.lang.String` or `javax.servlet.jsp.jstl.fmt.LocalizationContext`
Set by	<fmt:setBundle>, Deployment Descriptor, `Config` class
Used by	<fmt:message>, <fmt:formatNumber>, <fmt:parseNumber>, <fmt:formatDate>, <fmt:parseDate>

<fmt:message> actions retrieve localized messages from a resource bundle. That resource bundle is stored in a read-only object known as a localization context, which also keeps track of the locale that yielded the resource bundle. The localization context's resource bundle is used by <fmt:message> and its locale is used by JSTL formatting actions.

When a <fmt:message> action searches for a resource bundle, it turns to the FMT_LOCALIZATION_CONTEXT configuration setting if you don't specify the <fmt:message> bundle attribute and if the <fmt:message> action doesn't reside in the body of a <fmt:bundle> action. <fmt:setBundle> is the only JSTL action that sets the FMT_LOCALIZATION_CONTEXT configuration setting. You can temporarily override that configuration setting with <fmt:bundle>, which creates a localization context of its own. (<fmt:bundle> does not set the FMT_LOCALIZATION_CONTEXT configuration setting.)

The value of the FMT_LOCALIZATION_CONTEXT configuration setting can be a string representing a resource bundle base name, or it can be an instance of javax.servlet.jsp.jstl.fmt.LocalizationContext.

See "Localization Context Lookup" on page 268 for more information about <fmt:setBundle> and the FMT_LOCALIZATION_CONTEXT configuration setting.

JSTL Internationalization Actions

<fmt:setLocale> Configures a locale for <fmt:message> and formatting actions

Syntax:[14]

```
<fmt:setLocale value [scope] [variant]/>
```

Description:

The <fmt:setLocale> action sets the FMT_LOCALE configuration setting, which is used by I18N and formatting actions to locate resource bundles and formatting locales. You specify the locale by setting the required value attribute, with a string or an instance of java.util.Locale.

Attributes:

Attribute[a]	Type	Description
value	String or java.util.Locale	A value that specifies a locale. That value can be a Locale object or a string consisting of a two-letter language code and an optional two-letter country code. The language and country codes can be separated by either a hyphen or an underscore.
variant	String	A string representing a vendor- or browser-specific variant, such as WIN for Windows or MAC for Macintosh.
scope	String	The scope of the scoped variable whose name is specified by the value attribute; default is page scope.

a.   static I *dynamic*

---

14. Items in brackets are optional.

Constraints and Error Handling:

- If you specify `null` or an empty string for the `value` attribute, the associated <fmt:setLocale> action will store the default locale in the `javax.servlet.jsp.jstl.fmt.locale` configuration variable.

- If you specify an invalid `value` attribute, <fmt:setLocale> will throw an `IllegalArgumentException`.

In a Nutshell:

The <fmt:setLocale> action sets a locale for any action that establishes a localization context and *disables browser-based locale settings for those actions*. Place this action at the beginning of a JSP page, before any action that establishes a localization context.

You specify a locale with the `value` attribute, which can be a string or an instance of `java.util.Locale`. That string represents a language and, optionally, a country. The language and country are separated by a hyphen or an underscore; for example, you can specify `value='es'` for Spanish or either `value='es-MX'` or `value='es_MX'` for Mexican Spanish.

If a locale is stored in the FMT_LOCALE configuration variable, JSTL uses that locale for formatting actions and also to locate a resource bundle for <fmt:message> actions. The <fmt:setLocale> action, given a valid `value` attribute, stores a locale in that configuration variable, like this:

```
<fmt:setLocale value='en-US' scope='session'/>
```

Optionally, you can set the value of the FMT_LOCALE configuration setting in a business component, such as a servlet, life-cycle listener, custom action, or bean; for example, a custom action could set the locale for session scope like this:

```
import javax.servlet.jsp.jstl.core.Config;
...
Config.set(pageContext, Config.FMT_LOCALE,
        new java.util.Locale("en-US"),
        PageContext.SESSION_SCOPE);
...
```

The preceding code fragment, which uses the `Config` class to set the FMT_LOCALE configuration setting, is functionally equivalent to the <fmt:setLocale> action used above. You can also set a locale for your application by specifying a context initialization parameter in your deployment descriptor (`WEB-INF/web.xml`) for the FMT_LOCALE configuration setting like this:

```
<web-app>
  ...
  <context-param>
    <param-name>
      javax.servlet.jsp.jstl.fmt.locale
    </param-name>

    <param-value>
      en-US
    </param-value>
  </context-param>
  ...
</web-app>
```

<fmt:setBundle>	Creates a localization context for <fmt:message> and JSTL formatting actions

Syntax:[15]

<fmt:setBundle basename [var] [scope]/>

Description:

The <fmt:setBundle> action does three things:

1. Searches for a resource bundle, using the basename attribute.

2. Stores that resource bundle, along with the locale used to locate it, in a localization context.

3. Stores that localization context in the FMT_LOCALIZATION_CONTEXT configuration setting, or if you specify the var attribute, stores the localization context in a scoped variable whose name is specified by the var attribute.

Subsequently, <fmt:message> actions and formatting actions access the localization context: <fmt:message> uses its resource bundle to localize messages, whereas formatting actions use its locale to format and parse numbers, currencies, percents, and dates.

---

15. Items in brackets are optional.

Attributes:

Attribute[a]	Type	Description
basename	String	The base name of a resource bundle; for example if a resource bundle is specified by the properties file `com/acme/resources/Resources_fr.properties`, then the base name is `com.acme.resources.Resources`.
var	String	The name of a scoped variable that references a localization context that contains a reference to the resource bundle loaded by the <fmt:setBundle> action.
scope	String	The scope of the variable whose name is specified by the `var` attribute, or if `var` is not specified, the scope of the `FMT_LOCALIATION_CONTEXT` configuration setting. The default scope is page.

a.   static | *dynamic*

Constraints and Error Handling:

- If the `basename` attribute is `null` or empty or <fmt:setBundle> cannot find a resource bundle, <fmt:setBundle> creates an empty localization context, meaning a localization context with a `null` resource bundle and locale.

In a Nutshell:

You use the <fmt:setBundle> action to specify a resource bundle that <fmt:message> actions use to localize their messages. You specify a resource bundle base name with the `basename` attribute, like this:

```
<fmt:setBundle basename='messages' scope='request'/>
```

The <fmt:setBundle> action in the preceding line of code locates a resource bundle from information in the action's mandatory `basename` attribute (`messages`) and the user's preferred locale and stores that resource bundle in the `FMT_LOCALIZATION_CONTEXT` configuration setting for request scope. Subsequently, in the absence of other <fmt:setBundle> actions, <fmt:message> actions in the same request will use the `messages` resource bundle to localize their messages, as long as those <fmt:message> actions do not specify their `bundle` attribute.

You can also use <fmt:setBundle> to store a localization context in a scoped variable by specifying the `var` and `scope` attributes, like this:

```
<fmt:setBundle basename='messages' var='msgs' scope='request'/>
```

The <fmt:setBundle> action in the preceding line of code, like the first code fragment in this section, locates a resource bundle using the value of the action's mandatory basename attribute (messages) and stores that resource bundle in a localization context. The difference between the two uses of <fmt:setBundle> is that the preceding line of code stores the localization context in a scoped variable whose name is msgs. That scoped variable is stored in request scope. Subsequently, <fmt:message> actions in the same request can access that localization context like this:

```
<fmt:message key='login.page.title' bundle='${msgs}'/>
```

The <fmt:message> action in the preceding code fragment accesses the msgs localization context by specifying that scoped variable for the <fmt:message> bundle attribute.

If you specify the var attribute, but not the scope attribute, the localization context created by <fmt:setBundle> is stored in page scope.

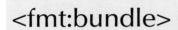	Creates a localization context for <fmt:message> actions and JSTL formatting actions that reside in the body of the action

Syntax:[16]

```
<fmt:bundle basename [prefix]>
    body content, presumably with other I18N and formatting actions that use the
    bundle specified with the mandatory basename attribute
</fmt:bundle>
```

Description:

The <fmt:bundle> action does three things:

1. Searches for a resource bundle, using the basename attribute
2. Stores that resource bundle in a localization context
3. Stores that localization context in the <fmt:bundle> action's tag handler

Subsequently, only <fmt:message> actions and formatting actions *within the body of the <fmt:bundle> action* will use the localization context created by the <fmt:bundle> action.

---

16. Items in brackets are optional.

Attributes:

Attribute[a]	Type	Description
basename	String	The base name of a resource bundle; for example if a resource bundle is specified by the properties file `com/acme/resources/Resources_fr.properties`, then the base name is `com.acme.resources.Resources`.
prefix	String	A prefix that's prepended to message keys specified by `<fmt:message>` actions that reside in the body of the `<fmt:bundle>` action that specified the `prefix` attribute.

    a.   static | *dynamic*

Constraints and Error Handling:

• If the `basename` attribute is `null` or empty or `<fmt:bundle>` cannot find a resource bundle, `<fmt:bundle>` creates an empty localization context.

In a Nutshell:

The `<fmt:bundle>` action finds a resource bundle specified by the `basename` attribute and stores that resource bundle in a localization context. The localization context is used by `<fmt:message>` actions and formatting actions only within the body of the `<fmt:bundle>` action; for example,

```
<fmt:bundle basename='app'>
   <fmt:message key='login.title'/>
   <fmt:message key='login.welcome'/>
   <fmt:formatNumber value='10000' type='currency'/>
</fmt:bundle>
```

In the preceding code fragment, both the `<fmt:message>` actions and the `<fmt:formatNumber>` action use the localization context created by their enclosing `<fmt:bundle>` action. The `<fmt:message>` actions look up localized messages in the localization context's resource bundle, whereas the `<fmt:formatNumber>` action uses the localization context's locale as its formatting locale.

You can also specify a *prefix* for `<fmt:bundle>` actions that have a body. Prefixes are used for long keys; for example, the code fragment below specifies a prefix:

```
<fmt:bundle basename='app' prefix='com.Acme.application.'>
   <fmt:message key='login.title'/>
   <fmt:message key='login.welcome'/>
</fmt:bundle>
```

Prefixes are prepended to message keys for <fmt:message> actions in the body of the <fmt:bundle> action, so the preceding code fragment is equivalent to the code fragment listed below:

```
<fmt:bundle basename='app'>
   <fmt:message key='com.Acme.application.login.title'/>
   <fmt:message key='com.Acme.application.login.welcome'/>
</fmt:bundle>
```

<fmt:message	Retrieves a localized message from a resource bundle

Syntax:[17]

Syntax #1: Without a body

```
<fmt:message key [bundle] [var] [scope]/>
```

Syntax #2: With a body that specifies message parameters

```
<fmt:message key [bundle] [var] [scope]>
    <fmt:param> actions
</fmt:message>
```

Syntax #3: With a body that specifies a message key and, optionally, message parameters

```
<fmt:message [bundle] [var] [scope]>
    key
    optional <fmt:param> actions
</fmt:message>
```

Description:

The <fmt:message> action extracts a localized message from a resource bundle and sends it to the current `JspWriter` (which in most cases displays the message in the browser) or stores it in a scoped variable specified with the `var` attribute, and optionally, the `scope` attribute.

---

17. Items in brackets are optional.

Attributes:

Attribute[a]	Type	Description
key	String	The message key used by <fmt:message> to extract localized messages from a resource bundle.
bundle	Localization-Context	<fmt:message> actions extract localized messages from a resource bundle stored in an instance of `Localization-Context`.
var	String	The name of a scoped variable that references a localized message.
scope	String	The scope of the scoped variable whose name is specified by the `var` attribute; default is page scope.

   a.   static | *dynamic*

Constraints and Error Handling:

- If you specify the `scope` attribute, you must also specify the `var` attribute.

- If you specify a `null` or empty key, the <fmt:message> action will generate an error message of the form ??????.

- If the <fmt:message> action cannot locate a valid localization context, an error message of the form ???<key>??? is generated, where <key> represents the value of the key attribute.

In a Nutshell:

You can specify message keys with the key attribute, like this—

```
<fmt:message key='messages.loginPage.title'/>
```

—or within the body of <fmt:message> actions, like this:

```
<fmt:message>
   messages.loginPage.title
</fmt:message>
```

   The resource bundle used by the <fmt:message> actions in the two preceding code fragments is the resource bundle stored in the localization context that is stored in the `FMT_LOCALIZATION_CONTEXT` configuration setting (See "<fmt:setBundle>" on page 498 for more information about that configuration setting). You can also specify a localization context explicitly, with the `bundle` attribute, like this:

```
<fmt:message key='msgs.greeting' bundle='${aLocalizationContext}'/>
```

The <fmt:message> action in the preceding code fragment specifies a localization context stored in a scoped variable named `aLocalizationContext`. That localization context can be created with <fmt:setBundle> or a business component, such as a servlet, life-cycle listener, or custom action.

If a <fmt:message> action resides in the body of a <fmt:bundle> action, that <fmt:message> action extracts localized messages from the resource bundle stored in the localization context established by its enclosing <fmt:bundle> action. If the enclosing <fmt:bundle> action specifies a `prefix` attribute, enclosed <fmt:message> actions prepend that prefix to their message keys. See "<fmt:bundle>" on page 500 for more information about the <fmt:bundle> action.

<fmt:message> actions can also display compound messages. A compound message is a message that contains parameters that are specified at runtime. Those parameters are specified with <fmt:param>, like this:

```
<jsp:useBean id='now' class='java.util.Date'/>

<fmt:message key='footer.messages.todaysDate'>
   <fmt:param value='${now}'/>
</fmt:message>
```

The preceding code fragment specifies a date as a parameter to the compound message corresponding to `footer.messages.todaysDate`. That compound message is specified like this in a properties file:

```
footer.messages.todaysDate=Today is: {0}
```

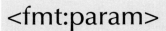 **<fmt:param>**   Supplies a parameter for an enclosing <fmt:message>

Syntax:

Syntax #1: Without a body

```
<fmt:param value/>
```

Syntax #2: With a body

```
<fmt:param>
    value
</fmt:param>
```

Description:

The <fmt:param> action specifies a parameter for an enclosing <fmt:message> action.

Attributes:

Attribute[a]	Type	Description
value	Object	This attribute specifies a parameter for an enclosing <fmt:message> action. You can also specify parameters in the body of <fmt:param> actions.

> a.   static | *dynamic*

Constraints and Error Handling:

- <fmt:param> actions must reside in the body of a <fmt:message> action.

In a Nutshell:

Each <fmt:param> action specifies a single parameter for a compound message. That compound message is retrieved from a resource bundle by an enclosing <fmt:message> action. The first <fmt:param> action contained in the body of a <fmt:message> action specifies the first parameter for that compound message, the second <fmt:param> action specifies the second parameter, and so on; for example, for this compound message in a resource bundle—

```
message=There are {0} parameters in this message: the second is \
{1} and the third is {2}.
```

— if you specify parameters like this—

```
<fmt:message key='message'>
   <fmt:param value='THREE'/>
   <fmt:param value='THE SECOND PARAMETER'/>
   <fmt:param value='THE THIRD PARAMETER'/>
</fmt:message>
```

—then the <fmt:message> action in the preceding code fragment will generate the following text: There are THREE parameters in this message: the second is THE SECOND PARAMETER and the third is THE THIRD PARAMETER.

You do not have to specify a <fmt:param> action for every parameter in a compound message, but it is recommended that you do so. If you do not specify a <fmt:param> action for every parameter, no substitution is made for unspecified parameters; for example, if you specify only two parameters for the compound message in the code fragment above, like this—

```
<fmt:message key='message'>
   <fmt:param value='TWO'/>
   <fmt:param value='THE SECOND PARAMETER'/>
</fmt:message>
```

—then the <fmt:message> action in the preceding code fragment will generate the following text: There are TWO parameters in this message: the second is THE SECOND PARAMETER and the third is {2}.

JSP 1.2 does not support JSTL Expression Language (EL) expressions, so you cannot specify an EL expression in the body of a <fmt:param> action (or any action, for that matter). For example, that means you can do this:

```
<fmt:param value='${param.amount}'/>
```

but you cannot do this:

```
<fmt:param>
    ${param.amount}
</fmt:param>
```

Instead, you must do this:

```
<fmt:param>
    <c:out value='${param.amount}'/>
</fmt:param>
```

JSP 2.0 will support the JSTL Expression Language, which means you will be able to specify EL expressions directly within the body of a <fmt:param> action.

<fmt:requestEncoding> Sets the request's character encoding

Syntax:[18]

```
<fmt:requestEncoding [value]/>
```

18. Items in brackets are optional.

Description:

The <fmt:requestEncoding> action sets an HTTP request's character encoding.

Attributes:

Attribute[a]	Type	Description
value	String	The character encoding that the servlet container uses to decode request parameters.

a. static I *dynamic*

In a Nutshell:

Imagine that you have two JSP pages: one that contains an HTML form, which we'll call the *form page*, and another that is specified as the form's action, which we'll call the *action page*. Now imagine that your *form page* is localized for Chinese, and that you set the response charset for that page to Mainland Chinese (charset=GB2312).

When the form is submitted, the *action page* is loaded and accesses the request parameters to find out what the user entered in the form. Will those request parameters be decoded properly? The answer for most browsers is no, because most browsers do not specify the Content-Type request header and therefore the application cannot determine the request encoding. To force your browser to properly decode those request parameters, you must specify the *action page's* request encoding so that it matches the *form page's* response encoding. That's exactly what <fmt:requestEncoding> does. All you have to do is use the <fmt:requestEncoding> action at the top of your *action page* before you access request parameters.

There are two ways to use the <fmt:requestEncoding> action. If you know the response encoding of the *form page*, you can specify that charset with the <fmt:requestEncoding> action's value attribute. If you don't know the response encoding of the *form page*, don't specify the value attribute and the <fmt:requestEncoding> action will figure out what to do.

At this point you may wonder how the <fmt:requestEncoding> action knows the charset to use if you don't specify it with the value attribute. The answer is that <fmt:requestEncoding> retrieves that charset from a session attribute. That attribute was created by the JSTL internationalization actions in the *form page*; therefore, for <fmt:requestEncoding> to work properly, *you must use JSTL internationalization actions in the form page if you don't specify the <fmt:requestEncoding> action's* value *attribute*.

Exposed Classes

JSTL exposes two classes for internationalization:

- `javax.servlet.jsp.jstl.fmt.LocaleSupport`

- `javax.servlet.jsp.jstl.fmt.LocalizationContext`

The `LocaleSupport` class lets you extract localized messages from resource bundles; `LocalizationContext` objects store a resource bundle and the locale used to locate that resource bundle.

LocaleSupport
A class that lets you retrieve localized messages from a resource bundle

Definition:

```
class LocaleSupport {
    public static String getLocalizedMessage(PageContext, String key)
    public static String getLocalizedMessage(PageContext, String key,
                                String basename)
    public static String getLocalizedMessage(PageContext, String key,
                                Object[] args)
    public static String getLocalizedMessage(PageContext, String key,
                                Object[] args, String basename)
}
```

Description:

The four methods of the `LocaleSupport` class let you extract localized messages from resource bundles, just like <fmt:message> actions do. You can use those methods in a custom action; for example see "I18N Custom Actions" on page 293 for a discussion of a custom action that uses the `LocaleSupport` class to localize error messages.

A class that stores a resource bundle and a locale	LocalizationContext

Definition:

```
class LocalizationContext {
    public LocalizationContext()
    public LocalizationContext(ResourceBundle bundle, Locale locale)
    public LocalizationContext(ResourceBundle bundle)

    public Locale getLocale()
    public ResourceBundle getResourceBundle()
}
```

Description:

In all likelihood, you will never have to deal with an instance of LocalizationContext directly, although you may want to create one in a business component, such as a servlet, servlet filter, or life-cycle listener.

The LocalizationContext class provides three constructors. The no-argument constructor creates an empty LocalizationContext instance with a null resource bundle and a null locale. JSTL uses that constructor when <fmt:bundle> or <fmt:setBundle> cannot find a resource bundle.

You can also create a localization context with a resource bundle and a locale. The constructor that takes those two arguments simply assigns the resource bundle and locale to the localization context's member variables. The constructor that just takes a resource bundle stores the resource bundle and its locale in the localization context.

11.7 Formatting Actions

The JSTL formatting actions parse and format numbers, currencies, percents, and dates. Four configuration settings support these actions.

Overview of the JSTL Formatting Actions

Table 11.17 lists the JSTL formatting actions.

Table 11.17   Formatting Actions

Action	Description
<fmt:formatNumber>	Formats a numeric value as a number, currency, or percent in a locale-dependent manner.
<fmt:parseNumber>	Parses a string representation of a number, currency, or percent in a locale-dependent manner.
<fmt:formatDate>	Formats a date, time, or both in a locale-dependent manner.
<fmt:parseDate>	Parses the string representation of a date, time, or both in a locale-dependent manner.
<fmt:timeZone>	Sets a time zone used by formatting actions in the body of the <fmt:timeZone> action.
<fmt:setTimeZone>	Sets the FMT_TIME_ZONE configuration setting, which stores a time zone used to parse and format dates.

JSTL Formatting Configuration Settings

The following configuration settings support the JSTL formatting actions:

- FMT_TIME_ZONE
- FMT_LOCALE
- FMT_FALLBACK_LOCALE
- FMT_LOCALIZATION_CONTEXT

The FMT_TIME_ZONE configuration setting is listed in Table 11.18.

Table 11.18   FMT_TIME_ZONE

Config Constant	FMT_TIME_ZONE
Variable Name	javax.servlet.jsp.jstl.fmt.timeZone
Type	java.lang.String or java.util.TimeZone
Set by	<fmt:setTimeZone>, Deployment Descriptor, Config class
Used by	<fmt:formatDate>, <fmt:parseDate>

The <fmt:formatDate> and <fmt:parseDate> actions require a time zone to format and parse times, respectively. If you do not specify the timeZone attribute for those actions and those actions do not reside in a <fmt:timeZone> action, they will use the time zone stored in the FMT_TIME_ZONE configuration setting. That configuration setting can be set in a number of different ways; one way to set it is with the <fmt:setTimeZone> action. You can also set the FMT_TIME_ZONE configuration setting with a context initialization parameter or in a business component. See "Configuration Settings" on page 230 for more information on how to do that.

The <fmt:formatNumber>, <fmt:parseNumber>, <fmt:formatDate>, and <fmt:parseDate> actions use the locale stored in the FMT_LOCALIZATION_CONTEXT configuration setting if they do not reside in a <fmt:bundle> action and the parseLocale attribute was not specified (for <fmt:parseNumber> and <fmt:parseDate>).

The locale stored in the FMT_LOCALE configuration setting is used by the <fmt:formatNumber>, <fmt:parseNumber>, <fmt:formatDate>, and <fmt:parseDate> actions when those actions do not reside in a <fmt:bundle> action and the localization context in the FMT_LOCALIZATION_CONTEXT configuration setting has not been set or does not have a locale. See "<fmt:bundle>" on page 500 for more information about the <fmt:bundle> action, and see "JSTL Internationalization Configuration Settings" on page 494 for more information about the FMT_LOCALE and FMT_LOCALIZATION_CONTEXT configuration settings.

The <fmt:formatNumber>, <fmt:parseNumber>, <fmt:formatDate>, and <fmt:parseDate> actions use the locale stored in the FMT_FALLBACK_LOCALE configuration setting as a last resort to locate a formatting locale. See "JSTL Internationalization Configuration Settings" on page 494 for more information about the FMT_FALLBACK_LOCALE configuration setting, and see "Formatting Locale Lookup" on page 354 for more information about how formatting actions look up a locale.

JSTL Formatting Actions

Formats a numeric value as a number, currency, or percent in a locale-dependent manner	<fmt:formatNumber>

Syntax:[19]

Syntax #1: Without a body

---

19. Items in brackets are optional.

```
<fmt:formatNumber value [type] [pattern] [currencyCode]
    [currencySymbol] [groupingUsed] [minIntegerDigits]
    [maxIntegerDigits] [minFractionDigits] [maxFractionDigits]
    [var] [scope]/>
```

Syntax #2: With a body that specifies a numeric value to format

```
<fmt:formatNumber [type] [pattern] [currencyCode]
    [currencySymbol] [groupingUsed] [minIntegerDigits]
    [maxIntegerDigits] [minFractionDigits] [maxFractionDigits]
    [var] [scope]>
    value
</fmt:formatNumber>
```

Description:

The <fmt:formatNumber> action formats a numeric value in a locale-dependent manner as a number, currency, or percent. You can specify that numeric value with the `value` attribute or in the body of the <fmt:formatNumber> action. By default, <fmt:formatNumber> sends its output to the current `JspWriter`, but if you specify the `var` attribute, and optionally, the `scope` attribute, <fmt:formatNumber> stores its output in a scoped variable instead.

Attributes:

Attribute[a]	Type	Description
value	String or Number[b]	The numeric value formatted by <fmt:formatNumber>.
type	String	A string that specifies how the numeric value is formatted. Valid values are `number`, `currency`, or `percent`; the default is `number`.
pattern	String	A custom formatting pattern. This attribute takes precedence over the `type` attribute.
currencyCode	String	A string that indirectly specifies a currency symbol. Currency codes are defined by ISO 4217. This attribute is applied only if you are using JDK 1.4 or later and the `type` attribute is `currency`. This attribute takes precedence over the `currencySymbol` attribute if you are using JDK1.4 or a later version of the JDK.
currencySymbol	String	A string that directly specifies a currency symbol. This attribute is applied only when the `type` attribute is `currency`. This attribute takes precedence over the `currencyCode` attribute if you are using JDK1.3 or an earlier version of the JDK.

Attribute[a]	Type	Description
groupingUsed	String	A string that specifies whether the grouping separator is used to separate thousands (or ten thousands for some locales); the default is `true`.
minIntegerDigits	String	The minimum number of integer digits in the formatted output.
maxIntegerDigits	String	The maximum number of integer digits in the formatted output.
minFractionDigits	String	The minimum number of fraction digits in the formatted output.
maxFractionDigits	String	The maximum number of fraction digits in the formatted output.
var	String	The name of a scoped variable. If you specify this attribute, <fmt:formatNumber> stores its output in a scoped variable whose name is specified with this attribute; otherwise, <fmt:formatNumber> sends the formatted output to the current `JspWriter`.
scope	String	The scope of the scoped variable whose name is specified by the `var` attribute; default is page scope.

a. static | *dynamic*
b. The `Number` class is from the `java.lang` package.

Constraints and Error Handling:

- If you specify the `scope` attribute, you must also specify the `var` attribute.
- You must specify a valid ISO 4217 currency code for the `currencyCode` attribute.
- If you specify a string for the `value` attribute and it cannot be parsed into a valid number, <fmt:formatNumber> will throw a `JspException`.
- If you specify something other than `number`, `currency`, or `percent` for the `type` attribute, <fmt:formatNumber> will throw a `JspException`.

In a Nutshell:

The <fmt:formatNumber> action formats numbers, currencies, and percents differently for different locales; for example:

```
<fmt:setLocale value='en-US'/>
English: <fmt:formatNumber value='1255.23'/>
```

```
<fmt:setLocale value='de-DE'/>
German: <fmt:formatNumber value='1255.23'/>
```

In the preceding code fragment, <fmt:formatNumber> formats the string "1255.23" as 1,255.23 for English and 1.255,23 for German.

Most of the time, the value that you specify for <fmt:formatNumber> will probably be a variable that you read from a data store, such as a database or flat file, so <fmt:formatNumber> lets you specify its value as a scoped variable; for example:

```
<%-- Typically, the numericValue scoped variable would be calcu-
lated or created from a value stored in a data store; here, <c:set>
is used in the interest of simplicity --%>

<c:set var='numericValue' value='234682.155'/>
<fmt:formatNumber value='${numericValue}'/>
```

Besides specifying a value with the value attribute, you can also specify a value in the body of the <fmt:formatNumber> action. That feature is useful for computed values, such as those produced by a custom action; for example:

```
<fmt:formatNumber>
   <acme:getSomeNumericValue/>
</fmt:formatNumber>
```

You can specify whether <fmt:formatNumber> formats its value as a number, currency, or percent with the type attribute, like this:

```
<fmt:formatNumber value='1255.23'/>
<fmt:formatNumber value='1255.23' type='currency'/>
<fmt:formatNumber value='.2348' type='percent'/>
```

For the U.S. English locale, the preceding code fragment will produce the following output: 1,255.23 $1,255.23 23%. If you don't specify the type attribute, as is the case for the first line of code in the preceding code fragment, that attribute defaults to number. Notice that <fmt:formatNumber> formats percents by multiplying the value by 100 and adding a locale-dependent percent symbol.

Most of the <fmt:formatNumber> attributes are used to control exactly how numbers, currencies, and percents are formatted; for example:

```
<fmt:formatNumber value='1255.23'
      minIntegerDigits='5'
    minFractionDigits='5'
         groupingUsed='false'/>
```

For the U.S. English locale, the preceding code fragment formats the specified value like this: 01255.23000.

With the currencySymbol attribute, you can *directly* specify the currency symbol that <fmt:formatNumber> uses to format currencies, like this:

Constraints and Error Handling:

- If you specify the scope attribute, you must also specify the var attribute.
- If you specify a value attribute that is null or an empty string and you specify the var attribute, the scoped variable identified by the var attribute will be removed.
- If you specify the parseLocale attribute as null or as an empty string, that attribute will be ignored.
- If you specify the pattern attribute as null or as an empty string, that attribute will be ignored.
- If an exception occurs during parsing, it will be caught by the action and rethrown as a JspException. The message of that JspException will include the value that was to be parsed and the original exception will be provided as the root cause.
- If you do not specify the parseLocale attribute and <fmt:parseNumber> cannot locate a suitable locale, <fmt:parseNumber> will throw a JspException. That exception will contain the value that was to be parsed.

In a Nutshell:

Sometimes you need to manipulate numeric values that are already formatted as numbers, currencies, or percents. For those types of use cases, you can use <fmt:parseNumber> to parse the original formatted value. You can then adjust the numeric value that <fmt:parseNumber> produces and subsequently use <fmt:formatNumber> to reformat the adjusted numeric value. For example, the following code fragment uses <fmt:parseNumber> in the manner described above:

```
<c:set value='$1,255.23' var='formattedCurrency'/>


<fmt:parseNumber value='${formattedCurrency}'
                 type='currency'
          parseLocale='en-US'
                  var='parsedCurrency'/>

<c:set value='${parsedCurrency + 250}' var='updatedAmount'/>

<fmt:setLocale value='en-US'/>
<fmt:formatNumber value='${updatedAmount}' type='currency'/>
```

The preceding code fragment uses the <c:set> action to create a scoped variable that references a formatted currency, but that formatted currency could come from anywhere, perhaps from a Web Service. The <fmt:parseNumber> action parses that formatted currency, using the U.S. English locale and stores the resulting numeric value in a scoped variable named parsedCurrency. Subsequently, the <c:set> action adds 250 to that parsed amount and stores the resulting value in a scoped variable named updatedAmount. Finally, the <fmt:formatNumber> action reformats the updated amount as U.S. currency. The output of the preceding code fragment is $1505.23.

The <fmt:parseNumber> action can be rather picky about the value it parses—if its value does not match the attributes that you specify, <fmt:parseNumber> will throw an exception. In the preceding code fragment, if the parsed currency is not formatted correctly, <fmt:parseNumber> throws an exception; for example, if you specify that formatted currency as 1,255.23 instead of $1,255.23, <fmt:parseNumber> will throw an exception because it cannot parse the specified value as U.S. currency. If <fmt:parseNumber> throws an exception, check the formatting of the value specified for <fmt:parseNumber>.

Like <fmt:formatNumber>, <fmt:parseNumber> has a type attribute that you can set to number, currency, or percent. Unlike <fmt:formatNumber>, <fmt:parseNumber> has a parseLocale attribute that you can use to specify the locale that <fmt:parseNumber> uses to parse its value. The parseLocale attribute was used in the preceding code fragment.

The <fmt:parseNumber> action also has an integerOnly attribute. If you set that attribute to true, <fmt:parseNumber> will only parse the integer portion of its numeric value. You can also specify custom parsing patterns with the pattern attribute, just like you can specify custom formatting patterns for <fmt:formatNumber>.

<fmt:formatDate>	Formats a date, time, or both, in a locale-dependent manner

Syntax:[21]

```
<fmt:formatDate value [type] [dateStyle] [timeStyle]
    [pattern] [timeZone] [var] [scope]/>
```

---

21. Items in brackets are optional.

Description:

The <fmt:formatDate> action formats an instance of java.util.Date in a locale-dependent manner. You specify that date with the value attribute. By default, <fmt:formatDate> sends its output to the current JspWriter, but if you specify the var attribute, <fmt:formatDate> stores its output in a scoped variable instead.

Attributes:

Attribute[a]	Type	Description
value	java.util.Date	A date that <fmt:formatDate> formats.
type	String	A string that specifies how the date is formatted. Valid values are date, time, or both; the default is date.
dateStyle	String	A string that specifies how the date portion of the value attribute will be parsed. Valid values are default, short, medium, long, and full; the default is default (which is the same as medium). This attribute is only applied if the type attribute is missing or set to date or both.
timeStyle	String	A string that specifies how the time portion of the value attribute will be formatted. Valid values are default, short, medium, long, and full; the default is default (which is the same as medium). This attribute is only applied if the type attribute is set to time or both.
pattern	String	A custom formatting pattern. This attribute takes precedence over the type, dateStyle, and timeStyle attributes.
timeZone	String or java.util.TimeZone	A time zone that <fmt:formatDate> uses to format the value attribute.
var	String	The name of a scoped variable. If you specify this attribute, <fmt:formatDate> stores the formatted output in a scoped variable whose name is specified with this attribute; otherwise, <fmt:formatDate> sends the formatted output to the current JspWriter.
scope	String	The scope of the scoped variable whose name is specified by the var attribute; default is page scope.

a. static | *dynamic*

Constraints and Error Handling:

- If you specify the `scope` attribute, you must also specify the `var` attribute.

- If you specify a `value` attribute that is `null` and you specify the `var` attribute, the scoped variable identified by the `var` attribute will be removed.

- If you specify the `timeZone` attribute as `null` or as an empty string, it will be ignored.

- If <fmt:formatDate> cannot determine a formatting locale, it formats the ouput with the `toString` method.

In a Nutshell:

The <fmt:formatDate> action formats an instance of `java.util.Date` and outputs a string representation of that formatted date. You can create a `Date` instance with <jsp:useBean>, like this:

```
<jsp:useBean id='now' class='java.util.Date'/>
<fmt:formatDate value='${now}'/>
```

In the preceding code fragment, <jsp:useBean> creates an instance of `java.util.Date`, representing the current date and time, which is subsequently formatted by <fmt:formatDate>. You can also create a `Date` instance with the <fmt:parseDate> action; see "<fmt:parseDate>" on page 522.

The <fmt:formatDate> action will format the same date differently for different locales; for example, if the current date is the 1st of June 1998, the preceding code fragment will output `Jun  1,   1998` for U.S English; for France French, the preceding code fragment will output `1 juin 1998`.

All instances of `java.util.Date` contain date and time information. The <fmt:formatDate> action lets you format the date portion, the time portion, or both the date and time with the <fmt:formatDate> `type` attribute; for example:

```
<jsp:useBean id='now' class='java.util.Date'/>

<fmt:formatDate value='${now}'/>
<fmt:formatDate value='${now}' type='time'/>
<fmt:formatDate value='${now}' type='both'/>
```

If you don't specify the `type` attribute, it defaults to `date`. In the preceding code fragment, if the locale is U.S. English and the current time and date is 3:55:41 P.M. on the 15th of May 2002, the first <fmt:formatDate> action will format that date like this: May 15, 2002. The second <fmt:formatDate> action in the preceding code fragment formats only the time portion of the date and produces this output: 3:55:41 PM. The last <fmt:formatDate> action formats both the date and time, like this: May 15, 2002 3:55:41 PM.

The <fmt:formatDate> dateStyle and timeStyle attributes let you specify a locale-dependent predefined formatting style for dates and times, respectively; for example:

```
<jsp:useBean id='now' class='java.util.Date'/>
<fmt:formatDate value='${now}' type='time' timeStyle='short'/>
```

The preceding code fragment formats the current time in short format. If the current time is 4:05 in the afternoon, the output of the preceding code fragment for U.S. English will be 4:05 PM. Table 8.4 on page 334 illustrates the various styles for dates and times.

In addition to the predefined date and time styles, you can also specify a custom pattern with the <fmt:formatDate> pattern attribute, like this:

```
<jsp:useBean id='now' class='java.util.Date'/>
<fmt:formatDate value='${now}' pattern='MM/dd/yy, hh:mm'/>
```

For the U.S. English locale, on the 5th of May 2002 at 4:15 P.M., the preceding code fragment will produce this output: 05/15/02, 04:15. Table 8.5 on page 337 lists the valid characters that constitute a custom date and time pattern.

You can also specify a time zone with the <fmt:formatDate> timeZone attribute, and <fmt:formatDate> will format its date relative to that time zone; for example:

```
<jsp:useBean id='now' class='java.util.Date'/>
<fmt:formatDate value='${now}' type='time' timeStyle='short'/>
<fmt:formatDate value='${now}' type='time' timeStyle='short'
          timeZone='America/Los_Angeles'/>
```

If your server resides in the U.S. Eastern time zone and the current time is 5:00 in the afternoon, the first <fmt:formatDate> action in the preceding code fragment will output 5:00 PM for the U.S. English locale, whereas the second <fmt:formatDate>, which interprets the time relative to the U.S. Pacific time zone, will produce this output: 2:00 PM.

`<fmt:parseDate>`

Parses the string representation of a formatted date or time, or both, in a locale-dependent manner

Syntax:[22]

Syntax #1: Without a body

```
<fmt:parseDate value [type] [dateStyle] [timeStyle]
    [pattern] [timeZone] [parseLocale] [var] [scope]/>
```

Syntax #2: With a body that specifies a date string to parse

```
<fmt:parseDate [type] [dateStyle] [timeStyle]
    [pattern] [timeZone] [parseLocale] [var] [scope]>
    value
</fmt:parseDate>
```

Description:

The `<fmt:parseDate>` action is the inverse of `<fmt:formatDate>`: it parses a string representing a formatted date, time, or both, into its original, unformatted form. You can specify that string with the `value` attribute or in the body of the `<fmt:parseDate>` action. By default, `<fmt:parseDate>` sends its output to the current `JspWriter`, but if you specify the `var` attribute, `<fmt:parseDate>` stores its output in a scoped variable instead.

Attributes:

Attribute[a]	Type	Description
value	String	A string that `<fmt:parseDate>` parses as a date, time, or both.
type	String	A string that specifies how the `value` attribute is parsed. Valid values are `date`, `time`, or `both`; the default is `date`.

---

22. Items in brackets are optional.

Attribute[a]	Type	Description
dateStyle	String	A string that specifies how the date portion of the `value` attribute will be parsed. Valid values are `default`, `short`, `medium`, `long`, and `full`; the default is `default` (which is the same as `medium`). This attribute is applied only if the `type` attribute is missing or set to `date` or `both`.
timeStyle	String	A string that specifies how the time portion of the `value` attribute will be parsed. Valid values are `default`, `short`, `medium`, `long`, and `full`; the default is `default` (which is the same as `medium`). This attribute is applied only if the `type` attribute is set to `time` or `both`.
pattern	String	A string that specifies a custom parsing pattern. This attribute takes precedence over the `type`, `dateStyle`, and `timeStyle` attributes.
timeZone	String or java.util.TimeZone	Specifies a time zone that <fmt:parseDate> uses to parse the time portion of the `value` attribute.
parseLocale	String or java.util.Locale	Specifies a locale whose formatting styles and formatting symbols for dates and times are used to parse the `value` attribute.
var	String	The name of a scoped variable. If you specify this attribute, <fmt:parseDate> stores its output in a scoped variable whose name is specified with this attribute; otherwise, <fmt:parseDate> sends the parsed result to the current `JspWriter`.
scope	String	The scope of the scoped variable whose name is specified by the `var` attribute; default is page scope.

a. static | *dynamic*

Constraints and Error Handling:

- If you specify the `scope` attribute, you must also specify the `var` attribute.

- If you specify a `value` attribute that is `null` or an empty string and you specify the `var` attribute, the scoped variable identified by the `var` attribute will be removed.

- If you specify the `timeZone` attribute as `null` or as an empty string, it will be ignored.

- If you specify the `parseLocale` attribute as `null` or as an empty string, it will be ignored.

- If an exception occurs during parsing, it will be caught by the action and rethrown as a `JspException`. The message of that `JspException` will include the value that was to be parsed, and the original exception will be provided as the root cause.

- If you do not specify the `parseLocale` attribute and <fmt:parseDate> cannot locate a suitable locale, a `JspException` will be thrown. That exception will contain the value that was to be parsed.

In a Nutshell:

The <fmt:parseDate> action parses a string into an instance of `java.util.Date`. Because <fmt:formatDate> does not accept a string value for the `value` attribute—<fmt:formatDate> only formats instances of `java.util.Date`—<fmt:parseDate> is commonly used to parse a string to provide a `Date` instance for <fmt:formatDate>, like this:

```
<fmt:parseDate value='06/01/98'
               var='parsedDate'
          dateStyle='short'/>


<fmt:formatDate value='${parsedDate}'/>
```

In the preceding code fragment, <fmt:parseDate> parses the string `06/01/98` and creates a `java.util.Date` instance that it stores in a scoped variable named `parsedDate`. Subsequently, <fmt:formatDate> formats that `Date` instance. The output of the preceding code fragment for the U.S. English locale is `Jun 1, 1998`.

The following <fmt:parseDate> attributes let you specify how the string that <fmt:parseDate> parses is interpreted: `dateStyle`, `timeStyle`, and `parseLocale`. You must make sure that those attributes match the string that <fmt:parseDate> parses; for example, in the following code fragment <fmt:parseDate> will throw an exception:

```
<%-- This code fragment throws an exception --%>
<fmt:parseDate value='06/01/98'
          dateStyle='long'/>
```

In the preceding code fragment, the <fmt:parseDate> `dateStyle` attribute is set to `long`, but the string that <fmt:parseDate> tries to parse is formatted with the *short* format for dates. Because of that mismatch, <fmt:parseDate> will throw an exception.

You must also make sure that the parse locale used by <fmt:parseDate> matches the value that <fmt:parseDate> parses; for example, the following code fragment also throws an exception:

```
<%-- This code fragment throws an exception also --%>
<fmt:parseDate value='06/20/98'
          dateStyle='short'
          parseLocale='fr-FR'/>
```

In the preceding code fragment, the string that <fmt:parseDate> tries to parse is formatted as MM/dd/yy, where M represents the month, d represents the day, and y represents the year. But because the parseLocale attribute is set to France French and because dates in that locale are formatted as dd/MM/yy, the <fmt:parseDate> action will not be able to parse its string (20 is not a valid month), and therefore that action will throw an exception.

For dates and times that are not formatted according to one of the standard formats—see Table 8.4 on page 334 for more information about those standard formats—you can specify a custom pattern with the <fmt:parseDate> pattern attribute, like this:

```
<fmt:parseDate value='06/20/98, 10:25'
            pattern='MM/dd/yy, hh:mm'/>
```

If you specify a custom pattern, as in the preceding code fragment, you must make sure that the pattern matches the string that <fmt:parseDate> tries to parse. For example, in the preceding code fragment, if you change the pattern to MM/dd/yy, hh:mm:ss, the <fmt:parseDate> action will throw an exception.

Establishes a time zone for <fmt:formatDate> and <fmt:parseDate> actions in the body of the <fmt:timeZone> action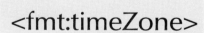

Syntax:

        <fmt:timeZone value>
            body content, presumably with <fmt:formatDate> or <fmt:parseDate> actions
        </fmt:timeZone>

Description:

The <fmt:formatDate> and <fmt:parseDate> actions format and parse dates, respectively, according to a time zone. One way to specify that time zone is with the <fmt:timeZone> action, which establishes a time zone for <fmt:formatDate> and

<fmt:parseDate> actions that reside in the body of the <fmt:timeZone> action. You specify that time zone with the <fmt:timeZone> action's value attribute, which can be either a string or an instance of java.util.TimeZone.

Attributes:

Attribute[a]	Type	Description
value	String or java.util.TimeZone	Specifies the time zone used by <fmt:formatDate> and <fmt:parseDate> actions in the body of the <fmt:time-Zone> action. If you specify the time zone as a string, you must use a time zone ID supported by the Java platform, such as America/Denver.

   a. static | *dynamic*

Constraints and Error Handling:

- If you specify the value attribute as null or an empty string, <fmt:timeZone> uses the GMT time zone.

In a Nutshell:

You can use the <fmt:timeZone> action to specify a time zone for <fmt:parseDate> and <fmt:formatDate> actions, like this:

```
<jsp:useBean id='now' class='java.util.Date'/>

<fmt:timeZone value='America/New_York'>
   <fmt:formatDate value='${now}'
                   type='time'
              timeStyle='full'/>
</fmt:timeZone>
```

In the preceding code fragment, if the current time is 10:30 A.M. MDT, the <fmt:formatDate> action will produce this output: 12:30:00 PM EDT.

You can override the time zone specified with the <fmt:timeZone> action with the timeZone attribute for <fmt:formatDate> and <fmt:parseDate>; for example:

```
<jsp:useBean id='now' class='java.util.Date'/>

<fmt:timeZone value='America/New_York'>
   <fmt:formatDate value='${now}'
                   type='both'
              timeStyle='full'/>

   <fmt:formatDate value='${now}'
                   type='both'
              timeZone='America/Denver'
```

```
            timeStyle='full'/>
</fmt:timeZone>
```

In the preceding code fragment, the first <fmt:formatDate> action formats the current date and time for U.S. Eastern Time, whereas the second <fmt:formatDate> formats the current date and time for Mountain Daylight Time.

Establishes a time zone for <fmt:formatDate> and <fmt:parseDate> actions	**<fmt:setTimeZone>**

Syntax:[23]

<fmt:setTimeZone value [var] [scope]/>

Description:

The <fmt:formatDate> and <fmt:parseDate> actions format and parse dates, respectively, according to a time zone. One way to specify that time zone is with the <fmt:setTimeZone> action, which stores a time zone in the FMT_TIME_ZONE configuration setting or, if you specify the var attribute, a scoped variable. You specify that time zone with the value attribute, which can be either a string or an instance of java.util.TimeZone.

Attributes:

Attribute [a]	Type	Description
value	String or java.util.TimeZone	A time zone used by <fmt:formatDate> and <fmt:parseDate> actions. If you specify the time zone as a string, you must use a time zone ID supported by the Java platform, such as America/Denver.
var	String	The name of a scoped variable. If you specify this attribute, <fmt:setTimeZone> stores the specified time zone in a scoped variable whose name is specified with this attribute; otherwise, <fmt:setTimeZone> stores the time zone in the FMT_TIME_ZONE configuration setting.
scope	String	The scope of the scoped variable named by the var attribute, or if that attribute is not specified, the scope of the FMT_TIME_ZONE configuration setting; default is page scope

23. Items in brackets are optional.

a. static | *dynamic*

Constraints and Error Handling:

• If you specify the value attribute as null or an empty string, <fmt:timeZone> uses the GMT time zone.

In a Nutshell:

The <fmt:setTimeZone> action stores a time zone in the FMT_TIME_ZONE configuration setting or in a scoped variable. This action is useful if you need to set a time zone for <fmt:formatDate> and <fmt:parseDate> actions that span one or more JSP pages. There are a number of ways that you can use <fmt:setTimeZone>; here are some examples:

```
<fmt:setTimeZone value='America/New_York'/>
<fmt:setTimeZone value='America/New_York' scope='request'/>
<fmt:setTimeZone value='America/New_York' var='timeZone'/>
<fmt:setTimeZone value='America/New_York' var='timeZone'
                 scope='session'/>
```

In the preceding code fragment, the first line of code sets the America/New_York Time time zone for the current JSP page. It does that by storing the time zone in a configuration variable named FMT_TIME_ZONE in page scope, which overrides the configuration setting of the same name in that scope. If the FMT_TIME_ZONE configuration setting was previously set for a scope other than page scope, that setting will be restored when the current JSP page is no longer active. See "Configuration Settings" on page 230 for more information about JSTL configuration settings.

The second line of code in the preceding code fragment stores the America/New_York time zone in the FMT_TIME_ZONE configuration variable for request scope, making that time zone the default for the current HTTP request. If the FMT_TIME_ZONE configuration setting was previously set for session or application scope, that setting will be restored when the current HTTP request is finished.

The last two lines of code in the preceding code fragment store the America/New_York Time time zone in a scoped variable. The third line of code stores that scoped variable in page scope, and the last line of code stores that scoped variable in session scope. You can access that scoped variable like this:

```
<fmt:formatDate value='${now}'
                type='both'
            timeZone='${timeZone}'
                timeStyle='full'/>
```

11.8 Database Actions

JSTL database actions let you connect to a database, query a database, update a database, and execute database transactions.

Overview of JSTL SQL Actions

Table 11.19 lists the JSTL database actions.

Table 11.19   Database Actions

Action	Description
<sql:setDataSource>	Stores a data source in a scoped variable or the SQL_DATA_SOURCE configuration setting.
<sql:query>	Queries a database and stores the query result in a scoped variable.
<sql:update>	Updates a database with a Data Manipulation Language (DML) command or a Data Definition Language (DDL) command.
<sql:param>	Sets SQL parameters for enclosing <sql:query> and <sql:update> actions.
<sql:dateParam>	Sets SQL date parameters for enclosing <sql:query> and <sql:update> actions.
<sql:transaction>	Establishes a transaction for enclosed <sql:query> and <sql:update> actions.

JSTL database actions are discussed in "Database Actions" on page 356. This section provides summaries for each of those database actions.

JSTL also exposes two interfaces and a single class in the javax.servlet.jsp.jstl.sql package, as discussed in "Exposed Classes and Interface" on page 541.

JSTL SQL Configuration Settings

The following configuration settings are supported by JSTL for SQL actions:

- SQL_DATA_SOURCE
- SQL_MAX_ROWS

The SQL_DATA_SOURCE configuration setting is listed in Table 11.20.

Table 11.20   SQL_DATA_SOURCE

Config Constant	SQL_DATA_SOURCE
Name	javax.servlet.jsp.jstl.sql.dataSource
Type	java.lang.String or javax.sql.DataSource
Set by	<sql:setDataSource>, Deployment Descriptor, Config class
Used by	<sql:query>, <sql:update>, and <sql:transaction>

The SQL_DATA_SOURCE configuration setting specifies a data source used by <sql:query>, <sql:update>, and <sql:transaction> actions. You can specify that configuration setting in a deployment descriptor or business component, or in a JSP page with the <sql:setDataSource> action. The SQL_DATA_SOURCE configuration setting can be specified as an object that implements the javax.sql.DataSource interface or as a string that represents a JNDI resource or JDBC parameters.

The SQL_MAX_ROWS configuration setting is listed in Table 11.21.

Table 11.21   SQL_MAX_ROWS

Config Constant	SQL_MAX_ROWS
Name	javax.servlet.jsp.jstl.sql.maxRows
Type	java.lang.String or java.lang.Integer
Set by	Deployment Descriptor, Config class
Used by	<sql:query>

The SQL_MAX_ROWS configuration setting lets you specify a maximum limit for database queries; for example, if you specify a value of 25 for the SQL_MAX_ROWS configuration setting, database queries performed by the <sql:query> action will be limited to 25 rows. There are no JSTL actions that set the SQL_MAX_ROWS configuration setting, so you must specify that configuration setting in a deployment descriptor or in a business component with the Config.set methods.

JSTL SQL Actions

Exposes a data source	<sql:setDataSource>

Syntax:[24]

    <sql:setDataSource {dataSource | url [driver] [user] [password]}
        [var] [scope]/>

Description:

The <sql:setDataSource> action stores a data source in a scoped variable or in the SQL_DATA_SOURCE configuration variable. JSTL implementations may choose to expose an existing data source with the exact same characteristics instead of creating a new one.

Attributes:

Attribute[a]	Type	Description
dataSource	java.lang.String or javax.sql.DataSource	A string or a scoped variable that references a string or an instance of java.sql.DataSource. If you specify a string, it must represent either a JNDI relative path to a data source or a comma-separated combination of JDBC url and, optionally, driver, user, and password.
url	String	A JDBC url, e.g.: jdbc:mysql://localhost/core-jstl
driver	String	A JDBC driver, e.g.: org.gjt.mm.mysql.Driver
user	String	A user name.
password	String	The user's password.
var	String	The name of a scoped variable that references the data source.
scope	String	Specifies the scope of the variable whose name is specified with the var attribute; otherwise, specifies the scope of the SQL_DATA_SOURCE configuration setting. The default is page scope.

a.   static | *dynamic*

24. Items in brackets are optional.

Constraints and Error Handling:

- If the `dataSource` attribute is `null`, `<sql:setDataSource>` will throw an exception.

In a Nutshell:

You can do two things with `<sql:setDataSource>`:

- Specify a data source with a Java object or a string representing a JNDI relative path or JDBC parameters
- Store that data source in a scoped variable or the `SQL_DATA_SOURCE` configuration setting

You can specify your data source with the `dataSource` attribute, which can be either a string or an instance of `javax.sql.DataSource`. If it's the latter, `<sql:setDataSource>` uses it as is; if it's the former, `<sql:setDataSource>` first assumes the string represents a relative path to a JNDI resource. If `<sql:setDataSource>` cannot find that resource, it then assumes that the string represents JDBC parameters and tries to establish a JDBC connection. You can specify JDBC parameters with the `url` attribute and, optionally the `driver`, `user`, and `password` attributes.

Typically, `<sql:setDataSource>` creates the data source that it stores in a scoped variable or the `SQL_DATA_SOURCE` configuration setting; however, if a data source exists with the exact same characteristics, JSTL implementations are *encouraged* to expose the existing data source instead of creating a new one. That lets you put an `<sql:setDataSource>` action at the top of all your JSP pages (or include a JSP page with an `<sql:setDataSource>` action) without having to worry about creating unnecessary duplicates of that data source. Realize however, that JSTL implementations do not *have* to expose existing data sources in this manner—they are only encouraged to do so.

Here's how you tell `<sql:setDataSource>` where to store your data source: If you specify the `var` attribute, `<sql:setDataSource>` will store that data source in a scoped variable whose name corresponds to the value of that attribute. By default, `<sql:setDataSource>` stores that scoped variable in page scope, but if you specify the `scope` attribute in conjunction with the `var` attribute, you can store that scoped variable in request, session, or application scope. If you use `<sql:setDataSource>` to store a data source in a scoped variable as described above, the `<sql:query>`, `<sql:update>`, and `<sql:transaction>` actions must specify that data source explicitly with their `dataSource` attributes.

If you don't specify the `var` attribute, `<sql:setDataSource>` stores the data source in the `SQL_DATA_SOURCE` configuration setting. If you don't specify the `var` or the scope attributes, that configuration setting applies to page scope, but you can specify a different scope with the scope attribute. (Note that if you specify both the var and scope attributes, <sql:setDataSource> will store a data source in a scoped variable as discussed in the preceding paragraph, instead of storing it the SQL_DATA_SOURCE configuration setting). If you use <sql:setDataSource> to store a data source in the <sql:setDataSource> configuration setting, <sql:query>, <sql:update>, and <sql:transaction> can implicitly access that data source without having to specify their dataSource attributes.

Executes a database query	**<sql:query>**

Syntax:[25]

Syntax #1: Without a body

    <sql:query sql var [scope] [dataSource] [startRow] [maxRows]/>

Syntax #2: With a body, specifying SQL query parameters

    <sql:query sql var [scope] [dataSource] [startRow] [maxRows]>
        <sql:param> or <sql:dateParam> actions, or both
    </sql:query>

Syntax #3: With a body, specifying an SQL statement and optional query parameters

    <sql:query var [scope] [dataSource] [startRow] [maxRows]>
        SQL query statement
        optional <sql:param> or <sql:dateParam> actions, or both
    <sql:query>

Description:

The <sql:query> action executes a database query and stores the result of that query in a scoped variable that you specify with the var attribute.

25. Items in brackets are optional.

Attributes:

Attribute[a]	Type	Description
sql	String	An SQL query statement, which can optionally be specified in the body of the action.
dataSource	String or javax.sql.DataSource	A string or a scoped variable that references a string or an instance of javax.sql.DataSource. If you specify a string, it must represent either a JNDI relative path to a data source or a comma-separated combination of JDBC url and, optionally, driver, user, and password.
startRow	int	The starting row for the query. The first row of a query is designated with the value 0; the last row is $n-1$, where n equals the number of rows in the query. The default value is 0.
maxRows	int	The maximum number of rows in the query. By default, database queries are not limited.
var	String	The name of a scoped variable that contains the query result. The type of that scoped variable is javax.servlet.jsp.jstl.sql.Result.
scope	String	The scope of the scoped variable whose name is specified by the var attribute; default is page scope.

a.   static | *dynamic*

Constraints and Error Handling:

• If the dataSource attribute is null, <sql:query> will throw an exception.

• The maxRows attribute must be ≥ 1.

• If the dataSource attribute is specified, the action must not be contained in the body of an <sql:transaction> action.

In a Nutshell:

The <sql:query> action executes a database query and stores the result in a scoped variable. That scoped variable, whose name is specified with the var attribute, is an object whose type is javax.servlet.jsp.jstl.sql.Result, which is easier to work with than java.sql.ResultSet. See "Result" on page 541 for an exact definition of the javax.servlet.jsp.jstl.sql.Result interface, and see

"Accessing Query Properties" on page 382 for more information about the use of that interface in practice.

The query specified by the `sql` attribute can contain parameter markers, specified with a question mark, that identify prepared statement parameters. For every parameter marker in an SQL query, there should be a corresponding <sql:param> or <sql:dateParam> action, or a custom action that supplies a parameter to its enclosing <sql:query> (or <sql:update>) action. See "Implementing Database Custom Actions" on page 418 for more information about implementing custom tags that supply SQL parameters to enclosing <sql:query> (or <sql:update>) actions.

You can also specify values for the `startRow` and `maxRows` attributes to limit the size of your query. Those attributes can be used to prevent so-called runaway queries, and they can also be used to scroll through large query results. See "Scrolling Through Large Queries" on page 385 for more information on the use of those attributes.

You can specify the `dataSource` attribute as either a string or an instance of `javax.sql.DataSource`, the same way you specify the `dataSource` attribute for the <sql:setDataSource> action; see "<sql:setDataSource>" on page 531 for more information about that action. If an <sql:query> action is nested in an <sql:transaction> action, that <sql:query> action must not specify the `dataSource` attribute. See "<sql:transaction>" on page 537 for more information about the <sql:transaction> action.

Updates a database	<sql:update>

Syntax:[26]

Syntax #1: Without a body

```
<sql:update sql [var] [scope] [dataSource]/>
```

Syntax #2: With a body, specifying SQL update arguments

```
<sql:update sql [var] [scope] [dataSource]>
    optional <sql:param> or <sql:dateParam> actions, or both
</sql:update>
```

---

26. Items in brackets are optional.

Syntax #3: With a body, specifying an SQL statement and optional update arguments

```
<sql:update [var] [scope] [dataSource]>
    SQL update statement
    <sql:param> or <sql:dateParam> actions, or both
</sql:update>
```

Description:

The <sql:update> action executes a database update with a Data Definition Language (DDL) command (insert, update, or delete rows) or with a Data Manipulation Language (DML) command (create, alter, or drop tables).

Attributes:

Attribute[a]	Type	Description
sql	String	An SQL update statement, which can optionally be specified in the body of the action.
dataSource	String or javax.sql.DataSource	A string or a scoped variable that references a string or an instance of javax.sql.DataSource. If you specify a string, it must represent either a JNDI relative path to a data source or a comma-separated combination of JDBC url and, optionally, driver, user, and password.
var	String	The name of a scoped variable that contains the number of rows affected by the database update.
scope	String	The scope of the scoped variable whose name is specified by the var attribute; default is page scope.

a. static | *dynamic*

Constraints and Error Handling:

- If the dataSource attribute is null, <sql:update> will throw an exception.

- If you specify scope, you must also specify var.

- If the dataSource attribute is specified, the action must not be contained in the body of a <sql:transaction> action.

In a Nutshell:

The <sql:update> action is almost identical to <sql:query>, except that <sql:query> performs database queries and <sql:update> performs database updates. Also, <sql:update> does not have `startRows` and `maxRows` attributes, and the `var` attribute for <sql:update> is not required. Other than those differences, the two actions have nearly identical behavior: both let you specify an SQL query or update statement with an attribute or in the body of the action.

The `update` statement specified by the `sql` attribute can contain parameter markers, specified with a question mark, that identify prepared statement parameters. For every parameter marker in an SQL update statement, there should be a corresponding <sql:param> or <sql:dateParam> action, or a custom action that supplies a parameter to its enclosing <sql:update> action. See "Implementing Database Custom Actions" on page 418 for more information about implementing custom tags that supply SQL parameters to enclosing <sql:update> or <sql:update> actions.

You can specify the `dataSource` attribute as either a string or an instance of `javax.sql.DataSource`, the same way you specify the `dataSource` attribute for the <sql:setDataSource> action; see "<sql:setDataSource>" on page 531 for more information about that action. If an <sql:update> action is nested in an <sql:transaction> action, that <sql:update> action must not specify the `dataSource` attribute. See <sql:transaction> below for more information about the <sql:transaction> action.

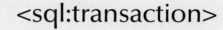

Performs a database transaction	**<sql:transaction>**

Syntax:[27]

```
<sql:transaction [dataSource] [isolation]>
    <sql:update> or <sql:query> actions, or both
</sql:transaction>
```

Description:

The <sql:transaction> action wraps a database transaction around <sql:update> and <sql:query> actions.

---

27. Items in brackets are optional.

Attributes:

Attribute[a]	Type	Description
dataSource	String or javax.sql.DataSource	A string or a scoped variable that references a string or an instance of `javax.sql.DataSource`. If you specify a string, it must represent either a JNDI relative path to a data source or a comma-separated combination of JDBC url and, optionally, driver, user, and password.
isolation	String	An isolation level for a transaction. Valid values are `read_committed`, `read_uncommitted`, `repeatable_read`, and `serializable`. The default isolation level is the isolation level originally set (presumably by the database) for the data source.

a.   static | *dynamic*

Constraints and Error Handling:

- If the `dataSource` attribute is `null`, <sql:transaction> will throw an exception.

- <sql:update> and <sql:query> actions in the body of an <sql:transaction> action must not specify a data source.

In a Nutshell:

If your database does not support transactions, <sql:transaction> will throw an exception; otherwise, the <sql:transaction> start tag saves the current autocommit mode, opens a database connection and disables autocommit. When the <sql:transaction> action completes, it closes the connection and restores the original autocommit mode.

If you specify a transaction isolation level with the `isolation` attribute, the <sql:transaction> start tag saves the current isolation level and sets the transaction isolation level to the value specified with the `isolation` attribute. When the <sql:transaction> action completes, it restores the original isolation level.

If all of the enclosed <sql:update> and <sql:query> actions execute successfully, the <sql:transaction> end tag commits the transaction; otherwise, if an exception is thrown, <sql:transaction> catches the exception, executes a rollback, and rethrows the exception.

Because <sql:transaction> manages database connections, enclosed <sql:update> and <sql:query> actions must not specify a data source; if they do, that error will be caught by the JSTL tag library validator.

Specifies an SQL parameter for enclosing <sql:query> or <sql:update> actions	**\<sql:param\>**

Syntax:

Syntax #1: Without a body

```
<sql:param value/>
```

Syntax #2: With a body, specifying an SQL query argument

```
<sql:param>
    value
</sql:param>
```

Description:

The <sql:param> action specifies an SQL parameter for an enclosing <sql:query> or <sql:update> action.

Attributes:

Attribute[a]	Type	Description
value	Object	This attribute specifies an SQL parameter for an enclosing <sql:query> and <sql:update> actions. That value can also be specified in the body of the <sql:param> action.

a.   static | *dynamic*

Constraints and Error Handling:

- If you specify a `null` value for the `value` attribute, the corresponding parameter is set to the SQL value NULL.

In a Nutshell:

The <sql:param> action lets you specify an SQL parameter for an enclosing <sql:query> or <sql:update> action. You can specify that parameter with the <sql:param> action's `value` attribute, or you can specify it in the body of the <sql:param> action.

If you want to specify an SQL date, time, or timestamp and you want to specify that parameter with an instance of `java.util.Date`, you must use the

<sql:dateParam> action instead of <sql:param>; see <sql:dateParam> below for more information about the <sql:dateParam> action.

# <sql:dateParam>	Specifies an SQL date, time, or timestamp parameter for enclosing <sql:query> or <sql:update> actions

Syntax:[28]

```
<sql:dateParam value [type]/>
```

Description:

Converts an instance of `java.util.Date` into an object suitable for an SQL date, time, or timestamp parameter and passes that object to an enclosing <sql:query> or <sql:update> action.

Attributes:

Attribute[a]	Type	Description
value	java.util.Date	A parameter corresponding to an SQL date, time, or timestamp.
type	String	The type of values that the `value` attribute represents; valid attributes are `date`, `time`, or `timestamp`. The default value is `timestamp`.

a.   static | *dynamic*

Constraints and Error Handling:

• If you specify a `null` value for the `value` attribute, the corresponding parameter will be set to the SQL value NULL.

In a Nutshell:

If you want to specify an SQL date, time, or timestamp parameter for <sql:query> or <sql:update> actions with an instance of `java.util.Date`, you must use <sql:dateParam> instead of <sql:param>. Depending on the value of the `type` attribute, <sql:dateParam> converts an instance of `java.util.Date` into an

---

28. Items in brackets are optional.

instance of java.sql.Date, java.sql.Time or java.sql.Timestamp and passes that object to its enclosing <sql:query> or <sql:update> action.

Exposed Classes and Interface

JSTL exposes two interfaces and one class for database access: Result and SQLExecutionTag (interfaces) and ResultSupport (class). The interfaces and the class are exposed by being placed in javax.servlet.jsp.jstl.sql. This section defines the interfaces and the class and also discusses the rationale for exposing them. Table 11.22 lists the interfaces and the class.

Table 11.22   Exposed Classes Interfaces and for Database Access

Name	Interface or Class	Description
Result	Interface	Represents a query result.
SQLExecutionTag	Interface	The interface implemented by <sql:query> and <sql:update>.
ResultSupport	Class	A support class for the Result interface.

The interfaces and the class listed above are described below.

An interface for accessing query results   # Result

Definition:

```
interface Result {
    public java.util.SortedMap[] getRows()
    public Object[][] getRowsByIndex()
    public String[] getColumnNames()
    public int getRowCount()
    public boolean isLimitedByMaxRows()
}
```

Description:

The Result interface provides a simpler and more user friendly mechanism than java.sql.ResultSet for accessing database queries.

The result of a database query executed by <sql:query> is an object of type Result. See "Accessing Query Properties" on page 382 for more information about how you can access a result's properties in JSP pages.

SQLExecutionTag
The interface implemented by <sql:query> and <sql:update>

Definition:

```
interface SQLExecutionTag {
    public void addSQLParameter(Object value)
}
```

Description:

Both the <sql:query> and <sql:update> tag handlers implement the SQLExecutionTag interface. That interface allows <sql:query> and <sql:update> to receive SQL parameters.

The SQLExecutionTag interface is exposed (in other words, it resides in the javax.servlet.jsp.jstl.sql package) so that you can implement custom actions that pass SQL parameters to <sql:query> and <sql:update>. See "Implementing Database Custom Actions" on page 418 for more information about how you can implement such a custom tag.

ResultSupport
A support class for the Result interface

Definition:

```
class ResultSupport {
    public static Result toResult(java.sql.ResultSet rs)
    public static Result toResult(java.sql.ResultSet rs, int maxRows)
}
```

Description:

The JSTL expert group thought that the `java.sql.ResultSet` interface was too difficult for page authors to work with, so they defined a simpler interface: `javax.servlet.jsp.jstl.sql.Result`. The `ResultSupport` class provides two methods to convert result sets into results. Those methods are used by the JSTL reference implementation, and the JSTL expert group thought that you might have some use for those methods also, so the `ResultSupport` class was placed in the `javax.servlet.jsp.jstl.sql` package.

11.9 XML Core Actions

The XML core actions comprise three actions that let you parse XML, evaluate XPath expressions and display the result, and set scoped variables specified with XPath expressions. Table 11.23 lists the XML core actions.

Table 11.23 XML Core Actions

Action	Description
<x:parse>	Parses an XML document.
<x:out>	Outputs the result of an XPath expression.
<x:set>	Sets a scoped variable's value to the result of an XPath expression.

Parses an XML document and stores the result in a scoped variable	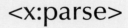

Syntax:[29]

    Syntax #1: Without a body; specifying an XML document as a `String` or `Reader`

        `<x:parse xml [systemId] [filter] {var [scope] | varDom [scopeDom]}/>`

---

29. Items in brackets are optional.

Syntax #2: With a body; specifying an XML document in the action's body

```
<x:parse [systemId] [filter] {var [scope] | varDom [scopeDom]}
    xml
</x:parse>
```

Description:

The <x:parse> action parses an XML document that you specify with the xml attribute or in the body of the <x:parse> action. The result of the parsed document is stored in a scoped variable, which you can specify with either var and scope attributes or the varDom and scopeDom attributes.

The <x:parse> action does not perform validation against DTDs or Schemas.

Attributes:

Attribute[a]	Type	Description
xml	String or java.io.Reader	A string or a reader that represents an XML document that's parsed by <x:parse>. **Note:** This attribute does *not* represent a filename.
systemId	String	The system identifier used to resolve external entities.
filter	org.xml.sax.XMLFilter	A SAX filter that filters the document as it's parsed.
var	String	The name of a scoped variable that references an object that represents the parsed XML document.
scope	String	The scope of the scoped variable whose name is specified by the var attribute; default is page scope.
varDom	String	The name of a scoped variable that references a DOM tree structure representing the parsed XML document.
scopeDom	String	The scope of the varDom scoped variable; default is page scope.

a.   static | *dynamic*

Constraints and Error Handling:

- If you specify a null value or an empty string for the xml attribute, <x:parse> will throw a JspException.

- If you specify a `null` value for the `filter` attribute, <x:parse> will not perform any filtering.

In a Nutshell:

There are a few things to keep in mind when you use the <x:parse> action:

- *The `xml` attribute does not represent a filename.* It must be a string or a reader whose content represents an XML document. Typically, this means that you will use <c:import> to convert an XML document to a string or a reader, which is subsequently specified as the <x:parse> action's `xml` attribute.

- *Do you want <x:parse> to use DOM?* The <x:parse> action stores the result of a parsed XML document in a scoped variable. You can specify that variable with the `var` attribute, and you can optionally specify that variable's scope with the `scope` attribute. If you use the `var` attribute (and optionally, the `scope` attribute), it's up to the JSTL implementation to decide what type of object to use for that scoped variable, so it may be a DOM tree structure or it may be another data type—presumably more efficient—that is specific to your JSTL implementation. If you specify the `varDom` attribute (and optionally, the `scopeDom` attribute), you will force the JSTL implementation to use a DOM tree structure.

- *Do you want to filter for performance?* For large XML documents, it can be inefficient to store the parsed document in a data structure, whether it's DOM or not. If you only access a subset of the data stored in an XML document, you can use a SAX filter, which you specify with the <x:parse> `filter` attribute; <x:parse> uses that filter to filter the parsed document. The entire document is still parsed, but only the filtered subset is stored in a data structure.

Evaluates an XPath expression, coerces that expression to a string, and sends the result to the current `JspWriter`	

Syntax:[30]

```
<x:out select [escapeXml]/>
```

---

30. Items in brackets are optional.

Description:

The <x:out> action is analogous to the <c:out> action, which evaluates an EL expression and sends the result to the current JspWriter. The <x:out> action does the same, except that it evaluates an XPath expression.

Attributes:

Attribute[a]	Type	Description
select	String	An XPath expression.
escapeXml	boolean	Determines whether some characters are converted to character entity codes; see "The <c:out> Action" on page 102 for more information about those characters and their entity codes.

a. static | *dynamic*

In a Nutshell:

The <x:out> action is similar to <c:out>. Both actions evaluate an expression, coerce that expression to a string, and send the result of that evaluation to the current JspWriter, but <c:out> evaluates an EL expression whereas <x:out> evaluates an XPath expression. By default, both actions escape certain characters, but you can defeat that functionality by specifying false for the escapeXml attribute. See "<c:out>" on page 469 for more information about XML escaping. The <x:out> action does not let you specify a default value, as is the case for the <c:out> action.

<x:set>   Evaluates an XPath expression and stores the result in a scoped variable

Syntax:[31]

```
<x:set select var [scope]/>
```

Description:

The <x:set> action is analogous to the <c:set> action, which evaluates an EL expression and stores the result in a scoped variable. The <x:out> action does the same, except that it evaluates an XPath expression.

---

31. Items in brackets are optional.

Attributes:

Attribute[a]	Type	Description
select	String	An XPath expression.
var	String	The name of the scoped variable in which the result of the XPath expression is stored.
scope	String	The scope of the scoped variable whose name is specified by the `var` attribute; default is page scope.

a.   static | *dynamic*

11.10 XML Flow Control Actions

The XML flow control actions mimic the flow control actions from the JSTL Core library, except that the XML flow control actions operate on XPath expressions instead of EL expressions. See "General-Purpose Actions" on page 469, and see "Conditional Actions" on page 474 for more information about the corresponding actions from the Core library.

Table 11.24 lists the XML flow control actions. For each of the actions listed in Table 11.24, there is a corresponding action from the Core library.

Table 11.24   XML Flow Control Actions

Action	Description
\<x:if\>	Represents a simple conditional statement depending on whether an XPath expression is true or false.
\<x:choose\>	Sets the context for mutually exclusive conditional statements—meaning that \<x:choose\> actions can only contain \<x:when\> and \<x:otherwise\> actions that choose one of several alternatives depending on whether an XPath expression is true or false.
\<x:when\>	Represents one alternative in the body of an \<x:choose\> action.
\<x:otherwise\>	Represents the default alternative in the body of an \<x:choose\> action.
\<x:forEach\>	Iterates over a set of nodes returned from an XPath expression.

<x:if>   Evaluates its body content if a specified XPath expression is true

Syntax:[32]

Syntax #1: Without a body, stores the test result in a scoped variable

```
<x:if select var [scope]/>
```

Syntax #2: With a body that's evaluated if the test condition is true.

```
<x:if select [var] [scope]>
    body content
</x:if>
```

Description:

The <x:if> action evaluates an XPath expression and coerces the result to a `boolean` value. If that value is `true`, the <x:if> action evaluates its body content, if present; if not, the body content is ignored. You can also store the boolean result of that expression in a scoped variable that you specify with the `var` attribute, and optionally, the `scope` attribute. The <c:if> action works the same way, except that you specify an EL expression instead of an XPath expression.

Attributes:

Attribute[a]	Type	Description
select	String	An XPath expression that <x:if> coerces to a `boolean` value. If that value is `true`, the <x:if> action evaluates its body content; if not, the body content is ignored.
var	String	A scoped variable that stores the boolean result of the XPath expression specified with the `select` attribute.
scope	String	The scope of the scoped variable whose name is specified by the `var` attribute; default is page scope.

a.   static | *dynamic*

Constraints and Error Handling:

- If you specify the `scope` attribute, you must also specify the `var` attribute.

---

32. Items in brackets are optional.

In a Nutshell:

As with the <c:if> action, you can store the result of the expression in a scoped variable. You specify the name of that scoped variable with the `var` attribute and its scope with the `scope` attribute.

Provides a context for <x:when> and <x:choose>	`<x:choose>`

Syntax:

```
<x:choose>
    nested <x:when> actions and an optional <x:otherwise> action
</x:choose>
```

Description:

The <x:choose> action provides a context for mutually exclusive conditions. The body of this action can only contain whitespace, one or more nested <x:when> actions, and an optional <x:otherwise> action.

Attributes: none

Constraints and Error Handling:

- The body of an <x:choose> action can only contain whitespace, one or more <x:when> actions, and an optional <x:otherwise> action. The <x:otherwise> action, if present, must be the last action in the body of the <x:choose> action.

In a Nutshell:

The body of an <x:choose> action can contain multiple <x:when> actions and an optional <x:otherwise> action. The body content of the first <x:when> action whose `select` attribute represents a true XPath expression is evaluated, and the other <x:when> actions and optional <x:otherwise> action are ignored. If none of the <x:when> actions have a true XPath expression, the body content of the optional <x:otherwise> action, if present, is evaluated.

An alternative in a <x:choose> action	`<x:when>`

Syntax:

```
<x:when select>
    body content
</x:when>
```

Description:

The body content of an <x:when> action is evaluated if that action's XPath expression—specified with the select attribute—is true and the action is the first <x:when> action—contained in an <x:choose> action—whose XPath expression evaluates to true.

Attributes:

Attribute[a]	Type	Description
select	String	An XPath expression.

    a.   static | *dynamic*

Constraints and Error Handling:

- All <x:when> actions must reside in the body of an <x:choose> action.
- All <x:when> actions must appear before the <x:otherwise> action, if present.

In a Nutshell:

You specify an XPath expression with the select attribute, which <x:when> coerces to a boolean value. If that value is true and the <x:when> action is the first <x:when> action whose XPath expression evaluates to true, its body content is evaluated.

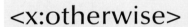

<x:otherwise>

The alternative if no <x:when> actions in the same <x:choose> have true XPath expressions

Syntax:

```
<x:otherwise>
     body content
</x:otherwise>
```

Description:

The body content of an <x:otherwise> action is evaluated only if none of the preceding <x:when> actions contained in the same <x:choose> action evaluated to true. The <x:otherwise> action, like the <c:otherwise> action, represents default behavior for mutually exclusive conditional statements.

Attributes: none

Constraints and Error Handling:

- An <x:otherwise> action must reside in the body of an <x:choose> action and must be the last action contained in the body of that <x:choose> action.

Iterates over a node-set returned from an XPath expression   <x:forEach>

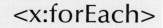

Syntax:[33]

```
<x:forEach select [var]>
    body content
</x:forEach>
```

Description:

The <x:forEach> action iterates over a node-set returned from an XPath expression. The body content of the <x:forEach> action is evaluated for every node in the node-set.

Attributes:

Attribute[a]	Type	Description
select	String	An XPath expression.
var	String	The name of the scoped variable representing the current item of the iteration.

a.   static | *dynamic*

Constraints and Error Handling:

- If the XPath expression specified with the select attribute is null or an empty string, <x:forEach> will throw a JspException.

In a Nutshell:

Like <c:forEach>, the <x:forEach> action iterates over a collection of objects. For <x:forEach>, that collection is a node-set that is the result of an XPath expression.

---

33. Items in brackets are optional.

The <x:forEach> action is a poor cousin of the <c:forEach> action. The latter offers six attributes and numerous amenities such as iterating over a range of items in a collection, iterating over integer values, and accessing a status variable. The <x:forEach> action, by contrast, offers only two attributes and none of the amenities listed above that are provided by the <c:forEach> action.

It's important to understand that <x:forEach> sets the *context node* for XPath expressions inside its body content; for example, the following code fragment iterates over nodes from an XML Rolodex:

```
<x:forEach select='$document//contact'>
   <table>
      <tr>
         <td>First Name:</td>
         <td><x:out select='firstName'/></td>
      </tr>

      <tr>
         <td>Last Name:</td>
         <td><x:out select='lastName'/></td>
      </tr>

      <tr>
         <td>Email:</td>
         <td><x:out select='email'/></td>
      </tr>

      <tr>
         <td>Work Phone:</td>
         <td><x:out select='phone[@type="work"]'/></td>
      </tr>
   </table>
</x:forEach>
```

In the preceding code fragment, every time the <x:forEach> action iterates over its body, it resets the context node. This feature simplifies XPath expressions within the body of <x:forEach> because they don't have to specify an absolute path. Because <x:forEach> sets the context node, the need to specify the var attribute, which specifies the name of a scoped variable that refers to the current item of the iteration, is greatly diminished.

11.11 XML Transform Actions

The XML transform actions let you transform XML with XSTL. Table 11.25 lists the XML transform actions.

Table 11.25   XML Transform Actions

Action	Description
<x:transform>	Transforms an XML document, using an XSLT stylesheet.
<x:param>	Specifies a parameter for an XSLT transformation.

Transforms an XML document, using an XSLT stylesheet	**<x:transform>**

Syntax:[34]

>   Syntax #1: Without a body

```
<x:transform xml xslt [xmlSystemId] [xsltSystemId]
    [{var [scope] | result}]/>
```

>   Syntax #2: With a body that specifies transformation parameters in the body

```
<x:transform xml xslt [xmlSystemId] [xsltSystemId]
    [{var [scope] | result}]>
    <x:param> actions
</x:transform>
```

>   Syntax #3: With a body that specifies an XML document and optional transformation parameters in the body

```
<x:transform xslt [xmlSystemId] [xsltSystemId]
    [{var [scope] | result}]>
    xml
    optional <x:param> actions
</x:transform>
```

---

34. Items in brackets are optional.

Description:

The <x:transform> action transforms an XML document, using an XSLT stylesheet.

Attributes:

Attribute[a]	Type	Description
xml	String, java.io.Reader, javax.xml.transform.Source, org.w3c.dom.Document, or an object exported by <x:set> or <x:parse>	The XML document that <x:transform> transforms.
xslt	String, Reader, or java.xml.transform.Source	The XSLT stylesheet that's applied to the XML document specified with the xml attribute.
xmlSystemId	String	A system identifier for parsing the XML document.
xsltSystemId	String	A system identifier for parsing the XSLT stylesheet.
result	javax.xml.transform.Result	An object that captures the transformation result.
var	String	The name of a scoped variable that references the transformed XML document.
scope	String	The scope of the scoped variable whose name is specified by the var attribute; default is page scope.

a.   static | *dynamic*

Constraints and Error Handling:

• If the XML document specified with the xml attribute is null or an empty string, <x:transform> throws a JspException.

• If the XSLT document specified with the xslt attribute is null or an empty string, <x:transform> throws a JspException.

In a Nutshell:

By default, <x:transform> sends the transformed XML document to the current JspWriter. You can specify the name of a scoped variable that references an org.w3c.dom.Document object representing the transformed document with the var attribute. You can also specify a scope for that variable with the scope attribute.

You can also save the transformed XML document in an object whose type is javax.xml.transform.Result by specifying the object's name with the result attribute.

Additionally, you can specify URIs for the xmlSystemId and xsltSystemId attributes, which are used to locate external entities for the XML document and XSLT stylesheet, respectively.

Specifies a parameter for an XSLT transformation 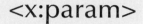 **\<x:param\>**

Syntax:

Syntax #1: Without a body, with a value specified by the value attribute

```
<x:param name value/>
```

Syntax #2: With a body, specifying a value in the body of the action

```
<x:param name>
    value
</x:param>
```

Description:

The \<x:param\> action specifies a parameter for an XSLT transformation.

Attributes:

Attribute[a]	Type	Description
name	String	The name of the transformation parameter.
value	Object	The value of the transformation parameter.

   a.   static | *dynamic*

In a Nutshell:

All \<x:param\> actions must reside in the body of an \<x:transform\> action; the former sets a transformation parameter for the latter. You must specify the name of the parameter with the name attribute. You can specify the value of the parameter with the value attribute or in the body of the \<x:param\> action.

SETTING UP THE MySQL DATABASE USED IN THIS BOOK

Topics in This Chapter

- Download and Install MySQL
- Download and Install a JDBC Driver for MySQL
- Create a MySQL Database for Core JSTL Examples
- Populate the MySQL Database Used in Core JSTL Examples

Appendix

All of the code examples in "Database Actions" on page 356 use the MySQL database management system (DBMS).[1] This appendix shows you how to download and install that DBMS and a corresponding JDBC driver, and how to create and populate the database used in this book.

To configure MySQL for the database examples in this book, you must perform the following steps:

1. Download and install the MySQL database management system
2. Download and install a JDBC driver for MySQL
3. Create the database used in this book's database examples
4. Populate the database created in the preceding step

To run this book's database examples, you must also download the code for those examples. See "The Book's Web Site" on page xiv for information about downloading the code examples discussed in this book.

This appendix discusses each of the preceding steps in the order they are listed.

---

1. An exception is the example in "Executing Database Transactions" on page 411.

A.1 Download and Install MySQL

The MySQL database management system is one of the most popular open source database management systems. That popularity stems from the fact that MySQL is free, fast, and reliable. You can read more about MySQL at the following URL:

```
http://www.mysql.com
```

The database examples in this book were tested with MySQL version 3.23.49 on Windows XP, and the instructions in this appendix pertain to that operating system. MySQL runs on many other operating systems, including Windows 95/98/2000/NT, Linux, Solaris, Mac OS, and OS/2. If you are using an operating system other than Windows XP, you can use this appendix as a guide and consult `http://www.mysql.com` for instructions specific to your operating system.

You can download MySQL at the following URL:

```
http://www.mysql.com/downloads/mysql-3.23.html
```

When you access the preceding URL, you should see a Web page like the one shown in Figure A–1. Scroll down that page to find download areas for the operating systems supported by MySQL.

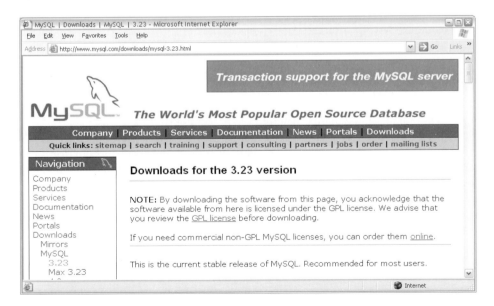

Figure A–1   The MySQL Download Page

For Windows 95/98/NT/2000/XP, you will download a ZIP file; for MySQL version 3.23.49, that ZIP file is named `mysql-3.23.49-win.zip`. After you download the ZIP file, you should create a directory—`C:\mysql` works best—and unzip the ZIP file in that directory.[2] When you are done, you should have a directory with the files shown in Figure A–2.

Figure A–2   The MySQL Directory and Its Contents

Next, you need to run the MySQL setup program; the icon for that program is circled in Figure A–2. That setup program will launch InstallShield to install MySQL. Installation is easy; just follow the instructions in the install wizard. After installation, the install wizard may ask you to reboot your computer.

That's all there is to downloading and installing MySQL; however, to run the database examples in this book, you need a JDBC driver. The next section shows you how to download and install a JDBC driver for MySQL.

---

2. You can use the Java `jar` command to unzip the MySQL ZIP file, like this:
    `jar xvf mysql-3.23.49-win.zip`. If you install MySQL in a directory other than
    `C:\mysql`, you will have extra work to do—see the MySQL installation documentation.

A.2 Download and Install a JDBC Driver for MySQL

You can download a freely available JDBC driver for MySQL at the following URL:[3]

```
http://prdownloads.sourceforge.net/mmmysql/mm.mysql-
2.0.14-you-must-unjar-me.jar
```

When you access the URL listed above, you should see a Web page that looks like the one shown in Figure A–3.

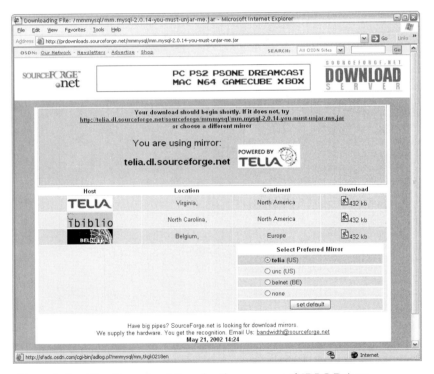

Figure A–3   The Download Page for the mm.mysql JDBC Driver

If you click on one of the icons in the Download column of the table in the Web page shown in Figure A–3, the download will be initiated. When the download is finished, you should have the following file:

```
mm.mysql-2.0.13-you-must-unjar-me.jar
```

---

3. That driver requires JDK1.1 or later.

As the name of the file suggests, you must unjar it. The easiest way to do that is with the Java `jar` command, like this:

```
jar xvf mm.mysql-2.0.13-you-must-unjar-me.jar.
```

When you unjar that file, a directory named `mm.mysql-2.0.13` will be created; it will contain a file named `mm.mysql-2.0.13.jar`. All you need to do is specify that file in your `CLASSPATH` environment variable, or alternatively put the file in your `$JAVA_HOME/jre/lib/ext`, where `$JAVA_HOME` is the directory in which you installed the Java Development Kit (JDK).

A.3 Create a MySQL Database for Core JSTL Examples

To create the database used in this book's examples, you must be running MySQL and you must start the MySQL administrative tool.

When you install MySQL, you can specify whether you want MySQL to start when you boot your computer. If you chose not to start MySQL at startup, you will need to start it manually. To do that, go to the `$MY_SQL/bin` directory (where `$MY_SQL` is the directory in which you installed MySQL—presumably that directory is `C:\mysql`)—and double-click on the icon for the MySQL administrative tool, which is circled in Figure A–4.

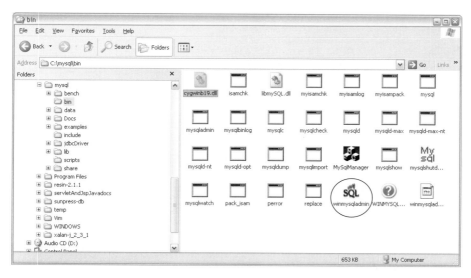

Figure A–4   The MySQL `bin` Directory and the MySQL Administrative Tool

If you chose to start MySQL when you boot your computer, you should see a stop-light in your task bar. If you click on that stoplight, you will see a pop-up menu with a `Show me` menu item. If you select that menu item, the MySQL administrative tool window will open.

After you start the MySQL administrative tool, either by double-clicking the icon circled in Figure A–4 or by selecting the menu item in your task bar, you should see a window like the top picture in Figure A–5.

You need to create one database for this book's database examples, so click on the Database tab in the MySQL administrative tool, and you should see something similar to the bottom picture in Figure A–5.

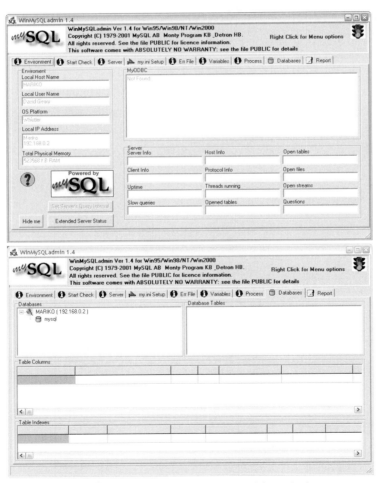

Figure A–5   The MySQL Administrative Tool for Windows

To create a database, right-click on your computer's name (that name is MARIKO in Figure A–6) and a pop-up menu will appear. Select Create database from that pop-up menu and type the name of the database in the dialog box that is displayed, as shown in the top picture in Figure A–6. You need to create a database named core-jstl.

When you have created the database, your MySQL administrative tool should look like the bottom picture in Figure A–6.

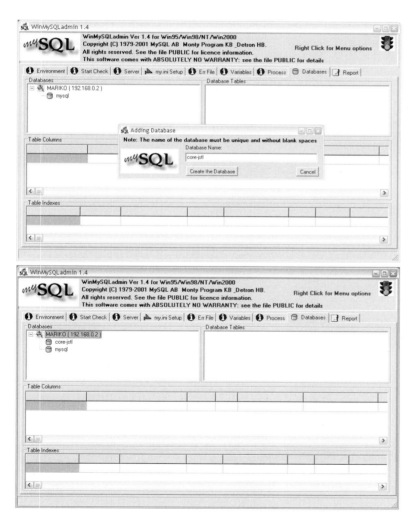

Figure A–6   Creating the Core JSTL Database

A.4 Populate the MySQL Database Used in Core JSTL Examples

After you have downloaded and installed the MySQL DBMS and the associated JDBC driver and have created the database used in this book, as discussed in the preceding sections, you need to populate that database. If you download this book's source code, you will find instructions on how to populate that database in the README file in the top-level directory that's created when you unjar the JAR file containing the book's source code. Those instructions tell you to run a Java program that populates the core-jstl database. Once you have populated the database, you are ready to run all of the examples in the book that use that database.

Although it's not necessary to understand the Java program that creates the Core JSTL database, that program is listed in Listing 1 for completeness.

Listing A.1   *Populating the core-jstl Database*

```java
import java.sql.Connection;
import java.sql.DriverManager;
import java.sql.Statement;
import java.sql.SQLException;

public class CreateDB {
   private Connection conn;
   private Statement stmt;

   public static void main(String args[]) {
      new CreateDB();
   }
   public CreateDB() {
      try {
         loadJDBCDriver();
         conn = getConnection("core-jstl");
         stmt = conn.createStatement();

         createTables(stmt);
         populateTables(stmt);

         stmt.close();
         conn.close();
      }
      catch(SQLException ex) {
         ex.printStackTrace();
      }
   }
```

```java
private void createTables(Statement stmt) {
    System.out.println("Creating Tables");
    try {
        stmt.execute("CREATE TABLE Customers (" +
                    "Cust_ID          INTEGER, " +
                    "Name             VARCHAR(25), " +
                    "Phone_Number     VARCHAR(25), " +
                    "Street_Address   VARCHAR(50), " +
                    "City             VARCHAR(50), " +
                    "State            VARCHAR(30))");

        stmt.execute("CREATE TABLE Orders (" +
                    "Order_Number     INTEGER, " +
                    "Order_Date       DATE, "    +
                    "Cust_ID          INTEGER, " +
                    "Amount           FLOAT, "   +
                    "Description      VARCHAR(30))");

        stmt.execute("CREATE TABLE Accounts (" +
                    "Cust_ID          INTEGER, " +
                    "Balance          FLOAT)");
    }
    catch(SQLException ex) {
        ex.printStackTrace();
    }
}
private void populateTables(Statement stmt) {
    System.out.println("Populating Tables");
    try {
        stmt.execute("INSERT INTO Customers VALUES " +
            "(1,   'William Dupont', '(652)488-9931', " +
            "'801 Oak Street', 'Eugene', 'Nebraska')," +

            "(2,   'Anna Keeney', '(716)834-8772', " +
            "'86 East Amherst Street', 'Buffalo', 'New York')," +

            "(3,   'Mariko Randor', '(451)842-8933', " +
            "'923 Maple Street', 'Springfield', 'Tennessee')," +

            "(4,   'John Wilson', '(758)955-5934', " +
            "'8122 Genessee Street', 'El Reno', 'Oklahoma')," +

            "(5,   'Lynn Seckinger', '(552)767-1935', " +
            "'712 Kehr Street', 'Kent', 'Washington')," +

            "(6,   'Richard Tattersall', '(455)282-2936', " +
            "'21 South Park Drive', 'Dallas', 'Texas')," +
```

Listing A.1	*Populating the core-jstl Database (cont.)*

```
"(7,  'Gabriella Sarintia', '(819)152-8937', " +
"'81123 West Seneca Street', 'Denver', 'Colorado')," +

"(8,  'Lisa Hartwig', '(818)852-1937', " +
"'6652 Sheridan Drive', 'Sheridan', 'Wyoming')," +

"(9,  'Shirley Jones', '(992)488-3931', " +
"'2831 Main Street', 'Butte', 'Montana')," +

"(10, 'Bill Sprague', '(316)962-0632', " +
"'1043 Cherry Street', 'Cheektowaga', " +
"'New York')," +

"(11, 'Greg Doench', '(136)692-6023', " +
"'99 Oak Street', 'Upper Saddle River', " +
"'New Jersey')," +

"(12, 'Solange Nadeau', '(255)767-0935', " +
"'177 Rue St. Catherine', 'Montreal', 'Quebec')," +

"(13, 'Heather McGann', '(554)282-0936', " +
"'7192 913 West Park', 'Buloxie', 'Mississippi')," +

"(14, 'Roy Martin', '(918)888-0937', " +
"'5571 North Olean Avenue', 'White River', " +
"'Arkansas')," +

"(15, 'Claude Loubier', '(857)955-0934', " +
"'1003 Rue de la Montagne', " +
"'St. Marguerite de Lingwick', 'Quebec')," +

"(16, 'Dan Woodard', '(703)555-1212', " +
"'2993 Tonawonda Street', 'Springfield', " +
"'Missouri')," +

"(17, 'Ron Dunlap', '(761)678-4251', " +
"'5579 East Seneca Street', 'Kansas City', " +
"'Kansas')," +

"(18, 'Keith Frankart', '(602)152-6723', " +
"'88124 Milpidas Lane', 'Springfield', 'Maryland')," +

"(19, 'Andre Nadeau', '(541)842-0933', " +
"'94219 Rue Florence', " +
"'St. Marguerite de Lingwick', 'Quebec')," +
```

Listing A.1 *Populating the core-jstl Database (cont.)*

```
            "(20, 'Horace Celestin', '(914)843-6553', " +
            "'99423 Spruce Street', 'Ann Arbor', 'Michigan')");

        stmt.execute("INSERT INTO Orders VALUES " +
"(1,  '2002-05-20', '1', '129.99', 'Wristwatch'), " +
"(2,  '2002-05-21', '1', '19.95',  'Coffee grinder'), " +
"(3,  '2002-05-24', '1', '29.76',  'Bath towel'), " +
"(4,  '2002-05-23', '1', '39.34',  'Deluxe cheese grater'), " +
"(5,  '2002-05-22', '2', '56.75',  'Champagne glass set'), " +
"(6,  '2002-05-20', '2', '28.11',  'Instamatic camera'), " +
"(7,  '2002-05-22', '2', '38.77',  'Walkman'), " +
"(8,  '2002-05-21', '2', '56.76',  'Coffee maker'), " +
"(9,  '2002-05-23', '2', '21.47',  'Car wax'), " +
"(10, '2002-05-21', '2', '16.80',  'Tape recorder'), " +
"(11, '2002-05-24', '2', '25.44',  'Art brush set'), " +
"(12, '2002-05-22', '3', '47.63',  'Game software'), " +
"(13, '2002-05-23', '3', '93.96',  'Furby collection'), " +
"(14, '2002-05-20', '4', '81.27',  'CD Player'), " +
"(15, '2002-05-21', '4', '66.83',  'Microphone'), " +
"(16, '2002-05-23', '4', '75.91',  'Dish set'), " +
"(17, '2002-05-22', '4', '32.67',  'Electric toothbrush'), " +
"(18, '2002-05-24', '5', '17.45',  'Case of mouthwash'), " +
"(19, '2002-05-20', '5', '88.81',  'Vacuum cleaner'), " +
"(20, '2002-05-21', '5', '29.13',  'Fine chocolates'), " +
"(21, '2002-05-21', '5', '77.02',  'Computer monitor arm'), " +
"(22, '2002-05-22', '6', '119.11', 'Tennis shoes'), " +
"(23, '2002-05-23', '7', '107.96', 'Beanie Baby collection'), " +
"(24, '2002-05-22', '7', '101.97', 'Humidifier'), " +
"(25, '2002-05-22', '7', '223.55', 'Exercise bike'), " +
"(27, '2002-05-24', '7', '49.42',  'Coffee maker')");

        stmt.execute("INSERT INTO Accounts VALUES " +
            "(1,  '1245.97'), "  + "(2,  '130400.00'), " +
            "(3,  '28745.88'), " + "(4,  '125863.32'), " +
            "(5,  '25.99'), "    + "(6,  '891.34'), "    +
            "(7,  '924.76'), "   + "(8,  '1578.22'), "   +
            "(9,  '1258.77'), "  + "(10, '259876.33'), " +
            "(11, '125866.09'), " + "(12, '159.88'), "    +
            "(13, '590886.22'), " + "(14, '678231.44'), " +
            "(15, '245.33'), "    + "(16, '8999.06'), "   +
            "(17, '1342.82'), "   + "(18, '197312.33'), " +
            "(19, '907310.21'), " + "(20, '921345.33')");
    }
    catch(SQLException ex) {
        ex.printStackTrace();
    }
  }
}
```

Listing A.1 | *Populating the core-jstl Database (cont.)*

```
private void loadJDBCDriver() {
   try {
      Class.forName("org.gjt.mm.mysql.Driver").newInstance();
   }
   catch(Exception e) {
      e.printStackTrace();
   }
}
private Connection getConnection(String dbName) {
   Connection con = null;
   try {
      con = DriverManager.getConnection(
            "jdbc:mysql://localhost/" + dbName);
   }
   catch(SQLException sqe) {
      System.out.println("Couldn't access database " + dbName);
   }
   return con;
}
}
```

The preceding Java program loads the MySQL JDBC driver and creates a connection to the core-jstl database. Subsequently, the program creates and populates the tables for that database.

Index

informIT